Daoism in Modern China

This book questions whether temples and Daoism are two independent aspects of modern Chinese religion or if they are indissolubly linked. It presents a useful analysis as to how modern history has changed the structure and organization of religious and social life in China, and the role that Daoism plays in this.

Using an interdisciplinary approach combining historical research and field-work, this book focuses on urban centers in China, as this is where sociopolitical changes came earliest and affected religious life to the greatest extent and also where the largest central Daoist temples were and are located. It compares case studies from central, eastern, and southern China with published evidence and research on other Chinese cities. Contributors examine how Daoism interacted with traditional urban social, cultural, and commercial institutions and pays close attention to how it dealt with processes of state expansion, commercialization, migration, and urban development in modern times. This book also analyses the evolution of urban religious life in modern China, particularly the ways in which temple communities, lay urbanites, and professional Daoists interact with one another.

A solid ethnography that presents an abundance of new historical information, this book will be of interest to academics in the field of Asian studies, Daoist studies, Asian religions, and modern China.

Vincent Goossaert is Professor of Daoism and Chinese Religions at Ecole Pratique des Hautes Etudes, PSL, France.

Xun Liu is Professor of History at Rutgers University, USA.

Routledge Studies in Taoism

Series editors:

T.H. Barrett, School of Oriental and African Studies, University of London; Russell Kirkland, University of Georgia; Benjamin Penny, Australian National University; and Vincent Goossaert, École Pratique des Hautes Études.

The *Routledge Studies in Taoism* series publishes books of high scholarly standards. The series includes monographic studies, surveys and annotated translations of primary sources and technical reference works with a wide scope. Occasionally, translations of books first published in other languages might also be considered for inclusion in the series.

Daoism in History
Essays in Honour of Liu Ts'un-yan
Edited by Benjamin Penny

Daoist Ritual, State Religion, and Popular Practices
Zhenwu Worship from Song to Ming (960–1644)
Shin-Yi Chao

The Emergence of Daoism
Creation of Tradition
Gil Raz

Daoism in Japan
Chinese Traditions and Their Influence on Japanese Religious Culture
Edited by Jeffrey L. Richey

Daoism in Modern China
Clerics and Temples in Urban Transformations, 1860–Present
Edited by Vincent Goossaert and Xun Liu

Daoism in Modern China

Clerics and Temples in Urban
Transformations, 1860–Present

Edited by
Vincent Goossaert and Xun Liu

LONDON AND NEW YORK

First published 2021
by Routledge
2 Park Square, Milton Park, Abingdon, Oxon OX14 4RN

and by Routledge
605 Third Avenue, New York, NY 10158

Routledge is an imprint of the Taylor & Francis Group, an informa business

British Library Cataloguing-in-Publication Data
A catalogue record for this book is available from the British Library

Library of Congress Cataloging-in-Publication Data
Names: Goossaert, Vincent, editor. | Liu, Xun, 1959- editor.
Title: Daoism in modern China: clerics and temples in urban transformations, 1860–present / edited by Vincent Goossaert and Liu Xun.
Description: Abingdon, Oxon; New York: Routledge, 2021. | Includes bibliographical references and index.
Identifiers: LCCN 2020052010 | ISBN 9781138889415 (hardback) | ISBN 9781315712895 (ebook)
Subjects: LCSH: Daoism--China. | Religion and culture--China.
Classification: LCC BL1925 .D365 2021 | DDC 299.5/140951--dc23
LC record available at https://lccn.loc.gov/2020052010

ISBN: 978-1-138-88941-5 (hbk)
ISBN: 978-0-367-76597-2 (pbk)
ISBN: 978-1-315-71289-5 (ebk)

Typeset in Times New Roman
by Deanta Global Publishing Services, Chennai, India

Contents

List of illustrations   vii
Acknowledgments   ix
Notes on contributors   x

Introduction   1

PART I
Historical overview   9

1   Urban Daoists, from 1860 to the present   11
    VINCENT GOOSSAERT

2   The Martial Marquis Shrine: politics of temple expropriation
    and restitution, and struggles of Daoist revival in
    contemporary Nanyang   52
    XUN LIU 劉迅

PART II
Spirit-writing temples and their networks   81

3   The Jin'gaishan network: a lay Quanzhen Daoist organization
    in modern Jiangnan   83
    VINCENT GOOSSAERT

4   The Dao in the Southern Seas: the diffusion of the Lüzu cult
    from Meizhou to Bangkok   120
    YAU CHI-ON 游子安

PART III
Householder urban Daoists 159

5 **The modern transformations of the Old Eastern Peak temple in Hangzhou** 161
FANG LING

6 **Zhengyi Daoists and the Baoqing Pier neighborhood in modern Hankou** 213
MEI LI 梅莉 AND XUN LIU 劉迅

Index 265

Illustrations

Tables

1.1	Number of Registered Daoists and Temples in Selected Cities	26
1.2	Rituals Performed By Master Zhou Caiyuan in July 2011	36
1.3	Rituals Performed at Suzhou Chenghuangmiao in July 2011	37
4.1	Simplified Representative Table of Lüzu's Divine Prescriptions in Guangdong and Southeast Asia	136
4.2	Lüzu Scriptures Printed in/Sent from Bangkok's Zanhuagong	141
5.1	List of Rituals Offered at the Temple in 2012, with Price (in Yuan) and complete name as per the temple's liturgical manuals	184

Map

| 5.1 | Location of the Dongyue associations | 197 |

Figures

2.1	Overview of the Martial Marquis Shrine compound in *Wolonggangzhi*	58
2.2	Zhu Zongchang (seventh from left) and fellow Daoist clerics (third and fifth from left) with the Nanyang Museum staff in 1961 in Zhang Xiaogang, *Wangshi ruge*, p. 9	71
5.1	Old Dongyue temple layout in *Wulin jinxiang xuzhi*, p. 563. This map does not show the entrance hall Jianing baodian built in 1809, destroyed in 1929, and later restored; it was thus likely drawn before 1809	167
5.2	Old Dongyue temple Daoists burning spirit money, 2009. At the end of the ritual of merit for the Dongyue Emperor's birthday, the Daoists send him their pledges of faith, in the form of spirit money. © Fang Ling	181
5.3	Certificate (*zhizhao*) issued at the Old Dongyue temple. © Fang Ling	201

6.1   A view of a harbour landing. Baidu.com open source image,
       accessed on Sept 12, 2020   223
6.2   A sketch of Baoqing neighborhood location marked; Map
       prepared by Mei Li in Sept. 2017   224
6.3   Water route from Xinhua to Hankou via Zi and Yangzi Rivers
       (Google Maps with watery route marked by Mei Li and Xun Liu,
       Sept, 2017). For a recent study of the commercial navigation on
       the Zi and other major waterways in Hunan, see Huang Juan,
       "Hunan jindai hangyunye yanjiu"   226
6.4   Baoqing Daoists performing a rite on Mount Wudang, summer
       2009 © Xun Liu   247

Acknowledgments

We gratefully acknowledge the support given to the "Temples, Urban Society and Taoists" project conducted between 2007 and 2011 by the Chiang Ching-kuo International Foundation for Scholarly Exchange as well as the French Agence Nationale de la Recherche.

This volume is dedicated to our friend and colleague Mei Li, who was a cherished member of this project and left this world very prematurely in March 2020.

Notes on contributors

FANG Ling (PhD, EPHE, Paris, 2001) is a research fellow at CNRS, member of the Groupe Sociétés, Religions, Laïcités (CNRS-EPHE). Her research deals with Chinese sacred medicine, local cults, and the religious practices of the Chinese in France.

Vincent GOOSSAERT (PhD, EPHE, Paris, 1997) was a research fellow at CNRS (1998–2012) and is now Professor of Daoism and Chinese religions at EPHE, PSL; he has served as dean of its graduate school (2014–2018). His research deals with the social history of Chinese religion in late imperial and modern times. He is coeditor of *T'oung Pao*, a leading journal in sinology established in 1890.

Xun LIU (PhD, University of Southern California, USA, 2001) is a professor of late imperial and modern China at Rutgers University, New Brunswick, New Jersey, and served as the founding director of Rutgers Center for Chinese Studies (2014–2017). His publications cover Daoist inner alchemy and bodily practices, and social and cultural history of Daoism in local society from the late Ming to present China. He is currently completing a monograph on the social history of Daoist temples and local society in Nanyang of North China from the late Ming to the early twentieth century.

MEI Li (PhD, Wuhan University, China, 2003) was a professor of historical geography at the Institute of Modern History and senior editor at the *Journal of Central China Normal University* (Humanities and Social Sciences Edition) at Central China Normal University, Wuhan, China. She published several influential monographs on the pilgrimage and local cults centered on Mount Wudang during the Ming and Qing eras. She was working on the history of Zhengyi Daoist ritualists in Central Hunan migrant communities in late Qing and modern Wuhan before her untimely death in the early spring of 2020.

YAU Chi-on (PhD, Chinese University of Hong Kong, 1994) is Associate Professor, Department of Chinese Literature, Chu Hai College of Higher Education and Associate Director, The Centre for Hong Kong History and Culture Studies, Chu Hai College of Higher Education. His research deals with the modern history of Chinese religions, especially in the Cantonese world.

Introduction

"Wherever there is a Daoist, a temple soon follows" 先有道士後有廟. So goes the common saying among the Daoists. Indeed, the modern history of Chinese temples and that of the Daoists seem to go hand in hand. Yet, while both temples and Daoists serve Chinese society, the relationship between the two has yet to be thoroughly analyzed. Most temples, now as before, operate without a Daoist, and many Daoists do not work in temples. So, are temples and Daoists two independent aspects of modern Chinese religion? Are they indissolubly linked? If so, what factors helped forge such a link? How have Daoists and temples fared through the political, social, and cultural changes in modern China?

This volume attempts to shed new light on these and other issues through an interdisciplinary approach combining historical research (tapping on archival resources and recently published material) and fieldwork. It focuses on urban centers because this is where sociopolitical changes came earliest and affected religious life to the greatest extent; it is also where the largest central Daoist temples were and are located. The chapters examine how Daoism interacted with traditional urban social, cultural, and commercial institutions and pay close attention to how it dealt with processes of state expansion, commercialization, migration, and urban development in modern times. By comparing their case studies from central, eastern, and southern China with published evidence and research on other Chinese cities, the authors reach larger conclusions as to how modern history has changed the structure and organization of religious and social life in Chinese cities, and the role therein of Daoism, in particular.

We examine the evolution of urban religious life in modern China, particularly the ways in which temple communities, lay urbanites, and professional Daoists interact with one another. We look at major Daoist sacred sites (both Quanzhen 全真 monasteries and Zhengyi 正一 temples) and their function as central institutions structuring local religious systems (training other clerics, organizing the large-scale festivals, etc.), but also at clerics working for neighborhood temples or trade and professional guild shrines either as resident specialists or as occasional ritual service providers. While there is a trend among lay temple leaders to marginalize and even replace religious professionals like Daoists, the latter still manage to retain control over important material and symbolical resources.

The political changes during the twentieth century have deeply changed relationships between lay institutions and clerics; yet, the question remains whether lay people or Daoist clerics can or should control temple life. These questions were addressed repeatedly from the last years of the Qing empire through the early Republican and the socialist periods, all the way to the present post-Maoist era. Our chapters follow these moments in sequence. Instead of a more conventional schematic tradition vs. modernity narrative, we offer a more complex and interesting story of continuous negotiation and reinvention over some 150 years.

Historiography

A recent state of the field essay by one of us has outlined how modern history (transformations between the late imperial period and the present) has long been a neglected part of Daoist studies, which have traditionally been strong on textual studies of early scriptures, and on fieldwork-based investigations of ritual and other local practices in rural areas understood as the living tradition, sometimes even within a perspective of salvage anthropology.[1] While these studies are fundamental and must continue, new developments since the early 2000s, such as wider availability of sources materials (archives and local historical records) and an interest among scholars in China in religion as part of local history, have seen the field develop rapidly and strongly. Our volume is part and parcel of this larger movement, and it tries to showcase some of the best studies that have been published so far. It is a result of a cooperative project entitled "Temples, Urban Society and Taoists" conducted between 2007 and 2011 with the generous support of the Chiang Ching-kuo International Foundation for Scholarly Exchange as well as the French Agence Nationale de la Recherche. This volume builds on other publications also stemming directly from that project, including a volume of primary source materials in Chinese forthcoming from the Religious Culture Press 宗教文化出版社 in China, and a special issue of the journal *Daoism: Religion, History and Society* 道教研究學報.[2]

This new research trend that combines social and local history with Daoist studies is also embedded within a larger scholarly interest in the religious history of modern China, and of the first half of the twentieth century, in particular.[3] Rapidly growing interest and studies in the current religious revival and development throughout the Chinese world have led scholars to discard a simplistic opposition between tradition and modernity and to trace the roots of the contemporary evolutions. Many of these roots were found in the effervescent situation of the Republican period that witnessed not only widespread attacks on and destructions of local religion by the modernizing state and anti-superstition campaigners but also vibrant religion innovations: new cults, organizations, rituals, and ideas. While studies of the modern transformations have tended so far to pay particular attention to Christianity and Buddhism, Daoism was by no means a sideshow in that larger history. Therefore, while remaining ever keenly aware that it is self-defeating to isolate Daoism from the larger religious ecology of China, we have provided an intentionally Daoist perspective on the larger religious developments that have been taking place from the end of the empire to the present day. We hope that these Daoist stories add nuance, depth, and richness to the growing and larger picture of contemporary religious revival in China.

Definitions

We need to define from the outset the object of our enquiry. By Daoists we mean, in a broad definition, all professional or amateur providers of services (such as rituals and teachings) identified as Daoist by themselves and/or their clients. While this definition casts a wider net than those used by historians who look specifically to people with an ordination in either the Zhengyi or Quanzhen tradition, it allows us to embrace the continuum of the specialists teaching Daoist techniques and providing Daoist ritual services to urban communities; in any case, most of the specialists living in or employed by temples who are discussed in the present volume are Daoist by any definition. Defining urban can be trickier, as we are fully aware that the urban vs. rural divide has been a rhetorically loaded category in modern China, often serving as a foil for modern rationality vs. backward superstition; furthermore, moving beyond rhetoric and looking at actual situations lead us to discover and argue alternatively for a rural-urban continuum extending from the major metropolises and their suburbs to smaller cities, townships, and large villages. Our focus here is clearly on the largest cities such as Shanghai, Suzhou, Hangzhou, Wuhan, Guangzhou, and Hong Kong, as well as sub-provincial centers such as Nanyang, while remaining aware of the dynamic circulations between these centers and their own peripheries.

We do not mean that these large cities were home to a specific form of Daoism or that there is such a thing as a distinctive "urban Daoism." By contrast, we look at dynamics of change caused by urbanization and other modern processes, how they impact Daoists and their practices and organizations in the urban setting, or indeed how Daoists face and experience the extremely rapid urban expansion. The specific conditions of urban life do not create just new constraints (temple seizures, zoning rules against temples, smaller public spaces for rituals, de-territorialization of identities and social bonds) but also new aspirations and possibilities. Indeed, throughout Asia, cities have been places of religious affirmation and innovations through the modern period.[4] We aim to show that China and Daoism are no exception.

This volume, which has a strong social-historical focus, does not deal with the evolving contents of the Daoist ideas, teachings, and self-cultivation practices. These equally important issues have been addressed by other recent volumes, and we will return to them in future projects.[5] Similarly, we look less at liturgy, which tends to be conservative (even though denying its modern changes would be a flagrant mistake), than at the social context of rituals: who pays for and organizes Daoist rituals in modern Chinese cities, and where does it take place? Daoists today need access to (and ideally control over) temples to be able to perform their rituals and be recognized, but those with rights and authority over temples may have other agendas. Taking our hint from Kenneth Dean's idea of Daoism as one of the liturgical frameworks that organizes and structures Chinese local societies, we endeavor to explore how this (in relation to other) framework adapts to the social, political, and economical transformations that have shaped modern Chinese cities, notably the sweeping movements of temple appropriation, destruction, and reconstruction.[6]

Structure of the volume

Part I, "Historical Overview," provides a historical framework for looking at our case studies, at two levels: first at the most general level of the Chinese world, and second, with a case study, located in Nanyang 南陽 in Central China, so as to place the various types of Daoist institutions and their trajectories through the history of modernization and urbanization.

Chapter 1, "Urban Daoists, from 1860 to the Present," provides an analytical background for the whole volume by describing the various configurations for Daoism in Chinese cities by the late Qing period – central temples, neighborhood and guild temples staffed by Daoists, entrepreneurial Daoist ritual services centers, and lay spirit-writing halls – and the way these types experienced diverging trajectories through the upheavals of the twentieth century down to the present. The chapter concludes by presenting four general models through which Daoist temples adapted to the modern changes (first during the Republican period, then during the socialist period): (1) the classical model of the central temple ordering networks of lower-order neighborhood and guild temples, and negotiating with the state and local elites; (2) the Daoist association model of the temple as a conservatory of Daoist culture providing services to individuals; (3) the entrepreneurial temple ran by closed groups of devotees expanding through charity and ritual services; and (4) the community temple that builds up legitimacy by identifying itself as Daoist (yet often keeps the Daoists at a distance). This line of analysis will contribute to understanding not only what was lost in the process but also how Daoist clerics, rituals, and communal forms of organizations resisted or weathered the twentieth-century modernization processes and embodied tradition and, actually, in an urban context, adapted and invented new ways of operating. The following chapters in the book provide cases for several of these models.

Chapter 2, "The Martial Marquis Shrine: Politics of Temple Expropriation and Restitution, and Struggles of Daoist Revival in Contemporary Nanyang," traces the history of Daoists and their former temples in Nanyang, a prefectural seat and regional trade town located in the upstream Han River valley, from the 1980s to the present. In that city, the Quanzhen Daoist lineages and their temples had developed over the late imperial period close interactive ties with the local elite, guilds, cults, and local community. But, contrary to the story in other cities (such as those discussed in Chapters 5 and 6), the revival after 1980 has run into tall and seemingly insurmountable obstacles: the initial outright seizure of the temple by the local government in 1949, and the continued occupation and repurposing of the temple complex as municipal museum and tourist site from the early 1950s to the present, even though such occupation and repurposing are directly at odds with the post-Mao era CCP and state policies of religious liberalization and temple repatriation. As a result, Daoists who used to run the famed Wuhou ci 武侯祠, a temple in honor of the late Eastern Han era brilliant strategist and loyal minister Zhuge Liang, have never managed to date to recover their temple in spite of their sustained activism and mobilization. The story tells us that the local government's secularizing agenda and entrenched political interests have often proven too overwhelming for any Daoist revival to thrive.

Part II, "Spirit-Writing Temples and Their Networks," is devoted to one of the most important types of Daoist temples that developed in Chinese cities during the late imperial and modern periods. These temples are organized around the worship of deities that communicate with humans through spirit-writing (*fuji* 扶乩) séances and answer individual queries. These divine-human communications and revelations often result in full-fledged scriptures and other sacred texts. Such temples and their communities engage as a rule in charitable activities and thus form a nexus for community organization. The two chapters in this section deal with such networks of temples devoted to the same deity (Patriarch Lü 呂祖) in two different areas.

Chapter 3, "The Jin'gaishan Network: A Lay Quanzhen Daoist Organization in Modern Jiangnan," describes the emergence during the turn of the nineteenth century of a major spirit-writing cult to Patriarch Lü at Jin'gaishan 金蓋山 (a hill just south of Huzhou, northern Zhejiang province) and its subsequent growth into a dense network that by the first half of the twentieth century included over 70 branches in all the major cities of the Jiangnan region, notably Shanghai. These urban branches had genealogies that listed thousands of members, most of them members of the local elites. Through a combination of internal and external sources (revealed texts, liturgical manuals, newspapers, archival documents, ethnography, etc.), the chapter describes the activities of the branch temples (ritual, self-cultivation, charity, and predication), their place in local religious life, and the process of their demise after 1949, to be followed by present-day renewal in some of the branches. This dense description provides new perspectives on the importance of Daoist temples in urban Jiangnan between the late Qing and the Republican period and what is left of this historical moment.

Chapter 4, "The Dao in the Southern Seas: The Diffusion of the Lüzu Cult from Meizhou to Bangkok," tells a story that dovetails with the previous chapter as it starts with temples dedicated to the same deity, with similar patterns of urban development and elite membership, this time in the Hakka area of Meizhou, and then in the Chaozhou area of southern China. Because of the dense migrant networks of the Chaozhou people, this cult soon spread to Southeast Asia, particularly Thailand, where it has since flourished without interruption. Bringing a transnational and diasporic dimension to the volume, the chapter explores how the cult came to be a central institution in the lives of the Chinese settlers in Bangkok, and then it was brought back from there to the mainland in the 1980s.

Finally, Part III, "Householder Urban Daoist," looks at a different facet of urban Daoists: the married priests who are affiliated with urban temples (usually owned by local communities) but do not own or run them.

Chapter 5, "The Modern Transformations of the Old Eastern Peak Temple in Hangzhou," based on several years of intense fieldwork and archival documentation, explores the modern history of a temple that used to be one of the most famous in the Jiangnan region and now struggles to revive. The Old Eastern Peak temple 老東嶽廟 in the suburbs of Hangzhou was up to 1949 the locus of a huge network of lay devotional associations that converged during the seventh month to participate in the Eastern Peak festival, where local deities and their human servants came to pay homage to their overlord, the God of the Eastern Peak. This was managed by a very large and influential family of Daoist priests, the Zheng. The local power of the Zheng caused their brutal downfall after 1949, and the temple was closed and razed down in 1958 as part of the struggle against "reactionary societies." Yet, the temple was rebuilt during the 1990s and now employs some of the Zheng as ritual specialists. This fascinating story encapsulates many elements of the story where the respective roles of Daoists priests, village leaders, and religious activists had to be reinvented through the contemporary revolutionary struggles, yet it also shows remarkable resilience at the level of ritual and worldviews of the believers.

Chapter 6, "Zhengyi Daoists and Daily Life in the Baoqing Pier Neighborhood in Modern Hankou," based on archival and textual sources, and fieldwork notes, retraces the origins and history of the Zhengyi Daoist householders' settlement and practice among the central Hunanese migrant community in Hankou (Wuhan) from the nineteenth century to the present. The authors examine the various roles these Daoist householders played in the daily life of the Hunanese migrant laborers, merchants, and sojourners in the modernizing city, and pay particular attention to these householders' negotiation with the state's changing regulatory framework, new urban planning and development, increasing social mobility of the younger generations, and the post-Maoist economic reforms in order to survive and thrive in the swiftly changing social, economic, and cultural settings of Wuhan.

Notes

1 Goossaert, "L'histoire moderne du taoïsme. État des lieux et perspectives."
2 Fang & Goossaert, eds. *Zhongguo xiandangdai chengshi daojiao ziliaoji*; Lai, Fang & Goossaert (eds.), "Special Issue on Urban Daoism."
3 Goossaert, Kiely & Lagerwey (eds.), *Modern Chinese Religion II: 1850–2015*; Nedostup, *Superstitious Regimes*; Poon, *Negotiating Religion in Modern China*; Katz, & Goossaert, *The Fifty Years that Changed Chinese Religion, 1898–1948*; Katz & Goossaert, eds., *Gaibian Zhongguo zongjiao de wushinian*; Katz, *Religion in China and Its Modern Fate*.
4 van der Veer (ed.), *Handbook of Religion and the Asian City*.
5 See notably Liu & Palmer, eds. *Daoism in the 20th Century*; Liu, *Daoist Modern*.
6 Dean & Zheng, *Ritual Alliances of the Putian Plain*.

References

Dean, Kenneth & Zheng Zhenman 鄭振滿. *Ritual Alliances of the Putian Plain,* Volume I: *Historical Introduction to the Return of the Gods,* and Volume II: *A Survey of the Village Temples and Ritual Activities*. Leiden: Brill, 2010.

Fang Ling 方玲 & Vincent Goossaert 高萬桑, eds. *Zhongguo xiandangdai chengshi daojiao ziliaoji* 中國現當代城市道教資料集. Beijing: Zongjiao wenhua chubanshe, in press (2 vols.)

Goossaert, Vincent & David A. Palmer *The Religious Question in Modern China*. Chicago: University of Chicago Press, 2011.

Goossaert, Vincent, Jan Kiely & John Lagerwey, eds. *Modern Chinese Religion II: 1850–2015*. Leiden: Brill, 2015, 2 vols.

Goossaert, Vincent. "L'histoire moderne du taoïsme. État des lieux et perspectives", *Etudes chinoises*, XXXII(2), 2013, pp. 7–40.

Katz, Paul R. & Vincent Goossaert, eds. *Gaibian Zhongguo zongjiao de wushinian* 改變中國宗教的五十年，1898–1948. Taipei: Academia Sinica, Institute of Modern History, 2015.

Katz, Paul R. & Vincent Goossaert. *The Fifty Years that Changed Chinese Religion, 1898–1948*. Ann Arbor: AAS, 2021.

Katz, Paul R. *Religion in China and Its Modern Fate*. Waltham: Brandeis University Press, 2014.

Lai, Chi-Tim, Fang Ling & Vincent Goossaert, eds. "Special Issue on Urban Daoism," *Daoism: Religion, History and Society*, 4, 2012.

Liu, Xun & David Palmer, eds. *Daoism in the 20th Century: Between Eternity and Modernity*. Berkeley: University of California Press, 2012.

Liu, Xun. *Daoist Modern. Innovation, Lay Practice, and the Community of Inner Alchemy in Republican Shanghai*. Cambridge (MA): Harvard University Asia Center, 2009.

Nedostup, Rebecca. *Superstitious Regimes. Religion and the Politics of Chinese Modernity*. Cambridge (MA): Harvard University Asia Center, 2009.

Poon, Shuk Wah. *Negotiating Religion in Modern China: State and Common People in Guangzhou, 1900–1937*. Hong Kong: Chinese University Press, 2011.

van der Veer, Peter, ed. *Handbook of Religion and the Asian City*. Berkeley: University of California Press, 2015.

Part I
Historical overview

1 Urban Daoists, from 1860 to the present

Vincent Goossaert

This chapter provides a bird's-eye view of the situation of Daoists in Chinese cities from the turn of the twentieth century to the 2010s, which will serve as the background and analytical framework for the case studies in the following chapters. It starts with an ideal-typical description of four types of situations where the Daoists interacted with temples and urban society before the twentieth-century revolutions: (1) central temples managed by elite clerics; (2) temple or territory-based priests; (3) the clerical underclass; and (4) lay (nonprofessional) Daoists. We will attempt to illustrate these types with examples taken from the cities we are focusing on in this volume, notably Hangzhou, Guangzhou, Wuhan, Nanyang, and Shanghai. The modern transformations of Daoism in these cities were marked by both common trends, shaped by a common political framework, and by the strong resilience, as well as setback or failure of different local religious systems: we will try to highlight both. The aim is thus not to tell a national narrative but to outline the main parameters for variation.

The second section will focus on changes during the Republican period, following how connections between the four types of Daoists evolved under new political, social, and economic circumstances. Finally, the third section will examine the contemporary situation and explore what the present-day policies and rapid urbanization has meant for large clerical temples, community temples, home-based Daoists, lay groups, and their multifaceted interconnections. This overview takes a very large definition of Daoists, encompassing all who claimed or claim to be Daoists and provide services accordingly, such as performing rituals, teaching self-cultivation techniques, or operating temples. It pays particular attention to their place in communal religious life and festivals.

The structure of the urban Daoist Clergy ca. 1900

Elite Daoists and central temples

Late imperial urban Daoism was characterized, at least in the more densely populated, prosperous areas, by a small clerical elite controlling "central temples"[1] around which were built networks of home-based Daoists (for whom the central temple could serve as a training and ordination center) and lay groups that organized festivals and processions. In every major city there were one or two such central temples, managed by the local Daoist elites who maintained close links with local government officials and the economic and cultural elites. The temples of the City God (Chenghuangmiao 城隍廟) and of the Eastern Peak (Dongyuemiao 東嶽廟) often played the role of central temple. The Daoist elites who controlled these temples belonged to one of the two major clerical orders: the Quanzhen 全真 and the Zhengyi 正一. Although these two orders are organized in different ways, their liturgy is to a large extent similar, and we will not dwell on their differences here.[2]

The term "central temples" refers both to these temples' physical location typically in the center of the cities and to their being at the core of various socioreligious networks that managed flows of religious specialists, devotees, money, services, and knowledge. The number of central temples varies according to the precise criteria we choose to define them: the largest cities could have two or even three; but one central temple was probably most common. Smaller towns may have none.

Some of these central temples were remnants of the old Tang-, Song-, and Yuan-dynasty systems of one official Daoist temple for each county and prefecture. The name of the official temple varied under the Tang and Song dynasties, but it was renamed as Xuanmiaoguan 玄妙觀 in 1295 under the Yuan dynasty. Other such central temple as the City God or Eastern Peak temples were originally established between the Song (960–1279) and the Ming (1368–1644) dynasties. Even when the central temple was called by another name, it could have the City God or (more often) the Eastern Peak as its most vibrant cult. The City God temples, central to Daoism in many if not most modern Chinese cities, were both official temples that the local officials regularly visited and the institutional organizers of mammoth popular processions, *sanxunhui* 三巡會, held three times a year (on Qingming, 7/15 and 10/1) to the *litan* 厲壇 outside the city walls (to sacrifice to local hungry ghosts) and back, involving the whole city's population, guilds, neighborhoods, devotional associations, and more.[3] Furthermore, these central temples were points of contact with Daoists in other provinces and with centers of authority, such as the Zhang Heavenly Master 張天師 headquarters on Longhushan 龍虎山, the center of an empire-wide Daoist bureaucracy[4] or the major Quanzhen monasteries and the networks built and maintained by ordination and consecration procedures. They also were places of articulation with the state, since these were as a rule the institutions that housed the local Daoist official (*daoguan* 道官). These central temples can be understood as key nodes in a Daoist bureaucratic structure governing local society.[5]

Daoist central temples, like the largest Buddhist monasteries, were controlled by elite clerical lineages. We can define late imperial elite Daoists with four criteria: formal affiliation with the state (a key element in defining elites of any kind in Chinese society), notably through court-appointed positions as Daoist officials; a role in training (including managing ordinations) and regulation over local clerics; an organization in lineages (*fapai* 法派, *zongpai* 宗派) with written genealogies recording the transmission of rights and privileges;[6] and control over central temples. These various criteria are obviously interrelated, and all supposed significant accumulation of resources to sustain them; as a result, less economically developed districts often did not have any elite Daoists.

Through its legislation and administrative practice, the Qing state recognized and reinforced the social stratification of the Daoist clergy.[7] It did so by cooperating with elite Daoists while ignoring and occasionally repressing non-elite ones (who were not recorded by the imperial administration). Elite Daoists were comprised of the abbots and managers of central temples and officials in both the Heavenly Master's own administration (*faguan* 法官) and in the state's system of Daoist officials.[8] Many (including some Zhengyi Daoists) were celibate. These elite Daoists enjoyed high social prestige and close relationships with the state and local elites. As a result, elite Daoists fully participated and shaped elite culture and lifestyles: we see them even engaging in local politics and leading charities, providing well-paid ritual services for officials and rich merchants, and engaging in medicine and high-brow self-cultivation with a few select disciples; they socialized with local officials and upper gentry members over tea flowers, or wine, and in poetry, music, and other literary and artistic pursuits, and in cases of Zhengyi Daoists, even intermarrying with them. Biographies of Qing Daoists in local gazetteers (*difangzhi* 地方志) feature a large share of such elite Daoists remembered by gentry friends and clients for their cultural achievements as much as for their ritual practices. In such families, it was not uncommon to have among their membership both laureates of civil service examinations and Daoists, when they were not the same persons who acquired both qualifications. Consider for instance the case of Jiang Zhaozhou 姜肇周 (1867–1933), a *xiucai* (laureate of the first degree) from a prominent Shanghai family who later succeeded his father as a Daoist and even Daoist official.[9] While there was a rather dense presence of Daoist elites in the richest part of the empire, such as in Jiangnan cities, they were largely absent from large tracts of the rural north and center.

A survey of the Buddhist and Daoist officials listed in the administrative geographical section of the *Gujin tushu jicheng* 古今圖書集成 (1725) shows that of 1,582 documented jurisdictions (counties, prefectures), 497 had a functioning local Daoist official[10] – among whom 59 were located in City God temples and 20 in Eastern Peak temples.[11] This proportion, projected at 31% for the whole empire, climbed as high as 55% for the combined provinces of Jiangsu, Anhui, and Zhejiang. These show that in rich Jiangnan, there was a larger pool of elite Daoists who could fill these offices and play intermediaries between local officials and local populations. In those central temples that were managed by Daoist officials, the central part of the temple was devoted to the higher Daoist gods (City Gods, Eastern Peak, Jade Emperor 玉皇, etc.) and their subaltern deities worshipped by the public, but side courtyards were the Daoists' residence with their own shrines as well as offices for conducting Daoist rituals and bureaucratic business. With local officials often devolving to the Daoists the management of temples inscribed in the register of sacrifice 祀典, the Daoist cooperation with local officials was not limited to the City God temples; it was also the rule for a number of cults such as Wenchang 文昌 (after he entered the register in 1801) and the Fire God 火神.[12]

Let us see a couple of examples of these central temples, to flesh out our ideal-typical discussion above. One very well-documented example is the City God temple in Hangzhou, which housed the provincial, prefectural, and county (for the two counties, Renhe and Qiantang, based in Hangzhou) City Gods.[13] Located atop Wushan 吳山 (the hill within the walled city), the City God temple was an impressive complex of shrines (the main building, now turned into a museum, is still a landmark) that featured prominently in all descriptions of Hangzhou urban life. It was managed by an alliance of several Zhengyi Daoist sublineages, *fang* 房 (15 during the early Qing, but only 11 of them were still there by the late eighteenth century). Each *fang* owned property and monopolistic rights to perform rituals in certain places. The organization of central temples under various *fang* is typical, as evidenced most extensively in Zhengyi temples.[14] But the large Quanzhen lineage based in Weiyushan 委羽山 (Huangyan county, southern Zhejiang) that controlled most Quanzhen temples in southern and central Zhejiang from the nineteenth century onward was also divided into multiple *fang*, with each of them controlling its own temples.[15] During the seventeenth and eighteenth centuries, each of the Wushan City God temple's Daoist sublineages would send one Daoist to serve in the Longhushan staff, and some went from there to serve among the Daoist chaplains to the Qing emperor in the Forbidden City.[16] They were thus well connected to other elite Daoists throughout China, by networks of crossed discipleship, intermarriage, scholarly friendships, and shared professional experience in Beijing, Longhushan, or elsewhere. Under the Daoists' leadership and in close cooperation with the city's guilds, the temple not only organized official rites for the City God, and the huge popular procession, but also staged judicial rituals in which urbanites could come any day to seek justice. This temple was home to a large number of devotional associations, and in the adjacent temples and shrines that covered the hill, had charitable clinics, spirit-writing altars, year-round opera and other entertainment, and more.

A second example is the Xuanmiaoguan in Nanyang. Studies on the history of this major Quanzhen monastery in southern Henan province by Xun Liu shows that it has always been, through the Qing and Republican period, closely associated with local officials and governance. At key points in local history, such as the post-1644 reconstruction of local society,[17] the armed resistance against invading Nian and Taiping armies during the 1850s and 1860s,[18] and implementation of post-1898 reforms such as building schools,[19] the monastic leaders worked closely with local officials to provide services (setting up a militia, building a school, setting up a hospital) and thus served as local leaders.[20] These monastic leaders were also part of an empire-wide Quanzhen elite and were invited in other major monasteries, in Beijing and elsewhere, to take over abbotships or preside over consecration ceremonies. At the same time, the Xuanmiaoguan also played a key role in local festivals in Nanyang and around, and was at the center of pilgrimage networks to nearby Wudangshan.

Temple managers and home-based clerics

Below the elite layer was a much larger strata of local temple managers and home-based (*huoju* 火居, *sanju* 散居) Daoists, ministering to the common folk, without large symbolical or material resources, but with established rights over temples and/or traditionally delimited territories.[21] The division of urban (as well as rural) areas into territories, each of which belonged to a Daoist family or a troupe of Daoist ritualists having a monopolistic right to perform rituals within the territory, was a widespread phenomenon, also observed among Buddhists.[22] For instance, in Anqing, the then capital of Anhui province, 17 leading Daoist families had a territory of their own in the city; only the celibate Quanzhen Daoists of the main temple (the Youshengguan 佑聖観) could perform anywhere.[23] Similar situations were also seen in places such as Wuhan,[24] Shangyu (a smaller city between Hangzhou and Ningbo),[25] and Liancheng (Fujian), where the City God temple Daoists had a monopoly over the whole city.[26] In Jiangnan, these territories or groups of families were called *mentu* 門圖/徒 or *menjuan* 門眷,[27] and they characterized the organization of most religious professions, including Daoists, Buddhists, ritual musicians, and even spirit-mediums.

While the management of such complex systems of rights was largely a question of the Daoists negotiating among themselves, it often was the elite Daoists', especially the local Daoist officials', role to adjudicate conflicting claims and disputes. For instance, an 1882 newspaper report discusses the Suzhou prefecture Daoist official who requested the Jiangsu governor's help in imposing his authority over home-based local Daoists, and backing up his power to regulate their right to practice.[28] Very interestingly, the Republican-period local Daoist associations did the same thing and tried to prevent from performing rituals nonregistered persons without a territory or affiliated families of their own.[29] But, as late imperial officials perpetually oscillated between supporting elite Daoists and disclaiming all Daoist efforts at self-management, we also see the Huian (Quanzhou area) magistrate striking down, in a proclamation dated 1909 and prompted by protests of local gentry, all Daoist claims over territorial monopolies.[30] During the Republican period, Daoist territorial monopolies were specifically targeted by local authorities in Wuhan.[31]This late Qing and early Republican governments' efforts in denying Daoist claim to territorial monopoly reflects the modernizing state's new penchant for totalistic dominance of society, and its instinctual tendency to control and manage religion.

Whether or not the city was divided into territories for Daoist rituals, a very large number of temples varying in size from small to large, generally belonging to neighborhood associations, guilds, or other communal institutions, employed Daoists, either to reside permanently (as *zhuchi* 住持) often on a contractual basis and under the close supervision of lay community leaders or to come and officiate during festivals.[32] In Taiwan, a long-established pattern is that Daoists control very few temples, but many local temples retain a Daoist family that has a monopoly to perform rituals in the contracted temple, and that routinely has one of its family members available in the temple for providing small-scale rites on demand or on appointment.

The Daoists established in the local community could thus either reside and work in a community temple by contract or live and work in a temple they (or more precisely, their lineage) had built and owned, or work from their own homes. Indeed, many of the at-home Daoists quite frequently set up shops and operated in city centers. The home-based Daoists in Guangzhou, called *namo xiansheng* 喃無先生, have been studied in great detail by Lai Chi Tim.[33] As Lai shows, in 1936, there were over such 270 shops, called *namo daoguan* 喃無道館, where patrons could meet with the Daoists to organize a ritual. Some of these Daoists later migrated to Hong Kong, and such *namo daoguan* are active now in downtown Hong Kong, selling ritual services as well as paper offerings and other material for funeral rituals and commemorative places for ash-urns or tablets to be placed in temples. In the Shanghai area, the shops were also called *daoguan* or *daoyuan* 道院, and operated along similar lines; however, whereas the Guangzhou *namo daoguan* were all specialized in either death rituals or rituals for the living, the Shanghai-area *daoguan* typically offered the whole range of ritual services – they tended, however, to be distinguished by their geographical origin, as they served different migrant communities.[34] Moreover, some *daoguan*, especially in Shanghai, and as early as the 1870s, operated like businesses, promoting new cults and personalized services, thus prefiguring the storefront ritual services shops that have become commonplace in Taiwanese cities. Before 1949, a Shanghai proverb went: "every street has a Daoist spirit-writing hall, and every alley has a home-based Daoist ritual shop" (路路見道堂,条条有道房).[35] Such entrepreuneurial ventures established by Daoists, Buddhists, or spirit-mediums, often in a rented-out store or room, were colloquially known in Shanghai as *fodian* 佛店, "Buddha shops," and much criticized in the press.

Mei Li and Xun Liu's chapter on the home-based Hunan Daoists in Hankou (the commercial part of Wuhan), Chapter 6, offers many parallels with the Guangzhou situation. These Daoists were intimately embedded in the Hunan merchant community in the bustling harbor city, and they were known as the Baoqing 寶慶 troupes, from the name of the Baoqing pier used by the Hunan timber merchants and laborers; the Daoists themselves also engaged in the timber business and in particular in the important coffin trade. In addition, they also organized and led annual pilgrimage composed largely of Hunan immigrants in Wuhan to the Southern Peak. Thus, the home-based Daoist communities, in Hankou as in Guangzhou, and presumably in many other cities, were organized as a profession in close connection with other trades (such as the funeral industry) and intimately engaged with the social, economic, and religious life of the Hunan immigrant community, rather than as a religious community of recluses in contemporary Wuhan.

Daoists in central temples and their counterparts in community and guild temples or ritual shops all offered ritual services for local communities and individuals; the largest celebrations, such as the *jiao* 醮 offerings on a city-wide scale, were often the preserve of the central temples. Central temple Daoists (and this often held true for Buddhists as well) shared one common ritual tradition with their temple- and home-based coreligionists, and often trained them,[36] but often distinguished themselves by a different musical style. The much-discussed question of the interplay between temple/monastic and local vernacular ritual and music is played out differently in each local context, but a very common pattern is that the central temple Daoists' ritual music was accompanied with only drums and bells, and performed in a very dignified style, whereas their local temple and at-home counterparts would typically add much string and pipe (絲竹) instrumental music and flourish widely used in local opera and entertainment quarters.[37] Such adoption by vernacular Daoists of the more boisterous and entertaining performance style from local drama is a clear sign of their closeness and embeddedness in local society and culture. For instance, in Chengdu as well as many other parts of Sichuan, a difference was observed between *jingtan* 靜壇 (celibate Daoists living in the major monasteries such as Qingyanggong 青羊宮, which served as a Chengdu central temple) and *xingtan* 行壇 (vernacular performers).[38] Descriptions of Shanghai Daoism also sharply contrast the *yuandao* 院道 (Daoists having rights in a given temple) to the home-based ritualists, even though some of the latter may be part of a temple troupe.[39] Whereas lay patrons of rituals would often not know much about liturgy, such a basic difference in musical performance style would be obvious and was part of how people distinguished Daoists. This difference between central temple clerics and other Daoists was more important than that between Quanzhen and Zhengyi Daoists.[40]

The clerical underclass

Further down on the Daoist clerical hierarchical ladder and in a marginal situation were Daoists without their own territory or temple, including mendicant wandering clerics. For instance, an early nineteenth-century source describes Daoists gathering each morning at one gate in Suzhou, waiting for a day job of helping to perform small rituals, in stark contrast to the few rich and influential elite Daoist families in the same city.[41] The situation was still basically the same in the early 1950s: the Daoist association counted two types of Daoists, the temple-based ones (*daofang daoshi* 道房道士), and those who were hired on call (called *ben fuying* 奔赴應) for a day job (they had to bring their own costumes, too!); the former were naturally richer and more respected.[42] In various parts of China, those Daoists with an established hereditary position holding monopolistic rights (over temples and/or territories) were clearly distinguished from those without such a position (very often politely referred to as "guest masters" *keshi* 客師), whom they employed on a regular or ad hoc basis.[43] Among all of these categories, we find clerics affiliated with Quanzhen and Zhengyi[44] as well as clerics not affiliated with either of these China-wide traditions.

Another type of marginal Daoists commonly seen in modern cityscapes were those engaged in fund-raising for repairing or building their own temple, either locally or visiting large cities with larger numbers of potential wealthy donors. One extreme example is Wang Mingzhen 王明真 (?–1873), a Quanzhen cleric from a Hangzhou temple (the Xianzhen daoyuan 顯真道院) that had been burned down by the Taiping in 1861. Wang, imitating many other Daoist and Buddhist clerics in similar predicaments, engaged in fund-raising in Shanghai and then back in Hangzhou, and even started a hunger strike, which ended tragically. The money he raised in the process was used by his disciple to build a small temple that later evolved into the Shanghai Baiyunguan 白雲觀.[45]

In contrast to the elite Daoists, who were registered with the state, and thus had privileges that they transmitted down to their successors in their lineage, most Daoists were not registered, and usually not organized in lineages. Though they could transmit their practice to sons or disciples, and knew the transmission lines over a few generations, these transmissions were not embedded in a larger lineage with genealogies, ancestor worship, and common property. As such, they operated wholly below the radar of the state. Notably, official sources such as the local gazetteers hardly ever mention the vernacular priests, even though they do appear frequently here and there either in the polemical literature (where they are categorized often not as Daoists but as spirit-mediums, *shiwu* 師巫) or in anecdotes[46]; even then, such mentions only make full sense when illuminated by present-day ethnography of these specialists. Elite Daoists, to highly varying degrees in each place, did have relationships with local unofficial Daoists, but unfortunately, there does not seem to remain any archives of the Daoist officials that would help us understand the nature of such relationships.

The Daotan 道壇

Besides, and quite independent of the three-tiered professional clergy discussed above, the nineteenth century saw a massive expansion of a distinct type of Daoist institution, mostly but not exclusively, in urban settings: spirit-writing groups of lay people worshipping Daoist saints, notably Lü Dongbin 呂洞賓, Wenchang, and Doumu 斗姆(姥). Names for such groups are many (such as *daotang* 道堂, or *xiantan* 仙壇). I use *daotan* here as a generic term. Some of these groups produced texts – liturgy, hagiography, self-cultivation manuals, scriptures, morality books – and they represent a major source of modern Daoist textual production. These lay persons also devoted themselves to self-cultivation as well as charity. While their Daoist identity varied – some explicitly claimed to be Quanzhen Daoists, others created their own lineage and kept separate from Daoist clerical institutions – most claimed to be Daoists, while often being very syncretic, advocating for the union of the Three Teachings.

The ritual practice of the *daotan* also varied to a great extent, some only chanting scriptures for themselves, while others learned and practiced Daoist liturgy and offered services (death rituals, even *jiao* offerings) to nonmembers. There is a common pattern among the *daotan* to begin as a closed group not open to outsiders and focused on self-cultivation, gradually opening up and providing more and more services to the local community. In any case, because the leading/senior *daotan* members tended to be members of the upper class, they performed for free, and thus claimed a higher status than the professional clerics.[47]

During the Republican period, as legal constraints on such groups radically diminished, many coalesced into large networks with a common identity, state registration, institutional charters and regulations, and sets of scriptures. These networks have recently attracted scholarly attention under the category of "redemptive societies."[48] Redemptive societies have played a key role in diffusing Daoist self-cultivation techniques and texts during the twentieth century.[49] Meanwhile, the local *daotan* (affiliated or not to a larger network) has continued to be the most common form of lay Daoist group in most Chinese cities through 1949 (when they were suppressed), and outside of the mainland to the present day. As Yau Chi-on's chapter shows, *daotan* were also very apt at creating transnational networks in Chinese diasporic communities, and have even been able to transmit their network back to the Mainland after the 1980s.

All Chinese cities had large numbers of *daotan*. Chapter 3 tells the story of a network of *daotan* closely associated with the Quanzhen order, active throughout Jiangnan, including in Shanghai. Another well-studied case is that of Guangzhou. Starting about the mid-nineteenth century, spirit-writing halls, mostly devoted to Lü Dongbin, flourished in the city, offering cures and setting up charitable activities, as well as producing large amounts of spiritual and self-cultivational literature.[50] While the groups were put down after 1949, some have resurfaced since the 1990s, under the umbrella of the Daoist association. Many of them had set up branches in Macao and Hong Kong during the Republican period. These branches have since spawned about 200 new groups. While they tended to be rather inward-turned groups of same-minded businessmen during their early phases, they, however, beginning in the 1960s, began to expand, building larger and larger temples, setting up (and monopolizing) the Hong Kong Daoist Association, making large amounts of money on funeral services, and becoming a prime source of donations for the reconstruction of Daoist temples in the mainland since the 1980s.

Temples and Daoist culture in late imperial cities

The broad classification sketched above does not do justice to the very rich variety of urban Daoism in the cities under study, but at least it suggests how different types of Daoists played different parts in producing, transmitting, and spreading Daoist culture in urban areas. Most aspects of Daoism could be found in central temples: large community rituals and opera; individual healing or exorcistic rituals; diffusion of Daoist books and self-cultivation techniques; spirit-writing (that was conducted in most central temples, either Zhengyi or Quanzhen); and charitable activities such as free clinics or soup kitchens (often conducted by dedicated gentry groups in close collaboration with Daoists at the central temples).[51] These central temples also housed all the major Daoist cults of the modern period, including the Jade Emperor, the Eastern Peak, Doumu, and Lü Dongbin to name just the most ubiquitous ones. By contrast, the local temples, the ritual shops set up by home-based Daoists, and the *daotan* usually offered only some of these services and specialized either in certain cults or in certain types of ritual services (funeral, healing, and spirit-writing, etc.). At the same time, these various actors cooperated with one another to an important extent, as we find them linked by all kinds of networks, with various types of Daoists co-celebrating during large festivals. The sociopolitical changes of the twentieth century radically changed this organization, affecting the different actors in very different ways, as we will now see.

The Republican period

The organization of urban Daoism was deeply affected by sociopolitical changes that began in 1898 and continued over the last decade of the Qing imperial rule, and the Republican era, including the centrifugal Beiyang regime and the unified Nationalist Nanking regime. While the religious policies of this period have been well explored elsewhere,[52] we would like here to outline their impact on urban Daoism. First, beginning around 1902, temple property began to be appropriated on a large scale for building modern schools which were often set up within temple buildings, using either part or whole of the temple as classrooms, and part or all of the temple lands as the school's endowments.

Temple appropriation was a complex, highly localized process, and resulted in very different outcomes in different cities. First, whereas the process was rather slow and usually not violent in conservative Beijing,[53] it was very brutal and early in Guangzhou, where 570 temples were confiscated and then auctioned by the revolutionary city authorities in 1923.[54] Second, the types of temples targeted by the process of temple appropriation varied between places and periods, but Daoist temples (in the largest sense of the term, including territorial temples) were as a rule affected earlier, and to a greater extent, than Buddhist ones. This is borne out by a tabulation of the known details of temple appropriation in Shanghai municipality (including both the city and its rural suburbs).[55] While our source's classification between "Buddhist" and "Daoist" temples is open to discussion, the fact remains that by the 1930s the local community temples seem to have been appropriated to a greater extent than those owned and managed by the Buddhist clergy. This can be explained by several factors, including better Buddhist association-led organization and resistance after 1912, and much more well-established and argued Buddhist property claim cases which the local courts more likely upheld than those cases involving the Daoist and community temples.

Not only were many community temples that either hired Daoists as managers or invited Daoists to perform regularly ruined and taken over (partly or entirely), but even some powerful central temples were also targeted in many cases. In some places, central temples, presumably precisely because they were at the core of the traditional socioeconomic "nexus of power," were aimed for destruction as early as the 1911 revolution or shortly thereafter. One case in point is the Xuanmiaoguan in Guangzhou, which served up to 1911 as the top-ranking temple for Zhengyi Daoists both in and around the city: it was entirely appropriated and transformed into a school around 1920.[56] The seizure of temple lands and the decline of the supporting territorial groups (whose property was also often seized) affected the possibility to maintain Daoists in the temples. For instance, between 1909 and 1934, the landholdings of the Xuanmiaoguan in Nanyang declined from 7,700 mu 畝 to 3,000 mu,[57] and comparable figures of confiscated temples and properties obtained for many other central temples; many had to rent out more and more of the temple buildings to shops in order to survive.

Furthermore, during the height of the anti-superstition fever at the beginning of the Nanking period, some local authorities zealously implemented the November 1928 "Standards to determine the temples to be destroyed and those to be maintained," *Shenci cunfei biaozhun* 神祠存廢標準, which called for the suppression of temples which did not exactly fit a narrow definition of orthodox Daoism or Buddhism.[58] For instance, in 1936, the Kunming municipal government seized 61 temples and produced a detailed justification based on the different articles in the "Standards," explaining for each seized temple (including several major Daoist temples such as the Yuhuangge 玉皇閣 and Zhenqingguan 真慶観) why they were not "religious" enough and too "popular" (a code word for vulgar) to qualify for preservation.[59]

Many of the central temples targeted for suppression were City God temples. Under the imperial regime, these temples were entirely protected by local officials who used them as part of their governance. Yet, during the post-Taiping period, we already witness a trend toward privatization as, in some places, the costs of repairing the City God and other official temples were entirely borne by gentry-led institutions (such as the Reconstruction bureaus, Shanhouju 善後局). As a consequence, such gentry institutions often took over the temple and sidelined the Daoists previously retained to reside and work there.[60] But, an even more radical turn came in 1912 when local officials who had hitherto protected the City God temples turned against them under the new Republican regime, and led in person the efforts to destroy them.[61] The 1926–1928 Northern Expedition campaign was a second moment of massive vandalism, when City God temples were very often a prime target.[62] This is only logical in that as key foci for the traditional socioreligious organization of urban society, the City God temples were seen by the reform-minded modernizing Republican regime as a prime obstacle to its program of building of a new society.[63]

Even in those cases where the City God temples and other central temples were not destroyed, local officials withdrew patronage and participation (even though in rural areas, county officials sometimes maintained minimal participation), as did local *yamen* employees who were among the key organizers of central temples rituals and festivals during the late Qing era. Temple life and festivals depended entirely upon local powerholders (guilds, lineages).[64] While some managed to continue staging the festivals and processions up to the time of the Japanese invasion in 1937, most of the central temples could no longer revive or return to their former richly vibrant, and multifaceted religious world of the mid-nineteenth century. For instance, the Guangzhou City God temple resisted several attempts at destruction by revolutionaries in 1911–1912 before it passed under the control by local merchants who protected it against the KMT policy of nationalizing all temples. But the merchant protection came at a cost: the City God temple now had to limit its ritual services to individuals only.

Another noted case is the City God temple in Shanghai. Up to the early nineteenth century, the temple was managed by an alliance of powerful Daoist lineages which seemed to have been in charge of all major temple rebuildings and extensions. But after the opening of Shanghai as a treaty port and the subsequent rise of the city as an economic powerhouse, the temple gradually came under the control of a large alliance of commercial guilds. These guilds continuously built meeting halls, shrines, teahouses, and other shops on the huge temple premises (notably the large gardens behind the central shrines).[65] What has survived of the City God temple and reopened since 1995 is only the inner core of the pre-1949 massive temple complex which used to own the entire sprawling tourist commercial district around it today. As a result, the guild managers came to control the nomination of the Daoists for residence and work at the temple ever more closely. For instance, in 1896, the temple shopkeepers petitioned the magistrate to expel (for alleged sexual promiscuity) the two managers of the temple's two Daoist sublineages (*fang*) who had been previously nominated by gentry leaders.[66]

This lay merchant control further intensified during the Republican period: in 1913, the guild leaders decided to sack one of the Daoist managers whom they considered corrupt, and to replace him with a young Daoist (presumably one who would follow their orders), a move that was endorsed by the magistrate.[67] After the disastrous fire of 1924, the temple came under the total control of local strongmen (notably leaders of the notorious Green Gang 青幫 mafia) who set up a board of trustees, *dongshihui* 董事會. The Daoists, who now had to pay rents and fees to the board of trustees, were very bitter about their disempowerment, something they still discuss to this day. To a certain extent, the temple's new board of trustees supported the festivals and thrice-yearly processions, but that was nonetheless discontinued from 1912 to 1919, and then again from 1927 to1934, and finally stopped after 1937, even though during that period, the leaders of the temple's devotional associations managed to have a ritual performed at a cemetery, with Daoists officiating, in lieu of the full procession and sacrifice to wandering ghosts.[68]

Finally, some Republican local governments even tried to ban all home-based Daoists, and force them to take on other jobs. This provoked concerted and usually effective reactions among the Daoists. In 1927, Suzhou, the provisional KMT government (which had just taken hold of the city during the Northern Expedition), issued a ban on Daoists; the Xuanmiaoguan manager convened over 2,000 Daoists and produced a well-argued public document, which resulted in the ban being canceled.[69] A very similar ban took place in 1936 Guangzhou, where all the *namo daoguan* joined in a collective petition to the local government and succeeded in having the ban lifted.[70] Again, in Wuhan, the home-based Daoists, if not outright banned, were registered and submitted to all manners of intrusive controls and limitations.[71]

In terms of the overall organization of urban Daoism, these processes had at least three major consequences. First, they ushered in a deep shift in Daoism's economic basis. As both temple lands and the property of the various devotional associations, *shenhui* 神會, that organized the biggest festivals were appropriated, temple economy and communal festivals were thrown into chaos. For instance, from the funds appropriated for school buildings in Sichuan during the 1902–1905 period, we find that large sums came from *qingjiaohui* 清醮會 that organized the large communal yearly Daoist ritual for their territorial God.[72] Only a minority of well-protected temples could keep enough lands to sustain themselves, while most had to rely entirely on fees from their ritual services to survive.[73]

In spite of varied attempts at restraining and/or taxing rituals, including funeral services, Daoists remained in high demand up to the 1950s, and it does not seem that their numbers declined during the Republican period, by contrast to the number of their temples.[74] But, as the number of temples declined and difficulty of operating temples increased, many Daoists increasingly turned to setting up their own individual and commercialized private ritual shops. This trend toward a bifurcation of individual Daoist operators and communal temples has become the norm in Hong Kong and much of Southeast Asia, and also (albeit for different reasons) in Taiwan. At the same time, many temple-based Daoists trained lay practitioners in liturgy, before or after being expelled from their temple. For instance, Stephen Jones has shown how Daoists running temples such as City God temples in northern Chinese cities passed on their ritual skills to village amateur groups that still perform them today.[75] Thus, the end of temple-based ritual services did not necessarily mean the end of the rituals themselves.

As a result, the Daoist groups with the greatest resources and most able to organize rituals and charity during the 1920s and 1930s were now the lay *daotan*. Because the *daotan* rarely held much property, but depended on regular contributions and extraordinary donations from well-off members, and also because they were registered with the state not as communal institutions but as private charities or social groups, they were much less susceptible to confiscations. As a result, they became dominant actors on the urban religious scene, and in some cases actually took over ruined temples, which they repaired; they also sometimes joined the Daoist association. Chapter 3 provides a detailed case study of one network of lay Daoists altars in Jiangnan and its rise to prominence during the late Qing and Republican period, but comparable cases can be observed throughout China. The case of Hong Kong is also to a large extent comparable. When many communal temples were nationalized in 1928 (Chinese merchants elites pressured the colonial government to pass this law, inspired by the KMT policies),[76] and their income were siphoned into merchant-run charities, religious innovation shifted to private *daotan* (many of them initially created as branches of earlier *daotan* in Guangzhou), which after the 1950s turned more and more public and offered an ever-increasing array of ritual and charitable services.[77]

Second, the new sociopolitical context provoked the reorganization of the local Daoist clergy. Whereas Daoist elites up to 1912 were the managers of central temples, usually with close links to officialdom, power brutally shifted to newly formed Daoist associations, either entirely local or local branches of China-wide associations.[78] Only such institutions were recognized by local officials. But, it is important to note that the leaders of the post-1912 Daoist associations were not part of the state administration the way late Qing Daoist officials were; as a result, their elite status declined to an important extent, amounting to no more than a well-organized social organization or group. Some, because of their personal charisma, maintained a high profile, but as a whole, the urban Daoist leadership mostly ceased to be part of the urban elites.

In some places, it was the old elites who managed to seize control of the new Daoist associations (such as in Suzhou, where the abbots of the Xuanmiaoguan became in charge), but in others, the power shift was quite remarkable. For instance, in Hangzhou, the central temple during the Qing period was the Wushan City God temple. While it was mostly spared until the 1940s (the temple and adjacent ones on Wushan still had 52 Daoists in 1950; it was destroyed in 1958),[79] it lost much of its power and prestige. In its place, Quanzhen leaders emerged and successfully established new temples and eventually dominated the local Daoist scene, even though Quanzhen Daoists were always in a minority in the city. The key figure in this process was Li Lishan 李理山 (1873-1956).[80] A Quanzhen Daoist from Nantong (Jiangsu) and thus not a local, Li became in 1919 the manager of the Fuxingguan 福星観, a temple atop Yuhuangshan 玉皇山, a hill near West Lake and long an important pilgrimage spot, but only a promi-nent Daoist temple that ordained and consecrated Quanzhen clerics since after the post-Taiping reconstruction. Li, a renowned bibliophile, doctor, martial art-ist, and activist impressed politicians and foreign visitors, and gained the trust of Hangzhou businessmen. Under Li's vigorous leadership, the Fuxingguan reclaimed several dilapidated and ruined Daoist temples (included a fair num-ber of formerly Zhengyi-managed ones), and restored or rebuilt them as its own branches. Li also managed the Hangzhou Daoist association, established charities (he was concurrently president of the Hangzhou Red Cross society), and ran a publication program. He became such a prominent local religious figure that he became a key target for political attacks after 1949, was sentenced to ten years in 1951, and died in jail around 1956.

The example of Li Lishan shows that the story of urban Daoism during the Republican period is not only one of destruction and fatal decline; besides the pro-liferation of new or recent *daotan*, some old temples did well and actively partici-pated in social and economic reforms. This is also the case of the Xuanmiaoguan in Nanyang which, under successive abbots, established schools, clinics, and cooperative farms and thus maintained a high profile until 1949.[81] What most spectacularly declined during the period was the huge *saihui* 賽會 festivals organ-ized by the central temples where Daoist rituals were at the center of urban life.

The history of festivals during the Republican period has not been much explored yet, but from the scattered available evidence, the decline in urban con-texts is quite clear.[82] We have seen that the mammoth processions of the City Gods stopped in many cities where these temples were expropriated. Other processions were affected as well. Outright police bans were often ignored by temple lead-ers; for instance, Ai Ping and Yu Zhejun's studies of processions in Republican-period Shanghai suggests that in spite of political leaders' stern determination to abolish all processions, police forces were too few to effectively enforce the ban. When the police efforts to enforce the ban led to shootings, all parties had to come to compromises.[83] And, while special efforts at enforcement were deployed in 1912–1915 and 1927–1931, they were followed by periods when police forces were mostly resigned to let processions go in spite of the bans. But, factors other than brute force worked against the *saihui*. In Hangzhou, for instance, even townships around the city proper had mostly stopped their largest *saihui* by the 1930s, because of both political pressure, with KMT activists present at every festival propagandizing and threatening local leaders,[84] and because the traditional silk merchants who used to patronize and underwrite the festivals were ruined by severe rural economic downturn, and therefore could no longer bankroll them.[85] There were still some occasions (with official support such as prayers for rain, for peace, or for the salvation of dead KMT soldiers)[86] during the 1930s when Daoists could preside over massive city-wide rituals, but this was not the norm anymore.

The case of Suzhou is very revealing. In the city, many processions had stopped in 1912, if not a few years earlier, including those organized by the four City Gods temples (for the Suzhou prefecture and the three affiliate counties all based in the city), which were famous throughout Jiangnan for their magnificence. By contrast, in the countryside around Suzhou the processions continued through 1937. Yet, a severe drought in July 1934 created a whole new situation, where the local government, wary of igniting riots in a tense social situation, let people organize rain-praying rituals and processions downtown, on an ever-increasing scale, until it actually rained, and a few days afterward when processions took place all over the city to thank the gods. Many of these processions, which had not been held for 20 years, resumed and for most of the time included a visit to the Suzhou central temple, the Xuanmiaoguan. The four City gods also resumed their procession, led by the Daoist in charge of one of their temples, followed by the neighborhoods' Earth Gods.[87]

Thus, the Republican period saw a growing divide between city and countryside in terms of public religious life, and Daoism in particular; but, memories of the place of Daoist ritual in urban life were still very vivid by the 1930s and 1940s, and large-scale celebrations uniting local temples and neighborhoods around the Daoist central temples could be revived as soon as the circumstances allowed it. These changes took place very rapidly, and also varied from one city to the next. At the same time as territory-based festivals declined, pilgrimages flourished, helped by better public transport and by the fact that pilgrim groups were mostly voluntary and did not depend on landed resources. For instance, in Shanghai, Suzhou, and other Jiangnan cities, many groups organized the pilgrimage to Maoshan 茅山 up to the Japanese invasion in 1937, and resumed in 1945.[88] At the same time as fewer festivals were celebrated in the cities, bus lines, tramways, and trains (sometimes with special service for festivals) took urbanites to suburbs where they could join large-scale celebrations.[89]

The contemporary mutations of urban temples and their ritual services[90]

On the mainland, temples and *daotan* were closed gradually after 1949 (the latter usually more brutally repressed); while some central temples transformed into offices of the local branch of the Daoist Association (Daojiao xiehui 道教協會,

Table 1.1 Number of Registered Daoists and Temples in Selected Cities

	1912	1929	1950	1953	1956	1958
Hangzhou			287/78		183/?	
Wuxi		?/78		?/40		?/24
Wuhan	?/114		233/85			

Sources: Cao Benye and Xu Hongtu, *Hangzhou Baopu daoyuan*, 104–8; Qian Tiemin & Ma Zhenyuan, *Wuxi daojiao keyi*, 3; Wang Ping, "Daojiao."

established in 1957) continued to operate up to 1964. Most of the Daoists, both home- and temple-based, had to return to secular life, often becoming musicians or actors in the official troupes under the cultural affairs bureau, clerks, schoolteachers, and even laborers. While some of them have been able to return to Daoism after 1980, many, including former managers of prestigious temples, are now humble home-based priests (Table 1.1).

Temples started to reopen in 1979, and Daoism has since then revived in Chinese cities. Yet, while the temples were always autonomous, before 1949 hierarchical systems linked them together. The reorganization of the temples and of Daoism during the contemporary period has put an end to this organization, replacing it with a bureaucratic management that functions according to a completely different logic.

The expansion of religious practices in public spaces in the People's Republic is just as spectacular in the urban world as in the rural world but differs markedly in its modalities. While the rural world is characterized above all by the renewal of communal forms of religion (such as the temples of local saints, lineages, pilgrimages, etc.), these communal forms are heavily constrained in the largest cities for reasons of both politics (the laws forbidding religious activities outside the duly recognized "places of religious activity" are more strictly applied there) and urban planning. In the cities, we are witnessing rather an expansion of new forms of religiosity organized in dynamic networks that are largely deterritorialized (Confucian movements, lay Buddhism, house churches, new religious movements centered on body techniques), and are developing outside fixed visible structures such as temples.[91] While in some rural areas (especially in the province of Fujian) the number of temples has returned to the level that prevailed before the devastations of the twentieth century (an average of one temple per hundred families), the proportion remains infinitely lower in the large cities.[92] This separation between city and country is one of the most significant results of Chinese modernity.

However, two factors are trending once again to favor the activity of temples in the large contemporary cities: the expansion of the cities themselves, whose suburbs constantly absorb numerous villages along with their temples; and a political shift, irregular and strongly variable from one place to another, but nonetheless perceptible everywhere, which tends to favor "Chinese" religions such as Buddhism and Daoism over the various forms of Christianity in the contexts of both popular and state-sanctioned cultural and religious nationalism. Previous research on this increase in urban temples has mainly dealt with Buddhist temples;[93] here we focus on the place occupied by Daoist temples in urban religious life.

Yet, this revival of Daoism in urban contexts is very different from the situation before 1949. The fourfold typology we have described above (central temples; territorial priests; underclass clerics; and amateur *daotan*) has been replaced with a new twofold typology: the temples affiliated with the Daoist Association and their registered priests, and the community temples which work with home-based priests.

Let us look first at the major temples managed by the Association and its official clergy before tackling the case of the community temples and home-based Daoists in the next section. The Daoist Association under the People's Republic was first established in the year of 1957 and remained in operations until 1966 when the outbreak of the Cultural Revolution put an end to it. It was re-founded in 1980. Since then, one of its main tasks has been to negotiate with the authorities for the return of the large number of temples confiscated since 1949.[94] There are now more than a thousand temples affiliated with the Association. Although the most important decisions (concerning what is or is not allowed in the temples) are made by the government and its Religious Affairs Offices at various levels of the administrative hierarchy, the Daoist Association manages the temples on a day-to-day basis in the framework established by the state and under its control. Among these temples, two situations must be distinguished: first, quite a few former major central temples, in particular the large Quanzhen monasteries prior to 1949 were among the first to be reopened after 1980. This preference accorded to the Quanzhen is linked to the overrepresentation of the order among the leaders of the Daoist Association, as well as to the fact that its major temples are often more separate from the fabric of urban society than the major Zhengyi temples. These temples, the restoration of which has often received financial support from the state, play several roles at once: as headquarters of the local Daoist Association, places of training (they accommodate the Daoist seminaries) and even consecrations since 1989, and tourist destinations.

The return of the City God and other central temples mostly associated with Zhengyi Daoists took place later and has been less common and more difficult than that of the Quanzhen monasteries, even though not all Quanzhen monasteries had it easy as shown in the case study by Xun Liu in this volume. They were often destroyed by the revolution of 1911–1912, or during the Northern Expedition of 1926–1928, precisely because they were at the heart of the traditional social structures of the cities that the revolutionaries wanted to eliminate and replace with the new institutions of the nation-state. They are still used today, in most cases, as museums or schools. The City God temple in Shanghai, one of the very first to reopen, was entrusted to the Daoist Association in 1994; the one in Xi'an followed in 2003, and the one in Guangzhou in 2010.[95] The temple of the Eastern Peak in Beijing, initially opened as a museum in 1999, was finally partly turned over to Daoists, who have been able to carry out rituals there since 2008. It must be emphasized that, while a certain number of the central temples from before 1949 have now become temples directly managed by the Daoist Association, this is not true of all of them; others have been destroyed or are still occupied by other institutions (the Wushan City God temple in Hangzhou is run as a museum and exhibition hall, even though as of 2009, a new statue had been placed in a corner where people do burn incense), or have been rebuilt outside the Daoist Association and have become community temples.

The model developed by the major temples managed by the Daoist Association is that of a conservatory and a showplace for "Daoist culture," often understood as being the heart of traditional Chinese culture in the broadest sense (more on this model in the conclusion). The role of the major Daoist temples as showcases for a modern religious culture is very similar to that of the major Buddhist temples. Moreover, like their Buddhist counterparts, they are called on to play a role of the official representative of a religion by delivering its official position on major events (such as the return of Hong Kong to Chinese sovereignty, major diplomatic events, the 2008 Olympic Games, and civic responses to natural disasters) and by organizing ceremonies, meetings, or billboard campaigns that demonstrate Daoist support for the party and the government.

However, an important difference between the major Daoist and Buddhist temples lies in the role played by the laity. The groups of lay Buddhists (*jushi* 居士), who play a major part in the large monasteries where they organize lectures, training, and other dissemination activities,[96] have no direct equivalent in the major Daoist temples. The Daoist Association issues lay membership cards to a range of people (including spirit-mediums, who of course are not recognized as such, but for whom the "lay Daoist" card constitutes a sort of protection).[97] Abbots and other eminent Daoists also have personal disciples, often quite numerous. These disciples have sometimes become disciples after a healing and personal tragedies or pivotal events. They learn diverse individual techniques from their masters, or simply ask them for advice on a regular basis. These disciples help the temple in various ways (such as gifts, political support, help with festival organization), but have not been collectively organized as a lay group with its specific activities, as their Buddhist counterpart has. The organized groups with the strongest presence in the temples, as we shall see, are pious associations issuing from local community structures, which do not present themselves as being "lay Daoist" or "Daoist followers." Instead, they often seek to replace the Daoists in serving the local community.

The major temples managed by the Association have to play their role as showcases of Daoist culture while struggling to be economically self-sufficient; they survive on the income from a combination of admission tickets, sale of religious products (incense, spirit-money, books, talismans, and souvenirs), donations, and payments for rituals. In the 1980s, the Daoists in these temples were paid directly by the Association and did not have much interest in integration into the local religious culture; with the end of state subsidies in the 1990s, the temples had to find other sources of financing (although the Daoists in these temples remain employees) and approach other local religious actors.[98] The Zhengyi Daoists in the official temples now collaborate with the home-based Daoists who work without any temple affiliation[99] and call on the latter for help in large-scale rituals for which the Daoists resident in the temple often find themselves to be short-handed.

Relations between the major temples of the Association and the local religious actors also depend on their location. In very touristy locations such as the City God temple in Shanghai or the Xuanmiaoguan in Suzhou, the flow of visitors (many of whom are tourists) is sufficient to finance the operation of the temple. Others, such as the City God temple in Suzhou (which is just a few hundred meters away from the Xuanmiaoguan), do not sell admission tickets, and seem more open to pilgrimage groups (*xianghui* 香會)[100] from local society. Relations with the *xianghui* are a thorny question for the major Daoist temples, particularly but not exclusively in the largest cities of Jiangnan. The religious culture of this region has produced since at least the Song dynasty an extremely rich tradition of devotional associations, the majority of which are made up of women. Often originally territorial (representing a village or a neighborhood), these groups are increasingly purely voluntary (their members have moved to different places while maintaining the coherence of the group). The groups have been enriched since the 1990s with former peasants whose land was bought up for property or industrial development, and who now have regular income and a lot of free time to spend on religious activities. The traditional role of women (and of grandmothers in particular) to represent and pray for the whole family before the gods has not been eroded by the rise of the single-child family.

These groups often visit the major temples, both Buddhist and Daoist. Their visits to the Daoist temples are often conceived as a visit to the highest divinities of the pantheon. Thus the leaders of a group observed at the City God temple in Suzhou in June 2009 told us they had come for an audience with the Jade Emperor, which is to say Heaven, at the top of the pantheon; the temple's Daoists carried out their standard ritual sequence (which lasts about 3 hours) for this kind of groups: the convocation of the divine emissaries (*fafu* 發符), the offering to Heaven (*zhaitian* 齋天), and the sending of the memorial (*biaochao* 表朝).[101]

Many of these groups come to a given temple once a year. Sometimes, if the group requests it in advance, the Daoists of the temple will organize a ritual for them (which does not prevent them from criticizing the group's practices), and sometimes not; their attitude toward the groups can sometimes be haughty and condescending. Moreover, whereas the community temples often provide spaces for the pilgrimage groups (dormitories, canteens, rooms where the groups can practice the recitation of the names of the Buddha and prepare spirit-money), this is almost never the case in the major temples managed by the Daoist Association. The rising price of the visit is another factor that has begun to keep the pilgrimage groups away from the major official temples. Thus, the itinerary of pilgrims around the largest temples (both Buddhist and Daoist) in Hangzhou at the time of the New Year, which had remained unchanged for several centuries, is changing now because of the extremely high price of admission to the most tourist-frequented temples. These groups are now increasingly turning to community temples instead.

The Daoists in the major temples therefore have mixed feelings about these pilgrimage groups and their leaders (*xiangtou*). Many of the latter are often (but not necessarily) spirit-mediums (women or more rarely, men) who officiate in village and suburban communities in order to heal illnesses and deal with unexplained misfortune, and also act as religious intermediaries, bringing many patrons (individually or collectively) to the Daoists. Even though the *xiangtou* (of whom a substantial number are lay members of the Daoist Association) are not normally possessed and do not behave as spirit-mediums during their visits to the Daoist Association's major temples (possession can nonetheless happen at any moment), their identity as spirit-mediums remains problematic, because possession and spirit-mediumship remain illegal and also displease certain Daoists – their opposition has a long history going back over two millennia. While cooperation between Daoists and spirit-mediums is natural and unproblematic in many rural parts of China, it does not fit in with an officially encouraged representation of "Daoist culture" that is exhibited in the major urban temples.[102]

The community temples

In contrast with the major temples, heirs to the pre-1949 central temples that seek to define a Daoist identity, the community temples do not aim to define and spread Daoism, but rather to serve the local community. It is true that the Daoist Association has restored some old neighborhood temples, such as the Renweimiao 仁威廟 in Guangzhou, restored by the Association in 2003, which for centuries had been an important neighborhood temple but which also attracts the faithful from all of western Guangzhou, and from the adjacent Pearl River delta districts of Nanhai, Panyu, and Shunde.[103] However, what we call the community temples are directly controlled not by the Daoist Association but by neighborhood associations or by a lineage: one often finds active or retired Party cadres (or their relatives) among their leaders. Many of them concern only the residents of a neighborhood, such as the Earth God temples, but for some temples, the network of the devotees is much wider than the neighborhood and stretches out over one or several regions.

Most community temples work in close cooperation with the home-based Daoists. The home-based Daoists are now again, as they have been throughout history, much more numerous than temple-based ones in many cities; for instance, in the Pudong area of Shanghai, as of 2007, the local Daoist association had registered 45 temple-based (in 7 temples) and over 200 home-based priests.[104] Yet, in the vast majority of cases, the traditional regulation of home-based clerics through monopolistic territories has disappeared, and in any case is discouraged by the Daoist association.

During the reconstruction process, some temples changed managers, like the Lao Dongyuemiao 老東嶽廟 temple in the northwestern suburbs of Hangzhou, once a great central temple and one of the most important centers of the worship of the God of the Eastern Peak in the Jiangnan area, discussed in detail in Chapter 5. This temple was managed for centuries by the Zheng 鄭 clan, which in 1949 still included around a hundred Daoist masters. The Zheng clan formed a majority in the village and dominated local life. The temple was closed for political reasons in 1958, and then completely destroyed in 1959, and some of the Daoists were sentenced to prison while others were labeled "counter-revolutionaries." The Zheng clan lost all its power in the village. In the 1980s, the temple was rebuilt by the village; some of the Zheng family Daoists who had survived the mass movements have since been employed by the village to carry out rituals, but they no longer play any part in the management of the temple, and relations with the village leaders are far from good.

Some community temples have been able to survive or be rebuilt after the Cultural Revolution, essentially due to their being located on the edges of the cities. Since the beginning of the economic reforms, China has experienced extremely rapid urbanization, in the course of which the countryside around the cities has been gradually transformed into urban neighborhoods. While the Daoist Association of Shanghai states it has 22 temples under its authority, only 3 of them are situated in the old city center of Shanghai. Urbanization leads to the destruction and rebuilding of neighborhoods, many of which have completely disappeared. However, in the old rural or suburban villages, certain temples have been moved or rebuilt; some village committees have made safeguarding the village temple their number one priority when discussing development with higher authorities, and have succeeded.[105] Even when they fail to maintain their temple, and in spite of the inflow of migrants who often outnumber original villagers, the latter often strive to maintain a sense of their corporate religious identity, such as in a Shanghai neighborhood where during the 1990s villagers would come every year to burn incense in the hundreds in front of a condominium built on the site of their former temple. Other cases of villages absorbed into Shanghai show that villagers who could not rebuild their temple put their gods in side shrines of the nearest City God temples managed by Daoists and continued their worship there.[106]

One also sees the joining together of small separate temples into a bigger collective temple, as is the case, for example, with the Yuhuanggong 玉皇宫 near Suzhou. This temple of over 4,000 square meters, inaugurated in 2008 in the new high-tech industrial zone, brought together all the old temples of the zone, in particular the Earth God temples of the constituent villages, as these territorial gods are extremely important to the former residents. These temples had been rebuilt by the villagers in the 1980s, then destroyed (together with the villages themselves) in a major real estate development in the 1990s. These village temples were first relocated as a cluster of small shrines around an old local temple; this was in turn destroyed in the late 2000s and moved to the entirely new Yuhuangong managed by the Daoist association. Dozens of village territorial gods are thus now housed in small cubicles lined around the Daoist temples, and villagers relocated to new high-rise apartment buildings nearby rent a room in the temple as their communal space on the day when they perform a ritual, in negotiation with the Daoists who would like to "improve" their rituals and practices. One reason why villagers want to keep their territorial shrine is that this is where they report the death of villagers to the gods in the course of funerals. Urbanites have lost the memory of the Earth

God with whom they were registered for their territorial identity, but most newly urbanized villagers seem still intent on maintaining this bond.[107]

A large number of temples rebuilt locally by lay communities without any official permission or support have sought to obtain a permit, which was made compulsory by the 1994 "Regulations on the management of places of religious activity." (*Guowuyuan guanyu zongjiao huodong changsuo guanli tiaoli* 國務院關於宗教活動場所管理條例). To this end, they often seek to become affiliated with the Daoist Association (or in some cases, with the Buddhist Association), while maintaining more autonomy – to a degree that varies according to local situations – than the major temples directly managed by the Association. In certain places, in accordance with the 2005 law on religious matters (*Zongjiao shiwu tiaoli* 宗教事務條例), and with consideration underway at the State Administration of Religious Affairs in Beijing of the possibility of recognizing the category of "popular beliefs" (*minjian xinyang* 民間信仰) independent of the five official religions, some local authorities accept the registration of temples in the category of "popular beliefs." However, in most cases, the Daoist Association remains the favored means for a community temple to obtain recognition from the state.

Relations between the community temples and the Daoist Association, when they are affiliated with it, cover a wide range, depending on the persons involved, from open tension to simple taxation (affiliation in exchange for a substantial financial contribution) to confident cooperation – the case of Wenzhou is a good example of such confident cooperation, in stark contrast to the provincial capital of Hangzhou where tension prevails. Some leaders of the local branches of the Daoist Association make no secret of their dissatisfaction with the forms of popular and local religion that are expressed there, and would like to reform them. These leaders believe that a Daoist temple should be managed by Daoist masters, and not by the laity. Moreover, control over the sometimes considerable resources and income generated by the temples increases tension between the Daoist Association and the communities that manage the temples. The leaders of the community temples, some of whom have a very entrepreneurial approach (some temples are contracted out to managers, or actively recruit visitors from other religious sites) take a jaundiced view of the Daoist Association's desire to access and even control the finances of the temples. This is why some major temples with resident Daoists are not affiliated with the Association and have not even the slightest desire to become affiliated. Thus no compromise has ever been found between the Daoist Association and the Lao Dongyuemiao, despite the very important role the temple plays in the religious life of Hangzhou, and the sheer size of its pilgrimage; *de facto*, as with most community temples, it is not an authorized place of worship.

Moreover, it seems that the criteria used to assess requests for affiliation with the Daoist Association, and thus for recognition as a "place of religious activity," serve in the end the government's purpose of limiting the number of community temples. Required from the latter are modern management methods and an excellent condition and outward appearance of the buildings, so that small, impecunious temples have little chance of being accepted. Some of them, conscious of not having the financial resources that would make it possible to satisfy the demands of the Association, do not even make a request. Some have tried to seek affiliation, but have failed. Such is the case of the Sanfangmiao 三方廟, an Earth God temple in the Lao Dongyuemiao area of Hangzhou, founded during the Song dynasty (see Chapter 5 for more details). The Daoists of the Lao Dongyuemiao are often invited to officiate there at the request of the residents. The leaders of the Sanfangmiao sought affiliation with the Daoist Association in order to receive financial assistance for the restoration, but the leaders of the Association were not interested. The temple then changed its name to Sanfangsi 三方寺 in order to take on a Buddhist appearance, but the Buddhist Association was not willing to recognize it either.

Daoist liturgy in an urban context

The contrast we have just outlined between two somewhat ideal but major kinds of Daoist temples expresses itself on several levels. The major temples of the Association are managed by Daoists and satisfy the ideals and needs of the Daoist Association and the state, while the community temples obey the local institutions (village and neighborhood governments, in particular) that control them. The former act as representatives of a modern and state-sanctioned Daoist culture, while the latter tend to justify themselves in terms of local culture and festivals, with some of them even asking for recognition of these festivals as "intangible cultural heritage" (*feiwuzhi wenhua yichan* 非物質文化遺產).[108] The former counts most of its visitors among the urban population and tourists, while the latter, even though it attracts groups of worshippers from afar, is solidly grounded in local community.

In fact, the major temples still do not have processions. For instance, the Daoists of the Shanghai City God temple have for several years asked for permission to once again organize the procession that has not taken place since 1949, but up to now (2017) has not obtained it. By contrast, the community temples usually manage to organize a procession inside their village or neighborhood. The most spectacular case is no doubt that of Quanzhou – a very particular case, since the city is classified as a historic city and is also located in Fujian, a province where the local authorities are the most open to the local temples, and where over half of the ancient neighborhood temples have been rebuilt and have organized processions with official approval.[109]

I would like to emphasize here the question of the ritual services provided by the Daoists in these various kinds of temples. The list of ritual services provided by the major temples managed by the Daoist Association are usually conspicuously displayed to visitors. The temples organize rituals according to the liturgical calendar, particularly for the birthdays of the gods. They also offer services at the request of the laity, divided into two categories: funeral rites, and prosperity rites for the living. Among the former, one does not find the entire "traditional" sequence (at least a whole day, with merit rituals in the morning and in the afternoon, and offerings for suffering souls in the evening) that is still practiced in people's homes by the home-based Daoists. The temples mostly offer segments of this sequence, some of which can be performed long after the death, in particular the "crossing of bridges" (*guoqiao* 過橋), which guides the soul of the deceased from the courts of Purgatory toward a good reincarnation, or a short version of the ritual for the salvation of all suffering souls.

Among the prosperity rituals, the most commonly practiced are the simple recitation of revealed texts, *jing* 經, or of litanies, *chan* 懺, and the offerings to Heaven (*zhaitian* 齋天) followed by the presentation of a request in the name of those who have requested the ritual. The Daoist association's regulations forbid "superstitious practices," including spirit-writing, spirit possession, and divination.[110] These regulations are applied with increasing tolerance: the sale by the temples of spirit-money and other paper offerings is now widespread, and one is allowed to burn them in the temple in a furnace fitted out for this purpose, which was rarely the case in the early 2000s. However, the range of rituals available in the major temples directly managed by the Association remains constrained and limited: one notices in particular the absence of any exorcism, healing, or judicial rituals (which are still frequent in the City God temples in Taiwan and in other parts of the Chinese world[111]), at least in any visible form; it is likely that these rituals are occasionally practiced at clients' request and in their homes or workplaces in secret. Moreover, we should note that manuals dealing with forbidden rituals (such as exorcism or spirit-writing) are freely on sale in the shops of some of the Association's temples.

The situation of the community temples is rather different. While the liturgy[112] is often the same (some major temples managed by the Association reconstituted their texts and their liturgical knowledge with the help of home-based Daoists during the 1980s),[113] the style and range of rituals practiced, as well as their social context, differ significantly. The Association's largest temples have a significant number of available Daoists and new equipment (vestments, musical instruments, paintings, and decoration); these Daoists often on Daoist Association's payroll can afford to emphasize correct appearance and discipline (*zhenggui* 正規) and are quick to criticize the loose style of the small temple and home-based Daoists. The traditional discourse on the superiority of the more disciplined temple Daoists persists despite the fact that the strictly celibate and ascetic way of life (including a program of regular meditation) is becoming increasingly rare among the Daoists living in urban temples.

The conditions under which rituals are supplied also differ between the two kinds of temple. Even more so than those of the Association temples, the Daoists who work in the community temples are frequently asked to officiate outside the temple (particularly for funeral rites in households or in nonreligious premises rented for that purpose), and collaborate constantly with home-based Daoists, who are rarely seen in city centers, but large numbers of whom work in suburban areas. There they also collaborate with other actors in local religious life, including spirit-mediums and groups of lay performers, such as women reciting sutras. Thus, a funeral ritual in a temple of the Daoist Association will take a few hours, with only the officiating Daoists and the close family in attendance; in the suburbs (whether in a community temple or in rented-out premises) it will take a whole day or two, with successive or concurrent rites performed by

Daoists (or Buddhists), sutra-chanting groups, numerous visitors, shared meals, etc. Naturally, for the families, the one does not exclude the other. For urbanites, whether to go to a major Association temple or to a community temple where Daoists work is not really an issue in itself. They go to one or the other according to its proximity to where they live, or according to the places they know: often they are guided and counseled in this approach by people who know the rituals, such as a spirit-medium.

The ritual practice of the temples has suffered major losses compared to the situation prior to 1949. The liturgy of the central temples was not separate from that of the Daoists of the small temples and the home-based Daoists; however, the very socioreligious function of the central temples made them the depositors and guarantors of certain major celebrations, such as city-wide *jiao* offerings. This tradition has to a large extent disappeared, along with the clerics who practiced it and the religious texts preserved by the central temples: these manuals were destroyed during the Cultural Revolution. Consequently, an important part of the ritual repertoire practiced in the temples before 1949 has disappeared[114]; thus, at the Lao Dongyuemiao, only one very old Daoist still knows how to make talismans. In some cases, the liturgical texts still exist, but there is no longer any Daoist who knows how to perform the ritual.[115] This is the case with the ordination rituals (one hardly ever sees a real Daoist ordination in urban areas any more) and with the great community celebrations, particularly to ward off natural disasters (fires, epidemics, etc.) that were the occasions for the largest Daoist rituals up until the middle of the twentieth century. The temples directly managed by the Daoist Association organize large collective rituals several times a year to which everyone can subscribe and participate, particularly for the salvation of the dead (*pudu* 普渡) in the middle of the seventh lunar month,[116] but the laity participates individually and not collectively as of old. These temples also organize major public rituals for the victims of natural disasters, such as after the 2008 Sichuan earthquake.

The renewal of the temples after 1980 necessitated a reintroduction of the liturgy, which in some cases came from home-based Daoists who had been better able than the major temples to conceal and preserve a portion of their possessions and texts. This reintroduction sometimes took place over great distances: thus the liturgy used at the Baiyunguan in Beijing is no longer the pre-1949 liturgy that included some Beijing music,[117] but was reintroduced from Zhejiang and Shaanxi. Taiwanese Daoists also played a role in reintroducing liturgical knowledge. Where the central temples once served as training centers for the local clergy, they are now turning away from that in order to transmit a uniform liturgy and music all over China, and sometimes try to impose it on the small temples controlled by the Association.[118] A similar process is underway in the Buddhist temples.[119] However, the role of the major temples in transmitting the liturgy is not only negative. The manuals (essentially scriptures and litanies for recitation) they have put together have been reproduced in large print runs and are sold in the temple shops, where the small community temple and home-based Daoists come to buy them as needed.

While we do not have quantitative research data available, the Daoists in the major temples whom we interviewed generally agree that they perform more and more rituals for the living (although certain temples, such as those of the Eastern Peak, remain associated with funeral rites). While there was a strong demand for funeral rites as soon as the temples reopened in the early 1980s, in particular from families wishing to do something for the souls of their dead who had suffered and been cremated during the Cultural Revolution (and therefore had not been able to benefit from a traditional burial),[120] it seems that the demands of the urban middle class now focus especially on rituals aimed at bringing health and well-being to increasingly isolated people.

In order to have an overview of rituals performed by Suzhou Daoists, Tao Jin and I have compiled the following tables (Tables 1.2–1.3) based on records collected from master Zhou Caiyuan 周財源 and from the Suzhou Chenghuangmiao.[121]

These tables show how ritually active these Daoist temples are, mostly working from suburban local communities who book and hire the temple priests. This hiring is done through the intermediary of local activists, *xiangtou*, who play a key role in the communal religious life in Suzhou, organize pilgrimages and rituals, and thus bring patrons to the Daoists on a regular basis. There is almost no large-scale *jiao* initiated by city residents, and almost all the *jiao* are patronized by farmers from the suburbs. Furthermore, women are no longer banned from attending *jiao*, and they have actually become the majority of participants in most *jiao*.

This evolution in the demand for ritual services (less variety, rituals above all for individuals and the living) is reflected in the cults within the temples. While the community temples have essentially maintained the cults that were active prior to 1949, the major temples directly managed by the Daoist Association have to some extent recomposed their cults to the detriment of local gods and in favor of cults that are to be found everywhere in China.[122] A particularly developed cult is that of Taisui 太歲 (the God of the planet Jupiter, who rules over all the deities of the

Table 1.2 Rituals Performed By Master Zhou Caiyuan in July 2011

Day	Address of the Patron	Daoists Performing	Type of Ritual	Main Rites Performed
5/24	郊区望亭	7	陪靈道場	三寶懺悔、九天生神煉
7/2	何山道院	客師	過關醮	過關
7/3	何山道院	客師	公醮	發符、供天、進表
7/4	何山道院	客師	公醮	發符、供天、進表
7/5	郊区望亭	7	賣回道場	迎真驅煞、供王
7/9	何山道院	客師	周年道場	咒食、虛皇懺悔
7/10	何山道院	客師	公醮	發符、供天、進表
7/13	市區蘇安新村	5	五七道場	召魂法、供王、虛皇懺悔
7/17	何山道院	客師	公醮	發符、供天、進表
	市区西花桥巷	7	五七道場	發符、供王、虛皇懺悔
7/24	何山道院	客師	公醮	發符、供天、進表
7/25	郊區望亭	7	五七道場	召魂法、亡誥斗、虛皇懺悔

Source: Tao Jin and Goossaert, "Daojiao yu Suzhou difang shehui," p. 105.

Table 1.3 Rituals Performed at Suzhou Chenghuangmiao in July 2011

Day	Address of the Patron	Participants	Type of Ritual	Main Rites Performed
7/13	上海青浦	60	超度祖先	發符、咒食、進表
7/14	蘇州婁葑	90	公醮	發符、供天、進表
7/16	蘇州陸慕	110	過關醮	過關、供天
7/17	蘇州虎丘	120	公醮	發符、供天、進表
	蘇州東港	110	公醮	發符、供天、進表
7/18	蘇州市區	獨醮	獨醮	發符、供天、進表
7/22	蘇州跨塘	70	公醮	發符、供天、進表
7/23	上海嘉定	110	公醮	發符、供天、進表
（火神聖誕）	蘇州虎丘	90	公醮	發符、供天、進表
7/24	蘇州市區	120	公醮	發符、供天、進表
（雷尊聖誕）	蘇州陸慕	200	公醮	發符、供天、進表
7/25	蘇州陸慕	120	公醮	發符、供天、進表
7/26	蘇州田涇	100	過關醮	過關、供天
7/28	蘇州相城	90	過關醮	過關、供天
7/30	上海青浦	90	公醮	發符、供天、進表

Source: Tao Jin and Goossaert, "Daojiao yu Suzhou difang shehui," p. 106.

sexagesimal cycle of the division of time, and who is himself under the authority of Doumu, the Mother of the Dipper stars). This cult, based on the rich Daoist notion of fundamental destiny, existed in the Daoist temples long before 1949, but it seems to have taken up a much larger place in the course of contemporary reconstruction and refitting, as it has in Taiwan and Hong Kong. It is a prime example of a cult practiced by people coming individually to the temple, rather than by a community: one prays to the stellar divinity responsible for one's own destiny (which does not prevent visitors often praying for their relatives). Moreover, the worship of Taisui does not require the mediation of a Daoist; the signs and the salespeople in the shop where one buys the paper offerings explain to the visitor how to proceed. Yet, in some temples at least, like in Nanyang's Xuanmiaoguan, Daoists try to register patrons who come to worship Taisui and to form a community on this basis.

Another service, which constitutes a sizeable source of income for the temples, is that of lamps inscribed with the client's name and lit for a year, and which collectively benefit from the rituals carried out by the temple's Daoists. These lamps can be lit for the dead, or, more and more frequently, for the living to strengthen or rectify his or her fate and fortune. Moreover, while the temples in the People's Republic (by contrast to Hong Kong and Taiwan) do not currently have permission to receive funerary urns, they offer rooms with plaques inscribed with the names of the dead where salvation rituals can be organized for them. The spread of this practice underlines the extent to which the new Daoist Association temples are oriented toward the satisfaction of individual needs without any community framework. In this, they follow a development comparable (even though its point of departure is very different) to the major Daoist temples in Hong Kong, which are also devoid of any community base, but which have found a niche in the market for religious services for individuals (funeral services and repair of individual destiny), and which also justify themselves by the promotion of "Daoist culture."[123]

The Daoists of the Association temples are to some extent at home; they are certainly under the control of the Association leadership and of the Office of Religious Affairs and subject to all sorts of regulations; however, prior to 1949, they were often (in the City God temples in particular) under tight and sometimes extremely intrusive control of the guilds and other institutions of the local elites. In the community temples, whether affiliated with the Association or not, the Daoists are generally, as they have been for centuries, employed by village chiefs or local entrepreneurs who are the real bosses of these temples. This employer-employee relationship inevitably generates economic disagreements, but also theological ones (the Daoists complain that the managers constantly make "mistakes" in the choice of divinities, in the writing of inscriptions, etc.), in contrast with home-based Daoists, who have always been much more free in their practices.

What has changed and now widely characterizes the contemporary situation is thus the severing of the link between the community temples and the major central temples directly managed by the Daoist Association. The latter are evolving from a role of structuring local religion toward serving as centers of religious services for individuals. The continuous decline throughout the twentieth century of territorial communities, both because the state appropriated their resources and prevented their organizing Daoist rituals and because ever-increasing social mobility makes corporate neighborhoods pooling large resources for festivals and rituals ever harder to sustain, has caused this bedrock of urban Daoism to crumble. Such de-territorialization of temple support has also been described for other parts of the Chinese world, notably Taiwan and Hong Kong, even though there the forcible population relocations by the PRC local governments were not a factor.[124] But even as neighborhood Daoist rituals are on the wane, voluntary associations and individuals still need the Daoists. Given the increasing numbers of home-based Daoists, and the vitality of the pilgrimage groups and the neighborhood groups that keep the community temples alive, the importance of Daoism in the largest cities in China still holds.

Conclusion: Temples and Daoists: Four models of adaptation to modernity

The brief survey above and the following chapters suggest that, among Daoists, various models for operating temples (some of which were first developed in Taiwan and Hong Kong) are now at work in the Chinese world: (1) the classical model of the central temple ordering networks of lower-order neighborhood temples, and negotiating with the state and local elites; (2) the Daoist association model of the temple as a conservatory of Daoist culture providing services to individuals; (3) the entrepreneurial temple ran by closed groups of devotees expanding through charity and ritual services; and (4) the community temple that builds up legitimacy by identifying itself as Daoist. These are of course ideal types that combine in multiple ways on the ground. This line of analysis will hopefully contribute to understanding how Daoist clerics, rituals, and communal forms of organization not only resisted or weathered the twentieth-century moderniza-tion processes and embodied tradition, but also, in an urban context, adapted and invented new ways of operating[125]; we should be as attentive to innovation as to loss in that process. I add without elaborating here that a similar analysis would be fruitful when looking at Buddhist institutions.

Model 1: The central temple

I have developed this model above and need not repeat its presentation here; let us simply mention that while its ideal is still alive and some major urban temples attempt to federate local Daoists and associations and organize large-scale, inclu-sive rituals, the pre-1949 systems of regulations (such as territories) and dense networks of associations on which they were based have vanished for good.

Model 2: The conservatory of Daoist culture

The model applied in the major temples managed by the Daoist Association is that of a conservatory and a showplace for "Daoist culture," often understood as being the heart of traditional Chinese culture in the broadest sense. This role expresses itself in the temple shops selling books and objects, where one finds as many items linked to *Yijing* and divination as to Daoism proper; in vegetarian restaurants and tea rooms within the temples where a Daoist aes-thetic is deployed; and in large boards offering representations of Daoist cul-ture that favor the major speculative texts (reinterpreted in the direction of the "Harmonious Society"), the arts and music, mythology and the main divini-ties, and the techniques of the body and of long life (*yangsheng* 養生). The Daoists themselves show visitors (who are essentially urbanites whose tradi-tional religious culture is now often weak because of the rarity of temples and religious festivals in the center of the city) the rudiments of the gestures to carry out in a temple: how to hold the incense sticks, how to bow to the divini-ties, etc. Moreover, certain temples such as the City God temple in Shanghai or the Qinciyang dian 欽賜仰殿 (dedicated to the Eastern Peak, the largest and most active Daoist temple in the municipality of Shanghai) fund a collection of books and manage a website on Daoist culture. One also sees appearing, since the beginning of the 2000s, traditional morality books (*shanshu* 善書) that are distributed for free in the Daoist temples, as has always been the case in Taiwan, Hong Kong, and the rest of the Chinese world.

One also finds treatment centers for "Daoist medicine": some Daoists today, as before 1949, have training in Chinese medicine and very much want to practice (a desire fueled by a genuine social demand for Daoist medicine),[126] but few have the qualifications that would allow them to practice legally, hence formulations under the heading of paramedicine, or even psychological counseling centers.[127] Some Daoists who obtained the right to practice in the 1980s have produced significant income for their temples by this means.

The adaptation of Daoist temples to modern urban life is a topic of vibrant debate within Daoist and academic circles, with optimists pointing out the many "modern" elements of Daoist temple life (harmony, attention to nature, etc.) and others remarking that to most Chinese, this lifestyle has become irrelevant and invisible.[128] The developmental path favored by the Daoist Association is that of tourism, so as to draw to the temples people with little prior interest in and knowledge of Daoism.[129] This is bolstered by a large output of ideological production, but also by training courses for the clergy who attend classes on temple and tourism management. But, some of the more spectacular productions of this drive have proved quite controversial; the huge touristic developments on Maoshan masterminded by the wildly entrepreneurial priest Yang Shihua 楊世華, for instance, as studied by Ian Johnson, have proved profitable so far (but based on speculative investment, and on revenue-sharing with nonreligious private and public outlets). Yet, with his focus on gigantic constructions, marketing the Maoshan brand, and selling retreats for superrich urbanites, Yang's vision has drawn criticism from with Daoist ranks as having very little Daoist content anymore.[130] The Maoshan case is not isolated, and scandals burst out every so often around reckless temple management. But, more sedate Daoist leaders also adapt by showcasing a modern, disciplined, patriotic Daoism.

Model 3: The entrepreneurial temple

The entrepreneurial ethos is absolutely not new to Daoist temples. As we have seen, in late imperial times, elaborate systems of regulations controlled the business of providing ritual services, and many Daoists set up their ritual service centers in cities to tap the market; many of these Daoists were also businessmen, selling not only services but also goods, such as in Wuhan where they controlled the coffin business. Similarly in Hong Kong, Daoists set up shops where they sell all goods and services (including brokering tombs and places for funerary tablets). The twenty-first-century capitalist fever that has engulfed China has unleashed this tradition and brought new developments. Whereas in the past profits were by and large aimed at temple building and development as well as charity, profit has now in some cases become an end in itself, with new temples being built purely as financial investment.[131] This is of course highly controversial, as are all forms of subcontracting of businesses in temples; Fang Ling provides a telling example in Chapter 5.

Model 4: The community temple with a Daoist identity

This model has been particularly prominent in Taiwan, maybe because the particular situation there where Daoists do not control temples, but are nonetheless very important actors on the religious scene. Daoist associations in Taiwan are mostly association of temple leaders, who are lay people, who in turn hire Daoists. Claiming a Daoist identity is an effective way for local temples to bolster their profile as centers of a world religion; in such temples, however, the main deities tend to remain their original local gods rather than the Heavenly worthies and immortals.[132] Similarly, Daoists tend to be hired without any significant power over temple management. The political situation in mainland China, where temples have, in many places, to register with the Daoist or Buddhist association in order to obtain official recognition, had led to a very similar process. In some places, such as Hangzhou documented in Chapter 5, the relationship is fraught (leading local temples to prefer to adopt a Buddhist identity), whereas in others, such as Wenzhou, it is more amicable and mutually beneficial. There, local temples continue to operate with a large degree of autonomy while maintaining good relationships with the Daoist association.

Much depends on which of these models is dominant in a given place: the situation of the Daoists (in charge, hired on contract, or barely tolerated); the range of rituals available (community-oriented, individual-oriented, or very little); the nature of the gods worshipped; and the relation with local communities and associations. This conditions temple life but also religious life outside the temple; the impossibility to use temples to perform rituals is a major impediment for some urban Daoists, as shown in Chapter 6. The wide range of possibilities has existed for a long time but the transformations of the modern and contemporary Chinese world has made some options more difficult to achieve, while others have become easier. There is little doubt that this array of possibilities will continue to evolve due to both political conditions and socioreligious changes.

Notes

1 I develop the concept of "central temple" (*hexin gongguan* 核心宮觀) in Goossaert, "Bureaucratie, taxation et justice." Dean & Zheng, *Ritual Alliances*, 8 use the same term to qualify temples at the core of ritual alliances in the Putian area (Fujian province).

2 On the construction of Quanzhen identities in the modern period, see Liu & Goossaert, eds. *Quanzhen Daoism in Modern Chinese History and Society*.

3 On late Qing and Republican period City God temples and their processions, see Chen Hsi-yuan, "Liji yu guijie"; Goossaert, "The Shifting Balance of Power in the City God Temples," "Managing Chinese Religious Pluralism."

4 Goossaert, "Bureaucratic Charisma"; "Qingdai Jiangnan diqu de Chenghuangmiao, Zhang Tianshi ji daojiao guanliao tixi."

5 I argue this for the Jiangnan area in Goossaert, "Bureaucratie, taxation et justice."

6 On the importance of lineages in defining clerical elites, see Goossaert, "Taoists, 1644-1850," 426–29 and "Les institutions lignagères."

7 On the late imperial state management of Daoists, see Goossaert, *Taoists of Peking*, 55–62 and "Taoism, 1644-1850," 416–36.

8 This system was comprised of the Daolusi 道錄司, with eight officials, at the capital, and one *daoji* 道紀 in each prefecture 府, one *daozheng* 道正 in each subprefecture 州, and one *daohui* 道會 in each county 縣.

9 Zhu Jianming and Tan Jingde, *Shanghai Nanhuixian Zhengyi pai*, 3.

10 This is an underestimate, for several reasons (incomplete data in the source, and Daoist officials who were actually concurrently responsible for several jurisdictions).

11 Even when the local Daoist official (if the position existed in practice) was not posted at the City God temple, the latter was still, in most cases, staffed by Daoists.

12 See for instance the discussion of the Fire God temple in Kunshan (southern Jiangsu) during the mid-nineteenth century, where the magistrate performed the prescribed

sacrifice, and the managing Daoists officiated a *jiao* offering at the same time and in cooperation with the magistrate: *Kunshan xian Chenghuangmiao xuzhi*, 63–64.

13 The key source is the 1789 gazetteer, *Wushan Chenghuangmiao zhi*, a very rich source on the life of the temple during the eighteenth century.

14 Qian Tiemin & Ma Zhenyuan, *Wuxi daojiao keyi*, 6–8.

15 Katz, "Jiangnan daojiao wangluo de fazhan" and Cao Benye & Xu Hongtu, *Wenzhou Pingyang Dongyue guan*; on the Buddhist monasteries in Jiangnan, also divided into *fang*, see Zhang Xuesong, *Fojiao fayuan zongzu yanjiu*.

16 *Wushan Chenghuangmiao zhi*, juan 5.

17 Liu, "General Zhang Buries the Bones."

18 Liu, "In Defense of the City."

19 Liu, "Jidai totomoni," "Quanzhen Proliferates Learning."

20 Liu, "Immortals and Patriarchs."

21 In his case study of Liancheng county (Fujian) Wei Deyu, "Ming yilai Zhengyipai" suggests that during the Qing period, Daoists moved from controlling temples to controlling territories.

22 Wang Jian, *Lihai xiangguan*, 56–57.

23 Zhan Shouzhen, "Anqing daoguan de jianzao yu chuanshuo" and "Anqing daojiao tanzhu ji keshi."

24 Mei Li, "Minguo nianjian Hankou difang zhengfu dui huoju daoshi de guanli."

25 Xu Hongtu & Shi Yuanshi, *Zhejiang sheng Shangyu xian Lingbao zhai tan keyiben huibian*, 7.

26 Wei Deyu, "Ming yilai Zhengyi pai daojiao de shisuhua."

27 Goossaert, "A Question of Control."

28 "Yanjin huoju 嚴禁伙居," *Shenbao*, GX8/3/13.

29 See Huang Xinhua, "Minguo nianjian Suzhou daojiao kao," 33 for such a regulation in 1937 Suzhou.

30 Zheng Zhenman & Dean, *Fujian zongjiao beiming huibian – Quanzhou fu fence*, n° 782.

31 Mei Li, "Minguo nianjian Hankou difang zhengfu dui huoju daoshi de guanli."

32 Among the publications on the role of neighborhood temples in the religious and social life of Chinese cities prior to 1949, mention must be made of the research on Beijing: Naquin, *Peking*; Schipper, "Structures liturgiques et société civile à Pékin"; and the project "Épigraphie et mémoire orale des temples de Pékin – Histoire sociale d'une capitale d'empire" directed by Marianne Bujard.

33 Lai Chi Tim, "Minguo shiqi Guangzhou shi" and *Guangdong difang daojiao*, chapter 5.

34 Zhu Jianming and Tan Jingde, *Shanghai Nanhuixian Zhengyi pai*, 1–3; Chen Yaoting, "Shanghai daojiao shi," 426–28.

35 Chen Yaoting, "Shanghai daojiao shi," 426–28.

36 Central temples Daoists often organized training courses for all local Daoists during the Republican period: see for instance Huang Xinhua, "Minguo nianjian Suzhou daojiao kao," 35 about Suzhou and Zhang Jianxin & Chen Yueqin, *Xi'an Baxian gong*, 96–97 about Xi'an.

37 Jones, *In Search of the Folk Daoists*, documents this point in detail for northern China.

38 Gan Shaocheng, *Qingchengshan daojiao yinyue yanjiu*, chapter 2.

39 Zhu Jianming & Tan Jingde, *Shanghai Nanhuixian Zhengyi pai*, 13.

40 Goossaert, "Quanzhen, what Quanzhen?"

41 *Wumen biaoyin*, 2.23.

42 Huang Xinhua, "Minguo nianjian Suzhou daojiao kao," 34.

43 Qian Tiemin & Ma Zhenyuan, *Wuxi daojiao keyi*, 5; Zhan Shouzhen, "Anqing daojiao tanzhu ji keshi."

44 With the possible exception of mendicant Zhengyi clerics, which I have never heard of.

45 Goossaert, "Starved of Resources," 106–8.

46 See for instance *Youtai xianguan biji*, n°209, where Yu Yue discusses different types of vernacular priests and confuses Daoists and spirit-mediums.

47 See for instance a detailed discussion of this for Shaoxing, Zhejiang province: "Wo zuo daoshi 我做道士," *Shenbao*, 1947.12.03.

48 Goossaert & Palmer, *Religious Question*, chapter 4; Palmer, Katz & Wang, eds., "Special Issue on Redemptive Societies."

49 Goossaert, "Self-cultivation market."

50 Shiga Ichiko, "Difang daojiao zhi xingcheng"; Lai Chi Tim, *Guangdong difang daojiao*, chapter 4; Lai, Yau & Wu, *Xianggang daojiao*, chapters 1 and 3.

51 One example among many of a charitable clinic was the one operated by the Lüzumiao 呂祖廟 on Wushan (Hangzhou): see *Hangsu yifeng*, 37.

52 Nedostup, *Superstitious regimes*; Poon Shuk-wah, *Negotiating Religion*; Goossaert & Palmer, *Religious Question*; Katz & Goossaert, *The Fifty Years that Changed Chinese Religion, 1898–1948*.

53 Goossaert, *Taoists of Peking*, 63–73; see however Fu Haiyan, "Geming, falü yu miaochan" for a detailed study of a brutal (but ultimately failed) takeover of a (Buddhist) Beijing temple in 1931.

54 Poon Shuk-wah, *Negotiating Religion*, chapter 2.

55 Zhang Hua, *Shanghai zongjiao tonglan*, 22–182 ("Buddhist" temples) and 228–329 ("Daoist" temples): these lists include 639 temples for which the date of appropriation is reasonably well documented, among many other less documented cases. The same data are discussed in more detail in Katz & Goossaert, *The Fifty Years that Changed Chinese Religion, 1898–1948*, chapter 1.

56 Lai Chi Tim, "Guangzhou Xuanmiaoguan kaoshi."

57 Liu, "Quanzhen Proliferates Learning."

58 Nedostup, *Superstitious regimes*, 78–88.

59 Xiao Jihong & Dong Yun, *Yunnan daojiao shi*, 142–59.

60 Goossaert, "The Shifting Balance of Power in the City God Temples."

61 Zheng Guo, "Jindai geming yundong."

62 Nedostup, *Superstitious regimes*, 68–74, 84, 96, 99, 106–7, 111–14, 125–26, and passim; Sha Qingqing, "Xinyang yu quanzheng."

63 Kang Youwei 康有為 himself, in his "fake" 1898 memorial on instituting a Confucian state religion (請尊孔聖為國教立教部教會以孔子紀年而廢淫祠摺) specifically targeted the City God temples for destruction: Jian Bozan et al., comp., *Wuxu bianfa*, 231.

64 Poon Shuk-wah, "Religion, Modernity, and Urban Space."

65 Su Zhiliang & Yao Fei, "Miao, xinyang yu shequ."

66 "Yushi beigao 羽士被告," *Shenbao*, GX22/10/23.

67 "Xiao daoshi jieguan miaochan 小道士接管廟產," *Shenbao*, 1913.7.4.

68 Chen Hsi-yuan, "Liji yu guijie," Yu Zhejun, "Volksreligion im Spiegel der Zivilgesellschaftstheorie," chapter 9; *Shenming yu shimin*.

69 Huang Xinhua, "Minguo nianjian Suzhou daojiao kao," 35.

70 Lai Chi Tim, "Minguo shiqi Guangzhou shi."

71 Mei Li, "Minguo nianjian Hankou difang zhengfu dui huoju daoshi de guanli."

72 Xu Yue, "Qingmo Sichuan miaochan xingxue."

73 Huang Xinhua, "Minguo nianjian Suzhou daojiao kao," 34 who opposes the *xianghuo daoyuan* 香火道院 (temples that had maintained enough of an endowment to live from) and the *jingji daoyuan* 經濟道院 (temples that had to rely entirely on fees and donations).

74 For Beijing, see Goossaert, *The Taoists of Peking*, 84–86.

75 Jones, *In Search of the Folk Daoists*, 146–48.

76 Goossaert & Palmer, *Religious Question*, 205–6.

77 Lai Chi Tim, Yau Chi-on & Wu Zhen, *Xianggang daojiao*, chapter 1.

78 On the Republican-period Daoist associations, see Goossaert, "Republican Church Engineering"; Liu, "Daoism from the late Qing to Early Republican Periods," 814–18.
79 Cao Benye & Xu Hongtu, *Hangzhou Baopu daoyuan*, 107–8.
80 Cao Benye & Xu Hongtu, *Hangzhou Baopu daoyuan*, 88–96, 125–26; Han Songtao, "Yuhuangshan daojiao."
81 Liu, "Quanzhen Proliferates Learning."
82 Goossaert, "The local politics of festivals," "Wanqing ji Minguo shiqi Jiangnan diqu de yingshen saihui."
83 Yu Zhejun, "Volksreligion im Spiegel der Zivilgesellschaftstheorie," chapter 10. Similar reports in Shen Jie, "Fan mixin," 56–62.
84 For a detailed discussion of how the KMT activists managed to disrupt the massive processions of village temples to Daoist central temples in townships around Suzhou during the 1930s, see Xiao Tian, "Shequ chuantong de jindai mingyun."
85 Li Xuechang & Dong Jianbo, "Hangxian yingshen saihui shuailuo."
86 Examples: a three-day ritual in Wuxi presided over by the 63rd Heavenly master Zhang Enpu 張恩溥 (1904–1969, titled 1924) for dead soldiers: Qian Tiemin & Ma Zhenyuan, *Wuxi daojiao keyi*, 15; rituals for peace presided over by Li Lishan in 1939 in Hangzhou, see Han Songtao, "Yuhuangshan daojiao."
87 Shen Jie, "Fan mixin." See also Nedostup, *Superstitious Regimes*, 136–37 on the massive rain-making *jiao* at the Xuanmiaoguan.
88 Goossaert & Berezkin, "The Three Mao Lords in modern Jiangnan."
89 See Poon, "Thriving" for a detailed discussion of a case from Guangdong.
90 This section is based on Goossaert & Fang, "Temples and Daoists in Urban China since 1980."
91 Goossaert & Palmer, *Religious Question*, chapters 10 and 11.
92 Dean, "Further Partings of the Way," observes that while the Daoist ritual networks have been reconstituted in rural areas, they are often no more than a memory in the cities.
93 Ji Zhe, "Buddhism in the Reform-Era China"; Ashiwa and Wank, "The Politics of a Reviving Buddhist Temple."
94 Lai Chi Tim, "Daoism in China Today, 1980–2002."
95 Fan Guangchun, "Urban Daoism, Commodity Markets and Tourism."
96 Fisher, "Universal Rescue."
97 We have seen this situation mostly in medium-size cities. It is probably less frequent in the major metropolises, but there again the situation varies enormously from one city to another.
98 Yang Der-Ruey, "The Changing Economy"; "The Education of Taoist Priests."
99 All the home-based Daoists we interviewed and followed belong to the Zhengyi order, which seems to be the rule in the major cities in Jiangnan. However, there are home-based Quanzhen Daoists (and indeed, Buddhists) in other parts of China.
100 This term, which is extremely common all over the Chinese world, can have various meanings; in Jiangnan it particularly denotes pious groups that have no temple but that make regular pilgrimages to temples.
101 This ritual is described in detail in Liu Hong, *Suzhou daojiao keyi yinyue*; see also Tao Jin & Goossaert, "Daojiao yu Suzhou difang shehui."
102 See a discussion of this issue in the context of the Maoshan cult and pilgrimage in Goossaert & Berezkin, "The Three Mao Lords in modern Jiangnan"; see also Yang Der-Ruey, "The Changing Economy."
103 Lai Chi Tim, "Xiandai dushi zhong daojiao miaoyu de zhuanxing."
104 Long Feijun, "Jiangyi Yubu, hefa danxin," 117.
105 Dean & Zheng, *Ritual Alliances*, 25–26 discuss this process in Putian (Fujian province).
106 Wang Honggang, "Shanghai nongcun chengshihua."
107 Goossaert, "Territorial cults and the urbanization of the Chinese world."

108 Thus a request was made for recognition of the major festival known as "audience and judgment" (*chaoshen* 朝審) of the Lao Dongyuemiao, which has not been able to be organized since 1949. On the role of the intangible cultural heritage in the rehabilitation of local cults, see Goossaert and Palmer, *Religious Question*, chapter 12.

109 Abramson, "Places for the Gods."

110　See the detailed 1998 regulations in "Zhongguo daojiao xiehui guanyu."

111　Katz, *Divine Justice*, chapter 7.

112 Liturgy is composed of all the rules and resources (texts, music, and informal rules) that make it possible to perform rituals.

113 See, for example, the reconstitution of the liturgy of a temple near Shanghai: Zhu Jianming and Tan Jingde, *Shanghai Nanhuixian Zhengyi pai*.

114 On the ritual services in the Daoist temples in Beijing prior to 1949, see Goossaert, *The Taoists of Peking*, chapter 6.

115 Zhu Jianming and Tan Jingde, *Shanghai Nanhuixian Zhengyi pai*, pp. 123–134. On the loss of contemporary Daoist liturgy in another context, see Jones, *In Search of the Folk Daoists*.

116 There are good descriptions in Cao Benye and Xu Hongtu, *Hangzhou Baopu daoyuan daojiao yinyue*.

117 Jones, *In Search of the Folk Daoists*; Goossaert, *The Taoists of Peking*.

118 Lai Chi Tim, "Contemporary Daoist Temples in Guangdong" which shows how, in affiliating themselves to the Daoist Association, local temples in Guangdong adopt cults and a liturgy that were unknown to them.

119 Tan Hwee-San, "Saving the Soul in Red China."

120 On the funeral reforms and their consequences, see Fang and Goossaert, "Les réformes funéraires" and Goossaert & Palmer, *Religious Question*, chapter 9.

121 Tao Jin & Goossaert, "Daojiao yu Suzhou difang shehui."

122 See, for example, a discussion of the differences between the divinities present in the Baiyunguan today and prior to 1949 in Li Yangzheng, *Xinbian Beijing Baiyunguan zhi*, chapter 3.

123 On the Hong Kong Daoist temples, which play an important part in the financing of temples in the People's Republic, see Lai Chi Tim, "Hong Kong Daoism," *idem* (ed), *Xianggang daotang keyi lishi yu chuancheng*, and Lai Chi Tim, Yau Chi-on & Wu Zhen, *Xianggang daojiao*.

124 Chipman's "The De-territorialization of Ritual Spheres" argues that large temples such as the Chaotiangong 朝天宮 in Beigang used to draw support mostly from subordinate neighborhood temples and now, like many other such temples, is mostly supported by volunteer associations from throughout the island (while the neighborhoods are still active in the temple festival), yet her fine discussion of the nature of the territorial link shows that de-territorialization does not necessarily mean a weakening of the bond with the temple. Furthermore, territorial groups are still well entrenched in Taiwan and major patrons of the Daoists' liturgical services. By contrast, Hong Kong corporate villages that as a rule organize regular massive *jiao* festivals are becoming fewer and fewer, as they sell their land to property developers.

125 For instance, Liu, "Quanzhen Proliferates Learning" studies how the Xuanmiaoguan actually played an active role during the Republican-period educational and other state-building reforms in Nanyang (southern Henan).

126 On the case of a contemporary Daoist doctor practicing in the largest Daoist temple in Wuhan, see Liu, "Abbot Huang Zongsheng."

127 At the Changchunguan in Wuhan, when we visited in 2007, a consulting room for life choices was run by a lay disciple of the monastery's abbess.

128 Johnson, "Two Sides."

129 On tourism and religion in contemporary China, see Oakes and Sutton, *Faiths on Display*.

130 Johnson, "Two Sides."

131 For a discussion of the creation of purely entrepreneurial temples, see Lang, Chan, and Ragvald, "Temples and the Religious Economy."
132 See for instance the case of the Baoangong 保安宮 in Taipei: Liao Wuzhi, *Xinxiu Dalongdong Baoangong zhi.*

Bibliography

Primary

Hangsu yifeng 杭俗遺風. Fan Zushu 范祖述. Ca 1850. Shanghai: Shanghai wenyi chubanshe, 1989.
Shenbao 申報. Shanghai: Shenbaoguan, daily, 1872–1949.

Secondary

Abramson, Daniel Benjamin. "Places for the Gods: Urban Planning as Orthopraxy and Heteropraxy in China," in Nihal Perera & Tang Wing-Shing (eds.), *The Transforming Asian City: Innovative Urban Planning Practices*, pp. 7–27. http://geog.hkbu.edu.hk /tacconf/PROCEEDING%20BOOK%20OF%20   TRANSFORMING%20ASIAN %20CITIES.pdf, accessed 5 August 2009.
Ai Ping 艾萍. "Minguo jinzhi yingshen saihui lunxi. Yi Shanghai wei gean 民國禁止迎神賽會論析. 以上海為個案," *Jiangsu shehui kexue* 江蘇社會科學, 5, 2010, pp. 216–21.
Anonymous "Zhongguo daojiao xiehui guanyu daojiao gongguan guanli banfa 中國道教協會關于道教宮觀管理辦法," *Zhongguo daojiao*, 4, 1998, pp. 19–21.
Ashiwa Yoshiko & David L. Wank. "The Politics of a Reviving Buddhist Temple: State, Association, and Religion in Southeast China," *Journal of Asian Studies*, 65(2), 2006, pp. 337–59.
Cao Benye 曹本冶 & Xu Hongtu 徐宏圖. *Hangzhou Baopu daoyuan daojiao yinyue* 杭州抱朴道院道教音樂. Taipei: Xinwenfeng, 2000.
Cao Benye 曹本冶 & Xu Hongtu 徐宏圖. *Wenzhou Pingyang Dongyue guan daojiao yinyue yanjiu* 溫州平陽東嶽觀道教音樂研究. Taibei: Xinwenfeng, 2000.
Chen Hsi-yuan 陳熙遠. "Liji yu guijie – Shilun youyi zai tan yu miao, guan yu min zhijian de Shanghai sanxunhui 厲祭與鬼節 – 試論游移在壇與廟、官與民之間的上海三巡會," *Paper for the "The Modern History of Urban Daoism" International Conference*, Tainan, 13–14 November 2010.
Chen Yaoting 陳耀庭. "Shanghai daojiao shi 上海道教史," in Ruan Renze 阮仁澤 & Gao Zhennong 高振農 (eds.), *Shanghai zongjiao shi* 上海宗教史. Shanghai: Shanghai renmin chubanshe, 1992, pp. 353–438.
Chipman, Elana. "The De-territorialization of Ritual Spheres in Contemporary Taiwan," *Asian Anthropology*, 8, 2009, pp. 31–64.
Dean, Kenneth & Zheng Zhenman. *Ritual Alliances of the Putian Plain*. Leiden: Brill, 2010, 2 vols.
Dean, Kenneth. "Further Partings of the Way: The Chinese State and Daoist Ritual Traditions in Contemporary China," in Yoshiko Ashiwa and David L. Wank (eds.), *Making Religion, Making the State: The Politics of Religion in Contemporary China*. Stanford: Stanford University Press, 2009, pp. 178–210.
Fan, Guangchun. "Urban Daoism, Commodity Markets and Tourism: The Restoration of the Xi'an City God Temple," in David A. Palmer and Xun Liu (eds.), *Daoism in the*

Twentieth Century: Between Eternity and Modernity. Berkeley: University of California Press, 2012, pp. 108–20.

Fang, Ling and Vincent Goossaert. "Les réformes funéraires et la politique religieuse de l'État chinois, 1900–2008," *Archives de Sciences Sociales des Religions*, 144, 2008, pp. 51–73.

Faure, David. *Emperor and Ancestor: State and Lineage in South China*. Stanford: Stanford University Press, 2007.

Fisher, Gareth John. "Universal Rescue: Re-making Post-Mao China in a Beijing Temple," PhD dissertation, University of Virginia, 2006.

Fu Haiyan 付海晏. "Geming, falü yu miaochan – Minguo Beiping Tieshansi an yanjiu 革命、法律與廟產—民國北平鐵山寺案研究," *Lishi yanjiu* 歷史研究, 3, 2009, pp. 105–20.

Gan Shaocheng 甘紹成. *Qingchengshan daojiao yinyue yanjiu* 青城山道教音樂研究. Taibei: Xinwenfeng, 2000.

Goossaert, Vincent & Fang Ling. "Temples and Daoists in Urban China since 1980," *China Perspectives*, 4, 2009, pp. 32–41.

Goossaert, Vincent & David A. Palmer. *The Religious Question in Modern China*. Chicago: University of Chicago Press, 2011.

Goossaert, Vincent. "Daoists in the Modern Chinese Self-Cultivation Market: The Case of Beijing, 1850–1949," in David Palmer & Xun Liu (eds.), *Daoism in the 20th Century: Between Eternity and Modernity*. Berkeley: University of California Press, 2012, pp. 123–53.

Goossaert, Vincent. "Détruire les temples pour construire les écoles: reconstitution d'un objet historique," *Extrême-Orient Extrême-Orient*, 33 (special issue *Religion, Education et Politique en Chine moderne*), 2011, pp. 35–51.

Goossaert, Vincent. "Les institutions lignagères des spécialistes religieux en Chine, 16e-21ème siècles," in Adeline Herrou & Gisèle Krauskopff (eds.), *Moines et moniales de par le monde. La vie monastique au miroir de la parenté*. Paris: L'Harmattan, 2010, pp. 305–18.

Goossaert, Vincent. "The Local Politics of Festivals: Hangzhou, 1850–1950," *Daoism Religion, History & Society*, 5, 2013, pp. 57–80.

Goossaert, Vincent. "Managing Chinese Religious Pluralism in the Nineteenth-Century City Gods Temples," in Thomas Jansen, Thoralf Klein & Christian Meyer (eds.), *Globalization and the Making of Religious Modernity in China*. Boston: Brill, 2014, pp. 29–51.

Goossaert, Vincent. "Quanzhen, What Quanzhen? Late Imperial Daoist Clerical Identities in Lay Perspective," in Vincent Goossaert & Xun Liu (eds.), *Quanzhen Daoists in Chinese Society and Culture, 1500–2010*. Berkeley: Institute of East Asian Studies, 2013, pp. 19–43.

Goossaert, Vincent. "A Question of Control: Licensing Local Ritual Specialists in Jiangnan, 1850–1950," in Liu Shufen & Paul R. Katz (eds.), *Xinyang, shijian yu wenhua tiaoshi. Proceeding of the Fourth International Sinology Conference* 信仰、實踐與文化調適. 第四屆國際漢學會議論文集. Taipei: Academia Sinica, 2013, pp. 569–604.

Goossaert, Vincent. "Qingdai Jiangnan diqu de Chenghuangmiao, Zhang Tianshi ji daojiao guanliao tixi 清代江南地區的城隍廟、張天師及道教官僚體系," *Qingshi yanjiu* 清史研究, 1, 2010, pp. 1–11.

Goossaert, Vincent. "Republican Church Engineering. The National Religious Associations in 1912 China," in Mayfair Mei-hui Yang (ed.), *Chinese Religiosities: Afflictions of Modernity and State Formation*. Berkeley: University of California Press, 2008, pp. 209–32.

Goossaert, Vincent. "The Shifting Balance of Power in the City God Temples, Late Qing to 1937," *Journal of Chinese Religions*, 43(1), 2015, pp. 5–33.

Goossaert, Vincent. "Starved of Resources. Clerical Hunger and Enclosures in Nineteenth-Century China," *Harvard Journal of Asiatic Studies*, 62(1), 2002, pp. 77–133.

Goossaert, Vincent. "Taoists, 1644–1850," in *Cambridge History of China*, vol. 9, part 2: *The Ch'ing Dynasty to 1800*. Cambridge: Cambridge University Press, 2016, pp. 412–57.

Goossaert, Vincent. *The Taoists of Peking, 1800–1949. A Social History of Urban Clerics*. Cambridge (MA): Harvard University Asia Center, 2007.

Goossaert, Vincent. "Territorial Cults and the Urbanization of the Chinese World. A Case Study of Suzhou," in Peter van der Veer (ed.), *Handbook of Religion and the Asian City*. Berkeley: University of California Press, 2015, pp. 52–68.

Goossaert, Vincent 高萬桑. "Wanqing ji Minguo shiqi Jiangnan diqu de yingshen saihui 晚清及民國時期江南地區的迎神賽會," in Paul R. Katz & Vincent Goossaert (eds.), *Gaibianle Zhongguo zongjiao de wushinian* 改變了中國宗教的50年. Taipei: Institute of Modern History, Academia Sinica, 2015, pp. 75–99.

Goossaert, Vincent & Rostislav Berezkin. "The Three Mao Lords in Modern Jiangnan. Cult and Pilgrimage between Daoism and *baojuan* Recitation," *Bulletin de l'EFEO*, 99, 2012–2013, pp. 295–326.

Goossaert, Vincent & Xun Liu, eds. *Quanzhen Daoists in Chinese Society and Culture, 1500–2010*. Berkeley: Institute of East Asian Studies, 2013.

Han Songtao 韓松濤. "Yuhuangshan daojiao jindai yilai zhi bianqian 玉皇山道教近代以來之變遷," *Daoism: Religion, History and Society*, 4, 2012, pp. 49–82.

Huang Xinhua 黃新華. "Minguo nianjian Suzhou daojiao kao 民國年間蘇州道教考," *Zhongguo daojiao* 中國道教, 4, 2008, pp. 33–36.

Ji, Zhe. "Buddhism in the Reform-Era China: A Secularised Revival?," in Adam Yuet Chau (ed.), *Religion in Contemporary China: Revitalization and Innovation*. London: Routledge, 2011, pp. 32–52.

Jian Bozan 翦伯贊 et al., comp. *Wuxu bianfa* 戊戌變法. Shanghai: Shenzhou guoguangshe, 1953.

Johnson, Ian. "Two Sides of a Mountain. The Modern Transformation of Maoshan," *Journal of Daoist Studies*, 5, 2012, pp. 89–116.

Jones, Stephen. *In Search of the Folk Daoists of North China*. Aldershot: Ashgate, 2010.

Katz, Paul R. *Divine Justice: Religion and the Development of Chinese Legal Culture*. London: Routledge, 2008.

Katz, Paul R. 康豹. "You *Weiyu dongtian Qiuzu Longmen zongpu* lai kan jindai Jiangnan daojiao wangluo de fazhan 由《委羽洞天邱祖龍門宗譜》來看近代江南道教網路的發展," in Fang Ling & Vincent Goossaert (eds.), *Zhongguo xiandangdai chengshi daojiao ziliaoji* 中國現當代城市道教資料集. Beijing: Zongjiao wenhua chubanshe, in press.

Katz, Paul R. & Vincent Goossaert. *The Fifty Years that Changed Chinese Religion, 1898–1948*. Ann Arbor: AAS, in press.

Lai Chi Tim 黎志添 (ed.). *Xianggang daotang keyi lishi yu chuancheng* 香港道堂科儀歷史與傳承. Hong Kong: Zhonghua shuju, 2007.

Lai Chi Tim 黎志添, Yau Chi-on 游子安 & Wu Zhen 吳真. *Xianggang daojiao: lishi yuanliu jiqi xiandai zhuanxing* 香港道教：歷史源流及其現代轉型. Hong Kong: Zhonghua shuju, 2010.

Lai Chi Tim 黎志添. "Guangzhou Xuanmiaoguan kaoshi 廣州元妙觀考釋," *Zhongyang yanjiuyuan Lishi yuyan yanjiusuo jikan* 中央研究院歷史語言研究所集刊, 75(3), 2004, pp. 445–513.

Lai Chi Tim 黎志添. "Minguo shiqi Guangzhou shi 'Namo daoguan' de lishi kaojiu 民國時期廣州市南嘸道館的歷史考究," *Zhongyang yanjiuyuan Jindaishi yanjiusuo jikan* 中央研究院近代史研究所集刊, 37, 2002, pp. 1–40.

Lai Chi Tim 黎志添. *Guangdong difang daojiao yanjiu: daoguan, daoshi, ji keyi* 廣東地方道教研究: 道觀、道士及科儀. Hong Kong: Chinese University Press, 2007.

Lai Chi Tim 黎志添. "Xiandai dushi zhong daojiao miaoyu de zhuanxing – cong cunmiao dao daoguan: yi Guangzhoushi Pantangxiang Renweimiao wei ge'an 現代都市中道教廟宇的轉型 – 從村廟到道觀. 以廣州市泮塘鄉仁威廟為個案," *Daoism: Religion, History and Society*, 4, 2012, pp. 127–73.

Lai, Chi Tim. "Contemporary Daoist Temples in Guangdong: A Construction of 'Daoist' Identity and Founding of New Daoist Temples," *Xianggang zhongwen daxue Daojiao wenhua yanjiu zhongxin tongxun*, 14, 2009, pp. 1–4.

Lai, Chi Tim. "Daoism in China Today, 1980–2002," in Daniel Overmyer (ed.), *Religion in China Today, China Quarterly*, 174, 2003 (also published as a book: Cambridge: Cambridge University Press, 2003), pp. 413–27.

Lai, Chi Tim. "Hong Kong Daoism: A Study of Daoist Altars and Lü Dongbin Cults," *Social Compass*, 50(4), 2003, pp. 459–70.

Lang, Graeme, Selina Chan and Lars Ragvald. "Temples and the Religious Economy," in Yang Fenggang and Joseph B. Tamney (eds.), *State, Market, and Religions in Chinese Societies*. Leiden: Brill, 2005, pp. 149–80.

Li Shiwei 李世偉. "Jieyan qian Taiwan xiandao tuanti de jieshe yu huodong, 1950–1987 解嚴前臺灣仙道團體的結社礜活動," in Chi Tim Lai 黎志添 (ed.), *Xianggang ji Huanan daojiao yanjiu* 香港及華南道教研究. Hong Kong: Zhonghua shuju, 2005, pp. 485–514.

Li Xuechang 李學昌 & Dong Jianbo 董建波. "Ershi shiji shangbanye Hangxian yingshen saihui shuailuo yinsu qianxi 二十世紀上半葉杭縣迎神賽會衰落因素淺析," *Huadong shifan daxue xuebao (Zhexue shehui kexue ban)* 華東師範大學學報(哲學社會科學版), 39(5), 2007, pp. 49–53.

Li Yangzheng 李養正. *Xinbian Beijing Baiyunguan zhi* 新編北京白雲觀志. Beijing: Zongjiao wenhua chubanshe, 2003.

Liao Wuzhi 廖武治, comp. *Xinxiu Dalongdong Baoangong zhi* 新修大龍峒保安宮志. Taipei: Baoangong, 2005.

Liu Hong 劉紅. *Suzhou daojiao keyi yinyue yanjiu: yi 'Tiangong' keyi weili zhankai de taolun* 蘇州道教科儀音樂研究: 以「天功」科儀為例展開的討論. Taipei: Xinwenfeng, 1999.

Liu, Xun. "Daoism from the late Qing to Early Republican Periods," in Vincent Goossaert, Jan Kiely & John Lagerwey (eds.), *Modern Chinese Religion II: 1850–2015*. Leiden: Brill, 2015, pp. 806–37.

Liu, Xun. "In Defense of the City and the Polity: The Xuanmiao Monastery and the Qing Anti-Taiping Campaigns in the Mid-Nineteenth Century Nanyang," *T'oung Pao*, 95, 2009, pp. 287–333.

Liu, Xun. "General Zhang Buries the Bones: Early Qing Reconstruction and Quanzhen Daoist Collaboration in Mid-Seventeenth Century Nanyang," *Late Imperial China*, 27(2), 2006, pp. 67–98.

Liu, Xun. "Immortals and Patriarchs: The Daoist World of a Manchu Official and His Family in Nineteenth Century China," *Asia Major* 3rd series, 17(2), 2004, pp. 161–218.

Liu Xun 劉迅. "Jidai to tomo ni: Zenshin dōshi Ri Sōyō to Jiki, Dōmeikai, oyobi Shinmatsu-Minsho Nanyō ni okeru kindaika kaikaku (1890 nendai – 1930 nendai) 時代とともに一全真道士李宗陽と慈禧,同盟會,および清末民初南陽における近代

化改革(1890–1930)," in Tanaka Fumio 田中文雄 & Terry Kleeman (eds.), *Dōkyō to kyōsei shisō* 道教と共生思想. Tokyo: Taiga Shobō, 2009, pp. 299–337.

Liu, Xun. "Profile of a Quanzhen Doctor Abbot Huang Zongsheng of Monastery of Eternal Spring in Wuhan," *Journal of Daoist Studies*, 1, 2008, pp. 154–60.

Liu, Xun. "Quanzhen Proliferates Learning: The Xuanmiao Temple, Clerical Activism, and the Modern Reforms in Nanyang, 1880s–1940s," in Vincent Goossaert & Xun Liu (eds.), *Quanzhen Daoists in Chinese Society and Culture, 1500–2010*, vol. 39. Berkeley: Institute of East Asian Studies, 2013, pp. 269–307.

Long Feijun 龍飛俊. "Jiangyi yubu, hefa danxin. Shanghai Chuansha Cao Suixin daozhang fangtan lu 絳衣禹步鶴發丹心 – 上海川沙曹歲辛道長訪談錄," *Shilin* 史林, 180, 2007, pp. 117–19.

Mei Li 梅莉. "Cong Minguo nianjian Hankou de sici dengji kan difang zhengfu dui huoju daoshi de guanli 從民國年間漢口的四次登記看地方政府對火居道士的管理," *Daoism: Religion, History and Society*, 4, 2012, pp. 251–86.

Naquin, Susan. *Peking: Temples and City Life, 1400–1900.* Berkeley: University of California Press, 2000.

Nedostup, Rebecca. *Superstitious Regimes. Religion and the Politics of Chinese Modernity.* Cambridge (MA): Harvard University Asia Center, 2009.

Oakes, Tim & Donald S. Sutton, eds. *Faiths on Display. Religion, Tourism, and the Chinese State.* Lanham: Rowman & Littlefield, 2010.

Palmer, David A., Paul R. Katz & Wang Chien-chuan, eds. "Special Issue on Redemptive Societies and New Religious Movements in Modern China," *Min-su ch'ü-i*, 172–173, 2011.

Poon, Shuk Wah. *Negotiating Religion in Modern China: State and Common People in Guangzhou, 1900–1937.* Hong Kong: Chinese University Press, 2011.

Poon, Shuk Wah. "Thriving under an Anti-superstition Regime: The Dragon Mother Cult in Yuecheng, Guangdong, during the 1930s," *Journal of Chinese Religions*, 43(1), 2015, pp. 34–58.

Qian Tiemin 錢鐵民 & Ma Zhenyuan 馬珍媛. *Wuxi daojiao keyi yinyue yanjiu* 無錫道教科儀音樂研究. Taibei: Xinwenfeng, 1999.

Schipper, Kristofer. "Structures liturgiques et société civile à Pékin," *Matériaux pour l'étude de la religion chinoise – Sanjiao wenxian*, 1, 1997, pp. 9–23.

Sha Qingqing 沙青青. "Xinyang yu quanzheng: 1931 nian Gaoyou 'Da Chenghuang' fengchao zhi yanjiu 信仰與權爭: 1931年高郵"打城隍"風潮之研究," *Jindaishi yanjiu* 近代史研究, 1, 2010, pp. 115–27.

Shen Jie 沈潔. "Fan mixin yu shequ xinyang kongjian de xiandai licheng – yi 1934 nian Suzhou de qiuyu yishi weili 反迷信與社區信仰空間的現代曆程——以1934年蘇州的求雨儀式為例," *Shilin* 史林, 2, 2007, pp. 44–63.

Shiga Ichiko 志賀市子. "Difang daojiao zhi xingcheng: Guangdong diqu fuluan jieshe yundong zhi xingqi yu yanbian 地方道教之形成：廣東地區扶鸞結社運動之興起與演變(1838–1953)," *Daoism: Religion, History and Society*, 2, 2010, pp. 231–67.

Su Zhiliang 蘇智良 & Yao Fei 姚霏. "Miao, xinyang yu shequ – Cong Chenghuang xinyang kan jindai Shanghai Chenghuangmiao shequ 廟, 信仰與社區 – 從城隍信仰看近代上海城隍廟社區," *Shehui kexue* 社會科學, 1, 2007, pp. 63–73.

Tan, Hwee-San. "Saving the Soul in Red China: Music and Ideology in the 'Gongde' Ritual of Merit in Fujian," *British Journal of Ethnomusicology*, 11(1), 2002, pp. 119–40.

Tao Jin 陶金 & Vincent Goossaert 高萬桑. "Daojiao yu Suzhou difang shehui 道教與蘇州地方社會," in Fan Lizhu & Robert Weller (eds.), *Jiangnan diqu de zongjiao yu gonggong shenghuo* 江南地區的宗教與公共生活. Shanghai: Shanghai renmin chubanshe, 2015, pp. 86–112.

Wang Honggang 王宏剛. "Shanghai nongcun chengshihua guochengzhong de zongjiao wenti yanjiu 上海農村城市化過程中的宗教問題研究," *Shijie zongjiao yanjiu* 世界宗教研究, 4, 2005, pp. 130–41.

Wang Jian 王健. *Lihai xiangguan: Ming Qing yilai Jiangnan Susong diqu minjian xinyang yanjiu* 利害相關: 明清以來江南蘇松地區民間信仰研究. Shanghai: Shanghai renmin chubanshe, 2010.

Wang Ping 王平. "Daojiao 道教," in *Wuhan shizhi, shehui zhi* 武漢市志.社會志. Wuhan: Wuhan daxue chubanshe, 1997, pp. 215–40.

Wei Deyu 魏德毓. "Ming yilai Zhengyi pai daojiao de shisuhua – dui Minxi huoju daoshi de diaocha 明以來正一派道教的世俗化 – 對閩西火居道士的調查," *Shehui kexue* 社會科學, 11, 2006, pp. 153–60.

Xiao Tian 小田. "Shequ chuantong de jindai mingyun. Yi Suzhou "Qionglong laohui" wei duixiang de li'an yanjiu 社區傳統的近代命運。 以蘇州穹窿老會為對象的例案研究," *Jiangsu shehui kexue* 江蘇社會科學, 6, 2002, pp. 141–47.

Xu Hongtu 徐宏圖 & Shi Yuanshi 石元詩. *Zhejiang sheng Shangyu xian Lingbao zhai tan keyiben huibian* 浙江省上虞縣靈寶齋壇科儀本彙編. Taibei: Xinwenfeng, 2006.

Xu Yue 徐跃. "Qingmo Sichuan miaochan xingxue ji youci chansheng de sengsu jiufen 清末四川廟產興學及由此產生的僧俗糾紛," *Jindaishi yanjiu* 近代史研究, 5, 2008, pp. 73–88.

Yang, Der-Ruey. "The Education of Taoist Priests in Contemporary Shanghai, China," PhD dissertation, London School of Economics and Political Science, 2003.

Yang, Der-Ruey. "The Changing Economy of Temple Daoism in Shanghai," in Yang Fenggang and Joseph B. Tamney (eds.), *State, Market, and Religions in Chinese Societies*. Leiden: Brill, 2005, pp. 113–48.

Yu, Zhejun. "Volksreligion im Spiegel der Zivilgesellschaftstheorie: Gottbegrüssungsprozession in Shanghai während der Republikzeit," PhD. dissertation, Leipzig University, 2010.

Yu Zhejun 郁喆雋. *Shenming yu shimin: Minguo shiqi Shanghai diqu yingshen saihui yanjiu* 神明與市民：民國時期上海地區迎神賽會研究. Shanghai: Shanghai Sanlian shudian, 2014.

Zhan Shouzhen 詹壽禎. "Anqing daoguan de jianzao yu chuanshuo 安慶道觀的建造與傳說" & "Anqing daojiao tanzhu ji keshi 安慶道教壇主及客師," *Anqing wenshi ziliao* 安慶文史資料, 25, 1994, pp. 108–12 & 116–18.

Zhang Hua 張化. *Shanghai zongjiao tonglan* 上海宗教通覽. Shanghai: Shanghai guji chubanshe, 2004.

Zhang Xuesong 張雪松. *Fojiao fayuan zongzu yanjiu* 佛教法緣宗族研究. Beijing: Zhongguo renmin daxue chubanshe, 2015.

Zhang Jianxin 張建新 & Chen Yueqin 陳月琴. *Xi'an Baxian gong* 西安八仙宮. Xi'an: Sanqin chubanshe, 1993.

Zheng Guo 鄭國. "Jindai geming yundong yu pochu mixin – yi Xuzhou Chenghuangmiao weizhu de kaocha 近代革命運動與破除迷信 – 以徐州城隍廟為主的考察," *Hefei shifan xueyuan xuebao* 合肥師範學院學報, 26(2), 2008, pp. 54–57.

Zheng Zhenman 鄭振滿 & Kenneth Dean 丁荷生, comp. *Fujian zongjiao beiming huibian – Quanzhou fu fence* 福建宗教碑銘彙編 – 泉州府分冊. Fuzhou: Fujian renmin chubanshe, 2004, 3 vols.

Zhu Jianming 朱建明 & Tan Jingde 談敬德. *Shanghai Nanhuixian Zhengyi pai daotan yu Dongyuemiao keyiben* 上海南匯縣正一派道壇與東嶽廟科儀本. Taipei: Xinwenfeng, 2006.

2 The Martial Marquis Shrine

Politics of temple expropriation and restitution, and struggles of Daoist revival in contemporary Nanyang

Xun Liu 劉迅

It was around noon on a hot July 31, 1988, when a few Daoist clerics led by Zhu Zongchang 朱宗長, a near-70-year-old Quanzhen Longmen lineage cleric, forced their way into the main temple (Dabaidian 大拜殿) in honor of Zhuge Liang 諸葛亮 (181–234) at the famed Martial Marquis Shrine (Wuhou ci 武侯祠) located on the Crouching Dragon Knoll (Wolonggang 臥龍崗) just outside the west city-gate of Nanyang. There some of them sat down on the floor while others squatted near the gate. Early that afternoon, when the workers of the Nanyang Museum 南陽博物館, which had been occupying the shrine and its main temple for office use, returned to work after their noon nap, they were surprised to find Zhu and his fellow Daoist clerics squatting in what was now their office. When told to leave, Zhu and his fellow Daoists refused, stubbornly staying their ground. Their claim was that the shrine had always been the property of Quanzhen Daoists and it should be returned to them as their rightful venue for conducting their religious activities. But the shrine had been occupied for nearly three decades by Nanyang Museum under the auspice of the Nanyang Prefectural Administration's Bureau of Cultural Affairs 南陽行政公署文化局. Under the Cultural Affairs Bureau's occupation, Zhu Zongchang, who had lived at the shrine for nearly six decades, was reduced to serving as a custodian in charge of sweeping the sprawling courtyard and cleaning toilets at the shrine.[1]

But taking such an open and bold stand against the museum that had occupied his shrine for three decades was not an easy decision for Zhu and his fellow Daoists. As one of the most senior clerics, Zhu had survived the War of Resistance and the Civil War and weathered a host of the post-1949 political movements from the Land Reform to the Great Proletariat Cultural Revolution. Though government archives do not give us any detailed description of his character, Zhu was by nature quiet, withdrawn, and aversive to confrontation, in the eyes of his fellow Daoists and activists. According to some of them, prior to the dramatic squatting at the shrine, Zhu had yielded to the pressuring tactics employed by the museum officials and aborted several earlier attempts to openly stake their claim to the shrine. But his clerical seniority and moral probity made him an indispensable leader among the Daoists and lay activists fighting to reclaim their beloved shrine. So after days of gentle pleading and reasoning by his own more assertive disciples like Liu Chengshan 劉誠山 and others, Zhu finally agreed to leading the Daoists in taking the dramatic stand at noon on that summer day.

The outcome of this brief protest squat was not unexpected. After Zhu and his fellow Daoists refused to leave, the museum security and staff members resorted to forcefully removing the Daoist squatters. Zhu and his fellow clerics tried to resist. In the ensuing scuffle, he and his men were physically assaulted and forcefully removed from the shrine. With bruises to both his heart and body, Zhu was escorted by a young Daoist nun to a secret hideout deep in the mountains north of the Nanyang where he would recuperate from his injuries.[2]

But the physical removal of Zhu Zongchang and the Daoists did not end the dispute. Indeed, the Nanyang Bureau of Cultural Affairs escalated the situation by issuing a decision to reject Zhu's petition for the return of the shrine and ordered Zhu dismissed from its staff and evicted from the shrine later that summer. Faced with mounting pressure, Zhu and his fellow Daoist clerics persisted in their claim. Several months later on a brisk November day, Zhu took the unusual measure of embarking on a protest tour by leaving Nanyang and traveling to Zhengzhou, the provincial capital and even Beijing to publicize the Nanyang Daoist plight and grievances. Zhu's departure put himself into de facto self-exile, an extraordinary gesture of protest against the Cultural Affairs Bureau's decision to evict him and deny him and his fellow Daoists the rightful claim to the shrine. As Zhu was most senior and esteemed Quanzhen Daoist cleric widely popular in Nanyang, his walkout created an immediate uproar among his fellow Daoist clerics and lay followers in the city.[3]

It also caused quite a stir among the Nanyang local officialdom. Keenly aware of the highly sensitive nature and political symbolism of Zhu's departure, the Nanyang prefectural Bureau of Ethnic and Religious Affairs 民族宗教事務處, a branch agency of Nanyang Prefectural Administration 南陽行政公署, charged with the task of managing all local religious affairs immediately filed an incident report to its superiors in the city: Liu Haicheng 劉海程, the deputy secretary of Nanyang Prefectural Committee of the Chinese Communist Party, and Shi Faliang 石發亮, the deputy commissioner of the Nanyang Prefectural Administration – two key local officials charged with overseeing religious affairs throughout Nanyang region. Citing the letter which Zhu had left behind, the bureau report explained that the reason why the senior Daoist prior had left was that despite his repeated petitions over the years to the Nanyang local government to implement the CCP's new religious policies of upholding religious freedom and returning religious venues to Daoism, the famed Martial Marquis Shrine had yet to be restituted to him and his fellow Daoists. Indeed, what triggered Zhu's action was the recent decision by the Nanyang Prefectural Administration's Bureau of Cultural Affairs, which not only rejected outright his petition for the temple's return but also forbade him to continue residing and practicing his Daoist religion there.

Despite his advanced age and hypertension, Zhu took the unusual gesture of leaving his beloved home temple and going into self-imposed exile and wander. In the months that followed, prior Zhu sent out a series of petition letters to a host of government bodies such as the National Political Consultative Council 全國政協, the Chinese Daoist Association 中國道協, the Religious Affairs Bureau of the State Council 國務院宗教局, the Henan Provincial Political Consultative Council 河南省政協, the Henan Provincial Daoist Association 河南省道協, and the Provincial Bureau of Religious Affairs 省宗教局, explaining the reasons of his self-imposed exile, and his frustration over the Nanyang government's failure to carry out the CCP's new liberalizing religious policy which called for the return of occupied and confiscated temples to Daoism and Buddhism. The highly sensitive political symbolism of Zhu's exile did not escape the Nanyang authorities. Cautioning their readers against the potential negative impact (*buliang yingxiang* 不良影響) on public opinion should anything unexpected happen to the senior Daoist during his wandering self-exile in the bone-chill winter of North China, the Bureau of Religious Affairs report went on to acknowledge the legitimate nature of Zhu's request, and called upon the authorities for an early decision to return the shrine to Zhu and his fellow clerics as both their Daoist religious real estate (*Daojiao fangchan* 道教房產) and Daoist ritual venues (*Daojiao huodong changsuo* 道教活動場所).[4]

The incidents of Zhu's squatting and then his self-imposed exile highlight the ongoing complicated politics of temple restitution and the dilemma of Daoist revival in post-Mao era Nanyang and beyond. Zhu's decision to leave his beloved Martial Marquis Shrine reveals a complex dynamic of local politics and a near-impossible negotiation among the demands of the new party-state policies on religion, the religious passions of Daoist clerics and their lay followers, the vested interests of local government agencies, and the commercial ventures of local and national real estate companies. With gradual religious liberalization and opening, which first began in the early 1980s, Daoist clerics in many places in China started to demand that their temples long expropriated and physically occupied by state agencies, factories, schools, and even local residents be returned to them as legitimate and legal venues for their religious activities and residence.

Drawing on local temple steles, government archives, memoirs, oral interviews, and more than a decade of fieldwork and research, I reconstruct the history of the post-Mao-era Daoist revival through several case studies of temple restitution struggles in Nanyang. In a way, this is a story of failure or setback about the Daoist revival in the post-Mao era in China. I hope to highlight the intricate dynamic of and ongoing challenges to the local Daoist clerical and lay efforts to revive Daoist monastic life, economy, and culture in Nanyang local society from the late 1970s to the present.

Reform and opening: Beginning of the religious revival

Beginning in the late 1970s, as China emerged from a decade of political tumults, economic stagnation, and religious persecution during the Cultural Revolution (1966–1976), the Communist Party and the country were faced with a major crisis of legitimacy and confidence. These years had devastated most Daoist temples and uprooted clerics in the country. To regain political legitimacy, restore people's confidence in the party, and alleviate social and political tension in the country, the Communist Party and the PRC state under the leadership of Deng Xiaoping began a host of reforms to rebuild the economy and to address a variety of ideological, social, and cultural issues left behind by the Cultural Revolution. Indeed, around 1981–1982, the Chinese Communist Party's powerful executive body, the Central Secretariat 中央書記處, held special internal sessions among its leading members to discuss the "religious question" (*zongjiao wenti* 宗教問題) during the socialist transitional period (presumably before the advent of the Communist period). Out of these high-level internal discussions, the Central Secretariat formulated and issued its authoritative directive as the new guiding policy in dealing with the religious question throughout China. Issued as the No.19th Directive of 1982 with the straightforward title, "Fundamental Perspectives and Basic Policy Regarding the Religious Question under Our Country's Socialist Period" (*Guanyu woguo shehuizhuyi shiqi zongjiao wenti de jiben guandian he jiben zhengce* 關於我國社會主義時期宗教問題的基本觀點和基本政策), the directive was transmitted to all levels and branches of the national and local party organizations and state agencies throughout China. While rendering a standardized criticism of religion as the primitive people's mystique about the natural phenomenon and as the reflection and result of underdevelopment of production and lack of scientific understanding, the 19th directive also openly acknowledged religion as an unavoidable historical necessity before the advent of communism, and as a living tradition among the Chinese people since antiquity. As such, the directive stressed to all levels of the party and the state agencies the vital importance to guarantee the freedom and rights of religious faith as both a principle and a means for their administration and management of religion. It stipulates that the new perspectives and policies were aimed at carrying out the party's fundamental task of "uniting all peoples (including the broad masses who believe in religions and those who do not) to strive together in building a strong and modernized socialist state" 當前的基本任務是團結全體人民[包括廣大信教和不信教的羣眾]為建設社會主義的強國而共同奮鬥. Further, the directive urges the national and local government agencies to create and provide the necessary physical and material conditions for the full implementation and realization of the party's new religious policy. Specifically, it stipulates that state agencies in charge of religious affairs must take effective measures in arranging and providing venues for religious activities. In some of the large and medium cities where there are religious venues which had been historically active and famous, and where religious devotees congregated in large numbers, the directive exhorts that government must restore these religious venues in a planned and step-by-step manner. As for those famous religious temples, synagogues, and churches with significant domestic and international influence and with great cultural relic value, they must be restored step by step and based on local conditions.[5] With the promulgation of the party's new directive on religion throughout the country in 1982, restoration and return of famous religious temples to clerics and their devotees became not only a priority of many local religious administration agencies but also an important yardstick of their success or failure in implementing the party's new policy on religion.

Yet, despite the party directive's apparent pressure, its implementation in Nanyang proved to be very difficult. Like everywhere else in China, Nanyang had witnessed several waves of severe religious persecution, which centered on state or collective confiscation and occupation of temples, and the suppression of the clerics such as prior Zhu of the Martial Marquis Shrine since 1949. Most of the local Daoist temples, such as the Martial Marquis Shrine, the Dark Mystery Temple (Xuanmiao guan 玄妙觀) located northwestern of Nanyang, the Sage of Medicine Shrine (Yisheng ci 醫聖祠) outside Nanyang's east gate, and the Shrine of Heavenly Consort (Tianhou miao 天后廟) at the city's south gate, were all appropriated by various Nanyang government agencies and local factories at various times after 1949. Most of the resident Daoists at these temples were forcefully removed and returned to their native villages and towns during land reform and collectivization campaigns in the 1950s. During the Cultural Revolution, the very few clerics who had managed to stay on at their temples as custodians and groundskeepers were now all expelled from these temples and forced to return to secular life in their hometowns or villages. While most of the small and less well-known Daoist temples in Nanyang suffered the fate of either disrepair or destruction due to urban expansion since 1949, the above-mentioned four temples managed to survive due to their relative fame and size. But by the early 1980s, they had all and each been repurposed as government offices, factory workshops, schools, and even residential quarters after their initial seizures.

The Martial Marquis Shrine, for example, was first appropriated by the Nanyang Prefectural government in 1949 as a production site for a factory that produced quilts and clothes but was later used in 1959 to house the newly established Nanyang Historical Museum 南陽歷史博物館, which changed its name to Nanyang Museum in 1965. Meanwhile, the occupied shrine was designated in 1963 by the Henan Provincial Government's Bureau of Cultural Affairs as one of its provincial-class Cultural Relics Preservation units 省級文物保護單位 in Henan. Such designation meant direct and additional funding by the provincial and prefectural governments for Nanyang Museum and the shrine which was now fully repurposed also as a cultural park, and a preservation center. By 1996, the whole shrine and its compound received an upgraded re-designation as a "national key unit of cultural relics preservation" 全國重點文物保護單位. This new designation and elevated status entitled the shrine to receive additional annual funding for cultural preservation and restorations from both the national and provincial governments.[6] These designations ignore the shrine's primary religious functions in history and choose instead to highlight its secular cultural and artistic values as relevant to the socialist state and people. Such designations also further serve to justify Nanyang Museum's physical occupation of the shrine as a center of culture, archaeology, relic preservation, and public recreation, while downplaying and even erasing the shrine's long history as a major venue of ritual activities and religious functions for both the imperial state and local society in Nanyang since the medieval times. The CCP state and local governments' physical occupation of temples also represents a culmination of a much longer pattern of state behavior and policy toward religion dating back at least to the late nineteenth century, when the Qing imperial state first began its modernization drive and reforms.[7]

With the rolling out of the new opening and reform policies in the early 1980s, restitution of these confiscated and occupied temples along with rehabilitation of persecuted Daoist clerics and their return to the temples became one of the key concerns for many of the PRC state's religious affairs authorities at all levels, as the party re-adopted its earlier position prior to the outbreak of the Cultural Revolution that all religious clerics, including the Daoists, were part of its United Front 統一戰線 for socialist revolution and construction. As such, they must not be seen and alienated as enemies of the state, but rather they were to be embraced as part of the citizenry of the new socialist republic. But the party's conciliatory policies toward Daoism and other religions also belied its underlying recognition of the declining ideological influence of communism and the resurging of religious passions and piety among ordinary people in China in the aftermath of the Cultural Revolution.

Yet, while easing decades of restricting and even repressive approach to religion, the 1982 directive remained guarded and vigilant against religion and its mass appeal and power, and made the implementation of the temple restitution policy at the local levels throughout the country open to and even dependent on local governmental interpretation and conditions. For instance, while the directive stresses the importance of restoring and rebuilding many historical well-known temples, it also prohibits local government from using state or collective resources for temple reconstruction, except those specially appropriated funds. Further, while the directive reiterates that religious freedom is a constitutionally protected right, it also stresses that all religious activities must be placed under the administrative leadership and management of local religious affairs agencies. The directive also stipulates that local government must take measures in preventing religious devotees from "excessively building temples in rural communities" 尤其要注意防止在農村濫修廟宇. While such extensive temple building was an expression of popular piety in the countryside, the directive censures it as a potential "waste of human, material and monetary resources and a hindrance to the construction of socialist material and spiritual civilization" 耗費人力物力財力, 妨礙社會主義物質文明和精神文明的建設 and urges local governments to assiduously prevail upon the zealous devotees to avoid it.[8] While such ambiguities, even contradictions in the language of the directive reflect the delicate balance which the party's central leaders and policy-makers were trying to strike between their Marxist atheistic ideology on the one hand, and their political interests and expediency on the other, they created real dilemma and obstacles for Daoist clerics and lay devotees in their struggle to reclaim their temples, and opened up gaping holes and grey areas for local governments and officials to obfuscate and even resist the state policy to return temple properties to the Daoists. It is under these weaknesses of the new liberalizing policy that the Daoist clerics and lay followers began their efforts to retrieve their temples in Nanyang in the 1980s.

Origins of the Martial Marquis Shrine and early Daoist inhabitation and activities

The bone of contention between prior Zhu and the Nanyang prefectural Bureau of Cultural Affairs was twofold: the Daoist claim to ownership of the Martial Marquis Shrine and its restitution to the Daoists; and the Daoist right to the shrine as the rightful venue for religious activities. But until the onset of the Great Leap Forward campaign in 1958, when Quanzhen Daoist clerics were expelled from the shrine and the Nanyang Museum moved in, the shrine had a long and uninterrupted history of Daoist inhabitation that dated back at the latest to the Southern Song era. Indeed, we know that the shrine remained under Daoist clerical management through the Yuan, Ming, Qing, and early Republican periods. (Figure 2.1)

The shrine's earliest roots dated to the pre-Tang era, when it was first built as a cottage (*maolu* 茅廬) in honor of Zhuge Liang, the legendary sagacious chief councilor and strategist of the Three Kingdoms era. The earliest known Daoist inhabitation of the shrine dates to the Southern Song era. The Southern Song field marshal Yue Fei 岳飛 (1103–1142), who was leading military campaigns in the 1130s against the Jürchen forces in the central plain, noted in a preface he allegedly composed in the fall of 1138 that he was at the time passing by Nanyang with his forces. As he stopped for a visit to the shrine in honor of Zhuge Liang, it began to rain. So he stayed for the night at the shrine. Late that night he held a lit candle to view the inscribed texts of Zhuge's two famous pronouncements composed on the occasions of launching his two expeditions against the rival Wei kingdom.

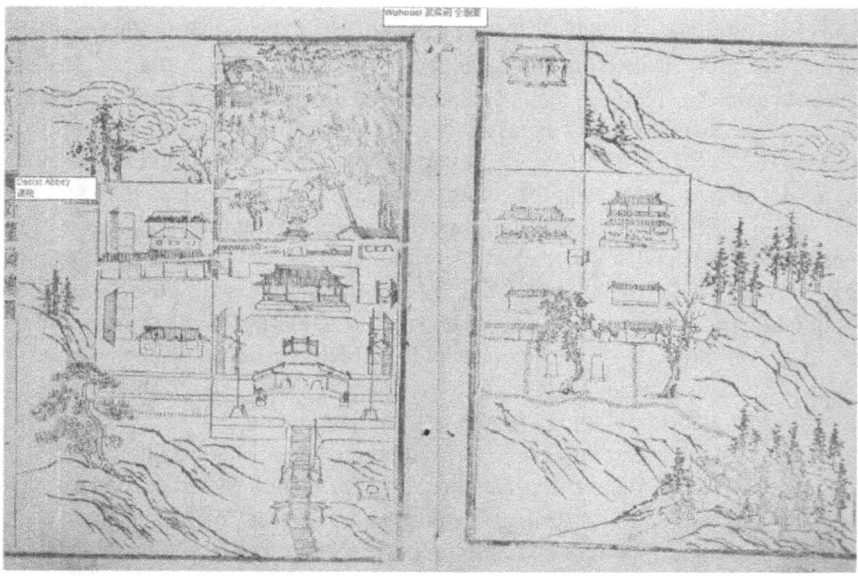

Figure 2.1 Overview of the Martial Marquis Shrine compound in *Wolonggangzhi.*

Yue wrote that he was so moved by Zhuge's unfailing loyalty to the Han imperial household and by his dogged determination to restore the Han that he shed tears like a rainfall. That night, he could not fall asleep and sat until dawn when he was served tea by a Daoist at the shrine. Afterward the Daoist produced some paper and asked him for his brushwork. Yue wrote that as he kept wiping off his tears, he wielded the brush in copying down Zhuge's pronouncements in his own cursive style of calligraphy. Afterward, he remarked that he felt quite relieved of the melancholic sentiments in his heart.[9]

If Yue Fei's account is credible, it highlights the two facts. First, Daoist clerics had already taken up residence at the shrine as early as the Southern Song era. Yue Fei's encounter with the Daoist cleric suggests that there was some form of the Zhuge cult already and that the Daoists there routinely received visitors, probably as part of their roles as the shrine-keepers. Second, as early as the twelfth century, the shrine's fame was already centered on the late Han era Martial Marquis and his political and military exploits. Indeed, Zhuge reportedly once lived as a hermit at the cottage on the shrine compound during the chaotic times of the late Han era before he was courted repeatedly by his patron Liu Bei 劉備 (161–223) to serve as the latter's chief strategist and prime minister. Zhuge Liang had been praised and worshipped early on for his profound political wisdom and sound military strategy, and most of all for his Confucian virtues of unswerving loyalty and righteousness.

Indeed, 160 years after Yue Fei's visit to the shrine in Nanyang, the ascending Yuan court gave the Zhuge cult in Nanyang a major boost. In the year of 1298, Lord Aqamad 阿哈馬, a Central Asian *darughachi* 達魯哈赤 (superintendent) of the Nanyang region,[10] and his fellow officials paid for a major renovation of the old cottage, expanding it into a much larger shrine with additional worship halls of Zhuge and other eminent statesmen and generals from Chinese history. After the completion of the shrine expansion, Lord Aqamad and his colleagues invited Zhang Zhihe 張志和, most likely a Quanzhen Daoist cleric loyal to the Mongols, from the Supreme Void Monastery (Taixu guan 太虛觀) in Hailiang 解梁 of Shanxi, to come to Nanyang and preside over the newly constructed shrine and manage the ritual services there. Unlike the Daoist cleric who served tea to Yue Fei, prior Zhang was the first known-by-name Daoist manager at the shrine. The fact that he was invited from the Shanxi to take over the operations of the shrine suggests that the Daoist inhabitation there may have been disrupted during the Song-Yuan transition. It's highly likely that the Daoists whom Yue Fei encountered on his stopover at the shrine may have been scattered by the time of the Mongol invasion of the central plains in the mid- to late thirteenth century, as Nanyang was geographically adjacent to Xiangyang, one of the hotly contested key strategic cities between the Southern Song and the Mongols. A decade or so later, in 1310, a local academy named after Zhuge Liang was also built alongside the east wing of the shrine. To ensure its sustained operations as an official shrine, the Central Asian *darughachi* of Nanyang prefecture decreed to set aside 400 mu 畝 of official farmland as the shrine's new endowment estate.[11]

Throughout the Ming and Qing era, it appeared that the shrine underwent numerous additional renovations and expansions. In addition to the worship of Laozi and a full pantheon of Daoist deities from the Jade emperor to Lord Guan Yu 關羽 (?–220), the shrine was composed of many additional halls in honor of famous kings, ministers, and generals in Chinese history such as Liu Bei 劉備 (161–223), the king of the Shu Kingdom and his loyal group of devoted generals from Guan Yu and Zhang Fei 張飛 (?–221) to Zhao Yun 趙雲 (?–229), Huang Zhong 黃忠 (?–220), and Ma Chao 馬超 (176–222). Another national hero and loyal general of the Southern Song court, Marshal Yue Fei was also prominently worshipped at the shrine. From the Yuan era onward, the shrine also housed the Nanyang prefectural school and the Zhuge Academy in its east wing, which consisted of a host of lecture halls, a library, and student dorms.

Since the Yuan era, the daily operation of the shrine had most likely remained in the hands of Daoists like Zhang Zhihe, as Daoist liturgical services and the state ritual worship of Zhuge Liang and other loyal generals at the shrine required their presence. Indeed, several accounts from the steles at the shrine and local gazetteers attest to the presence of the Daoist clergy at the shrine throughout the Ming and Qing periods. When Yang Shiqi 楊士奇 (1366–1444), the famous and powerful prime minister composed a stele inscription to commemorate a new construction of the main hall of worship of Zhuge Liang at the shrine, he specifically listed one Daoist official (*daoguan* 道官) Zhou Yuanchu 周元初 and another Daoist cleric Sun Daorong 孫道榮 as having helped "raising funds" (*quanyuan* 勸緣) for the newly built main temple.[12] Zhou's status as the Daoist official suggests that the shrine housed the Nanyang prefecture's Office of Daoist Discipline Office (Daoji si 道紀司), a branch of the Ming Central Office of Daoist Registrar (Daolu si 道錄司) based in the Ming capital and staffed by court-appointed ranking Daoist clerics from major Daoist temples throughout the empire. Indeed the fact that both Zhou and Sun helped raise construction funds for the new hall indicates that they and their fellow Daoist clerics may have been entrusted with the ongoing daily care and maintenance of the shrine.

Thirty years later, another mid-Ming stele inscription composed by a ranking official at Nanyang informs us of a possible presence of the Daoist shrine-keepers. In the early spring of 1476, Ren Yi 任義, a native from Yuci 榆次 of Shaanxi and a *juren* degree holder, was serving as a co-prefect of Nanyang prefecture (Nanyangfu tongzhi 南陽府同知). In such capacity, he was familiar with the conditions of the shrine in honor of Zhuge Liang located on the western suburbs of the prefectural town. Ren deplored the disrepair and decline of the once magnificent shrine and noted that it was so dilapidated and overgrown with thickets of grass and bushes that travelers and pilgrims who used to visit the shrine to pay homage to the famous Han statesman could hardly even locate it any longer from the nearby official highway which connected Nanyang to Luoyang in the north and Dengzhou 鄧州 and Mount Wudang 武當山 to the south. Saddened by this state of affairs, Ren and his colleagues at the Nanyang prefectural administration worked out a plan in the winter of 1477 to renovate the shrine so as to honor the memory of the loyal marquis and to attract the passing travelers back to the shrine.

In their renovation plan, they envisioned not only additional halls of worship and roofed verandas and fortified walls around them but also a Daoist community to maintain the renovated shrine (*shouyi daolü* 守以道侶). The renovation was completed early next spring. On the occasion, prefect Ren Yi lent his elegant calligraphic brushwork to a new signpost stele (*zhidaobei* 指道碑) to be planted at the nearby official highway and inscribed in the classic *li* calligraphic style (*lishu* 隸書) on the back of the new stele detailed directions informing the travelers of the exact location of the shrine, and a brief description of how the shrine had come to be renovated recently.[13] Another account which probably aimed at warding off itinerant Daoist clerics records an anecdote about a Daoist cleric who serendipitously took up residence at the shrine being awakened at night by the sounds of gatherings at the shrine. He was so frightened that he later moved out.[14]

It was also during the late Ming that the imperial court first began to standardize the annual sacrifice and ritual worship of Zhuge Liang at Nanyang. In the third moon of 1528 under the reform-minded Jiajing 嘉靖 emperor, Yang Yingkui 楊應奎, the prefect of Nanyang, finally received approval from the Board of Rites of his earlier request to add the Nanyang shrine and its worship of Zhuge Liang to the canon of the Ming state cult. The Board of Rites decree stipulated that the Nanyang local administration and its officials were to render both spring and autumn sacrifices to the marquis. It further set forth the sacrificial standards specifying exactly the ritual food and offerings to be proffered. Prior to that, local Nanyang administrators and officials had been conducting the spring sacrifice alone and they had done so by following local customs and without consulting the Ming state canon of sacrificial rites. Indeed, worship of Zhuge Liang by state officials had its roots in as early as the pre-Tang era. In Nanyang, alongside the official sacrifice and ritual worship of Zhuge, the locals were known to have practiced their own folk cult of the marquis ever since the Tang-Song era. Indeed, Cheng Jufu 程鉅夫 (1249–1318), the great early Yuan Confucian scholar, imperial academician, and ranking court official, had complained that during their annual sacrifice to honor the marquis, the Nanyang locals not only involved "shamans and witches," but they also made unregulated sacrificial offerings which he thought to be in violation of the state code of sacrifice and therefore offensive to the marquis.[15] Later accounts describe the local folk cult of the marquis as having centered on his thatched hut located in the center of the shrine where he reputedly lived as a hermit and a farmer before he accepted Prince Liu Bei's invitation to fight for and build the Shu kingdom. The cult also featured the offer of slaughtered animals at the annual spring sacrifice. The 1528 Ming court memorial seemed to have followed this local tradition of blood sacrifice, proffering a combination of one slaughtered pig, one slaughtered sheep, meat paste, fish paste, and pickled vegetables at the spring and autumn sacrifices.[16]

Though the stele records at the shrine make no mention of the Daoist clerical roles in either the state annual rites or the local cultic sacrifice at the shrine, evidence from other temples in Nanyang suggests that the resident Daoist clerics who had inhabited the shrine since the Southern Song must have been involved as the ritual assistants and even managers for both the official and the folk rites of sacrifice to the marquis.[17] Indeed, from the mid-Ming through the Qing and early Republican periods, we have indisputable evidence to show that at the latest from 1553 onward, the shrine was continuously inhabited and managed by at least seven generations of the Quanzhen Nanwu lineage (Nanwu pai 南無派) up until the year 1713 in the mid-Kangxi reign, and thereafter by 22 generations of the Longmen lineage (Longmen pai 龍門派) resident clerics until 1959 for a total of three centuries.[18]

By the late nineteenth century, the shrine had become one of the best-endowed Daoist temples in Nanyang. Aside from its 5,000 mu of premium endowment farmland, and more than a score of historical buildings and halls on its compound, the shrine also boasted of over 300 inscribed steles, some of which were attributed to Martial Marquis Zhuge and Marshal Yue Fei, and were nationally known. It derived a large portion of its revenue from frequent visits by officials, literati members, as well as commoners who came to pay homage to the Martial Marquis and other deities for a variety of purposes. During their visits, they made cash donations, ordered ritual services, or commissioned rubbings of many famous calligraphic inscriptions off the steles at the shrine. In such a way, the shrine's revenues enabled it to routinely house over a dozen and at times as many as more than a score of clerics, and support their livelihood from the late Ming era to the early twentieth century.[19] Many of the leading Quanzhen clerics active in the late Qing and early Republican periods, such as abbot Li Zongyang 李宗陽 (?–1939), began their clerical careers at the shrine.[20] Indeed, it was this long and deep history of Daoist inhabitation and upkeep of the shrine that was at the core of their sense of entitlement to, if not ownership of, the shrine as both the source of their livelihood and the venue of their residence and ritual practice.

However, despite centuries of their continuous working and living at the shrine, and their having weathered the late Qing and early Republican campaigns of temple expropriation and seizure, the Daoist rights to residence at the shrine proved no match to the unprecedented pressure of the Communist-led land reforms in the 1950s. On the eve of 1949, the Martial Marquis Shrine still owned over 5,000 mu of farmland and a large complex of halls totaling 257 chambers and rooms. At the time, as many as 22 Daoist clerics were in residence, each charged with taking care of the shrine buildings and their operations. But soon things began to change. With the Communist takeover in 1949, the Nanyang prefectural government set up its cadre training school on the shrine compound. Even while the government largely left the living quarters and the main shrine halls of worship alone, the resident Daoist clerics began to leave, with only 13 left at the shrine. But the subsequent land reform and the campaign against the so-called counterrevolutionaries in the early 1950s soon drastically reduced the clerical presence at the shrine down to only three, including Zhu Zongchang. During the Great Leap Forward campaign in 1958, Zhu and his two fellow Daoists were expelled from the shrine, and the Nanyang Museum moved in and took over the whole compound. There was a brief reprieve in 1961 when Zhu and his other two fellow Daoists Tian Chengquan 田成全 and Jia Zonggang 賈宗剛 were allowed back into the shrine to take up residence and work as the museum's custodians and groundskeepers.

They apparently proved themselves worthy of the new accommodation, and all three of them were selected as the model staff of the museum for the first quarter of 1961, as shown in a photo taken in March of 1961 celebrating the occasion. Another photo taken a month later in April shows the Daoist clerical trio dressed in their Daoist gowns and caps at a farewell party in honor of several departing museum staff (see Figure 2.2).[21] But despite their model behavior, the whole living quarters and the shrine halls of the Daoist cloister remained occupied by the Nanyang Museum as office space and storage houses. By 1963, with the launch of the Socialist Education campaign, Zhu and his fellow Daoists became easy targets for the CCP-mobilized anti-superstition movement, and they were ordered to stop all their religious activities at the shrine. By the start of the Cultural Revolution in 1966, two of the three Daoists had passed away, leaving Zhu to live and work there alone, a Daoist-turned-custodian at the shrine. In the subsequent tumultuous times, the whole shrine fell victim to the Red Guards who repeatedly raided and rampaged the shrine's halls of worship, destroying the statues of gods and ritual objects therein. Zhu was again expelled from the shrine and forbidden to continue his Daoist life. The end of the Cultural Revolution and the fall of the Gang of Four in 1976 brought Zhu back to the shrine, where he was allowed again to live and work as a groundskeeper and custodian.[22]

The Nanyang Museum and its entrenchment at the shrine

While Zhu was allowed to return to the shrine to live and work, the Cultural Affairs Bureau and the Nanyang Museum persisted in their denial of Zhu's petition for the return of the occupied shrine. But despite the increasingly liberal policies toward religion beginning from the early 1980s, the Nanyang Museum, now fully entrenched in its occupation of the shrine and clearly backed by the Nanyang municipal government, ignored and resisted all the relevant CCP and state directives requiring local governments to return occupied temple properties. Their persistent denial finally led to Zhu and his fellow Daoists' forceful entry into and dramatic sit-in at the shrine at the height of the summer of 1988. The subsequent removal of Zhu and his fellow Daoists from the shrine shortly thereafter not only highlighted the plight of the Daoists' struggle to reclaim what used to belong to him, but it also revealed long-term and deep-running post-1949 social and political changes which made the Daoist efforts to reclaim their shrine an insurmountable task.

In the nearly three decades running up to the summer of 1988, the Nanyang Museum had grown into a full-fledged leading cultural institution in the city and beyond. In the process, the shrine compound had also been transformed into a major public park open to the citizens of Nanyang. In the spring of 1959, the Nanyang government decided to turn the shrine complex into a public recreation park (Wolong gongyuan 臥龍公園). Along with that decision, the government also designated the shrine as the base for building the Nanyang Museum of History where Nanyang's extensive archaeological finds, especially the carved tomb bricks and stones of the Han era, as well as the historical buildings, steles, and other cultural relics at the shrine and from around the whole Nanyang prefecture were to be preserved, curated, and exhibited to the public. In addition, the museum was also put in charge of all investigation, preservation, surveys, and excavation of all the major historical and archaeological sites such as tombs and temples throughout the Nanyang area. Shortly after its formal establishment, the Nanyang Museum of History held one of its first public exhibitions on the history of Nanyang at the Daoist cloister in the west wing of the Martial Marquis Shrine in the early fall of 1959. By October that year, on the tenth anniversary of the People's Republic, the museum's exhibition had received a total of 40,000 visitors that included people from all walks of life and especially students from primary to high schools throughout the city.[23] In the three decades that followed, the Nanyang Museum continued as the main venue for curating, exhibiting, and preserving the city's rich archaeological findings. Throughout the 1960s and 1970s, as Mao Zedong and the CCP mounted even more intense political campaigns aimed at ridding the socialist republic of its so-called "feudal, bourgeois, and revisionist" legacies and building up the socialist and increasingly Maoist new culture, the museum, like all museums in all other places in China, also staged didactic and propagandistic exhibits that demonstrated the landlord exploitation and oppression of the peasantry, and the inevitable necessity and logic of the Communist-led peasant war over the KMT and its political and social allies.[24]

The early professionally curated exhibit made up of hundreds of archaeological findings, such as the Qin-Han era iron smelter, the Han tomb stones, and historical artifacts preserved at the shrine, marks the beginning of the newly founded museum's professional development as the major cultural affairs institution in the city, but more importantly, its exposure to and popularity among the public also signals a fundamental transformation of the shrine. It was by no sheer coincidence that the first major exhibit was held in the west wing of the shrine, where Zhu and his fellow Daoist clerics used to live and practice their Daoist faith. So it is quite poignant that alongside the museum's gradual professionalization and institutional growth was also a simultaneous process of disenchantment of the Martial Marquis Shrine's ritual and religious functions. As the museum mounted more and more curated displays and exhibits at the shrine, it was, to the general public, no longer a venue of ritual worship by either the imperial state or the local followers of the Martial Marquis. Rather, it was increasingly the Nanyang's new secular cultural space which featured carefully curated exhibitions of the city's rich and deep historical legacy, and increasingly its recent revolutionary heritage centered on the Communist-led struggle against the KMT and the landlord class.

Other social and political changes further ensured the ritual disenchantment of the shrine. Since its founding in 1959, the museum also managed to cultivate powerful patrons among the top echelons of the socialist state's cultural and political elite, including its top leaders such as Zhu Rongji 朱鎔基 and Hu Jintao 胡錦濤, who had visited the museum, respectively, in 1995 and 2007. These patrons' political and cultural influence helped solidify the museum's continued physical occupation and secularization of the shrine so much so that any challenge to the status quo would prove to be nearly impossible. Perhaps the most influential of all these patrons is none other than Guo Moruo 郭沫若 (1892–1978). Guo studied medicine in Japan in his youth. He later joined the KMT-led Northern Expedition against the warlord regime in the second Republican revolution. Active during the New Culture movement from the early 1900s through the 1920s, Guo became one of the leading Left-wing progressive writers and intellectuals while holding ranking positions in the KMT government and academia. In the post-1949 period, Guo served in a range of high-ranking positions of the new republic, including head of the Chinese Academy of Science, director of the National Institute of History, deputy premier of the State Council, director of the State Council's Commission on Culture and Education, and vice-chairman of the National Political Consultative Council from the 1950s until his death in 1978. In addition, Guo was a refined poet and calligrapher and exchanged poems with Mao himself. During the Cultural Revolution, Guo was closely aligned with Mao and the powerful Gang of Four led by Mao's wife Jiang Qing (1915–1991). But as a leading scholar of early Chinese history, archaeology, and linguistics, Guo showed a deep interest in the archaeological finds, especially the inscribed tomb stones and bricks unearthed from various sites in Nanyang. From 1959 through the 1970s, Guo composed in his flowing calligraphic style several placards to be hung at the entrance to the main hall of worship in honor of the Martial Marquis at the museum, and also offered advice and instructions on the interpretation of many of the archaeological finds held at the Nanyang museum.[25]

Guo's patronage is typical of the practice by many other political and cultural elite who visited the shrine in the pre-1949 and imperial times, but it also reflects the pattern of patronage by many other Communist elite who visited the museum and the shrine afterward. Like Guo, many of these post-Mao era officials and prominent writers, intellectuals, and entertainers left inscriptions composed in different calligraphic styles and expressing admiration for the loyal marquis. These inscriptions and visits, like those made during the late imperial era, add significantly to the prestige of the museum and repeatedly affirm the very reason for its continued occupation of the shrine.[26] So, as with its professional mission in building socialist culture and providing cultural service to the public, the Nanyang Museum's sustained pattern of cultivating powerful patrons among leaders at the national and provincial levels during their visits to the museum has not only fulfilled its obligations in educating the officials and the public about the history and cultural legacy of Nanyang, but it has also secured many influential allies whose visits and patronage of the museum ensured its continued occupation of the shrine.

Temple restitution work and its challenges in Nanyang

As the process of normalizing the occupation and repurposing of the Martial Marquis Shrine by Nanyang Museum moved on, the local government was faced with a new set of challenges with the CCP Central's more liberal policies on religion in the early 1980s. Like many other places in China, Nanyang experienced a robust religious revival starting at the end of the Cultural Revolution among all the state-recognized five religions: Protestantism, Catholicism, Buddhism,

Islam, and Daoism. In his 1980 report disseminated to all party and government cadres in Nanyang, the director of Nanyang CCP Department of United Front 統戰部), the party's overseer on all religious and ethnic issues in the region, provided startling official statistics on the massive growth in the number of religious devotees over a short span of time from 1979 to 1980. According to Mr. Zhang Jie, there were a combined total number of 46,000 Protestant, Catholic, Buddhist, and Daoist practitioners and devotees before 1949. Through a host of "religious reforms" and reorganization of the religions in the 1950s, the total number of those religious clerics and devotees fell to about 24,000 by 1960. But in the short time span from 1976 to 1980, the total number of Protestant, Catholic, Buddhist, and Daoist practitioners shot up to 75,000, tripling the 1960 figure. In Nanzhao 南召 county north of Nanyang city, there were formerly a total of 7,850 Protestants and Catholics, but by the summer of 1980, that number had increased to 25,000. According to Mr. Zhang, the religious revival had also affected the party's own rank and file. He gave an example of this threatening development to the party by citing rather revealing statements by several party members who apparently abandoned their faith in the party in favor of their newfound religious beliefs. One allegedly said: "I don't' believe in the party anymore, but I believe in my religion. I would rather give up my party membership card." Another stated: "It's meaningless to live my life within the party. It is much more meaningful to live a religious life."[27]

This extensive religious revival not only asserted individual rights to religious faith and practice which had been long reduced and even denied to the faithful since the 1950s, but it also soon began to focus on reclaiming temples and other religious properties either outright confiscated or occupied and repurposed for office and other uses by the state and other nonreligious entities throughout the country.

In Nanyang, the local government had earlier realized the importance of implementing the new party and state policies on returning occupied temples and religious properties and reopening them to religious practitioners and their followers. In Mr. Zhang Jie's 1980 report circulated among the local cadres, he urged fellow Nanyang officials to fully understand the danger of driving religious activities underground:

> Ever since the Cultural Revolution, our religious policies have been destroyed. We drove the priests, monks, and imams out of their churches, temples, and mosques. We forbade their devotees to follow their faith, and forced all religious activities underground. Instead of being stopped, they have since further developed and indeed, dramatically grown, leaving us in a very negative and awkward position.

As a solution, Mr. Zhang Jie suggested that the Nanyang government should implement the policies that both the central government and Nanyang's local government had issued regarding the reopening and returning a small number of temples, churches, and mosques to the devotees and practitioners. He specified that the scale and the number of these reopened temples, churches, and mosques must not exceed the limit set forth during the 1958 religious institutional reforms.[28]

But even the mild and cautious approach to temple restitution as suggested by Mr. Zhang proved to be challenging and ran into many unexpected problems when it came to Daoist efforts to reclaim their temples such as the Martial Marquis Shrine.

One of the problems involved in the return of temples had to do with the priority which was often influenced and even determined by the intensity and strength of the religious claimants, the most vigorous and assertive of which tended to be the Protestants and the Catholics, rather than the Daoists. A 1983 investigative report prepared by the Nanyang Ethnic and Religious Affairs Bureau singled out the Christian revivalists as the most zealous and proactive among all the religious sects in the various counties under Nanyang prefecture. Many Christian activists even openly challenged the local government officials in charge of religious affairs, and some went so far as to question the legitimacy of the Communist Party and the state-sanctioned official Patriotic Christian and Catholic Churches. For instance, one of the most assertive Catholic strongholds in Nanyang is Jin'gang 靳崗 diocese, located northwest of the Nanyang city. It is one of the oldest Catholic missions in China with roots dating back to the late Ming era. It developed into the most important Catholic diocese of central China by the mid-nineteenth century.[29] During the Cultural Revolution, the Jin'gang cathedral was completely appropriated and shut down. When it was reopened in 1980 as one of the authorized religious venues, many of the Catholics and devotees soon began to question and even challenge the legitimacy of the state-sanctioned bishop assigned to operate the church, alleging that he was "rejected by the Pope" and the newly reopened diocese was a "reformed Catholic church." Most militant activists told their fellow Catholics that the state-sanctioned church at Jin'gang had "betrayed and split the church," and that those joined it would not be able to ascend to the Heavens."[30] Though many of these openly rebellious Christian activists suffered punishments from hard labor in re-education camps to jail sentences, their religious militancy and fervor caught the attention of the local Nanyang government and forced its officials to prioritize the Protestant and Catholic demands for church restitution and more religious freedom above all other religions.[31] By comparison, Daoist clerics and their followers were not only far outnumbered by their Christian counterparts, but they were also lagging far behind in terms of intensity and vigor of their activism. The 1982 report prepared by the Nanyang Religious Affairs Bureau listed the total number of Protestants and Catholics throughout the whole Nanyang region as 136,681, where the same report recognized only 19 Daoist clerics. In terms of Daoist activism aimed at temple restitution as of 1983, the Nanyang government record does not contain any account of militant or even assertive demand by Daoist clerics. Indeed, as we have seen, the most assertive of the Daoist efforts to reclaim their temples as represented by the brief squatting of the Martial Marquis Shrine did not take place until the summer of 1988. As a result, Daoist clerics and their followers as a religious group weighed much less in the decision-making and policy-formulation processes of the Nanyang government and its officials.

Another problem which the Nanyang Daoist clerics faced in reclaiming their temple properties is the fact that most of the Daoist temples in the city of Nanyang were either appropriated or occupied by powerful government agencies and work units, a difficult situation with which neither the Christians nor Muslims nor Buddhists in the city had to deal with. The Catholic cathedral in Jin'gang was in the northwestern suburbs of Nanyang and was used as a storage depot by a local company during its appropriation from the late 1950s to 1980. Since it was not occupied by any government agency or work unit, it was a much easier decision for the Nanyang Religious Affairs Bureau to return it to the Catholic church in 1980 when the Nanyang government decided to reopen it to the Catholic followers for religious activities.[32] By contrast, the major Daoist temples in the city had all fallen to occupation and appropriation by Nanyang local government and its agencies since the early 1950s. The Martial Marquis Shrine aside, Nanyang's largest Daoist temple, the Monastery of Dark Mystery (Xuanmiao guan 玄妙觀) located on the northwestern corner of the city was appropriated by the Nanyang county government for use as office as early as 1949 when the city fell to the CCP-led People's Liberation Army. The Nanyang county government was by no means the first occupier of the Daoist monastery. Indeed, the Xuanmiao Monastery encountered its first occupier in the form of the Republican forces led by its leader Ma Yunqing 馬雲卿 (1877–1913) and his fellow anti-Manchu comrades and volunteers in the spring of 1912. Thereafter, from the establishment of the Republican regime under Yuan Shikai 袁世凱 (1859–1916) until 1949, the Quanzhen Daoist monastery in Nanyang experienced recurrent albeit partial and temporary occupation by a sleuth of warlord armies as well as Republican forces.[33] But none of the occupiers of the Daoist monastery could compare to the post-1949 Nanyang county government occupation in terms of scale. The pre-1949 warlord and Republican armies only took up portions of the Daoist monastery for use as either barracks or military operations headquarters,[34] whereas the post-1949 Nanyang county government appropriated the entire monastery as offices for its officials and staff, and as living quarters for their families. From the beginning of its occupation in 1949 to the present, the Nanyang county government and its successor has not only built several multi-leveled modern office buildings that erased and replaced original temples and dwarfed the surrounding shrines and halls of worship, but it has also carried out extensive remodeling and refurbishing of the original shrines and other temple buildings. These renovated temples and modern-styled office buildings have since totally changed the old Daoist monastery's traditional look and architectural style, highlighting the Daoist monastery's physical transformation from its former venue and function as a religious temple to its present-day status as both the physical base and organ of the secular government in Nanyang. As with the Martial Marquis Shrine, the Nanyang county government's appropriation and occupation of the Xuanmiao Monastery have since made it nearly impossible for its return to the Daoists. Persistent efforts by both Daoist clerics and their followers since the early 1980s have so far only resulted in partial reparation by the Nanyang government in the form of a new temple land located at the foothill of the Mount Solitude (Dushan 獨山) located in the northeastern rural suburbs of Nanyang city. The reparation deal was initially a concession made by the Nanyang government to the mounting pressure by the Daoists and their followers in the 1980s and early 1990s. Eager at the time for a venue to revive their ritual activities and daily religious routine, Liu Chengshan 劉誠山 (1933–2008), a leading young and energetic Quanzhen cleric and a protégé of prior Zhu Zongchang, and other Daoist activists and followers agreed to the deal in 1995. In 2000, under Liu's leadership and with funds raised from his followers, a new shrine was constructed at the designated lot at the foothill of Mount Solitude. But in the mind of Liu and his fellow Quanzhen Daoists, the rural location of the reconstructed Xuanmiao Monastery could hardly match the real market value and appeal of their old temple site located in a premium district and among their lay followers in downtown Nanyang. Their suspicion was confirmed later in the years running up to 2012 when Nanyang government hosted the National Peasant Sports Meet (Quanguo nongmin yundong hui 全國農民運動會). As such an occasion often involves major infrastructural investments by the central and provincial governments to construct new sports venues, local government often uses the occasion to piggyback some of its own urban expansion and renewal programs. Such urban expansion and renewal programs could not only add to the local party politicians' record of achievements, but they also provided opportunities for real estate developers for windfall profits. Beginning from the late 2000, the Nanyang city administration and its affiliate Wancheng District government (Wancheng qu zhengfa 宛城區政府) floated various urban renewal and development plans and initiatives that put the price of the downtown temple site in the range of several hundred millions yuan. One story related to me by some of the Daoist leaders who were given access to the Nanyang government initiatives and plans has it that the Wancheng Government demanded a 200 million yuan compensation to be paid by the Nanyang Daoist Association in exchange for its move-out and relocation to a newly planned government office park paid already with the central state funding on the eastern suburbs of the city.[35]

Yet the 1995 deal has since been cynically used by the Nanyang government as evidence of their sincere and full implementation of the party's policies on temple restitution. More importantly, the deal which was originally a temporary solution to the increasing demand for a ritual venue by the Daoists and their followers has since become Nanyang government's excuse and rationale for its intransigence to Daoists' continued demand for the return of the original downtown Xuanmiao Monastery.[36]

Another equally insurmountable problem faced by the Daoists in Nanyang is that the Daoist temple reclamation efforts may not fit into the local Nanyang government's overall modernization plan, especially its project for the city's cultural development in the post-Mao era. As Nanyang was either home or host to an array of historically prominent figures of Chinese history, its government has enjoyed a deep and large cultural legacy from which to draw while redefining its identity in the highly competitive national market for local culture and tourism in the post-Maoist era. As its counterparts among the second and third-tier cities in China vie with one another for cultural prestige, prominence, and tourism, Nanyang authorities have sought to promote tourism and local prestige by projecting the city as one of deep history and rich culture that are second to none in China. In constructing the city's cultural and historical image, Nanyang's local authorities and their cultural experts and scholars decided in the early 1980s to focus on a group of outstanding historical worthies (*lishi mingren* 歷史名人) as part of a comprehensive plan to represent the city's pinnacle achievements in moral and political philosophy, science, medicine, and commerce in early China. Known popularly as the Four Sages of Nanyang (Nanyang sisheng 南陽四聖), they are Fan Li 范蠡 (536–448 BC), the sage of commerce (*shangsheng* 商聖) and allegedly a native of Xichuan 淅川 in western Nanyang, Zhang Heng 張衡 (78–139), sage of science (*kesheng* 科聖) and a native of Nanyang, Zhang Ji 張機 (150–219), sage of medicine (*yisheng* 醫聖) and a native of Dengzhou south of Nanyang, and Zhuge Liang, sage of wisdom (*zhisheng* 智聖) who sojourned in Nanyang. After their first attempt in 1982, the Nanyang government successfully gained approval in the fall of 1986 by the State Council for listing their city on the national registry of the so-called National famous historical and cultural cities (*guojia lishi wenhua mingcheng* 國家歷史文化名城), a coveted status which not only ensured annual state funding for the repair and conservation of the historically and culturally significant sites and relics within the region, but it also rendered the city an attractive destination in the increasingly competitive market for commercial and cultural tourism. Nanyang made it into the national registry due in no small part to its government's active promotion of these historical figures. Later, the Nanyang government even lobbied the National General Postal Service to issue a set of four stamps in honor of the Four Sages of Nanyang in 2003. Since the sages' quartet was promoted for their secular cultural, material, and political achievements, or their perceived scientific inclination, it is perhaps not surprising that Nanyang's rich Daoist legacy and history were conspicuously absent from the Nanyang government's plan for the city's cultural development.[37] Indeed, the Martial Marquis Shrine where Zhuge Liang, the sage of political wisdom supposedly lived, figured in the government's application for entry into the registry not as a Daoist religious venue but rather as the historical and cultural site where Zhuge Liang once lived and achieved fame. While the Xuanmiao Monastery was not even mentioned in the city's original application for the registry, it did earn a mention in the State Council's approval notice which listed it as an "ancient relic site (*wenwu guji* 文物古跡)."[38]

Last but not the least, the variant and even conflicting intra-government interests and priorities also impeded the temple restitution work in Nanyang. In the case of the Martial Marquis Shrine, Nanyang prefectural government's Bureau of Ethnic and Religious Affairs 民族宗教事務處 and its Bureau of Cultural Affairs 文化處) and the latter's affiliate museums were often directly at odds with each other when it came to temple restitution work. Even the same government agency's policy and dealings with religion may fluctuate and change depending on the changing political conditions, institutional interests, and policy priorities.

Nanyang's Bureau of Cultural Affairs and its affiliate the Nanyang Museum's approach to religion experienced some interesting fluctuations and changes, due to the party's overall policies on religion and to the ebb and flow of its own institutional power and its prolonged entrenchment at the Martial Marquis Shrine. In the early 1950s, while the Communist-led land reform had earlier sent most of the resident Daoist clerics at the Martial Marquis Shrine packing, the Nanyang Museum which came to occupy the shrine shortly after 1949 seemed to have made practical arrangements to allow those Daoist clerics who either refused to be repatriated home or had no places to go after the land reform to stay on at the shrine, and assigned them temporary work as custodians and groundskeepers at the shrine-turned-museum. Indeed, in the aftermath of the Great Leap Forward and when the party relaxed its ideological zeal and political frenzy in the early 1960s, the museum even allowed Zhu Zongchang and his two other fellow Daoists to resume their routine worship and daily rituals at their old shrine. These Daoist-led ritual activities at the main hall of worship of the shrine were first resumed in October 1961 and carried on and off depending on the changing political climates until the breakout of the Cultural Revolution in 1966.[39] (Figure 2.2)

But by the early 1980s, when the new party and state policies promoting more open and liberalized space for religion were promulgated, the Nanyang Museum had become so fully and institutionally entrenched at the shrine that it had taken

纪念一季度先进生产者合影

Figure 2.2 Zhu Zongchang (seventh from left) and fellow Daoist clerics (third and fifth from left) with the Nanyang Museum staff in 1961 in Zhang Xiaogang, *Wangshi ruge*, p. 9.

up a much more intransigent stance toward the Daoist demands for temple restitution. This hardened position was most conspicuously demonstrated in the Nanyang Bureau of Cultural Affairs' resounding rejection to Zhu Zongchang's petition for the return of the shrine and its eviction of Zhu and his fellow Daoist squatters in the summer of 1988.

Meanwhile, in the aftermath of the Cultural Revolution, and perhaps impelled by the party's liberal policies toward religion, Nanyang's Bureau of Ethnic and Religious Affairs adopted a rather sympathetic, even accommodating, approach to temple restitution, at least in the case of the Martial Marquis Shrine beginning from the early 1980s through the 1990s. But the bureau's new stance was not entirely inspired by the party's new liberal religious policies alone. Indeed, evidence suggests that Zhu and his fellow Daoists' activism, indeed, their years of petitioning since the early 1980s, their dramatic collective squatting of the main worship hall at the shrine on July 31, 1988, and finally, Zhu's self-imposed exile in November of that year may have been the driving impetus behind the bureau's much softened approach. In its investigative report filed on December 16, 1988, one month after Zhu's self-imposed exile, the bureau not only acknowledged past wrongdoings against Daoism, but it also urged the Nanyang municipal government to fully carry out the party's new policies on religion by returning the shrine to Zhu and his fellow Daoists. In the report, the bureau unusually and specifically singled out Nanyang Museum and its supervising agency, the Bureau of Cultural Affairs, and censured both for continuing the occupation of the shrine and for failing to execute the party's key policy of temple restitution by refusing to return the shrine to Daoists promptly.[40]

But the inter-agency conflict did not really help the implementation of the party's policies of temple restitution. It remains unclear how Nanyang's Bureau of Cultural Affairs reacted to the criticism by the Bureau of Religious Affair. What is clear is that the criticism has so far failed to produce any visible change. Indeed, the Nanyang Museum has since remained steadfast in its occupation of the shrine, and its denial of Zhu and successive fellow Daoists' calls for the shrine's return as of today (2017).

Yet, faced with these obstacles in the 1980s, Zhu Zongchang and his fellow Daoists continued their campaign to reclaim the shrine. Their activism gained support among some officials within the National Bureau of Religious Affairs under the State Council. One deputy head of the bureau made visits to the shrine between 1985 and 1988 and required the Nanyang local government to pay due attention to the reopening of the shrine as a venue for religious and ritual activities. During his visit to the shrine in December of 1987, Mr. Jiang, a senior official from the Central Committee's Department of United Front, the party's central agency in charge of religious issues, gave specific instructions to the Nanyang government: "The Martial Marquis Shrine has been well-preserved. There are Daoist clerics here. The issue of its re-opening (for religious activities) must be considered."

But even these officials' directions fell on deaf ears when it came to returning the shrine to the Daoists, leaving Zhu Zongchang and fellow clerics in utter disappointment. After years of submitting petitions to the appropriate government agencies at various levels, Zhu opined in one of his petitions:

> The Nanyang City government has already implemented the policy by having returned properties to all four other religions, except to Daoism. The return of Daoist temple properties and its organization have all remained empty words. Despite the fact that temple restitution has remained our urgent wish, a dozen or so of our Daoist clerics have been continuously denied entry to the shrine. Even though I am presently an executive council member of the Henan provincial Daoist Association, and a member of the Nanyang Municipal Political Consultative Council, I have been reduced to merely a groundskeeper and forced to live outside the shrine!

Conclusion

Zhu died in the early 1990s without ever seeing the return of his beloved shrine. Indeed, Zhu's death had also lifted the political pressure upon the Nanyang local government. As none of his disciples and followers possessed the same charisma, authority, and influence as he did, Nanyang Daoist efforts to reclaim the shrine as their rightful property and venue for ritual activities have not been able to achieve the same intensity and power since.

As the history of the shrine shows that for a long period from the mid-Ming to the early Qing dynasty, the Martial Marquis Shrine enjoyed that status of an official temple which performed the spring and autumn state worships to Lord Zhuge based on the standards and regulations of the Ming and the Qing state canon of sacrifices. As these biannual rites were typically paid for by the local government, and attended by its leading officials, the shrine's resident Daoists who would often assist with and even officiate the ritual worships were thus quite intimately connected with the local Nanyang state and officials. In addition, the shrine also housed the state Office of Daoist Discipline whose court-appointed senior Daoist officials adjudicated all intra-Daoist disputes and litigations involving Daoist clerics. Further, the shrine's history also shows that the Quanzhen lineage clerics who resided at the shrine from the mid-Ming all the way to early 1950s were clearly also making accommodation for, if not outright organizing, local popular cults and devotional groups centered on the Martial Marquis at the shrine, which mirrors a central temple's key function in structuring and shaping popular and local ritual life and voluntary associations in both urban and rural areas in China.

Yet, the vicissitudes of the Martial Marquis Shrine's unsuccessful return to the Daoist also reveals how the power and prestige of such one-time central temple as defined by Vincent Goossaert in Chapter 1 of this volume could come undone and suffer irreparable damage and decline in the post-1949 China. As the case of the Martial Marquise Shrine in Nanyang demonstrates, Daoist revival at local levels in the post-Mao China can prove to be quite a thorny path. While factors such as state confiscation of temples count among the most devastating of all measures in destroying a religion, it is the state agencies' persistent physical occupation and repurposing of temples for other secular uses that has proved to be the most pernicious and obstructive to any Daoist efforts aimed at temple restitution in Nanyang. But the post-Mao era Daoist efforts to recover their temples must not be seen as merely a quarrel about the religious property or economic rights. It is about something more. Indeed, since modern states, from the late Qing dynasty through the Republic state to the People's Republic have consistently targeted religious properties, especially temples as a means to diminish and even destroy religion, it is therefore not surprising at all that successful temple restitution in the form of reclaimed, renovated, and reopened temples are often widely seen as a potent and physical symbol of Daoist religious revival.

Yet as we have seen, a swelter of challenges and problems, from local government indifference, state's appropriation and its entrenched occupation of the shrines, inter-agency rivalry and conflict, competitive influences by other religions, and Daoist institutional weakness and minority status have all combined to derail Zhu and his fellow Daoists' efforts to reclaim their shrine, making any successful Daoist temple recovery, and by extension Daoist revival at local level frustratingly elusive and rare in contemporary Nanyang, and perhaps in many other parts of China, too.

Notes

1 See Nanyang minzongchu (Dec 16, 1988), Nanyang Archives File 14-1-1-27, pp. 1–9.
2 This part of the event is based on my field interviews taking place since 2012 with Prioress Meng Yingxian 孟應仙, who together with Zhu Zongchang, Liu Chengshan, Zhang Zongwu 張宗武, Liu Zongchao 劉宗朝, Liu Zongdao 劉宗道, Zhou Yuanfu 周圓富, and Guo Chengxing 郭誠興 were among the closely knit group of Daoist clerics and lay activists advocating for the return of Daoist temples in Nanyang in the early 1980s.
3 See Zhu Zongchang, "Gei Henan sheng zhengxie de shenshushu (Petition to Henan Political Consultative Conference)" in appendix to Nanyang Archives File 14-1-1-21, pp. 148–49.
4 See Nanyang Minzongchu (Dec 14, 1988), Nanyang Archives File 14-1-1-21, pp. 146–47.
5 A hardcopy version of the directive is held at the Nanyang Municipal Archives, and a photocopy in my collection. For an online copy of the directive, access the following link at Baidu.com: https://baike.baidu.com/item/%E5%85%B3%E4%BA%8E%E6%88%9 1%E5%9B%BD%E7%A4%BE%E4%BC%9A%E4%B8%BB%E4%B9%89%E6% 97%B6%E6%9C%9F%E5%AE%97%E6%95%99%E9%97%AE%E9%A2%98%E7 %9A%84%E5%9F%BA%E6%9C%AC%E8%A7%82%E7%82%B9%E5%92%8C% E5%9F%BA%E6%9C%AC%E6%94%BF%E7%AD%96/4900600 (accessed on Sept 25, 2017). For English version of Directive 19, see "The Basic Viewpoint and Policy on the Religious Question During Our Country's Socialist Period, Document No. 19 (March 31, 1982), M.E. Sharpe, Inc., China Law and Government, 33.2 (Mar–Apr, 2000), pp. 17–34. For more in-depth analyses of the document and its impact on the post-Mao-era religious landscape, see Morrison "Religious policy in China"; Fenggang Yang, "Between Secularist Ideology and Desecularizing Reality"; Leung, "China's Religious Freedom Policy: The Art of Managing Religious Activity"; and H.H. Lai,

"Religious Policies in Post-Totalitarian China: Maintaining Political Monopoly over a Reviving Society."

6 See Zhu Zongchang, "Nanyang Wuhou ci daoyuan"; and also, Liu Xia, "Wuhou ci yu daojiao."

7 See Xun Liu, "Jidai totomoni."

8 See "Guanyu woguo shehuizhuyi shiqi Zongjiao wenti de jiben guandian he jiben zhengce" (Mar 1982), photocopy in my collection.

9 Yue Fei's handcopying of *Zhuge Pronouncements* in cursive style was re-carved onto a total of 21 steles in 1876 by Ren Kai 任愷, a famous calligrapher, an admirer of Yue's calligraphic style, and the presiding prefect of Nanyang in the 1870s. See both Ren Kai's epilogue (1876) and Yue Fei's epilogue composed in the fall of 1138 at the end of the latter's hand-copied *Zhuge Liang qianhou Chushibiao* 諸葛亮前後出師表, transcribed texts and stele inscription in Liu Yudong, et al., comp., *Wolonggang Wuhou ci beike*, pp. 278–79 and plates 82 and 83; and see also Nanyang Minzongchu (Dec 16, 1988), Nanyang Archives File 14-1-1-27, pp. 2–5.

10 In addition to his service in the Nanyang post, Aqamad later seemed to have risen to serve as a director of the Left and the Right Offices of the Henan provincial branch secretariat (Henan zuoyousi langzhong 河南行省左右司郎中) in 1304. See *Da Yuan shengzheng guochao dianzhang*, j. 6.

11 See Wang Qian, "Han chengxiang Zhuge Zhongwuhou ci bei," *Nanyang fuzhi* (hereafter, NYFZ, 1551), j.12: 92a-b.

12 See Yang Shiqi, "Dingjian Zhuge Kongming ci beiji," transcribed text and stele image in Liu Yudong, et al, comp., *Wolonggang Wuhou ci beike*, pp. 39–40, and plate #7.

13 See Ren Yi, "Shu zhidao beiyin," in WLGZ (1712), j.2: 25b-26b; and for the transcribed text of Ren Yi's inscription and photographs of the stele's front and back, see Liu Yudong, et al, comp., *Wolonggang Wuhou ci beike*, p. 43 and plate 8.

14 See Zhang Penghe, "Wuhou cimiao" in his *Zhongwu zhi* (1706): j.5: 38b.

15 See Cheng Jufu, *Chici Nanyang Zhuge shuyuan beiji*, in WLGZ (1712), 2.37a-41a.

16 See Yang Yingkui, *Chici Zhongwuhou miaogui wen jipin xiwen bei*, in WLGZ, 2.1b-9a.

17 For evidence of the Daoist temple managers and keepers' involvement in official and folk cults at other Nanyang temples, see Xun Liu, "Physicians, Quanzhen Daoists, and Folk Cult of the Sage of Medicine in Nanyang, 1540s–1950s."

18 See Xun Liu, "Quanzhen Nanwu Sect in Late Ming and Qing Nanyang."

19 Nanyang Minzongchu (Dec 16, 1988), Nanyang Archives File 14-1-1-27, pp. 1–9, and Xun Liu, "Quanzhen Nanwu Sect in Late Ming and Qing Nanyang." See also Zhu Zongchang, "Nanyang Wuhou ci daoyuan"; and Liu Xia, "Wuhou ci yu daojiao."

20 See Cao Tianduo, *Hansan zi Li Zongyang daoxing bei* (1941), stele rubbing in my possession; and see also, Xun Liu, "Jidai totomoni."

21 See Zhang Xiaogang, *Wangshi ruge*, pp. 9–10.

22 See Nanyang minzongchu (Dec 16, 1988), Nanyang Archives File 14-1-1-27, pp. 3–6.

23 See Zhang Xiaogang, *Wangshi ruge*, pp. 1–6.

24 For instance, to remind the public of the excess of the landlord class, a prime target amid the campaign to "exterminate the Four Olds" during the Cultural Revolution, the Nanyang Museum staged in the winter of 1969 the widely attended exhibition entitled "Rent-collection Yard (*shouzuyuan* 收租院)," which featured the heinous exploitation of peasants by the usurious Sichuan landlord and powerful hegemon Liu Wencai 劉文彩 (1887–1949), who allegedly exacted unbearably high rents on his poor tenant farmer in the pre-1949 Chengdu suburbs. See Zhang Xiaogang, *Wangshi ruge*, pp. 28–29.

25 For Guo's patronage of the Nanyang Museum, see Zhang Xiaogang, *Wangshi ruge*, pp. 2 and 37–38.

26 For a chronicle of the major visits to the museum and the shrine by prominent cultural figures and politicians in the post-Mao era, see Zhang Xiaogang, *Wangshi ruge*, pp. 46–172.

27 See Zhang Jie, "Dangqian zongjiao huodong qingkuang he jinhou yijian" (1980), Nanyang Archives, File 14-1-1-9.
28 See Zhang Jie, "Dangqian zongjiao huodong qingkuang he jinhou yijian."
29 For a brief history of the Jin'gang Catholic diocese, see Chai Junqing, "Jindai waiguo Tianzhujiaohui zai Henan huodong shulue."
30 See Nanyang diqu xingzheng gongshu zongjiao shiwuchu, "Nanyang diqu zongjiao qingkuang huibao tigang" (1982), Nanyang Archives, File 14-1-1-11a.
31 See Nanyang diqu xingzheng gongshu zongjiao shiwuchu, "Qingkuang fanying" (1983), Nanyang Archives, File 14-1-1-11b.
32 See Nanyang diqu xingzheng gongshu zongjiao shiwuchu (1982), Nanyang Archives, File 14-1-1-11a.
33 Yin Dejie, "Nanyang Xuanmiao guan."
34 Between the early 1910s and 1930s, parts of the Xuanmiao Monastery were successively seized and inhabited by several Beiyang and Republican military warlords and their troops. See Qiao Xinguang, "Beiyang junfa tongzhi shiqi Nanyang de lireng zhengshoushi"; Wang Baoqing, "Wo suo zhidao de Wu Qingtong"; Qiao Xinguang, "Junfa junzhan shiqi de Nanyang"; Zhang Hexuan, "Nanyang junfa Ma Wende"; Wang Zhi, "Qingmo Nanyang zhujun gaikuang"; and Shui Puci, "Liu Zhenhua zai Nanyang."
35 This is based on my field interviews with Daoist leaders in Nanyang since 2007.
36 This section on the Daoist struggle to reclaim the original site of the Xuanmiao Monastery is based on my field interviews since 2002 with several senior Daoist clerics who are still alive and active in Nanyang. At their request for anonymity, I have removed their real names to protect their identities, and instead refer to them as "Daoist clerics" or simply "Daoists in Nanyang" or "Nanyang Daoists" throughout this chapter.
37 See Nanyang shi renmin zhengfu (1986), "Guanyu zaici shenqing jiang Nanyang liewei guojia lishi wenhua mingdcheng de baogao ji fujian yi er," Nanyang Archives, File B2-1-1.2.
38 Guowuyuan (1986), "Guowuyuan pizhuan Jianshebu, Wenhuabu guanyu qing gongbu di'erpi guojia lishi wenhua mingcheng mingdan baogao—Di'erpi guojia lishi wenhua mingcheng jianjie," Nanyang Archives, File B2-1-1-1.
39 See Zhang Xiaogang, *Wangshi ruge*, p. 14.
40 See Nanyang Zongjiao shiwuchu, "Guanyu luoshi Wuhou ci Daojiao fangchan kaifang Daojiao huodong changsuo de qingkuang baogao," (1988) Nanyang Archives, File 14-1-1-14.

Reference works

Archival Materials

Guowuyuan 國務院. "Guowuyuan pizhuan Jianshebu, Wenhuabu guanyu qing gongbu di'erpi guojia lishi wenhua mingcheng mingdan baogao—Di'erpi guojia lishi wenhua mingcheng jianjie 國務院批轉建設部,文化部關於請公佈第二批國家歷史文化名城名單報告---第二批國家歷史 文化名城簡介," (Dec 8, 1986). *Nanyang Archives*, File B2-1-1-1.
Nanyang Daojiao xiehui 南陽道教協會. "Nanyang diqu Daojiao diyiji daibiao huiyi kaimuci 南陽地區道教第一屆代表會議開幕詞 [Remarks at the Opening Ceremony of the First Daoist Representative Congress of the Nanyang Prefecture]," (May 19, 1989). *Nanyang Archives*, File 14-1-1-28.
Nanyang diqu xingshu minzu zongjiao shiwuchu 南陽地區行署民族宗教事務處. Guanyu Fangchengxian Daojiao huodong qingkuang diaocha ji chuli yijian de baogao 關於方城縣道教活動情況調查及處理意見的報告 [A Report on the Investigation

of the Daoist Activities Situation in Fangcheng County and the Proposals for Its Handling]," (Feb 28, 1986). *Nanyang Archives*, File 14-1-1-17.

Nanyang diqu xingzheng gongshu zongjiao shiwuchu 南陽地區行政公署宗教事務處. "Nanyang diqu zongjiao qingkuang huibao tigang 南陽地區宗教情況彙報提綱 [An Outline Report on Religious Situation in Nanyang Prefecture]," (Jul 22, 1982). *Nanyang Archives*, File 14-1-1-11(a).

Nanyang Minzongchu 南陽民宗處. "Guanyu zongjiao fangmian jige wenti de diaocha baogao 關於宗教方面幾個問題的調查報告 [An Investigative Report on Several Religious Issues]," (Apr 4, 1988). *Nanyang Archives*, File 14-1-1-21.

———. "Guanyu Nanyang Wuhou ci daoren Zhu Zongchang chuzou de qingkuang baogao 關於南陽武侯祠道人朱宗長出走的情況報告 [Report on the Incident of Daoist Zhu Zongchang's Departure from Martial Marquis Shrine of Nanyang]," (Dec 14, 1988). *Nanyang Archives*, File 14-1-1-21.

———. "Guanyu kaifang Daojiao huodong changsuo Wuhou ci de qingkuang baogao 關於開放道教活動場所武侯祠的情況報告 [Report on the Conditions for Opening Martial Marquis Shrine as a Venue for Daoist Activities]," (Dec 16, 1988). *Nanyang Archives*, File 14-1-1-27.

———. "Nanyang diqu minzu zhongjiao shiwuchu 1986 gongzuo zongjie 南陽民族宗教事務處一九八六年工作總結 [A Summary of Nanyang Prefectural Ethnic and Religious Affairs Bureau's Work in 1986]," (Jan 7, 1987). *Nanyang Archives*, File 14-1-1-16.

Nanyang Zongjiao shiwuchu 南陽宗教事務處. "Guanyu kaifang zongjiao huodong changsuo Wuhou ci de qingkuang baogao 關於開放道教活動場所武侯祠的情況報告 [A Situational Report Regarding the Opening of the Martial Marquis Shrine as a Venue for Daoist Religious Activities]," (July 19, 1989). *Nanyang Archives*, File 14-1-1-27(a).

———. "Guanyu luoshi zongjiao tuanti fangchan zhengce de qingkuang he yijian 關於落實宗教團體房產政策的情況和意見 [Situation and Views Regarding the Implementation of the Policy of Returning Properties to Religious Groups]," (July 20, 1989). *Nanyang Archives*, File 14-1-1-27(b)

———. "Qingkuang fanying 情況反映 [Feedbacks on the (Religious) Situation]," (April 1, 1983). *Nanyang Archives*, File 14-1-1-11(b).

Nanyangshi Minzu zongjiao shiwuju 南陽市民族宗教事務局. "Jiaqiang lingdao, tongyi renshi, renzhenluoshi zongjiao tuanti fangchan zhengce 加強領導, 統一認識, 認真落實宗教團體房產政策 [Strengthen Leadership and Unify Understandings to Seriously Implement (Party's)policies Regarding Religious Groups' Properties]," (Oct 10, 1989), File 14-1-1-26(a).

Nanyangshi renmin zhengfu 南陽市人民政府. "Guanyu zaici shenqing jiang Nanyang liewei guojia lishi wenhua mingcheng de baogao ji Fujian yi er 關於再次申請將南陽列為國家歷史文化名城的報告及附件一二" (Sept 17, 1986). *Nanyang Archives*, File B2-1-1.2.

Nanzhaoxian minzu zongjiao shiwuju 南召縣民族宗教事務局. "Women shi zhenyang luoshi zongjiao tuanti fangchan zhengce de 我們是怎樣落實宗教團體房產政策的 [How We Have Implemented the Policy of Returning Properties to Religious Groups]," (1989). *Nanyang Archives*, File 14-1-1-26(b).

Zhonggong Nanyang diwei tongzhanbu Zhang Jie 中共南陽地委統戰部張傑. "Dangqian zongjiao huodong qingkuang he jinhou yijian 當前宗教活動情況和今後意見 [On the Situation of Current Religious Activities and Suggestions Going Forward]," (Nov 1, 1980). *Nanyang Archives*, File 14-1-1-9.

Zhonggong zhongyang shujichu 中共中央書記處. "Guanyu woguo shehuizhuyi shiqi Zongjiao wenti de jiben guandian he jiben zhengce 關於我國社會主義時期宗教問題的基本觀點和基本政策 [On Fundamental Perspectives and Basic Policy Regarding the Religion Question under Our Country's Socialist Period]," (Mar, 1982). *Nanyang Archives*, File 14-1-1-11. [English version published by M.E. Sharpe Inc. "The Basic Viewpoint and Policy on the Religious Question during Our Country's Socialist Period, Document No. 19 (March 31, 1982)," *Chinese Law and Government*, 33(2), 2000, pp. 17–34.]

Zhu Zongchang 朱宗長. "Gei Henan sheng zhengxie de shenshushu 給河南省政協的申述書 [Petition to Henan Political Consultative Conference]," (Undated). An appendix to *Nanyang Archives*, File 14-1-1-21, pp. 148–49.

Steles and Local Gazetteers

Cao Tianduo 曹天鐸. *Hansanzi Li Zongyang daoxing bei* 涵三子李宗陽道行碑 (1941). Stele rubbing in my possession.

Cheng Jufu 程鉅夫. "Chici Nanyang Zhuge shuyuan beiji 勅賜南陽諸葛書院碑記"(1311), *WLGZ* (1712), j.2:37a–41a.

Da Yuan shengzheng guochao dianzhang 大元聖政國朝典章. 2 volumes. Reprint edition. Taipei: Wenhai chubanshe, 1964.

Kang Konggao 康孔高 (1436), comp.; Jin Fu 金福 and Zhou You 周遊, suppl. *Nanyang fuzhi* 南陽府志 [Nanyang Prefectural Gazetteer, abbreviated as NYFZ 1436]. 8 of 12 juan. Microfilm held at Princeton University Library.

Kong Chuanjin 孔傳金 (1807), ed. *Nanyang fuzhi* 南陽府志 [Nanyang Prefectural Gazetteer, abbreviated as NYFZ 1807]. 6 juan. Harvard University Library.

Li Tinglong 李廷龍 (1577), ed. *Nanyang fuzhi* 南陽府志 [Nanyang Prefectural Gazetteer, abbreviated as NYFZ 1577]. 14 (18) juan. Microfilm held at Harvard University Library.

Luo Jing, *Wolonggang zhi* 臥龍岡志 (Abbreviated as WLGZ in text). 2 juan. Nanyang: Privately printed, 1712.

Ren Yi 任義. *Shu zhidao beiyin* 書指道碑陰 [Inscription for the Back of the Direction Stele, 1478]. *WLGZ*, j.2:25a-26b; and also WHCBK (2015), p. 43 and plate#8.

Wang Qian 王謙. "Han chengxiang Zhuge Zhongwuhou ci bei 漢丞相諸葛忠武侯祠碑," in *NYFZ* (1528), j.12: 92a-b.

Wang Weixin 王維新 and Tu Tengmao 塗滕茂 (1659), comp. *Nanyang fuzhi* 南陽府志. [Nanyang prefectural gazetteers, abbreviated as NYFZ 1659]. 13 juan. Peking University Library.

Yang Shiqi 楊士奇. "Dingjian Zhuge Kongming ci beiji 鼎建諸葛孔明祠碑記 [A Stele Record of the New Construction of the Worship Hall of Zhuge Kongming, 1444]," *WLGZ*, j.2:21a-24a; and also WHCBK, pp. 39–40 and plate#7.

Yang Yingkui 楊應奎 (1528), ed.; Zhu Shangwen 朱尚文 and Zhang Pei 張霈 (1554), suppl.; Zhang Jiamou 張嘉謀 (1939), ed./annot. *Ming Jiajing Nanyang fuzhi* 明嘉靖南陽府志 [Nanyang Prefectural Gazetteers of the Jiajing Reign, abbreviated in text as NYFZ 1528]. 12 juan. Rpt. Edition based on the 1942 reprint. Nanyang: Nanyang diqu shizhi biancuan weiyuanhui, 1984.

Yang Yingkui. *Chici Zhongwuhou miaogui jiwen jipin xiwen bei* 勅賜忠武侯廟規祭文祭品檄文碑 [A Stele of Imperially Bestowed Sacrificial Regulations, Sacrificial Eulogy, and Sacrificial Offerings for the Shrine of Loyal Martial Marquis] in *WLGZ*, j.2:1b-9a; and also *WHCBK*, pp. 63–65 and plates#1 and 14.

Zhang Penghe 張鵬翮. "Wuhou cimiao 武侯祠廟" in his . *Zhongwu zhi* 忠武志 (Abbreviated as ZWZ in text). 8 juan. Nanyang: Bingxuetang 冰雪堂, 1706. , j.5:38b.

Zhang Penghe 張鵬翮, comp. *Zhongwu zhi* 忠武志 (Abbreviated as ZWZ in text). 8 juan. Nanyang: Bingxuetang 冰雪堂, 1706.

Zhu Lin 朱璘 (1696). *Nanyang fuzhi* 南陽府志 (1696). [Nanyang Prefectural Gazetteers, abbreviated in text as NYFZ 1696]. 6 juan. Rpt. Edition. Taipei: Xuesheng shuju, 1968.

Zhuge Xi 諸葛羲 (1632). *Han chengxiang Zhuge Zhongwuhou ji* 漢丞相諸葛忠武侯集. 21 juan in *Daozang jiyao* 道藏輯要, ser. 26.

Secondary Works

Chai Junqing 柴俊青. "Jindai waiguo Tianzhujiaohui zai Henan huodong shulüe 近代外國天主教會在河南活動述略," *Yindu xuekan* 殷都學刊, 1, 1994, pp. 44–47.

Da Yuan shengzheng guochao dianzhang 大元聖政國朝典章. Reprint edition, 2 volumes. Taipei: Wenhai chubanshe, 1964.

Lai, H.H. "Religious Policies in Post-Totalitarian China: Maintaining Political Monopoly over a Reviving Society," *Journal of Chinese Political Science*, 11(1), 2006, pp. 55–77.

Leung, Beatrice. "China's Religious Freedom Policy: The Art of Managing Religious Activity," *The China Quarterly*, 184, Dec, 2005, pp. 895–913.

Liu Xia 劉霞. "Wuhou ci yu daojiao 武侯祠與道教," *Zhongguo daojiao* 中國道教, 4, 2006, pp. 36–37.

Liu, Xun. "Jidai to tomo ni: Zenshin dōshi Ri Sōyō to Jiki, Dōmeikai, oyobi Shinmatsu-Minsho Nanyō ni okeru kindaika kaikaku (1890 nendai – 1930 nendai) 時代とともに: 全真道士李宗陽と慈禧、同盟会、および清末民初南陽における近代化改革(一八九〇年代〜一九三〇年代〕" [Progressing with Times: Abbot Li Zongyang, Cixi, the Revolutionary Alliance, and Modern Reforms in Nanyang]" in Tanaka Fumio 田中文雄 and Terry Kleeman, eds., *Daoism and Kyosei (Co-Generativism) Thought* 道教と共生思想. Tokyo: Taige Press, 2009, pp. 299–337.

———. "Physicians, Quanzhen Daoists, and Folk Cult of the Sage of Medicine in Nanyang, 1540s-1950s," *Daoism: Religion, History and Society*, 6, 2014, pp. 269–334.

———. "Quanzhen Nanwu Sect in Late Ming and Qing Nanyang," *Paper Presented at the Fourth Nichibei Daoist Studies Conference Held at Pacific Lutheran University*, Tacoma, Washington, March 29–31, 2016.

Liu Yudong 柳玉東, Liu Xia 劉霞, et al. comp. *Wolonggang Wuhou ci beike* 臥龍岡武侯祠碑刻 (Abbreviated as WHCBK). Zhengzhou: Zhongzhou guji chubanshe, 2015.

Meng Yingxian 孟應仙. "Gaige kaifang yilai Nanyang Daojiao huifu chongjian de baogao 改革開放以來南陽道教恢復重建的報告 [A Report on Restoring and Reconstructing Daoism in Nanyang since the Reforms and Opening]," *Nanyang Daoist Association Annual Work Report Delivered on Behalf of Nanyang Daoist Association at the 2008 Nanyang Municipal Political Consultative Council*, 2008.

Morrison, Peter. "Religious Policy in China and Its Implementation in the Light of Document no. 19," *Religion in Communist Lands*, 12, Dec, 1984, pp. 244–55.

Nanyang daoxie 南陽道協. "Nanyang daojiao zongshu 南陽道教綜述," *Zhongguo daojiao*, 4, 2002, pp. 32–33.

Qiao Xinguang 喬新光. "Beiyang junfa tongzhi shiqi Nanyang de liren zhengshoushi 北洋軍閥統治時期南陽的歷任鎮守使," *Nanyang wenshi ziliao* 南陽文史資料 [Hereafter, *NYWS*], 2, 1986, pp. 28–31.

————. "Junfa hunzhan shiqi de Nanyang 軍閥混戰時期的南陽," *NYWS*, 2, 1986, pp. 40–49.

Shui Puci 水普慈. "Liu Zhenhua zai Nanyang 劉鎮華在南陽," *Henan wenshi ziliao* 河南文史資料 (hereafter *HNWS*), 48, 1993, pp. 154–59.

Wang Baoqing 王保慶. "Wo suo zhidao de Wu Qingtong 我所知道的吳慶桐,"*NYWS*, 2, 1986, pp. 34–38.

Wang Zhi 王直. "Qingmo Nanyang zhujun gaikuang 清末南陽駐軍概況," *Nanyangxian wenshi ziliao* 南陽縣文史資料, 6, 1992, pp. 57–59.

Yang, Fenggang. "Between Secularist Ideology and Desecularizing Reality: The Birth and Growth of Religious in Communist China," *Journal of Sociology*, 65(2), 2004, pp. 101–19.

Yin Dejie 殷德傑. "Nanyang Xuanmiao guan 南陽玄妙觀," *Wenshi zhishi* 文史知識, 5, 2008, pp. 153–55.

Xu Jiangwei 徐江偉. "Nanyang Wuhou ci yanjiu 南陽武侯祠研究," MA thesis, Yunnan University, 2016.

Zhang Hexuan 張和宣. "Nanyang junfa Ma Wende 南陽軍閥馬文德," *HNWS*, 14, 1985, pp. 83–86.

Zhang Xiaogang 張曉剛, ed. *Wangshi ruge: Nanyang shi bowuguan jian'guan wushizhounian jinianji-dashiji* 往事如歌: 南陽市博物館建館五十周年紀念集-大事記 (1959–2009). Xi'an: SanQin chubanshe, 2009.

Zhu Zongchang 朱宗長. "Nanyang Wuhou ci daoyuan 南陽武侯祠道院," *Zhongguo daojiao*, 3, 1989, p. 49.

Part II

Spirit-writing temples and their networks

3   The Jin'gaishan network

A lay Quanzhen Daoist organization in modern Jiangnan

Vincent Goossaert[1]

Jin'gaishan 金蓋山 is a hill (292 m high) situated some 8 km south of Huzhou 湖州, the center of a prosperous prefecture 府 (now a 市) in northern Zhejiang, adjacent to Hangzhou to the south and bordering lake Taihu on the north.[2] On the hill, at about mid-slope, is a Daoist temple, known by the names of (Gu) Meihuaguan (古)梅花觀 and Chunyanggong 純陽宮,[3] the latter name expressing its being dedicated to the cult of Lüzu 呂祖, i.e., Lü Dongbin 呂洞賓. It was originally built in the late eighteenth century by local lay devotees; shortly thereafter, under the leadership of Min Yide 閔一得 (1758–1836), it became a renowned center for Quanzhen Daoism, drawing large numbers of disciples from throughout the Jiangnan area. Min created for them a new lineage within the larger framework of the Longmen 龍門 lineage. One key characteristic of this lineage is that it was mostly composed of lay Daoists, that is, people living with their families and not professionally engaged in managing temples or performing rituals, yet claiming an explicit Quanzhen identity.[4]

Over the course of the nineteenth and twentieth centuries, this new lineage gradually developed into an original and fascinating organization (which I call the Jin'gaishan network) integrating over 70 branches throughout the Jiangnan region, most of them located in urban centers, at least until 1949. This large network, thanks to its multifaceted activities, from healing and spirit-writing to ritual services, was a major form of Daoism in urban Jiangnan, deserving study both in its own right and in comparison with other forms of modern urban religious organizations (such as redemptive societies 救世團體[5]) with which it shared a number of commonalities.

The study of Min Yide and his impressive scriptural legacy has been well advanced by scholars such as Monica Esposito and Mori Yuria 森由利亞.[6] Other scholars, notably Wu Yakui 吳亞魁 and Wang Zongyu 王宗昱, have focused on the institutional history of Quanzhen Daoism in the Jiangnan area, or Huzhou in particular, and have notably studied the genealogies produced by the lineage initiated by Min Yide.[7] This chapter, building on these very solid foundations, as well as some new sources (notably recently published temple gazetteers, spirit-writing collections, and early twentieth-century self-cultivation literature), tries to offer a social history of the network and to place it in a larger typology of religious organizations in modern Chinese society. It notably argues for the dynamism and creativity of the late imperial and Republican-period Lü Dongbin cult, showing, through this case study, how it could adapt to the new social and political conditions of the modern period through Republican and post-Mao changes.

The chapter begins with a background discussion of the Lü Dongbin cult in late imperial Jiangnan and the historical context for the rise of a spirit-writing cult on Jin'gaishan; it then sketches the history of the temple and that of the network of its branch altars that multiplied after the Taiping war and until 1949. In a next step, I examine the membership of this network and the various aspects of its activities – rituals, self-cultivation, and charity – and then describe the situation today based on fieldwork observations. Finally, I discuss the overlaps and commonalities with other modern urban religious organizations. Thus, this historical survey should allow us to identify the Jin'gaishan network as a specific type of Daoist network, distinct from clerical networks such as those discussed in the two preceding chapters.

The Lü Dongbin cult in late imperial Jiangnan

Before looking in detail at the Jin'gaishan temple, let us begin with a larger view of the Lü Dongbin cult in the whole Jiangnan area during the period. Lü Dongbin has been worshipped in countless shrines throughout China since the Song period;[8] his cult in Qing Jiangnan was thus by no means new. It took many different forms, including domestic worship among elites.[9] At the same time, the cult enjoyed full Daoist institutional support; it was particularly promoted by Quanzhen Daoists, even though it was not their monopoly, as we also find Lü's shrines in all Zhengyi-managed central temples in the Jiangnan area.

Two specific developments affected the development of the Lü Dongbin cult during the nineteenth century, and both directly illuminate the Jin'gaishan story. The first one is the 1804 imperial canonization of Lü Dongbin with the lofty title of Xieyuan zanyun chunyang yanzheng jinghua fuyou dijun 燮元贊運純陽演正警化孚佑帝君. This was the first such canonization of Lü since 1310 and was all the more remarkable since the title was awarded with reference to not only one temple where worship was mandated, as was usually the case with imperial canonizations, but one temple in each county throughout the empire was to be renovated and to receive official sacrifices.[10] The causes of this canonization are not known and await further research, but one inscription tells us that it was granted on the request of Jiang Sheng 姜晟 (1730–1810), a Suzhou native and long-time minister who memorialized on Lü's many miracles linked to water conservancy and flood control, for which Jiang was then in charge.[11] One cannot but observe that it took place during a period of intense canonization of Daoist deities (all honored with a *dijun* 帝君 Daoist title): Wenchang dijun in 1801 (who, very similarly, was also granted official sacrifices in each county), Xu Xun in 1803, and a further canonization for Guandi in 1814.[12]

We should note that these Daoist deities thus officially promoted during the Jiaqing reign were key deities in spirit-writing cults and morality book revelations, even though the imperial state never directly and explicitly condoned

spirit-writing. The status of the Lü Dongbin spirit-writing cult was highly ambiva-
lent indeed (and flies in the face of the classic scheme of official elite religiosity
vs. illegal popular religion) as spirit-writing was illegal, a fact regularly restated
by local prohibitions in late Qing Jiangnan,[13] even though the prohibition was
hardly enforced, at the same time as the Lü Dongbin temples where spirit-writing
took place were fully condoned by elite participation and official sacrifices.

In any case, the 1804 canonization did not spread the cult, which was already
firmly entrenched, but it certainly contributed to making it acceptable as a locus
for elite activism and organization. Local officials had to select one Lü Dongbin
temple in each jurisdiction for official sacrifices, in cooperation with Daoists and
local elites, a choice which may or may not correspond to the most active local Lü
Dongbin temple.[14] Furthermore, the officially sanctioned Lü Dongbin festivals,
around his birthday on 4/14, became in some cases major public holidays; one
1897 report described how all workers were given a day off on Lü's birthday in
Shanghai.[15]

The other and closely related trend affecting the Lü Dongbin cult from the
Qianlong period onward was the rise of large dedicated spirit-writing halls
devoted to Lü Dongbin and publishing corpuses of his revelations. This was by
no means an entirely new phenomenon: such halls and books have existed since
around the 1570s. The early (Song and Yuan) Lü Dongbin revelations, which
were not produced by spirit-writing, were by and large focused on *neidan* self-
cultivation. From the mid-eighteenth century onward, Lü increasingly reveals
scriptures characterized by a fuller religious discourse encompassing morality,
theology, eschatology, and social reform as well as self-cultivation.[16] At the same
time, comprehensive corpuses of Lü's revelation appear, the first one being the
Lüzu quanshu 呂祖全書 compiled in 1743 at a spirit-writing temple in Wuchang
(Hebei) called Hansangong 涵三宮. On top of earlier self-cultivation texts, this
compilation included recent revelations carrying a message of universal salvation, portraying Lü Dongbin as a savior of all humanity. During the succeeding
decades, this trend was amplified in other, similar Lü Dongbin spirit-writing halls
such as that Shao Zhilin and his master Cai Laihe 蔡來鶴 actually operated a
spirit-writing shrine dedicated to both Wenchang and Lüzu, named Guixiangji
桂香集 (within a temple named Tianxiangge 天香閣, on the southern shores of
the West Lake in Hangzhou), that published an enlarged *Lüzu quanshu* in 1775,
and the one established around 1798 in Beijing by the official Jiang Yupu 蔣予蒲
(1756–1819), that produced the *Daozang jiyao* 道藏輯要.[17]

The current historiography on spirit-writing in late imperial times has tended
to focus on spirit-writing as practiced in the private realm among elites. Indeed,
extant records suggest that in the Jiangnan area, this was an extremely common
activity among local elites,[18] geared toward self-cultivation and book writing.
This is understandable insofar as it is this type of spirit-writing that has produced most of the revealed books we now have. But the most common venue
for spirit-writing then as now was most likely not such elite private settings
but rather open spaces with regular séances, that is, dedicated shrines within
temples and/or charitable halls, *shantang* 善堂. In such contexts, spirit-writing

was aimed not at revealing texts, but rather at providing services to devotees, notably healing.[19] One artist's, Bao Tianxiao's 包天笑 (1879–1973), memoir tells how two types of spirit-writing altars (the vast majority of them devoted to either Lüzu or Jigong 濟公) were extremely common in late Qing Suzhou: public ones in the charitable halls, and private ones in homes, both training the sons of literati families to be mediums and decipher the god-prescribed drugs, *jifang* 乩方.[20]

Many Daoist temples in late imperial Jiangnan had a spirit-writing altar,[21] including the Shengzhenguan 上真觀 on Qionglongshan 穹窿山 near Suzhou, a preeminent center of Zhengyi Daoism in the whole Jiangnan area.[22] Descriptions of the Lü Dongbin temple festival in Suzhou mention that spirit-writing was a key part of the activities.[23] And, such spirit-writing altars were found everywhere in both urban and rural Jiangnan; an 1889 gazetteer of a township north of Shanghai describes how these altars became commonplace in each village from the Jiaqing period onward, with adepts (recruited from among the local gentry) identifying themselves as lay Daoists 夥居道士, organizing festivals and providing ritual services to local people.[24]

The Jin'gaishan network evolved in this context: its core temple, the Chunyanggong on Jin'gaishan was a large spirit-writing hall housed in a Lü Dongbin temple where officials came every year to sacrifice at the same time as a popular festival took place. This hall recruited disciples from among local elites who identified themselves as Daoists. Yet, on this basis, it developed in original directions through the nineteenth and twentieth centuries.

The early history of Jin'gaishan

The 1775 enlarged edition of the *Lüzu quanshu* was edited by Shao Zhilin 邵志琳 (1748–1810).[25] Lai Chi Tim has shown that one major purpose of this compilation, beyond claims that the original had become rare, was to include newly revealed texts and re-center it on the Jiangnan region: he counts 27 new texts revealed at 17 different spirit-writing shrines in Jiangnan, notably the shrines at Jin'gaishan – the Yunchaotan 雲巢壇 and the closely associated nearby shrine, Yiyuntan 怡雲壇 (or Yunyi caotang 雲怡草堂). Yet, the very active Lüzu spirit-writing center at Jin'gaishan that had by then failed to print most of its own texts, not to mention its own canon.[26] Shao was a regular visitor to Jin'gaishan and personally received an initiation from Lüzu there, as well as a divine order to print his scriptures. Shao Zhilin, like his master Cai Laihe and all other persons active in this project, was Jiangnan literati active in running charities, printing religious books, and establishing temples and spirit-writing shrines.[27] Remarkably, none of the nine texts revealed at Jin'gaishan during this period (second half of the eighteenth century) and included in the 1775 *Lüzu quanshu* (one of them also later included in the *Daozang jiyao*: *Jingshi gongguoge* 警世功過格) were included in later Jin'gaishan canons, discussed below. This suggests that from 1796 onward, when Min Yide took over the place, a very significant change of doctrinal as well as organizational course took place.

Shao's life is mostly known through a long biography in the 1821 *Jin'gai xindeng* 金蓋心燈.[28] In this work, much detail is provided about the vicissitudes of the spirit-writing shrines at Jin'gaishan during the 1770s, 1780s, and 1790s, where apparently severe conflicts opposed various parties, including various local families and Buddhist monks, over the control of the temple and its resources. Between 1787 and 1792, a temple to Lü Dongbin was built, with the name of Chongdetang 崇德堂. This was a new addition to a mountain already dotted with over a dozen small temples, retreats, and Buddhist hermitages. The Chongdetang was run by local lay devotees, and it provided miraculous healing and ritual services.[29] A detailed examination of this early stage of the story of Jin'gaishan will have to await a future publication.

The re-creation: Min Yide and the Chunyanggong

Min Yide was from a Huzhou gentry family; he was born in Renshi village 仁舍, some 10 km northeast of Jin'gaishan. He was cured of childhood illnesses by Quanzhen clerics on Tiantaishan 天台山 (central Zhejiang); he served as an official in Yunnan province for some time before returning home and settling on Jin'gaishan in 1796, where he took over the temple management and became a very successful intellectual leader and organizer. From 1796 onward, Min, whose lineage had long been involved in the mountain (having graves and private retreats there), oversaw a larger rebuilding of the Chongdetang now renamed Chunyanggong, and the temple was selected (among at least three other Lü Dongbin temples in Wucheng county) as the site for official sacrifices to Lü Dongbin, as mandated by the 1804 canonization.[30]

Min Yide had been an enthusiastic participant in spirit-writing cults to Lü Dongbin before settling on Jin'gaishan and continued there. There had been spirit-writing revelations on Jin'gaishan well before his arrival but, it seems that the spirit-writing cult really took off when Min Yide took over and oversaw the building of the Chunyanggong on a grand scale, with the spirit-writing hall, Yunchaotan (or Yunchao zongtan 宗), at its core.[31] As a result, Min was involved in the spirit-writing revelation and edition of several texts by Lü, which he compiled together with his own writings (including commentaries and essays) and other texts in two closely related collections, *Daozang xubian* 道藏續編 (23 texts) and *Gushu yinlou cangshu* 古書隱樓藏書 (37 texts, including all 23 texts from *Daozang xubian* and 14 others), both first published by the Chunyanggong in 1834, shortly before Min Yide's death.[32]

Min Yide's writings come with a lot of baggage; he was involved in a reinvention of Quanzhen Daoist doctrine and history – the latter expressed in the oft-quoted hagiographical work *Jin'gai xindeng*, which tells his vision of the history of the Longmen lineage, that Min first published in 1821.[33] This reinvention came about as the creative merging of two traditions (even though these traditions already had a long history of interaction elsewhere): the local spirit-writing cult to Lü Dongbin and Quanzhen Daoism. The latter was most probably introduced by Shen Yibing 沈一炳 (1708–1786), a local man who had become a Quanzhen

Daoist at Tiantaishan (some 250 km away) and had healed Min Yide and became his master.

But, we are not concerned with Min's writings here, rather by how the organization he created evolved with time. Min is credited with the creation of a sub-lineage of the Longmen lineage, called *fangbianpai* 方便派,[34] registering Daoists affiliated with the Yunchaotan. The term *fangbian* implies that its members are not held to the rules of celibacy and permanent vegetarianism observed by many members of the Longmen lineage. Indeed, throughout its nearly 200-year old history and to this day, most members are married, eat meat except on certain occasions,[35] and do not live from religious services, hence my term "lay Daoist." Indeed, some present-day members are local entrepreneurs, who are attracted to the Jin'gaishan tradition by its high cultural appeal. Nowadays, the Daoists in this tradition call themselves *si Longmen* 嗣龍門, which they consider as a distinctive term that sets themselves apart from other Quanzhen Daoists, and they wear, when performing rituals, a distinctive headgear (a flat blue cloth cap with a small wooden crown on top, held by a pin). They do not grow their hair long and wear distinctive vestments only when performing rituals.

During the early period, up to the Taiping war, the Chunyanggong and the community of the lay disciples of the Yunchaotan seem to have been, if not dominated, at least heavily invested in by the Min, who constituted one of the most prominent lineages in the rural areas south of Huzhou and around Jin'gaishan. As Wang Zongyu has noted, many members of the Min lineage in the two generations after Min Yide are listed in the genealogies of the Jin'gaishan lineage as disciples, and some of them were buried in the Chunyanggong cemetery along with a few other prominent Daoists.[36]

A turning point for Jin'gaishan, as for so many other religious organizations in Jiangnan, was the Taiping war that caused very extensive destructions – the Chunyanggong was burnt down – and disrupted religious networks and their economic basis; indeed, the whole Huzhou area was particularly affected during 1860–1863, and the population dropped. The Chunyanggong was rebuilt between 1864 and 1874 by members of the local elites (none of them from the Min lineage),[37] and it could recover some 200 mu of land along with urban real estate in Huzhou to support several Daoists in residence,[38] but most of the holdings of the impressive library that Min Yide had built up (the Gushu yinlou 古書隱樓) were lost forever.

The situation of the temple after the rebuilding is best documented in a gazetteer, the *Jin'gaishan zhi* 金蓋山志, compiled in 1883 and published in 1896. If the legacy of Min Yide is extolled throughout the book, his kin are hardly mentioned anymore; rather it is members of other prominent local lineages that feature as writers, patrons, and leaders. One powerful lineage is particularly in evidence: the Shen 沈 from nearby Zhudun 竹墩村 village, just a few kilometers south of Jin'gaishan, one of Huzhou's oldest (since the Song) and most prestigious lineages (that regularly intermarried with the Min).[39]

The preface of the *Jin'gaishan zhi* is signed by the Shen lineage's then most prominent member, Shen Bingcheng 沈秉成 (1823–1895), who was at a time governor-general 總督 of Jiangsu and Jiangxi – and also published in 1884 a lineage genealogy, the *Zhuxi Shen shi jiasheng* 竹溪沈氏家乘. Shen Bingcheng also authored various texts included in the *Jin'gaishan zhi*, prefaced the 1880 reprint of the *Jin'gai xindeng* (preface itself dated 1873), and wrote a biography of Min Yide.[40] We also see other Shens involved in the rebuilding of the Chunyanggong's various halls and shrines, presumably all from the same lineage.[41] Shen Bingcheng hints at a long-term commitment of his lineage to the Lü Dongbin cult by narrating, in both his prefaces (to *Jin'gaishan zhi* and *Jin'gai xindeng*), his Song-period ancestor's encounter with the immortal. Even more significantly, Min Yide's master, Shen Yibing, was also a Shen from Zhudun and was worshipped after his death both at Jin'gaishan and in various nearby villages.[42]

What we see at work in the nineteenth-century history of the Chunyanggong, then, is powerful local lineages (notably the Min and the Shen), the members of which shared the same religious culture characterized, among other things, by the cult of Lü Dongbin and a strong interest in self-cultivation, who patronized and maintained the temple as a community center with active official support. Some members of these lineages became full-time teachers there (teaching both Confucian and Daoist texts) and were worshipped after their death, not only as ancestors but also as Daoists. But, this is not the whole story, because there are certain aspects that the *Jin'gaishan zhi* does not discuss and that expand far beyond the landed elites living around Jin'gaishan: spirit-writing and the creation of branches. For, from the 1870s onward, the importance of the temple hinged on its being the center of an expanding regional network of affiliated spirit-writing branches.

The expansion of the network

Between the 1870s and the 1930s, the Yunchaotan on Jin'gaishan expanded by opening new "branch altars," *fentan* 分壇, throughout the Jiangnan area. These branches became part of a growing Jin'gaishan network, characterized by the altars' names having (with a few exceptions) *yun* 雲 as the second character (many members of these altars also took a Daoist name 道號 ending with *yun*). They maintained a close link to their "ancestral altar" (the Yunchao *zongtan*) by visiting regularly, notably every year on Lü Dongbin's birthday and contributing money. Individual members of the branch altars also traveled to the Yunchaotan, and could formally register as disciples there.[43] Often, a new branch was established by a member of an already existing branch who had to move for professional reasons. This was particularly the case of the ten branch altars that opened in Shanghai, most of them established by Huzhou people. The largest of them was the Jueyuntan 覺雲壇, which was established in 1888 at Langjiaqiao outside Shanghai East Gate 東門外郎家橋 by three Huzhou men (apparently, merchants).[44] They built a hall for the branch altar and invited masters from the Yunchaotan to celebrate a *jiao* 醮 offering on its inauguration.[45] The connection between Huzhou merchants in Shanghai and the Jin'gaishan remained very close throughout the late Qing and Republican periods.[46]

The establishment of new branches was not centrally planned and took a number of forms. Some of these branches also developed into a full-fledged Lü Dongbin temple, Chunyanggong 純陽宮.[47] Many were set up in the villages around Jin'gaishan, with smaller memberships; probably such branches were based within a preexisting temple that welcomed the group and created a side hall for them (this is a very frequent way of creating a spirit-writing hall in late imperial and modern China): examples include the Baoshougong 保壽宮 or the Tianyiyuan 天医院 (a temple that was run by Zhengyi Daoists), both near Huzhou city, or the Qizhen daoyuan 棲真道院 in Anji county 安吉縣 (in the western part of Huzhou prefecture). In some cases, branch altars actually took over Daoist temples that had run into hard times; for instance, Wu Yakui discusses the case of the Ziyangguan 紫陽觀 in Deqing, an old Zhengyi-run temple that was taken over after the Taiping by lay Quanzhen Daoists, who set up a Fanyuntan 梵雲壇 within it, that seems very much to have been part of the Jin'gaishan network even though it was not listed as such in the genealogies.[48] Indeed, the branch altars' economic basis (regular contributions from their members) was better suited to the post-Taiping situation than the land rent-dependent temple model, especially during the Republican period when temple landed endowments were encroached or seized by state agents or anti-superstition activists. Others branch altars, in the cities, were independently set up as a charitable hall, *shantang*. Accordingly, the known membership of these various branches ran between a few names and several hundreds.

Their geographical distribution shows that the majority was within Huzhou prefecture, notably in Huzhou city itself (ten branches) and the flourishing commercial townships nearby such as Nanxun 南潯 (four branches). Another major concentration was Shanghai, and less numerous branches could be found in southern Jiangsu, such as in Suzhou and Taicang 太倉, and in the Hangzhou area. The list of branches kept changing; while genealogies published during the 1920s and 1930s had between 50 and 60, and the ideal number of 72 branches is occasionally mentioned, I have based my research on Wang Zongyao's 王宗耀 recent work, which lists 69 of them.[49]

Quanzhen identity and genealogies

The members of the branch altars included some celibate Quanzhen clerics.[50] They were however only a tiny minority: the mainstay of this network was composed of married persons who had a nonreligious career in officialdom, the army, or commerce. Yet, these people were initiated within the Longmen lineage of clerical Quanzhen and claimed an explicit Quanzhen identity. Such a strong emphasis on Quanzhen orthodoxy and affiliation with the Longmen lineage was expressed by several means. First, a number of members went to undergo full Quanzhen consecration 受戒 at monastic centers, notably at Yuhuangshan 玉皇山 in Hangzhou, which emerged as a major center for Quanzhen Daoism in post-Taiping Jiangnan. The register of the 1896 consecration at Yuhuangshan lists, among its 346 consecrated Daoists, 13 who came from one of the Jin'gaishan network branches.[51]

Second, the network published large genealogies that squarely inscribed its members within the history of Quanzhen Daoism. The largest of these genealogies, with 1,885 names, is the *Daotong yuanliu* 道統源流 (1929).[52] While the data for ancient times is largely copied from earlier hagiographies and genealogies (notably Min Yide's *Jin'gai xindeng*), the names of persons born after the end of the eighteenth century are almost all those of the members of the lay communities of Jiangnan, drawn from the various altars which branched out from the Yunchaotan. A related work is the *Longmen zhengzong Jueyun benzhi daotong xinzhuan* 龍門正宗覺雲本支道統薪傳 (1927) listing around 500 names. It was compiled at the Jueyuntan, the Shanghai branch altar discussed above, and provides a generational chart up to the living members of the Shanghai altar along with biographies of the patriarchs.[53] A third cognate source is the annals of a branch altar (named Jueyunxuan 覺雲軒) in Zhuji 諸暨 county (central Zhejiang, quite a distance away from the core of the Jin'gaishan network), the *Jueyunxuan Yunxiao xuanpu zhi* 覺雲軒雲霄玄譜志 (1939). This document (discussed in more detail below) lists 1,001 names. These genealogies document members of their own Longmen sub-lineage but also provide some background information on the other major Quanzhen lineages, showing that these lay adepts saw themselves also as part of a larger Quanzhen community.[54]

Beside strong genealogical claims to Quanzhen identity, leading members of the Jin'gaishan network expressed their formal affiliation with Quanzhen Daoism in another way: to be part of the National Daoist Association 道教會 set up in Beijing in 1912 by leading Quanzhen clerics.[55] Yan Heyi 嚴合怡, the compiler of the *Daotong yuanliu*, set up the Wuxing 吳興 (the county around Huzhou) branch of the Association in 1912 – as well as the local branch of the Confucian Association 孔教會.[56] By doing this, Yan, and presumably other leaders of the Jin'gaishan network, clearly aligned themselves with the anti-superstitious reformism of these new associations.[57]

Such strong links with Daoist clerical institutions set the Jin'gaishan network apart from the majority of Lü Dongbin spirit-writing groups in Jiangnan (and elsewhere such as Beijing and Sichuan), among which our network was just a minority. These groups were very numerous but apparently rather small and fully independent, not affiliated with each other or with clerical institutions, by contrast to the Jin'gaishan network that could list memberships running in the thousands; as a result, such independent groups were also less stable over time than our network.

Membership: Local elites and women

Who were the members of the Jin'gaishan network branch altars? A fair proportion was composed of members of the local elites. The above-mentioned genealogies list large numbers of members of the gentry and officials, acting or retired.[58]

Rich merchants were also numerous; one typical example is Gao Fuzhen 高福箴 (1880–1949), who was a leader of the Jueyuntan in Shanghai, the Chunyanggong itself, and the Huzhou Chamber of Commerce during the Republican period.[59] There were also doctors, some of whom practiced within the branches as part of these branches' charitable services.[60] In cities, such as Shanghai, the branches largely recruited Huzhou people and may have been loci for Huzhou dialect and local culture, even though our sources are silent about this aspect; they were not exclusive however, and some members came from other areas.

The fact that the lineage offered full clerical prestige without the strictures of celibacy seems to have been a major attraction. For instance, Wang Laijue 王來覺 (?–1862), who was one of the Chunyanggong's leaders until he died during the Taiping assault on the temple, converted to Quanzhen Daoism during the Daoguang period. Wang saw his wife and children die during an epidemic, and he decided to turn his back on his earlier life to become a Buddhist monk. His mother managed to convince him to change his mind, and as a result, Wang became a member of the lay Quanzhen community.[61]

But, contrary to some late imperial spirit-writing groups that recruited exclusively among the upper gentry, the Jin'gaishan network was widely open to lower rural elites. The best description of initiation procedures, written by Qiu Shouming 丘壽銘, who was a member of one branch altar (the Guiyuntan 皈雲壇) in rural Huzhou before 1949, describes how his whole family, including his father and brothers, belonged to this branch.[62] To be admitted, one had to be "honest and literate" and to be presented by a current member; then one would receive one's name in the Longmen lineage through spirit-writing, as well as be assigned another current member as one's human master. Members who had been initiated received a certificate called *paidan* 派單.[63] All members could take part in the regular spirit-writing séances organized in the branch altars, but the member noting down the revelations, says Qiu, had to be highly literate; in his own branch altar during the 1920s, it was a former MP and then a lawyer.

The elite recruitment of the Jin'gaishan network was a constant characteristic, from the early days around Min Yide down to 1949. One fascinating early example, analyzed in loving detail by Xun Liu, the celebrated Hangzhou poet Chen Wenshu 陳文述 (1775–1845), shows how the network could draw such elite adepts.[64] Chen wrote an anthology of songs devoted to immortals who had lived in Hangzhou and their traces there, the *Xiling xianyong* 西泠仙詠 (1835). In a long preface to this work,[65] Chen provides a surprisingly candid spiritual autobiography, describing the various stages of his initiations in various spirit-writing altars devoted to Lü Dongbin and other immortals (most of which seem unconnected to the Jin'gaishan network), from a miraculous cure by an immortal in his youth to increasingly intense and systematic practices after his 40s. Chen, exhausted and ill after 20 strenuous years as an official, became interested in *neidan* 內丹 practice as a way of healing. He was introduced to an altar where he became a disciple and where the immortals then guided him in his *neidan* readings. His concubine, herself a disciple of Min Yide, initiated him in higher *neidan* practices (she was herself engaging in advanced meditative regimens) and Chen, who had been formally a disciple of Min since the latter had healed him in 1818 in Suzhou, renewed this relationship in earnest.[66] From then on, he traveled between various spirit-writing altars in Hankou, Suzhou, Shanghai, and Hangzhou, where he received further instructions and titles. He also saw to it that all female members of his extended family were initiated, and took other females as his own disciples. Chen shows in other prefaces and postfaces to this work that he was fully conversant with the Quanzhen scriptural legacy.

Chen Wenshu's account thus accounts for the high profile of Min Yide as a charismatic healer and teacher. It also documents the place of women in lay Quanzhen communities in general and in the Jin'gaishan network in particular. Indeed, one important aspect of the nineteenth-century Lü Dongbin spirit-writing cults was the production of manuals of female alchemy (*nüdan* 女丹). Although the tradition of *nüdan* predates the nineteenth century and was shared in modern times by female clerics and lay practitioners, the bulk of the *nüdan* manuals was produced during the nineteenth and twentieth centuries, often through spirit-writing, by lay Quanzhen communities (notably in Jiangnan and Sichuan) for their female members.[67] Min Yide himself edited two *nüdan* works as part of his collections.[68] Although details of how women practiced female alchemy within the framework of the Jin'gaishan network are unfortunately lacking, genealogies do show their massive presence. Indeed, Wu Yakui points out that after the turn of the twentieth century, women (most of them married, with their husbands often being members as well) actually outnumbered men in the genealogies, where they are listed separately.[69] The Jueyunxuan in Zhuji had 462 women out of its 1,001 members.[70] Meetings of the branch altars could be mixed gender, in an interesting contrast to some late imperial and early Republican spirit-writing halls in the Cantonese world, that insisted on excluding women, in order to establish their upper-class credentials.[71] And, it was often through their wives that male members of the elites came to join the network. One example is the famous KMT leader and lay Buddhist Dai Jitao 戴季陶 (1891–1949), who became a member just after his marriage in 1911.[72]

Ritual life

Some spirit-writing groups devoted to Lü Dongbin active in nineteenth and twentieth-century China had a rather anti-ritualist outlook, focusing on individual self-cultivation and limiting their rituals to simple scripture chanting in honor of Patriarch Lü.[73] This was not the case with the Jin'gaishan network as a whole (even though it might possibly have been the case with some of its members). Each altar maintained a regular liturgical program, and some members were hailed in the genealogies as having a solid training in liturgy. Genealogies show that at each branch altar, in each generation, a few members received ritual training from their elders and were recognized as *fashi* 法師, ritual masters. Specific liturgies mentioned encompass Thunder rituals 雷法 and "Zhengyi rituals."[74] Chen Wenshu duly mentions the liturgical registers (*lu* 籙) he received at various points.

The ritual life in a branch altar was described by Qiu Shouming.[75] Altars held daily services 朝晚科 when they were large enough to have a resident cleric, and all of them had three major festivals: the birthdays of the Jade Emperor 玉皇 (1/19), Lü Dongbin (4/14), and Doumu 斗姥 (9/9). Full members joined by wearing Daoist robes. Among them, a troupe of seven members well trained in liturgy would perform the ritual (essentially, reciting litanies, *chan* 懺) for two hours, and then all members would share a vegetarian meal. But, Lü Dongbin's birthday at the Yunchaotan was a special affair, with representatives of the network branches as well as local Huzhou gentry and officials (coming, until 1911, for the official sacrifice to Lü Dongbin) taking part in a massive celebration; large numbers of pilgrims arrived the day before (some of them ferried from Huzhou by the two boats the Chunyanggong owned) and stayed at the Chunyanggong's hostel. In all branches, during both festival and ordinary time, Lü Dongbin's oracles 靈簽 were in constant demand.

Beside regular celebrations, the branches also offered liturgical services to families, notably funerals. Lay Daoists often came to their own branch altar or to the Yunchaotan to perform funeral rituals for local families, and – in contrast to professional clerics – performed for free (the family providing a meal for them, and possibly making a donation to the branch itself). When the inviting family was from a rich merchant background, such services could be organized on a grand scale.[76] The liturgy, much like that performed by professional clerics, was the recitation of litanies during the day, and a salvation ritual 煉度 at night. Several members are said in the genealogies to have edited and transmitted the *Taiji lianke* 太極煉科,[77] which is the major salvation ritual performed by Zhengyi Daoists in Jiangnan,[78] so likely this was the liturgy used throughout the Jin'gaishan network. Indeed, the Jin'gaishan network does not seem to have ever brought much innovation in the field of liturgy,[79] using and disseminating established liturgical texts – by contrast to other Lü Dongbin spirit-writing groups in late Qing Jiangnan that did introduce new liturgies.[80] The Chunyanggong also sold to devotees copies of the *Yuhuang benxing jijing* 玉皇本行集經 and long-life certificates 長生疏牒.[81] Members who had donated to the branch altar had their tablet placed in the altar's *zutang* 祖堂 to be honored there after their death – a practice common to most if not all present-day lay Daoist groups throughout the Chinese world.

The altars also offered liturgical services to local communities, occasionally being invited to perform *jiao* offerings in village temples,[82] as they still do today. On these occasions, all members gathered at the altar according to their seniority and level of initiation. It is likely that some of the smaller branch altars did not have a disciple trained in performing *jiao* as a *gaogong* 高功, but these were occasions when different branch altars cooperated. Larger branch altars would send a *gaogong* to smaller ones to preside over the latter's celebration.[83]

Moreover, the prestige of Quanzhen liturgy caused independent spirit-writing altars to seek affiliation with the Jin'gaishan network, in order to gain training and initiation into that liturgy. This is what happened in 1894 at the Huiyun shantan 惠雲善壇 (Taicang, southern Jiangsu). This originally independent spirit-writing group gradually introduced a liturgy (*jingchan* 經懺), and invited Daoists from a Jin'gaishan branch altar, then Lü Dongbin ordered the group to be affiliated with the Yunchaotan.[84] So, one of the advantages of being affiliated with the

Jin'gaishan network was to be trained in Quanzhen liturgy and be able to provide members with liturgical services.

A similar process was observed a generation later at the Jueyunxuan in Zhuji (central Zhejiang). There a spirit-writing group was started in 1920, and it expanded to build a temple, named Yunxiaodian 雲霄殿, in 1924–1928 (more below).[85] Leaders of this group invited ritualists from other spirit-writing groups to perform a *jiao* in 1924, and they were so impressed with the performance of the Jin'gaishan network representatives that they invited them (being ordered to do so by Lü Dongbin as well) to teach them the full liturgical repertoire, including salvation rituals for funerals. As a result, they affiliated themselves with the Yunchaotan that regularly sent emissaries to check on their performance and in-house training. From then on, the group was overwhelmed with requests for rituals, which were, like in other branch altars, performed for free.

Part of the liturgical training provided by the Yunchaotan and other large branch altars to newly affiliated ones included the gift or sale of liturgical manuals. Such manuals printed by the Chunyanggong (some of them in the name of Min Yide's library, Gushu yinlou) seem to have been numerous[86] but few are left. In the collection of Wang Zongyao, which he very kindly showed to me, I have seen several such liturgical books, notably an 1869 edition of the *Nanji chengsheng jingchan* 南極長生經懺 published by the Gushu yinlou. A recent post on a blog maintained by adepts of the Jin'gaishan tradition also lists seven other liturgical manuals printed by the Chunyanggong between 1871 and 1887, comprising *Taiji jilian* manuals, litanies, and scriptures.[87] Several others are kept at the Shanghai library.[88] Yet other similar liturgical texts were privately published by prominent members of the Jin'gaishan network.[89] As a whole, from the extant examples, it seems the Jin'gaishan center and its branches printed and distributed significant amounts of liturgical works, some of which were standard texts, and some others were revealed by spirit-writing within the network.

If the ritual life of the Jin'gaishan branch altars was largely geared toward servicing the local communities, some members could have their own private ritual regimen. A fascinating case is that of Shen Bingcheng, already discussed as a major patron in the rebuilding of Jin'gaishan after the Taiping war. Shen became a member of the Jin'gaishan network together with his wife, and both recited the *Yuhuangjing* (that is, *Yuhuang benxing jijing*, which the network printed and distributed) daily, and regularly worshipped the Beidou.[90] He also supported a major charitable hall run by a branch altar in Huzhou, the Renjitang 仁濟堂. This kind of devotional life is classical among lay Daoists and does not seem specific to the Jin'gaishan network,[91] but it is noteworthy that our network welcomed and fostered this type of spirituality.

Self-cultivation, teachings, and books

The Jin'gaishan network was an important provider of liturgical services, but it was equally renowned for teaching and spreading self-cultivation techniques and theory, which is reflected in the network's editorial activities. The Chunyanggong itself and its branch altars were involved in two kinds of publishing enterprises: first, on their own corporate initiative they published genealogies, liturgical texts, and compilations of texts they received through spirit-writing. Second, members signing as initiates of the network, published or edited self-cultivation books on their own.[92] My discussion here is based on the certainly very incomplete corpus of such books I have identified so far.

The first publications of the Chunyanggong itself include the two large collections of texts compiled by Min Yide (*Gushu yinlou cangshu* and *Daozang xubian*, both first published at the temple in 1834). But, the Chunyanggong destruction by the Taiping was devastating, especially for its library. Its signature collection, Min Yide's *Gushu yinlou cangshu*, was republished in 1904, but the available reprints do not show which institution was responsible for this edition.[93] A second, augmented edition published in 1916 was edited by Wan Qixing 萬啟型 (a disciple of one of Min Yide's disciples), and paid for by the famous Daoist-cum-businessman-cum-reformist intellectual Zheng Guanying 鄭觀應 (1842–1921) and two of his friends.[94] Wan and Zheng were members of various Daoist spirit-writing cults in this area, and personal devotees of Lü Dongbin, but they are not listed in any Jin'gaishan network genealogy. It thus seems like the network lost some control over its own scriptural legacy in the sense that it was distributed by other groups (even though this may have been welcomed by members of the Jin'gaishan network). Zheng Guanying was involved in the republication of another major collection of *neidan* texts, the late Ming *Fanghu waishi* 方壺外史; on the 1915 punctuated reedition of this book, the punctuator signed on the book cover as "Tao Bennian, disciple of the Yunchao Gu Meihuaguan 雲巢古梅花觀弟子陶本念校," but the prefaces (both Zheng's and others) do not mention the Jin'gaishan network at all.[95] Thus, even though the Jin'gaishan network was always and still is closely associated with the teachings of Min Yide, this was by no means an exclusive association.

The Chunyanggong did not limit itself to publishing Min Yide's books. After the Taiping war, as we have seen, it published a number of (apparently all small-size) liturgical manuals, presumably in order to re-furnish branch altars that had their own working collections destroyed. It also published in 1896 a self-history, *Jin'gaishan zhi*, discussed above, and republished the *Jin'gai xindeng* in 1880.[96]

In terms of books published by the branch altars, we have already discussed the three genealogies that were produced by branches for distribution within the network. Given the primary importance of spirit-writing throughout the Jin'gaishan network, the number of known spirit-written texts published by members of the network is not very impressive; this is most probably explained by the fact that spirit-writing within the Chunyanggong and the branch altars was by and large devoted to healing and confirming new members rather than revealing full-fledged scriptures. Indeed, scholars have shown that this is often the case with spirit-writing halls in modern and contemporary times, which do not necessarily publish books.[97]

One revealed book, the *Xingmeng bian* 醒夢編, was published in 1904 by the Huiyuntan in Taicang. This collection is made up of short pronouncements on ethics and self-cultivation (of theoretical rather than practical interest) revealed by Ge

Xuan 葛玄; the language is rather abstruse and contents do not seem to differ particularly from many other morality books of the time. The postface explains that the Huiyuntan had long been involved in medical charity, but had been lacking in a universal message, an aspiration now fulfilled with this book. This is followed by poems revealed by the patriarchs of the Nanzong 南宗 and Quanzhen Daoist lineages. For its part, the Yunchaotan already had its universal message, in the shape of Lü Dongbin's scriptures contained in the *Gushu yinlou cangshu* (whether these scriptures were much read by members of the network or not is difficult to ascertain).

Besides publications made by a branch altar as such, some members of the various branch altars were very active as individuals in the thriving world of Daoist publishing, and authored or edited Daoist books signing with their identity as disciple of the Jin'gaishan network, or gave public lectures within the branch altars.[98] A late example is a certain Lu Qitu 陸淇圖, who was a disciple of the renowned doctor and self-cultivation practitioner Lin Pinsan 林品三 (1858–1936). In 1945, Lu prefaced an anthology of Lin's teachings (rather abstract pronouncements on cosmology and self-cultivation), in which he explained that he had been a member of a branch altar of the Jin'gaishan network for all his adult life, and as a result has been involved in reading, practicing, and taking part in self-cultivation groups. While he does not say that Lin Pinsan himself was an initiate, Lu Qitu praises the Jin'gaishan network as having brought the secrets of self-cultivation to all, "from the highest officials down to the coolies."[99]

This suggests that the Jin'gaishan network played a larger role in the dissemination within modern Jiangnan society of Daoist culture in general and self-cultivation in particular than the mere list of its known books would vouch for. Other types of institutions (publishers such as the Shanghai Yihuatang 翼化堂, lay communities around Chen Yingning 陳攖寧 (1880–1969), redemptive societies, etc.)[100] published much larger amounts of Daoist self-cultivation books than our Jin'gaishan network. But, Qiu Shouming notes that members of branch altars were trained in classical Daoist texts (*Laozi*, *Baopuzi*) and "Qiu Changchun's long-life techniques."[101] Pending the discovery of more information on how self-cultivation was taught within the branch altars,[102] it would seem that such teaching did reach much larger audiences than that of most Quanzhen clerical communities. While the Jin'gaishan network did not necessarily have a strong unified doctrinal identity, it seems to have been an important venue for distributing and teaching texts published by other institutions.[103]

Charity

Requests for instructions on alchemical practice at Lü Dongbin spirit-writing altars were closely related to concerns about good health. People such as Chen Wenshu were drawn into lay Quanzhen communities by miraculous cures.[104] Quanzhen altars cured individuals, but also diffused remedies revealed by immortals (many were printed out or given to newspapers), especially during outbursts of epidemics. Yau Chi-on's chapter in this volume shows how crucial revealed remedies were in the diffusion of the Lüzu cult in modern China. These altars worked as charitable halls and their leaders supported the free distribution of the remedies revealed by the immortals; this was for instance the case of the Huiyun shantan.[105] Medicine was often predominant, but charitable activities carried out by the Jin'gaishan network branches covered the whole range of *shantang* activities[106]: free clinics and distribution of medicine, but also kitchen soups, clothing for the poor, schools and orphanages, burying abandoned corpses, cherishing written characters (*xizi* 惜字), releasing animals (*fangsheng* 放生), lectures 宣講 on morality books and scriptures, etc.

As Wang Zongyu points out, the *shantang* set up by the Jin'gaishan network are discussed in the local gazetteers, but without any mention of their inner Daoist identity.[107] Many of the branches had both a name as a charitable hall and another name as a spirit-writing altar, with a frequent explanation that the former was "for the outside" and the latter "for the inside."[108] One example is the above-mentioned Renjitang, a charity in downtown Huzhou, that housed one of Huzhou's ten branch altars, the Suyuntan 夙雲壇.[109]

Another, probably the largest of all the charitable halls affiliated with the Jin'gaishan network, was the Weizhong shantang 位中善堂, which was the "outer" identity of the Jueyuntan in Shanghai. The Weizhong shantang notably ran a free clinic of Chinese medicine from its inception in 1888 to its forcible disbanding in 1955, and a free school from 1927 onward.[110] The Japanese occupation in 1937 caused major destruction, but operations restarted in 1941; reports to the Shanghai municipality during the 1945–1949 period list some 300–500 pupils enrolled in the school and 4,000–6,000 patients every month at the clinic.[111] It was a leading charitable institution associated with the Huzhou community in Shanghai, thus closely associating socioeconomical class, geographical origin, and religion.[112] The leaders then were all prominent businessmen, some (but not all) from Huzhou; the leader during the 1940s was Yao Xinzhi 姚鑫之 (1891–?; a prominent Shanghai local government official during the 1920s and then a leading philanthropist, also the president of another charity, the Mingde jiyi shanhui 明德集義善會). The Weizhong shantang took pride that all its charitable operations were paid for by monthly donations from the 70 plus members, and did not rely on either an endowment (it only owned the building in which it ran the school and clinic) or fundraising outside the group.

Documents related to these two institutions (the "inner" Jueyuntan and the "outer" Weizhong shantang) rarely put forward that they were actually one and the same, even though this is apparent enough from close reading; in a context hostile to "superstition," the spirit-writing and ritual activities of the group may have been downplayed in some public contexts, but that does not mean the group underwent a process of secularization.[113] In its regulations and reports to the Shanghai city hall, the Weizhong shantang never alludes to its religious nature, but the report of the PRC officer who oversaw its closure in 1955 says that by that time the Jueyuntan and its spirit tablets were still there; up to the beginning of the anti-reactionary sects campaign of 1950–1953, the place was providing funeral rituals and spirit-writing cures.[114]

Such a double identity was a widespread model, notably shared by many Jigong spirit-writing altars that developed in Jiangnan from 1860s onward, with their ancestral temple in Hangzhou.[115] Wang Chien-ch'uan 王見川, who has studied these Jigong altars, has shown that they not only operated on a totally similar model to the Jin'gaishan network altars but they also often mixed with them.[116] As Wang pointed out, some leading philanthropists were members in both networks, a notable example being Wang Yiting 王一亭 (1867–1938).[117] Wang Yiting (who originated from Huzhou) was a leading member of the Jishenghui 濟生會, an influential charity which was created in 1916 in Shanghai as the outer *shantang* identity of a Jigong spirit-writing hall, and also became a leader of the Jueyuntan during the 1920s. This was not an odd case: the three Jin'gaishan network genealogies all list names of members who also had a "Buddhist name 佛名" given by Jigong (whose lineage, Nanping 南屏派, itself a sub-lineage of the Linji lineage 臨濟宗, worked just like Lü Dongbin's Longmen lineage, with lay adepts being given a name through spirit-writing).[118] Several of the Jin'gaishan network branches received revelations from Jigong,[119] just as many Jigong altars also received revelations from Lü Dongbin. A rich merchant from Shanghai built a Jigong shrine within the Chunyanggong in 1903.[120] Even the names of their branches were similar, with many branches of the Jigong network being called X-yunxuan 口雲軒.[121]

The Zhuji local developments

The Jueyunxuan in Zhuji documents a very intimate mixing of the two networks – the Jin'gaishan and the Jigong networks. It was originally created as an independent spirit-writing group by a female spirit-medium, supported by her lineage, the Chen 陳, that sponsored the building of a shrine, first called Jueshishan shantan 覺世善善壇, near their ancestral hall.[122] This shrine experienced a spectacular development during the 1920s, with the creation of a full-fledged temple (the Xiaoxuandian) in 1924 and several affiliated associations 會, each with its endowments and regulations, some being charitable, while others liturgical. The temple was formally affiliated with the Jin'gaishan network, mostly because of their liturgical training as we have seen above, but also with the Jishenghui; this came about when a new county magistrate, himself a Jishenghui member, took office in 1923 and encouraged the group to set up the Jishenghui local chapter. As such it received numerous revelations from both Lü Dongbin and Jigong, some of which are published in its genealogy,[123] and the members were admitted in both the Longmen and the Nanping lineages. Moreover, the leading members, as documented in their biographies, were granted successive divine titles as officials in the celestial bureaucracy,[124] a continuous process of self-divinization that Philip Clart has shown is a key feature of popular Confucian spirit-writing groups in twentieth-century China.[125] Such grandiose self-divinization does not seem to be attested in other Jin'gaishan network branch altars that remained within the tradition where devotees are first and foremost disciples of Lü Dongbin under training and therefore should not glorify themselves.

The Jueyunxuan was located within the Zhuji county seat; it does not exist anymore. But, there were several other similar altars in Republican-period Zhuji, including the Songyunxuan 松雲軒 in Dasong village 大松村. The Songyunxuan does not exist anymore either, but one Daoist, Chen Yuansheng 陳圓勝 (aged 80 during our interview in December 2009), who was trained there in the 1940s (beginning aged only 10), is now the leading Daoist in a newly renovated temple nearby, the Zhishan daoyuan 芝山道院 (more on this later). Chen was the first Daoist of the 19th generation of the Longmen lineage in Zhuji, and acted as a medium in spirit-writing sessions at his altar before 1949. He recalls that at the time the altar was all-male, that many gods (and not only Lü Dongbin and Jigong) came down to the altar, and that many drug recipes were revealed to patients. The Zhishan daoyuan, where he now works, also used to have a spirit-writing altar during the Republican period, named Pujitang 普濟堂 and mentioned on a very recent stele inscription,[126] but none of the present temple managers recalls much of that. I ignore if this Pujitang is the same as the Pujiutang 普救堂, which is described in a 1925 description of religious life in Zhuji as the oldest and largest of the local spirit-writing halls, with thousands of initiates and branches (with names such as 慈雲軒 and 春雲軒) in all villages.[127] What we seem to have in Republican-period Zhuji, then, is a local religious landscape dominated by numerous spirit-writing halls (established by local female mediums) that provide healing and funeral services to villagers, and that during the 1920s affiliate themselves to the larger Jishenghui and Jin'gaishan networks, thus acquiring "orthodox" Daoist and Buddhist identities.

Since spirit-writing is not practiced anymore at the Zhishan daoyuan, Chen says that he is the only "proper Daoist" left (that is, registered in Heaven through spirit-writing) and all ritual documents sent to Heaven need to be signed with his name even if he is not performing in person. In any case, Chen has brought to this temple the practices of his first temple (Songyunxuan), and during rituals, the portraits of both Jigong and Lü Dongbin are displayed prominently on the altar. Thus, the Zhuji branch temples' tradition of worshipping the two saints is still alive and distinct from practice at Jin'gaishan, where Jigong is not worshipped anymore today. As Chen Yuansheng told me (interview, Dec. 1, 2009), "Jigong is like us, he is not a celibate (*chujia*) cleric."

Today, what is left?

The Chunyanggong was occupied by the Japanese in 1937, but was apparently well maintained up to the 1950s. The temple lands were nationalized in 1951–1952, with 11 Daoists receiving a small plot for themselves. The temple was turned into a sanatorium for cadres in 1962, and into a school in 1972; in between all its books and statues had been destroyed in 1968.[128] Activities at many branches continued until 1949 but stopped with the new regime – in some cases through repression in the framework of the 1950–1953 anti-"reactionary sects" campaign. I have found at least one clear case of a Jin'gaishan branch altar (the Jinyuntan 錦雲壇 in Xiaofeng county 孝丰縣, not far southwest of Huzhou) being eradicated among other redemptive societies ("reactionary sects" 反動會道門) just after 1949,[129] but it is quite possible that there were other cases – albeit not the Chunyanggong itself.[130] In Zhuji, it would seem that all the Lü Dongbin and Jigong altars were branded as reactionary and annihilated.[131]

The Chunyanggong began its revival around 1989 and was rebuilt gradually since then[132]; when I first visited in 2007, most halls had been very recently refitted. It has since then been the seat of the Huzhou branch of the Daoist Association. It was very quiet on ordinary days, but livened up during the festivals which are (like in many branch altars) Lü Dongbin's birthday, Yuhuang's birthday, and Doumu's festival. It was led by Ding Yongneng 丁永能 (1931–; became a Daoist in 1944), who has trained some 40 disciples, about 20 of whom (as of 2007) can perform rituals. The Longmen lay lineage is thus well alive: Wang Zongyao, a local entrepreneur, amateur historian, and secretary of the local Daoist Association, records in his privately published gazetteer of the temple tens of recent initiates. They all live at home (they do not have a home altar) and come to the temple on the 1st and the 15th of the month, and when they are needed to perform a ritual. They do death rituals in peoples' homes, and are occasionally invited to perform in village temples, but in temples not officially authorized (that is, in the vast majority of cases), they would only perform a small-scale short ritual.

Other branch altars also reopened as village temples during the same period.[133] The Chunyanggong Daoists keep a list of a dozen affiliated "branch altars" now active among the (at least) 69 that operated before 1949. The meaning of "branch altar" has changed though; if representatives do come to the Chunyanggong on Lü Dongbin's birthday, there does not seem to be any financial flow anymore. A few of the former branch altars are now thriving as village temples in rural Huzhou, and have grown as big as the Chunyanggong. Meanwhile, some Daoists trained at the Chunyanggong are hired as resident clerics by village temples that were never part of the pre-1949 Jin'gaishan network, thus creating a new kind of network. There is no spirit-writing going on publicly in any of these temples now, but some branch altars are said to practice anew in private, including one in Deqing and one in Anji – in this regard, the revival seems to lag behind the Lüzu cult in the Hakka heartland discussed in Yau Chi-on's chapter in this volume. As for the self-cultivation regimens, they seem in large part forgotten. Clearly, there is still a potential for reviving the network on a larger scale, a potential that is not fully actualized in the current complicated situation for local religion in the PRC.

I have visited in particular two branch altars within Huzhou: the Shanyuntan 善雲壇 and the Wanyuntan 萬雲壇. The former, opened around 2005, is located within the industrial township of Zhili 織里, a major center for the production of children's clothes. It is affiliated with the Huzhou Daoist Association, and thus has obtained formal authorization to operate as a temple. There are no Daoists in residence, and I am told that none of the Daoists who used to staff the temple before 1949 are still around. The temple is staffed by lay volunteers, but when devotees request a ritual, a phone call is given to the Chunyanggong, which sends Daoists to come over and perform the ritual. This temple is now officially called Shanyunguan 善雲觀 (this is part of a China-wide trend to give former temples 廟

or altars 壇 "proper" Daoist names as 觀 or 宮 to facilitate their official authorization), but informally it is known as Hongqiaomiao 虹橋廟 (documents burnt to be sent to the gods or the dead carry the temple seal that reads: Hongqiaomiao). Indeed, besides the central Daoist deities (Lü Dongbin, Yuhuang, etc.), it also hosts local deities such as Anlewang 安樂王.[134]

The second one is the Wanyuntan, located on a low hill just behind the township of Jingshan 菁山, not far south of Jin'gaishan. It has also been lavishly repaired, with a magnificent hall to Guanyin added to the older main hall (still called *tan*) devoted to Lü Dongbin; accordingly, the main festivals are Lü Dongbin's birthday and Guanyin's three festivals (on 2/19, 6/19, and 9/19). It has a lay Daoist in residence, but there too, Daoists are called from the Chunyanggong for performing rituals on demand.

A third cognate case is the Zhishan daoyuan, discussed above as having maintained the lay Quanzhen tradition in Zhuji. It is located in the busy industrial township of Datang 大唐鎮 (specialized in producing socks), a few kilometers away from Zhuji county. This is actually the only Daoist temple open in Zhuji as of late 2009, and as no local branch of the Daoist Association was established, the temple is listed as Buddhist by the local government, even though the Zhishan daoyuan welcomes visiting Daoist clerics to take residence (*guadan* 掛單). Apparently first built up during the Ming, it was named Shuihongmiao 水洪廟, and only got its more Daoist name of Zhishan daoyuan (from the name of a nearby hill) when it obtained an official authorization in 2004. It was first rebuilt in 1992 (with financial support from a local person living in Hong Kong) and was much enlarged in subsequent years. Its most active cult is that of Zhu laoxiangong 朱老相公 (that is, Zhu Biqing 朱碧清, 1503–1552, a doctor known for miraculous cures). Zhu is also worshipped in Taiwan (where his devotees say he has died, unlikely as it may seem) and a group of his devotees there came to the Zhishan daoyuan, on Zhu's order via his spirit-medium, and gave a large amount of money to enlarge his shrine; they also tried to revive spirit-writing, but the god answered that "time has not come yet."

Although I have never seen it listed as a Jin'gaishan branch altar, the temple is fully aware that its tradition originates from Jin'gaishan, and the temple's Daoists have been visiting there regularly. They confirm that their liturgy is the same, even though they do not have any text from before the Cultural Revolution and now use texts bought from the Baopu daoyuan 抱朴道院 in Hangzhou. They do not have a fully trained master 法師, so they essentially perform scriptures and litanies, yet they are in much demand. They do death rituals, but mostly rituals for the living, either in the temple or at people's homes (except *lidou* 禮斗, which they would only perform in the temple, because it necessitates a very pure ritual space). They would do *kaiguang* 開光 for local temples, and whole village three-day rituals, but they too, like at the Chunyanggong, are wary of performing in temples that have not obtained an official authorization.

The Zhishan daoyuan has in common with the two other cases to have been rebuilt on a rather grand and lavish scale with money (beside the Taiwanese donation) from local textile entrepreneurs, presumably through their wives, mothers, and daughters. The Zhishan daoyuan thus combines different types of religious traditions: a transnational cult to healing God Zhu, a lay Daoist ritual tradition, and neighborhood religious groups: the Earth God whose shrine is within the temple goes out in procession once a year, and a group of elderly sutra-chanting women is active in the temple, some of whom actually live in the temple's rooms, by contrast to the Daoists who live outside, with their families.

In sum, the Jin'gaishan network is alive and is now thriving in industrial townships where it has more leeway. In the pre-1949 period, it was largely urban (in Shanghai and Huzhou notably), but the urban branches are gone and largely forgotten. The tradition has retreated from city centers to the bustling peripheries.

The Jin'gaishan network in the modern religious landscape

Now that we have sketched a broad outline of the Jin'gaishan network's history and activities, it is time to try to place it in the larger religious landscape of which it was and is part. What kind of religious organization was and is the Jin'gaishan network? While presenting my research at conferences, I have met with the objection, particularly from Daoists, that it is indeed not part of Daoism but rather a sectarian movement using Daoist vocabulary. Such a remark speaks volumes about the recent and current political situation of Daoism, its complex relationship with groups that have been repressed, and the ban on spirit-writing still enforced to varying degrees in the PRC. But, the fact remains that most temples of the Jin'gaishan network now in activity are affiliated with the Daoist Association, that Min Yide is heralded as a key figure of "orthodox" Quanzhen Daoism, and that all members of the network, past and present, unequivocally present themselves as Daoists.

So rather than taking part in a debate on the definition of Daoism, I would like to explore the Jin'gaishan network as a specific type of lay Daoism in constant interaction with other forms of religious organization. This type is most easily defined by its organizational structure: a network of groups of active laypersons (typically between fifty and several hundred) initiated as Daoists, worshipping Lü Dongbin along with other deities (Daoist, Buddhist, and otherwise), pooling resources to build a temple, and providing charity as well as spirit-writing cures and ritual services (performed by some of them).

Did such a network have a common ideology that would underlie all its activities? There is a distinctive ideology at work in Min Yide's writings, which is clearly salvational and sees Lü Dongbin as a savior who will rescue humanity from delusion and suffering. It bases its world-saving program on individual self-cultivation by initiates, which enables them to both heal others and transform them by their example. While the Jin'gaishan network shared a lot with the thousands of other spirit-writing cults throughout China, the heritage of Min Yide was associated with Min's doctrinal innovations that hinged on his idea of *yishi* 醫世, "healing the world" (first expressed in a series of scriptures published in Min's *Daozang xubian* and *Gushu yinlou cangshu*), in which Lü Dongbin was seen as an universal savior.[135] I have no evidence documenting how this vision was received and understood in the twentieth-century branch altars, but it does offer clear continuities with many redemptive societies' message of saving the world, *jiushi* 救世 (albeit the Republican-period *jiushi* discourse was often more apocalyptic than Min Yide's). The introduction of the Jigong cult, itself also often associated with salvationist messages, within the Jin'gaishan network, certainly reinforced this vision. Yet, I would caution against projecting this ideology onto all the Jin'gaishan network members.

For one thing, the elite families that sustained the Jin'gaishan Chunyanggong, the Huzhou merchants who started new branches wherever their business took them, and the petty artisans, clerks, farmers, housewives, and others who became initiates in urban or rural branches did probably not understand the network, its doctrines, and its purposes in a uniform way. Even branches differed in significant ways, as we have seen in the case of the Zhuji branches, where the Jigong cult and local spirit-writing traditions brought a distinct flavor when compared with the other Jin'gaishan branches. Such diversity has been repeatedly observed among other spirit-writing groups and redemptive societies, where members join for a wide variety of reasons (interest in self-cultivation, social bonding, desire to study classical culture, healing, etc.) and hold very different views of the group.[136] The temples operating today are by and large local temples with sutra-chanting ladies and local deities, who call on the (lay) Daoists to perform standard rituals; it is hard to find a distinctive ideology at work in them. One thing the Jin'gaishan branches and members had in common, but also in common with numerous other modern religious groups, was a firm belief in lay activism: that members, alongside their professional and family life, could all become, with Lü Dongbin's help, agents of the transformation of this world, healing people, and restoring order to society.

For these reasons, the Jin'gaishan network constitutes a very interesting case study in the typology of Chinese religious groups. It was a late imperial creation linked to both the official cult (of Lü Dongbin) and the Daoist clerical establishment, but it evolved in several directions, in some cases interacting or mixing with early twentieth-century reformist movements and new religions, some of which we classify as redemptive societies. Many of these societies (which some Republican-period authors actually considered as the mainstay of Daoism[137]) did evolve from local spirit-writing halls. In between the traditional, small, independent spirit-writing hall, and the nation-wide redemptive societies, regional networks like the Jin'gaishan and the Jigong network offer a specific situation, with both late imperial and Republican-period characteristics. Both the Jin'gaishan and the Jigong network maintained close relationship with the clerical establishment (by contrast to redemptive societies) and organized pilgrimages (to the Jin'gaishan or to Jigong's stupa at the Hupaosi 虎跑寺 in Hangzhou). Both (along with many other spirit-writing groups) were willing to invest in local temples and repair them, or even take them over when the temple was ruined; for instance, the Jishenghui took over a large Daoist temple, the Yuxuguan 玉虚觀 near Nanjing during the 1920s.[138] They had large memberships (the Jishenghui had over a thousand members), collected donations from patients who were healed through spirit-writing that was used for charity, had a large female membership (that congregated separately in the case of some of Jigong's spirit-writing groups), and organized troupes performing liturgical services. All of this, argues Wang Chien-ch'uan, seems to have served as an organizational model for the slightly later Daoyuan 道院 (established 1921) and other redemptive societies.[139]

Because of this situation, the Jin'gaishan network offers various types of continuities between the late imperial world of elite piety and Republican-period new types of religious groups. While this is not surprising in itself, it can bring nuances to an historiography that tends to emphasize the ruptures of the early twentieth century, with the decline of traditional temple networks and the rise of new forms of lay Buddhism, redemptive societies, and other religious institutions. Among the leaders of the Jin'gaishan network, we find both late Qing traditional elites and new Republican elites. Whereas the Chunyanggong leaders were mostly retired local gentry up to 1910, one head of the Chunyanggong temple committee 董事會 (which was set up shortly after 1912) had returned from Japan where he had studied.[140] The Jin'gaishan branches, being rather open (conditions for membership were not demanding) and not exclusive, had members who were also part of other groups, including redemptive societies. In particular, some high-flying politicians and merchants were members of a very large array of religious groups, partly for the sake of extending their own social network, without usually being very much involved in any of them. It is probably in such terms that we may understand the membership in the Jin'gaishan network of such a prominent person as warlord (and Shandong native) Wu Peifu 吳佩孚 (1874–1939), who was also involved with several other Daoist groups and redemptive societies.[141]

Even more significant, leaders and activists carried ideas, texts, and practices from one group to the other. Cases include Yan Heyi, active in the Jin'gaishan network and the Confucian association, or the many leaders of both the Jin'gaishan network and the Jishenghui. Through such activists, the Jin'gaishan network that originated around Min Yide with an ideology defined quasi-exclusively in terms of Quanzhen Daoism, evolved in the direction of the redemptive societies.[142] They were in some cases seen as such by observers, including Communist cadres, who targeted some branches during the 1950–1953 anti-"reactionary sects" campaign, while other branches of the same network were merely labeled as local temples (which made their post-1978 revival much easier).

Last but not the least, continuities in models of organization offer tantalizing glimpses of how the Jin'gaishan network may have been one of the immediate sources of inspiration for the founders of the Republican-period redemptive societies. While the model of a spirit-writing hall devoted to Lü Dongbin recruiting among local elites and providing healing, training in self-cultivation, and practicing charity has been very common for centuries, what appears new in the case of the Jin'gaishan network is the large-scale integrated organization. I know of no spirit-writing cults outside of the Jin'gaishan network, its close relative the Jigong network, and the later redemptive societies, that published membership lists with thousands of members. Moreover, in places of highest concentration, like Huzhou or Zhuji, it would seem that the Jin'gaishan network branches were a dominant presence among local elites and in local political and economical life, in a way comparable to what other redemptive societies achieved in certain places.[143]

Clearly, the Jin'gaishan network expressed a form of Daoism favored by the local elites of modern Jiangnan, with an emphasis on charity and self-cultivation, organized around spirit-writing. In this respect, it resembles in many ways the lay Daoist groups of the Cantonese world (both in the Guangzhou-Hong Kong area and in the Chaozhou area), which also worshipped Lü Dongbin, combined an "inner" Daoist identity (either Quanzhen or Xiantiandao 先天道) with an "outer" identity as a charitable hall, and provided healing and liturgical services; a case study of such a group is explored in Yau Chi-on's chapter in this volume.[144] One key difference is that there does not appear to have existed in the Cantonese world a network with a central altar as was the case at the Jin'gaishan; probably the closest example is the constellation called Dejiao 德教, created in the Chaozhou area in 1939, that does organize its spirit-writing halls (worshipping notably Jigong and Lü Dongbin) in hierarchical networks. A closer parallel is a network of spirit-writing halls called *wenshe* 文社, established from the 1880s onward in Hunan and Jiangxi province, practicing Daoist rituals and affiliated with the Jingming lineage 淨明派.[145] Clearly, the social and political conditions of the last decades of the Qing made it possible to created such large networks.

The Lü Dongbin spirit-writing halls that have existed since at least the Ming dynasty and still thrive today, notably in Hong Kong, and form the matrix out of which the Jin'gaishan network emerged, have certainly long formed various kinds of informal circuits, with books and adepts circulating between various halls. But, the Jin'gaishan model of an organized network with a clearly identified center, common genealogies, regular exchanges, visits, and circulation of money is an original and significant feature of the Jin'gaishan network. While the coalescence of independent spirit-writing halls into networks was helped by the new religious policies of the Republican period and lies behind the rise of several redemptive societies as well as later organizations (such as the Cihuitang 慈惠堂 in post-1950 Taiwan), it remains that the Jin'gaishan network was conceived from the start as a centralized network.

But, we also see differences between the Jin'gaishan network and large hierarchical religious organizations such as the redemptive societies. By contrast to the latter, the former has maintained strong relationships with the Daoist clerical establishment rather than establishing an entirely independent clerical structure, and also with communal religion. Some of its branch altars operated as, or worked closely with, village temples. Whereas redemptive societies are entirely congregational (membership by individual choice), the Jin'gaishan network was in part embedded in the communal territorial dimension of Chinese religion. And indeed, that is what seems to be mostly left of it now.

Over the past two centuries, the Jin'gaishan network has evolved in different directions, between village religion and the world of cosmopolitan elites; it shows all the rich and complex potential for Daoism in modern Chinese society and its multifarious connections with the other forms of Chinese religiosity. The urban upper-class part of the network, with large downtown charitable halls and self-cultivation adepts, had for now disappeared, leaving the grassroots temples as inheritors of the two-centuries long tradition.

Notes

1 I am very grateful to Wang Zongyao for guiding me on my visits to Jin'gaishan in November 2007 and December 2009, and to Fang Ling, who also conducted fieldwork in Huzhou and shared her results with me, and did fieldwork with me in Zhuji. Paul Katz, Monica Esposito, Stephen Bokenkamp, and Daniel Burton-Rose commented on earlier drafts of this paper, which was presented at the "Popular Confucianism and Redemptive Societies" International Conference 「民間儒教與救世團體」國際學術研討會, Foguang University 佛光大學, June 9–10, 2009, and then at the "探古監今 – 全真道的昨天, 今天與明天" International Conference, Hong Kong, January 6–8, 2010. Wang Chien-ch'uan 王見川 and Lo Shih-chieh 羅士傑 helped with obtaining rare material. A preliminary analysis of part of the material used in the present article was included as part of my article "Quanzhen Clergy," and a shortened Chinese version was published as "Jin'gaishan wangluo."

2 In Qing times, Jin'gaishan was situated within Wucheng county 烏程縣. In 1912, Wucheng was merged with Gui'an 歸安縣, the other county based in Huzhou city, to form Wuxing county 吳興縣 (that was itself merged in Huzhou shi in 1981). To avoid confusion, I name Huzhou the area encompassing the city and Jin'gaishan throughout the chapter.

3 I use Chunyanggong throughout even when various sources use different names. It would appear that the name Meihuaguan appeared later than Chunyanggong.

4 For the notion of "lay Daoist/Quanzhen," see Goossaert, "Quanzhen Clergy," 741–47, and *Taoists of Peking*, 310–18. Lay Quanzhen (or more generally lay Daoist) is not an autonym but a scholarly concept; its applicability in the very vast and variegated world of spirit-writing cults to Lü Dongbin is contested by some scholars; while it is not applicable to all Lü Dongbin (or other) spirit-writing groups, I contend that it fits those of them, like the Jin'gaishan network halls, that claimed a Quanzhen identity.

5 On typologies of redemptive societies and other religious reform and revitalization movements of the Republican period, see Goossaert & Palmer, *Religious Question*, chapter 4.

6 Esposito, "La Porte du dragon," "Longmen Taoism," "Shindai ni okeru Kingaisan no seiritsu," "Shindai dōkyō to mikkyō," *Creative Daoism*; Mori, "Zenshinkyō Ryūmonha," "Ryo Dōhin to Zenshinkyō."

7 Wu Yakui, *Jiangnan Quanzhen Daojiao*, 280–96; "Lun Qingmo Minchu de Jiangnan Quanzhendao 'tan'"; Wang Zongyu, "Wuxing Quanzhendao."

8 Katz, *Images of the Immortal*; Ang, "Le culte de Lü Dongbin."

9 Liu, "Immortals and Patriarchs."

10 *Da Qing huidian shili*, 445:35, does not actually prescribe official sacrifices in these Lü Dongbin temples in all counties, but this is made clear in other sources (notably local gazetteers), which also add that these sacrifices were to be vegetarian. See also Wang, "Qingdai de Lüzu xinyang yu fuji."

11 *Chongxiu Fujiguan Lü zushi dadian ji* 重修福濟觀呂祖師大殿記, in Wu Yakui, comp., *Jiangnan daojiao beiji ziliaoji*, #93. This text, as well as several local gazetteers, lists Jiaqing 10 (1805) instead as 1804 as the date of the canonization.

12 *Da Qing huidian shili*, 438:978, 981, 983; 445:35. For further discussion of these events, see my "Spirit-writing, canonization and the rise of divine saviors: Wenchang, Lüzu, and Guandi, 1700–1858."

13 For instance, "Fanxian xinzheng 藩憲新政," *Shenbao*, GX5/11/21.

14 One detailed description of how a Lü Dongbin temple in the Hangzhou area was enlarged just after the canonization can be found in *(Jiaqing) Yuhang xianzhi*, 6.4a–b.

15 "Xiandan nianxiang 仙誕拈香," *Shenbao*, GX23/4/15 and "Xiandan renao 仙誕熱鬧," *Shenbao*, GX8/4/15.

16 Lai Chi Tim, "Ming Qing daojiao Lüzu jiangji xinyang de fazhan."

17 Esposito, "The Discovery of Jiang Yuanting's *Daozang Jiyao*"; Mori, "*Dōzō shūyō to Shō Yoho*," "Identity and Lineage," "Shinchō Zenshinkyō," "Shō Yoho no Ryoso." The best synthesis of the history of Lüzu canons is Lai, "Qingdai sizhong *Lüzu quanshu* yu Lüzu fuji daotan de guanxi."

18 See notably the many anecdotes collected and discussed in Xu Dishan, *Fuji mixin de yanjiu*. See also "Jixian yishi 乩仙逸事," *Shenbao*, GX1/9/27; "Jixian lingyi 乩仙靈異," *Shenbao*, TZ13/3/16 on literati private spirit-writing cults to Lü in the Suzhou area. See also my discussion of Yu Yue's 俞樾 (1821–1906) records of elite spirit-writing in my "Yu Yue (1821–1906) explore l'au-delà."

19 See "Wuzhong zaji 吳中雜記," *Shenbao*, GX4/6/20 on Lü Dongbin revealing cures in Suzhou during an epidemic.

20 *Chuanyinglou huiyilu*, 84–90.

21 Temple inscriptions tend not to mention this aspect (see however *Yongzhenguan jilüe* 永貞觀記略, in Wu Yakui, comp., *Jiangnan daojiao beiji ziliaoji*, #303, on a Shanghai spirit-writing temple), but anecdotes and newspaper reports frequently mention spirit-writing altars within Daoist temples.

22 *Qionglongshan zhi*, 1:73–80, has a preface (undated, early Qing) revealed by Lü Dongbin.

23 "Xiandan jisheng 仙誕紀盛," *Shenbao*, GX8/4/17; "Daishen quyue 待神去樂," *Shenbao*, GX7/4/15.

24 *Luodianzhen zhi*, 1:12. *Huoju* 夥居 (or 伙居), litt. companion, seems a different notion from the much more common and homophonous term 火居, home-dwelling.

25 Lai Chi Tim, "Qingdai sizhong *Lüzu quanshu*" and Yin Zhihua, "*Lüzu quanshu* de bianzuan he zengji" provide a very convenient list of the scriptures added to the 1775 edition when compared to the 1744 edition.

26 Lai Chi Tim, "Qingdai sizhong *Lüzu quanshu*," 196–202. The 1775 *Lüzu quanshu* editors note that they obtained most of the Jin'gaishan texts as manuscripts (prefaces to juan 43, 44).

27 On Shao Zhilin, see Goossaert, "Spiritual Techniques."

28 *Jin'gai xindeng*, 7.50a–52a.

29 See *Jin'gaishan zhi*, 16a–23a; the inscriptions in Wang Zongyao, *Gu Meihuaguan zhi*, 151–54; Lai Chi Tim, "Ming Qing daojiao Lüzu jiangji xinyang de fazhan," 161–63, and Xu Wei, "Wenben liuchuan yu keyi pinjie," 168–74, who discusses the liturgies revealed there and the ritual activities of the then Jin'gaishan leaders.

30 *(Guangxu) Wucheng xianzhi*, 6.9b–10a.

31 Yunchao seems to have been an alternative name for the Chunyanggong site since the Yuan period (Wang Zongyao, *Gu Meihuaguan zhi*, chapter 2), and locals still call the temple Yunchaomiao 廟. The hall devoted to spirit-writing within the temple was named Chaoluange 巢鸞閣 after its post-1864 reconstruction, so "Yunchaotan" became a name for a social institution rather than a specific place.

32 On scriptures revealed to Min Yide by spirit-writing around 1823, see Maruyama, "Qingchao Daoguang nianjian Jin'gaishan Lüzu daotan suo chuangzao zhi jingdian chutan."

33 Esposito, "Longmen Taoism," "The Longmen School."

34 The *fangbian fapai* is discussed in several of Min Yide's writings: see Wu Yakui, *Jiangnan Quanzhen daojiao*, 292; Liu Huanling, "Shixi Min Yide."

35 Wang Zongyao, *Gu Meihuaguan zhi*, 123, 133, quotes two cases of disciples of the network who were vegetarians, which shows how this was both rare and highly respected.

36 Wang Zongyu, "Wuxing Quanzhendao," 222–23. Wang Zongyao tells me that no heir of the Min Yide branch of the Min lineage is still living in Huzhou.

37 See the 1882 inscription "Jin'gaishan chongjian Chunyanggong ji 金蓋山重建純陽宮記" by the famous scholar Yu Yue in Wang Zongyao, *Gu Meihuaguan zhi*, 155–56 and in *Chunzaitang zawen* 4/1.2a–3b. Yu was from Deqing

德清, not far south of Jin'gaishan, but was not personally familiar with the place and the network.

38 Qiu Shouming, "Daojiao Huzhou Yunchao Chunyang gong," 118. These Daoists performed the regular daily services and birthday celebrations for Lü Dongbin and other immortals, but not rituals for private families, which were performed by members of the branch altars. Some of the Daoists in residence engaged in secluded self-cultivation.

39 Zhou Yangbo, *Cong shizu dao shenzu* on the history of the Shen, and p. 334 on four cases of marriage with the neighboring Min.

40 *Jin'gai xindeng*, appendix.6a–7a.

41 Among the many Shen, one of Shen Bingcheng's sons, Shen Ruilin 沈瑞麟 (1874-after 1935), a Republican-period official, also played a leading role in the network: Wang Zongyao, *Gu Meihuaguan zhi*, 124.

42 *Jin'gaishan zhi*, 2.19a.

43 Wu Yakui, "Lun Qingmo Minchu de Jiangnan Quanzhendao 'tan'," 4.

44 At least one of the leaders of the Huzhou tongxianghui 同鄉會 in Republican-period Shanghai, Pan Yihuan 潘益寰 (1872–?) was a member of the Jin'gaishan network: Wang Zongyao, *Gu Meihuaguan zhi*, 130.

45 Wu Yakui, "Lun Qingmo Minchu de Jiangnan Quanzhendao 'tan'," 6–8, *Jiangnan Quanzhen daojiao*, 256–60.

46 See for instance a report on how Huzhou merchants in Shanghai organized to pay for the burial of the victims of the Taiping war and organized a *jiao* offering for them at Jin'gaishan: "Quannang cheng shanju qi 勸囊成善舉启," *Shenbao*, TZ13/9/17.

47 For instance, the Jinyuntan 錦雲壇 in Xiaofeng county 孝丰縣 (in the western part of Huzhou prefecture).

48 Wu Yakui, *Jiangnan Quanzhen daojiao*, 251–52. The Fanyuntan is not listed in the genealogies or in Wang Zongyao, *Gu Meihuaguan zhi*.

49 Wang Zongyao, *Gu Meihuaguan zhi*, 175–79.

50 Wu Yakui, "Lun Qingmo Minchu de Jiangnan Quanzhendao 'tan'," 15–16 offers a list.

51 Besides these 13 unmistakable cases of altar name, it is quite possible that other Jin'gaishan network members listed their original institution under a temple name.

52 The best study of this text is Wang Zongyu, "Wuxing Quanzhendao."

53 This altar and its genealogy are discussed in Qing Xitai ed., *Zhongguo daojiao shi*, vol. 4, 298–304, but without reference to it being a lay spirit-writing altar. Wang Zongyao, *Gu Meihuaguan zhi*, also provides rich genealogical data, mostly culled from the *Daotong yuanliu* and *Longmen zhengzong Jueyun benzhi daotong xinzhuan* and completed by current membership.

54 On authoritative lists of Quanzhen lineages, see Goossaert, "Quanzhen Clergy," 731–32 and Wang Zongyu, "Wuxing Quanzhendao," 218.

55 On this association, see Goossaert, *Taoists of Peking*, 74–77.

56 Wu Yakui, "Lun Qingmo Minchu de Jiangnan Quanzhendao 'tan'," 5; Wang Zongyu, "Wuxing Quanzhendao," 217.

57 On the shared reformist outlook between the various religious associations established in 1912, see Goossaert, "Republican Church Engineering."

58 A list of officials is provided by Wu Yakui, "Lun Qingmo Minchu de Jiangnan Quanzhendao 'tan'," 13 and Wang Zongyu, "Wuxing Quanzhendao," 225. Some were acting officials in Huzhou, meaning that they converted not because of a family tradition but because they were exposed to the branches when posted in Huzhou.

59 Wang Zongyao, *Gu Meihuaguan zhi*, 93.

60 See the example of Jin Bengan 金本幹, in *Longmen zhengzong Jueyun benzhi daotong xinzhuan*, 439. Another case is Wang Laiyin 王來因 (died during the Guanxu period), who was the cantor 都講 at Chunyanggong and also the owner of a large drugstore: Wang Zongyao, *Gu Meihuaguan zhi*, 119.

61   Wang Zongyu, "Wuxing Quanzhendao," 229, quoting the *Jin'gaishan zhi*, 3.13b–14a, and Wang Zongyao, *Gu Meihuaguan zhi*, 117.

62   Qiu Shouming, "Daojiao Huzhou Yunchao Chunyang gong," 118–19.

63   A model of the *paidan* is provided at the beginning of *Longmen zhengzong Jueyun benzhi daotong xinzhuan*.

64   Liu, "An Intoning Immortal at the West Lake."

65   "Zixu 自敘," *Xiling xianyong*, 1a–11b.

66   Chen also discusses his relation to Min Yide in a preface dated 1832 to a compilation of Min's teachings on *neidan*, the *Jinxian zhizhi xingming zhenyuan*, collected by another disciple of Min, named Xue Yanggui 薛陽桂.

67   On the *nüdan* tradition, see Despeux, *Immortelles*, 163–82 and "Women and Daoism"; Valussi, "Men and Women," "Female Alchemy."

68   *Xiwang mu nüxiu zhengtu shize* 西王母女修正途十則 and *Nü jindan jue* 女金丹訣: the latter was revealed through spirit-writing by Sun Bu'er 孫不二 and received in 1799 in Hangzhou by one of Min Yide's disciples.

69   Wu Yakui, "Lun Qingmo Minchu de Jiangnan Quanzhendao 'tan'," 10–11.

70   My calculation based on *Jueyunxuan Yunxiao xuanpu zhi*, j. 5.

71   The *Longmen zhengzong Jueyun benzhi daotong xinzhuan*, "Liyan 例言," explains that men and women could congregate together at the Shanghai Jueyuntan. A Daoist from Zhuji (see below) recalls that some altars there were male-only, but it does not seem to have been typical of the Jin'gaishan network as a whole.

72   Wang Zongyu, "Wuxing Quanzhendao," 216. Dai was from a Huzhou family. See Scott, "The Buddhist Nationalism of Dai Jitao."

73   Esposito, "The Discovery of Jiang Yuanting's *Daozang Jiyao* in Jiangnan," 108–9.

74   Wu Yakui, "Lun Qingmo Minchu de Jiangnan Quanzhendao 'tan'," 16–17. Wang Zongyao, *Gu Meihuaguan zhi*, 119, documents a member who was famed for his exorcisms.

75   Qiu Shouming, "Daojiao Huzhou Yunchao Chunyang gong," 119–23.

76   Qiu Shouming, "Daojiao Huzhou Yunchao Chunyang gong," 120–21.

77   Wang Zongyao, *Gu Meihuaguan zhi*, 174–75.

78   A version of the *Taiji jilian* authoritative in modern Jiangnan was edited by the renowned Longhushan leader Lou Jinyuan 婁近垣 (1689–1776), see *Zangwai daoshu*, vol. 17.

79   The *Gushu yinlou cangshu* does not contain liturgical texts, except a few commentaries on incantations for individual use.

80   Cao Benye & Xu Hongtu, *Hangzhou Baopu daoyuan daojiao yinyue*, 156–64, discuss a salvation ritual revealed by Lü to a Hangzhou spirit-writing hall and that was in use in various Hangzhou Daoist temples. See also the discussion of a spirit-written liturgy for the salvation of the dead in Tao Jin, "Suzhou *Dadong wushang jiuji tianxian chuanjie keyi* chutan."

81   Wang Zongyao, *Gu Meihuaguan zhi*, 27.

82   Qiu Shouming, "Daojiao Huzhou Yunchao Chunyang gong," 121.

83   *Longmen zhengzong Jueyun benzhi daotong xinzhuan*, 1.35a discusses a member of a Shanghai branch altar invited in Beijing in 1923 to perform a ritual.

84   "Huiyun shantan chuangshi ji 惠雲善壇創始記," (dated 1903), *Xingmeng bian*, after main text.

85   "Longmen fachan zhi 龍門法懺志," *Jueyunxuan Yunxiao xuanpu zhi*, 4.37a–38b.

86   Wu Yakui, "Lun Qingmo Minchu de Jiangnan Quanzhendao 'tan'," 19–20, quotes the genealogies to the effect that the Yunchaotan and several branches printed a good number of standard scriptures (notably the *Yuhuang benxing jijing* 玉皇本行集經) and various litanies.

87   http://bbs.byscrj.cn/thread-1118-1-1.html, accessed May 18, 2009.

88   I have consulted at the Shanghai Library four different liturgical books (there certainly are more) printed by Jin'gaishan between 1873 and 1881, mostly preexisting books. The prefaces document how the Jin'gaishan lay Daoists retrieved copies of

these liturgical texts from bookstores or other places and had woodblocks carved for printing and distribution within the network.

89 For instance, the *Xuantian renwei shangdi baoen baochan* was edited and printed by Wang Laiyin (discussed above) and five other Longmen Daoists, and paid for by over 20 fellow lay Daoists.

90 *Daotong yuanliu*, 3.17–18; Wang Zongyao, *Gu Meihuaguan zhi*, 121; Wang Zongyu, "Wuxing Quanzhendao," 225. Shen Bingcheng wrote a biography of Min Yide, which was included in the 1904 reprint of the *Gushu yinlou cangshu*, prefatory material.

91 For an excellent discussion of another case of lay Daoist devotional life among high-ranking nineteenth-century officials, combining Lü Dongbin worship, an inclination toward Quanzhen identity, and scripture-recitation, see Liu, "Immortals and Patriarchs." Unfortunately, we do not seem to have any of Shen Bingcheng's private writings (poetry, diaries, prose collections, etc.) that would tell us more about his Daoist practice and involvement with the Jin'gaishan network.

92 Wang Zongyao, *Gu Meihuaguan zhi*, 172–75, has culled from the genealogies a list of books authored by disciples of the network; most of these books seem to be lost or at least absent from the major libraries and collections.

93 *Zangwai daoshu*, vol. 10 (based on a copy stored at the Shanghai library).

94 On Zheng Guanying's involvement with Daoist self-cultivation and spirit-writing, see Fan Chun-wu "Xiuzhen, feiluan yu banshan"; Goossaert, *Taoists of Peking*, 174, 328; Lai Chi-tim, "Zheng Guanying *xiandao*"; and Liu, *Daoist Modern*, 22–23.

95 I have not found Tao Bennian's name in the *Daotong yuanliu*.

96 This 1880 reprint is reproduced in *Sandong shiyi*, vol. 16.

97 For a discussion of the social role of spirit-writing in local society, see Katz, "Spirit-writing Halls."

98 See the public lectures given by a member of the Shanghai Huiyuntan 會雲壇, who was also a prominent lay Buddhist intellectual: "Jiangzuo 講座," *Shenbao*, 1944.09.07.

99 *Jiangxi Fenyi Lin Pinsan xiansheng yulu*, preface, 1–2. Lu Qitu was the manager of the medical charity ran by the Jueyuntan in Shanghai, the Weizhong shantang (see below); he is listed in a 1946 report to Shanghai municipality as being aged 68: Shanghai Municipal Archives, files Q6-9-79.

100 On all this, see Liu, *Daoist Modern*.

101 Qiu Shouming, "Daojiao Huzhou Yunchao Chunyang gong," 121–22.

102 An interesting note in a Jin'gaishan genealogy discusses a member who had been practicing on his own based on the classic *Lingbao bifa* 靈寶畢法, with unsatisfactory results, before he joined the network and was "corrected" in his practice: Wang Zongyao, *Gu Meihuaguan zhi*, 119.

103 Goossaert, *Taoists of Peking*, 306–19 discusses the role of several spirit-writing groups and redemptive societies in distributing and teaching Quanzhen Daoist texts in Beijing.

104 Wang Zongyao, *Gu Meihuaguan zhi*, 22–23, has a number of early nineteenth-century anecdotes of people going to the Chunyanggong to be healed either by Daoists there or by Lü Dongbin through spirit-writing.

105 "Huiyun shantan chuangshi ji 惠雲善壇創始記," (dated 1903), *Xingmeng bian*, after main text. The distribution of drugs based on recipes revealed by Lü Dongbin through spirit-writing was common among Lü Dongbin spirit-writing groups in the Cantonese world as well as in Jiangnan. The *Shenbao* carried a number of reports on this. An excellent general study on the role of the Lü Dongbin cult and spirit-writing in modern charity is offered by Yau Chi-on, *Shan yu ren tong*.

106 On *shantang* in late Qing society, see Leung, *Shishan yu jiaohua*; Fuma Susumu, *Chūgoku zenkai zendōshi kenkyū*.

107 Wang Zongyu, "Wuxing Quanzhendao," 230–31.

108 Wu Yakui, "Lun Qingmo Minchu de Jiangnan Quanzhendao 'tan'," 17–18.

109 Wang Zongyao, *Gu Meihuaguan zhi*, 119. Wang Zongyao tells me that nothing is left of the Renjitang. Its charitable activities are documented in numerous *Shenbao* reports, including its prominent role in raising funds for victims of the 1876–79 North China famine.

110 The Weizhong shantang is mentioned in a large number of *Shenbao* reports between 1900 and 1949, most often as a medical charity (offering drugs and vaccination, in some cases distributing drugs revealed by Lüzu along with morality books), or as one (in some cases featuring quite prominently) of the Shanghai charities that co-organized social events or coordinated charitable drives. "Zujieshang de daoshi 租界上的道士," *Shenbao*, 1929.11.19, also discusses how it employed Daoists and sold liturgical services.

111 Shanghai Municipal Archives, files Q6-9-79, Q115-25.

112 Tao Shuimu, "Beiyang zhengfu shiqi lü Hu Zheshang." On religious activities of the Huzhou community in Shanghai, see Liu Wenxing, "Jindai Hushe yu siyuan de hudong."

113 Leung, "Daotang hu? Shantang hu?" discusses at length the issue of the diverging charitable and spirit-writing identities of a Cantonese hall.

114 Shanghai Municipal Archives, files B2-2-73-14.

115 See for instance a report of spirit-writing séances in 1881 at the Wushan complex of temples in Hangzhou, where Lüzu and Jigong were invited together, and delivered warnings on impending epidemics and offered drugs to prevent devotees from dying: "Luanyu leilu 鸞諭類錄," *Shenbao*, GX7/+7/14.

116 Wang Chien-ch'uan, "Qingmo Minchu Zhongguo de Jigong xinyang yu fuji tuanti."

117 On Wang, see Katz, "Yige zhuming Shanghai shangren yu cishanjia de zongjiao shenghuo" and *Religion in China and its Modern Fate*, chap. 3.

118 Wu Yakui, "Lun Qingmo Minchu de Jiangnan Quanzhendao 'tan'," 13–14. The Nanping lineage is listed among lineages recognized in the *Daotong yuanliu*: Wang Zongyu, "Wuxing Quanzhendao," 218.

119 *Xingmenbian*, prefatory material, 1b. The Weizhong shantang housed a Jishenghui branch: "Yizheng liuxing zhi zuowen 疫症流行之昨聞," *Shenbao*, 1919.07.28.

120 Wang Zongyao, *Gu Meihuaguan zhi*, 26.

121 *Shenbao* reports from the late Qing and Republican periods have numerous instances of local elites, listed as members of a X-yuntan 口雲壇, giving to charities; some of the altars are indeed part of the Jin'gaishan network, but many are not. The fact that these people, who had other claims to social status, chose to be listed as disciple of an altar shows how being such a disciple brought respect.

122 *Jueyunxuan Yunxiao xuanpu zhi*; *Zhuji shehui xianxiang*, 86–7.

123 *Jueyunxuan Yunxiao xuanpu zhi*, j. 2.

124 *Jueyunxuan Yunxiao xuanpu zhi*, j. 6, 7.

125 Clart, "Confucius and the Mediums." On self-divinization, see Goossaert, *Bureaucratie et salut*.

126 *Chongjian Shuihongmiao beiji* 重建水洪廟記, 1994, on site.

127 *Zhuji shehui xianxiang*, 87.

128 Wang Zongyao, *Gu Meihuaguan zhi*, 27–29.

129 *Zhongguo huidaomen shiliao jicheng*, 439. Xiaofeng was merged into Anji county 安吉縣 in 1958. The Jinyuntan had been founded by Zhu Benci 諸本慈 (1863–1952), a heir to a local rich family who had also founded schools and orphanages: Wang Zongyao, *Gu Meihuaguan zhi*, 128–29.

130 In Changxing county 長興縣 (just west of Huzhou, where several Jin'gaishan branch altars were operating), a Longmendao 龍門道 was repressed and I do not know whether there is any connection with the Jin'gaishan (*Zhongguo huidaomen shiliao jicheng*, 435).

131 *Zhongguo huidaomen shiliao jicheng*, 454, documents the 1949–1953 repression in Zhuji, where a high number of spirit-writing halls were repressed, including the

Pujiutan, the Tongjueshan shantan 同覺善善壇 (a mistake for Jueshishan shantang?), the Chengyitan 誠一壇 (an early name for the Jueyunxuan), and others.

132 Monica Esposito (oral communication) visited and saw rituals there in 1989 and 1991, when the temple had not been rebuilt yet, and only opened for festivals.

133 The information in this section is based on my interviews on the field in November 2007 and December 2009, and Fang Ling's own fieldwork in April 2009. My warmest thanks to Dr. Fang for her help and for sharing her information with me.

134 I am yet to find any data on this temple in local gazetteers. Anlewang is a title of the well-known Jiangnan local god Jin zongguan 金總管.

135 Esposito, "Longmen Taoism"; Mori, "Ryo Dōhin."

136 Jordan & Overmyer, *The Flying Phoenix*.

137 Goossaert, "Daoists in the Peking Self-cultivation market."

138 *Chongjian Jinling Yuxu guan jishi zhengxin lu.*

139 Wang Chien-ch'uan, "Qingmo Minchu Zhongguo de Jigong xinyang yu fuji tuanti."

140 Wang Zongyao, *Gu Meihuaguan zhi*, 127.

141 On Wu Peifu's membership, see Wang Zongyu, "Wuxing Quanzhendao," 217; on his involvement in Beijing Daoism and redemptive societies, see Goossaert, "Daoists in the Peking Self-Cultivation Market."

142 This is comparable to the situation of several Daoist spirit-writing groups in Beijing, see Goossaert, *Taoists of Peking*, chapter 7.

143 Compare for instance with the Zailijiao 在理教 as studied in Jiang Zhushan, "1930 niandai Tianjin Duliu zhen."

144 Lai Chi Tim, *Xianggang daotang keyi lishi yu chuancheng, Guangdong difang daojiao yanjiu*, "Hong Kong Daoism"; Shiga Ichiko, *Kindai Chūgoku no shāmanizumu to dōkyō*, "Yibainian lai Guangdong diqu fuluan," "Mingokuki Kōshū no dōkyōkei zendō"; Leung, "Daotang hu? Shantang hu?"

145 Zhu Mingchuan, "Qingmo yilai de Guandi shengge yundong."

Bibliography

Primary

Chongjian Jinling Yuxu guan jishi zhengxin lu 重建金陵玉虛觀紀事徵信錄. Wang Lianyou 王蓮友. 1936 edition in *Zhongguo daoguan zhi congkan*, vol. 11.

Chuanyinglou huiyilu 釧影樓回憶錄. Bao Tianxiao 包天笑. In *Minguo biji xiaoshuo daguan* 民国笔记小说大观, vol. 4, Taiyuan: Shanxi guji chubanshe, 1999.

Chunzaitang zawen 春在堂雜文. Yu Yue 俞樾 (1821–1906). In *Chunzaitang quanshu* 春在堂全書, 1889 ed.

Da Qing huidian shili 大清會典事例. Shanghai: Shangwu yinshuguan, 1908.

Daotong yuanliu 道統源流. Yan Heyi 嚴合怡 (comp.). Wuxi: Zhonghua yinshuai ju, 1929.

Fanghu waishi 方壺外史. 1915 edition in *Sandong shiyi*, vol. 19.

Gushu yinlou cangshu 古書隱樓藏書. 1904 edition in *Zangwai daoshu*, vol. 10. See also modern edition by Beijing: Zongjiao wenhua chubanshe, 2010, 2 vols.

Jiangxi Fenyi Lin Pinsan xiansheng yulu 江西分宜林品三先生語錄. 1947 edition in *Sandong shiyi*, vol. 7.

Jin'gaishan zhi 金蓋山志. Li Zonglian 李宗蓮. 1896 original edition.

Jinxian zhizhi xingming zhenyuan 金仙直指性命真源. Xue Yanggui 薛陽桂. 1923 edition in *Daoshu jicheng* 道書集成, Beijing: Jiuzhou tushu chubanshe, 1999, vol. 49.

Jueyunxuan Yunxiao xuanpu zhi 覺雲軒雲霄玄譜志. Shen Rui 沈睿. 1939 edition in *Zhongguo daoguan zhi congkan*, vol. 22–23.

Longmen zhengzong Jueyun benzhi daotong xinzhuan 龍門正宗覺雲本支道統薪傳. Lu
    Benji 陸本基. 1927 original edition in *Zangwai daoshu*, vol. 31.
Luodianzhen zhi 羅店鎮志. Wang Shufen 王樹棻 et al., comp. 1889. in *Shanghai
    xiangzhen jiuzhi congshu* 上海鄉鎮舊志叢書, vol. 11. Shanghai: Shenghai shehui
    kexueyuan chubanshe, 2005.
Qionglongshan zhi 穹窿山志. Wu Weiye吳偉業 (1609–1672), Xiang Qiu 向球 and Li
    Biao 李標 compilers. 1674. Reprint *Zhongguo daoguan zhi congkan* 中國道觀志叢刊.
    Nanjing: Jiangsu guji chubanshe, 2000, vols. 14–15.
Sandong shiyi 三洞拾遺. Hefei: Huangshan shushe, 2005, 20 vols.
Shenbao 申報. Shanghai: Shenbaoguan, daily, 1872–1949.
(Guangxu) Wucheng xianzhi (光緒)烏程縣志. Zhou Xuejun 周學濬 et al., 1881.
Xiling xianyong 西泠仙詠. Chen Wenshu 陳文述 (1775–1845), 1835. *Wulin zhanggu
    congbian* 武林掌故叢編 edition.
Xingmeng bian 醒夢編. 1904 edition in *Ming Qing minjian zongjiao jingjuan wenxian*
    明清民間宗教經卷文獻, Wang Chien-ch'uan 王見川 and Lin Wanchuan 林萬傳
    (eds.). Taipei: Xinwenfeng, 1999, vol. 11.
Xuandu lütan Zhejiangsheng Guhang Yuhuangshan Fuxingguan chuanjielu
    玄都律壇浙江省古杭玉皇山福星觀傳戒錄. 1896. In Fang Ling 方玲 & Vincent
    Goossaert 高萬桑 (eds.), *Zhongguo xiandangdai chengshi daojiao ziliaoji*
    中國現當代城市道教資料集. Beijing: Zongjiao wenhua chubanshe, in press (2 vols.)
Xuantian renwei shangdi baoen baochan 玄天仁威上帝報恩寶懺. Undated edition in
    Zangwai daoshu, vol. 30.
(Jiaqing) Yuhang xianzhi (嘉慶)餘杭縣志. Zhang Ji'an 張吉安 et al. (eds.), *Zhongguo
    difangzhi jicheng – Zhejiang fuxian zhi ji* 中國地方志集成: 浙江府縣志輯, Chengdu:
    Ba Shu shushe, 1993, vol. 5.
Zangwai daoshu 藏外道書. Chengdu: Bashu shushe, 1992–1994, 36 vols.
Zhongguo daoguan zhi congkan 中國道觀志叢刊. Nanjing: Jiangsu guji chubanshe, 2000,
    36 vols.
Zhuji shehui xianxiang 諸暨社會現象 (*Zhuji minbao wuzhounian jiniance* 諸暨民報五周
    年紀念冊), Zhuji, 1925.

Secondary

Ang, Isabelle. "Le culte de Lü Dongbin sous les Song du Sud," *Journal asiatique*, 285(2),
    1997, pp. 473–507.
Cao Benye 曹本冶 and Xu Hongtu 徐宏圖. *Hangzhou Baopu daoyuan daojiao yinyue*
    杭州抱朴道院道教音樂. Taibei: Xinwenfeng chuban gongsi, 2000.
Clart, Philip. "Confucius and the Mediums: Is There a 'Popular Confucianism'?" *T'oung
    Pao*, LXXXIX(1–3), 2003, pp. 1–38.
Despeux, Catherine. *Immortelles de la Chine ancienne. Taoïsme et alchimie féminine.*
    Puiseaux: Pardès, 1990.
Despeux, Catherine. "Women in Daoism," in Livia Kohn (ed.), *Daoism Handbook*. Leiden:
    Brill, 2000, pp. 384–412.
Esposito, Monica. *Creative Daoism*. Wil/Paris: UniversityMedia, 2013.
Esposito, Monica. "The Discovery of Jiang Yuanting's *Daozang* Jiyao in Jiangnan. A
    Presentation of the Taoist Canon of the Qing Dynasty," in Mugitani Kunio 麥谷邦夫
    (ed.), *Kōnan dōkyō no kenkyū* 江南道教の研究. Kyoto: Jinbun kagaku kenkyūjo,
    2007, pp. 79–110.

Esposito, Monica. "La Porte du dragon : L'école Longmen du mont Jin'gai et ses pratiques alchimiques d'après le Daozang xubian (Suite au canon taoïste)," Ph.D. dissertation, Université Paris VII, 1993.

Esposito, Monica. "The Longmen School and Its Controversial History during the Qing Dynasty," in John Lagerwey (ed.), *Religion and Chinese Society*. Hong Kong: Chinese University Press, 2004, pp. 621–98.

Esposito, Monica. "Longmen Taoism in Qing China: Doctrinal Ideal and Local Reality," *Journal of Chinese Religions*, 29, 2001, pp. 191–231.

Esposito, Monica. "Shindai dōkyō to mikkyō: Ryūmon seijiku shinshū 清代道教と密宗—龍門西竺心宗," in Mugitani Kunio 麥谷邦夫 (ed.), *Sankyō kōshō ronsō* 三教交渉論叢. Kyoto: Jinbun Kagaku Kenkyūjo, 2005, pp. 287–338.

Esposito, Monica. "Shindai ni okeru Kingaisan Ryūmonha no seiritsu to Kinka shūshi 清代における金蓋山龍門派の設立と金華宗旨," in Kyōto Daigaku Jinbun Kagaku Kenkyūjo 京都大學人文科學研究所 (ed.), *Chūgoku shūkyō bunken kenkyū* 中國宗教文獻研究. Kyoto: Rinsen shoten, 2007, pp. 239–64.

Fan Chunwu 范純武. "Feiluan, xiuzhen, yu banshan: Zheng Guanying yu Shanghai de zongjiao shijie 飛鸞、修真與辦善：鄭觀應與上海的宗教世界," in Wu Jen-shu 巫仁恕, Lin May-li 林美莉 & Paul R. Katz (Kang Bao 康豹) (eds.), *Cong chengshi kan Zhongguo de xiandaixing* 從城市看中國的現代性. Nankang: Institute of Modern History, Academia Sinica, 2010, pp. 247–74.

Fuma Susumu 夫馬進. *Chūgoku zenkai zendōshi kenkyū* 中国善会善堂史研究. Kyoto: Dohosha shuppan, 1997.

Goossaert, Vincent. *Bureaucratie et salut. Devenir un dieu en Chine*. Genève: Labor & Fides, 2017.

Goossaert, Vincent. "Daoists in the Modern Self-Cultivation Market: The Case of Beijing, 1850–1949," in David Palmer & Xun Liu (eds.), *Daoism in the 20th Century: Between Eternity and Modernity*. Berkeley: University of California Press, 2012, pp. 123–53.

Goossaert, Vincent. "The Quanzhen Clergy, 1700–1950," in John Lagerwey (ed.), *Religion and Chinese Society*. Hong Kong: Chinese University Press and Paris, EFEO, 2004, pp. 699–772.

Goossaert, Vincent. "Republican Church Engineering. The National Religious Associations in 1912 China," in Mayfair Mei-hui Yang (ed.), *Chinese Religiosities: Afflictions of Modernity and State Formation*. Berkeley: University of California Press, 2008, pp. 209–32.

Goossaert, Vincent. "Spirit-Writing, Canonization and the Rise of Divine Saviors: Wenchang, Lüzu, and Guandi, 1700–1858," *Late Imperial China*, 36(2), 2015, pp. 82–125.

Goossaert, Vincent. "Spiritual Techniques among Late Imperial Chinese Literati," in Angela Hobart, Thierry Zarcone & Jean-Pierre Brach (eds.), *Spiritual Techniques*. Canon Pyon: Sean Kingston, forthcoming.

Goossaert, Vincent. *The Taoists of Peking, 1800–1949. A Social History of Urban Clerics*. Cambridge (MA): Harvard University Asia Center, 2007.

Goossaert, Vincent. "Yu Yue (1821–1906) explore l'au-delà. La culture religieuse des élites chinoises à la veille des revolutions," in Roberte Hamayon, Denise Aigle, Isabelle Charleux & Vincent Goossaert (eds.), *Misceallanea Asiatica*. Sankt Augustin: Monumenta Serica, 2011, pp. 623–56.

Goossaert, Vincent & David A. Palmer. *The Religious Question in Modern China*. Chicago: University of Chicago Press, 2011.

Goossaert, Vincent & Wu Yakui, trans. "Jin'gaishan wangluo. Jinxiandai Jiangnan de Quanzhen jushi zuzhi 金蓋山網絡：近現代江南的全真居士組織," in Zhao Weidong 趙衛東 (ed.), *Quanzhendao yanjiu* 全真道研究, 1. Jinan: Qilu shushe, 2011, pp. 319–39.

Jiang Zhushan 蔣竹山. "1930 niandai Tianjin Duliu zhen shangren de zongjiao yu shehui huodong canyu – yi 'Zaili jiao' weili 1930 年代天津獨流鎮商人的宗教與社會活動參與 –以在理教為例," in Wang Chien-ch'uan 王見川 & Jiang Zhushan (eds.), *Ming Qing yilai minjian zongjiao de tansuo – Jinian Dai Xuanzhi jiaoshou lunwen ji* 明清以來民間宗教的探索– 紀念戴玄之教授論文集. Taipei: Shangding wenhua chubanshe, 1996, pp. 266–91.

Jordan, David K. & Overmyer, Daniel. *The Flying Phoenix. Aspects of Chinese Sectarianism in Taiwan.* Princeton: Princeton University Press, 1986.

Katz, Paul R. *Images of the Immortal. The Cult of Lü Dongbin at the Palace of Eternal Joy.* Honolulu: University of Hawai'i Press, 1999.

Katz, Paul R. *Religion in China and Its Modern Fate.* Waltham (MA): Brandeis University Press, 2014.

Katz, Paul R. "Spirit-Writing Halls and the Development of Local Communities: A Case Study of Puli (Nantou County)," *Min-su ch'ü-i*民俗曲藝, 174, 2012, pp. 103–82.

Katz, Paul R. "Yige zhuming Shanghai shangren yu cishanjia de zongjiao shenghuo: Wang Yiting 一個著名上海商人與慈善家的宗教生活: 王一亭," in Wu Jen-shu 巫仁恕, Lin May-li 林美莉, & Paul R. Katz (Kang Bao 康豹) (eds.), *Cong chengshi kan Zhongguo de xiandaixing* 從城市看中國的現代性. Nankang: Institute of Modern History, Academia Sinica, 2010, pp. 275–96.

Lai Chi Tim 黎志添. *Guangdong difang daojiao yanjiu: daoguan, daoshi, ji keyi* 廣東地方道教研究: 道觀、道士及科儀. Hong Kong: Chinese University Press, 2007.

Lai Chi Tim 黎志添. "Hong Kong Daoism: A Study of Daoist Altars and Lü Dongbin Cults," *Social Compass*, 50(4), 2003, pp. 459–70.

Lai Chi Tim 黎志添. "Ming Qing daojiao Lüzu jiangji xinyang de fazhan ji xiangguan wenren jitan yanjiu 明清道教呂祖降乩信仰的發展及相關文人乩壇研究," *Journal of Chinese Studies* 中國文化研究所學報, 65, 2017, pp. 139–79.

Lai Chi Tim 黎志添. "Qingdai sizhong *Lüzu quanshu* yu Lüzu fuji daotan de guanxi 清代四種《呂祖全書》與呂祖扶乩道壇的關係," *Zhongguo wenzhe yanjiu jikan* 中國文哲研究集刊, 42, 2013, pp. 183–230.

Lai Chi Tim 黎志添, ed. *Xianggang daotang keyi lishi yu chuancheng* 香港道堂科儀歷史與傳承. Hong Kong: Zhonghua shuju, 2007.

Lai Chi-tim 黎志添. "Zheng Guanying *xiandao* yu *jiushi* de sixiang he shijian : jianping qidui Qingmi Minchu daojiao fazhan de yinxiang ji yiyi 鄭觀應「仙道」與「救世」的思想和實踐: 兼評其對清末民初道教發展的影響及意義," *Journal of Chinese Studies* 中國文化研究所學報 67, 2018, pp. 151-202.

Leung Angela 梁其姿. "Daotang hu? Shantang hu? Qingmo Minchu Guangzhou chengnei Xingong caotang de dute moshi 道堂乎?善堂乎?清末民初廣州城內省躬草堂的獨特模式," in Chen Yung-fa 陳永發 (ed.), *Ming-Qing diguoji qi jinxiandai zhuanxing* 明清帝國及其近現代轉型. Taipei: Yunchen congkan, 2011, pp. 395–434.

Leung Angela 梁其姿. *Shishan yu jiaohua. Ming Qing de cishan zuzhi* 施善與教化. 明清的慈善組織. Zhangjiakou: Hebei jiaoyu chubanshe, 2001.

Liu Huanling 劉煥玲. "Shixi Min Yide zhi Longmen fangbian famen 試析閔一得之龍門方便法門," *Zhongguo daojiao* 中國道教, 5, 2005, pp. 33–39.

Liu Wenxing 劉文星. "Jindai Hushe yu siyuan de hudong: yi Shanghai Shousheng'an shijian wei zhongxin 近代湖社與寺院的互動:以上海壽聖庵事件為中心," in Paul R. Katz & Vincent Goossaert (eds.), *Gaibian Zhongguo zongjiao de wushinian* 改變中國宗教的五十年, 1898–1948. Taipei: Academia Sinica, Institute of Modern History, 2015, pp. 427–93.

Liu, Xun. *Daoist Modern. Innovation, Lay Practice, and the Community of Inner Alchemy in Republican Shanghai.* Cambridge (MA): Harvard University Asia Center, 2009.

Liu, Xun. "Immortals and Patriarchs: The Daoist World of a Manchu Official and His Family in Nineteenth Century China," *Asia Major*, 3rd series, 17(2), 2004, pp. 161–218.

Liu, Xun. "An Intoning Immortal at the West Lake: Chen Wenshu and His Daoist Pursuits in Late Qing Jiangnan," *Cahiers d'Extrême-Asie*, 25, 2016, pp. 77–111.

Maruyama Hiroshi 丸山宏. "Qingchao Daoguang nianjian Jin'gaishan Lüzu daotan suo chuangzao zhi jingdian chutan: yi *Yuqing zanhua jiutian yanzheng xinyin jijing, Yuqing zanhua jiutian yanzheng xinyin baochan* wei zhongxin zhi tantao 清朝道光年間金蓋山呂祖道壇所創造之經典初探: 以《玉清贊化九天演政心印集經》、《玉清贊化九天演政心印寶懺》為中心之探討," *Daoism: Religion, History and Society* 道教研究學報, 7, 2015, pp. 171–200.

Mori Yuria 森由利亞. "Dōzō shūyō to Shō Yoho no Ryoso fukei shinkō 道藏輯要と蔣予蒲の呂祖扶乩信仰," *Tōhō shūkyō* 東方宗教, 98, 2001, pp. 33–52.

Mori Yuria 森由利亞. "Identity and Lineage: The *Taiyi jinhua zongzhi* and the Spirit-Writing Cult to Patriarch Lü in Qing China," in Livia Kohn and Harold D. Roth (eds.), *Daoist Identity: Cosmology, Lineage, and Ritual.* Honolulu: University of Hawai'i Press, 2002, pp. 165–84.

Mori Yuria 森由利亞. "Ryo Dōhin to Zenshinkyō: Shinchō koshū Kingaisan no jirei o chūshin ni 呂洞賓と全真教—清朝湖州金蓋山の事例を中心に," in Sunayama Minoru 砂山稔 et al. (eds.), *Kōza Dōkyō daiichikan: Dōkyō no kamigami to kyōten* 講座道教弟一巻:道教の神々と経典. Tokyo: Yūzan kaku, 1999, pp. 242–64.

Mori Yuria 森由利亞. "Shinchō Zenshinkyō no denkai to Ryoso fukei shinkō: Tensenkai no seiritsu wo megutte 清朝全眞教の傳戒と呂祖扶乩信仰—天仙戒の成立をめぐって," in Fukui Fumimasa hakushi koki/taishoku kinen ronshū kankōkai 福井文雅博士古稀・退職記念論集刊行会 (ed.), *Ajia bunka no shisō to girei* アジア文化の思想と儀禮. Tokyo: Shunjūsha, 2005, pp. 441–61.

Mori Yuria 森由利亞. "Shō Yoho no Ryoso fukei shinkō to Zenshinkyō 蔣予蒲の呂祖扶乩信仰と全眞教——『清微宏範道門功課』の成立をめぐって," in Horiike Nobuo 堀池信夫, Sunayama Minoru 砂山稔 (eds.), *Dōkyō kenkyū no saisentan* 道教研究の最先端. Tokyo: Taiga Shobō, 2006, pp. 82–108.

Mori Yuria 森由利亞. "Zenshinkyō Ryūmonha keifu kō 全眞教龍門派系譜考—『金蓋心燈』に記された龍門派の系譜に關する問題點について」道教文化研究會編," in Dōkyō bunka kenkyūkai 道教文化研究会 (ed.), *Dōkyō bunka e no tenbō* 道教文化への展望. Tokyo: Hirakawa, 1994, pp. 180–211.

Qing Xitai 卿希泰, ed. *Zhongguo daojiao shi* 中國道教史, vol. 4. Chengdu: Sichuan renmin chubanshe, 1995.

Qiu Shouming 丘壽銘. "Daojiao Huzhou Yunchao Chunyanggong 道教湖州雲巢純陽宮," in Zhejiang sheng zhengxie wenshi ziliao weiyuanhui 浙江省政協文史資料委員會 (ed.), *Zhejiang wenshi jicui* 浙江文史集粹, vol. 7, *Shehui minqing juan* 社會民情卷. Hangzhou: Zhejiang renmin chubanshe, 1996, pp. 116–23.

Scott, Gregory Adam. "The Buddhist Nationalism of Dai Jitao," *Journal of Chinese Religions*, 39(1), 2011, pp. 55–81.

Shiga Ichiko 志賀市子. "Difang daojiao zhi xingcheng: Guangdong diqu fuluan jieshe yundong zhi xingqi yu yanbian (1838–1953) 地方道教之形成: 廣東地區扶鸞結社運動之興起與演變," *Daoism: Religion, History and Society*, 2, 2010, pp. 231–67.

Shiga Ichiko 志賀市子. *Kindai Chūgoku no shāmanizumu to dōkyō: Honkon no dōtan to fūkei shinkō* 近代中国のシャーマニズムと道教: 香港の道壇と扶乩信仰. Tokyo: Bensei shuppan, 1999.

Shiga Ichiko 志賀市子. "Mingokuki Kōshū no dōkyōkei zendō: Shōkyū sōdō no katsudō, jigyō, to sono hensen 民國期廣州の道教系善堂--省躬草堂の活動,事業とその變遷," *Chūgoku – shakai to bunka* 中國- 社會と文化, 21, 2007, pp. 148–64.

Tao Jin 陶金. "Suzhou *Dadong wushang jiuji tianxian chuanjie keyi* chutan: Yi ge Qingdai Beijing yu Jiangnan wenren jitan jiaohu yingxiang de anli 蘇州『大洞無上九極天仙傳戒科儀』初探——一個清代北京與江南文人乩壇交互影響的案例," *Daoism: Religion, History and Society*, 5, 2013, pp. 111–41.

Tao Shuimu 陶水木. "Beiyang zhengfu shiqi lü Hu-Zhe shang de cishan huodong 北洋政府時期旅滬浙商的慈善活動," *Zhejiang shehui kexue* 浙江社會科學, 11, 2005, pp. 117–83.

Valussi, Elena. "Female Alchemy and Paratext: How to Read *nüdan* in a Historical Context," *Asia Major*, 3rd series, 21(2), 2008, pp. 153–93.

Valussi, Elena. "Men and Women in He Longxiang's *Nüdan hebian*," *Nan Nü – Men Women and Gender in China*, 10(2), 2008, pp. 242–78 (Special issue on "Women, Gender and Religion in Premodern China").

Wang Chien-ch'uan 王見川. "Qingdai de Lüzu xinyang yu fuji – yi Jiaqing huangdi cifeng wei kaocha zhongxin 清代的呂祖信仰與扶乩——以嘉慶皇帝賜封為考察中心," *Mazu yu minjian xinyang: yanjiu tongxun* 媽祖與民間信仰: 研究通訊, 4, 2013, pp. 28–39.

Wang Chien-ch'uan 王見川. "Qingmo Minchu Zhongguo de Jigong xinyang yu fuji tuanti: jiantan Zhongguo Jishenghui de youlai 清末民初中國的濟公信仰與扶乩團體-兼談中國濟生會的由來," *Min-su ch'ü-i* 民俗曲藝, 162, 2008, pp. 139–67.

Wang Zongyao 王宗耀. *Huzhou Jin'gaishan gu Meihuaguan zhi* 湖州金蓋山古梅花觀志. Privately printed, 2003.

Wang Zongyu 王宗昱. "Wuxing Quanzhendao shiliao 吳興全真道史料," in Poul Andersen & Florian Reiter (eds.), *Scriptures, Schools and Forms of Practice in Daoism: A Berlin Symposium*. Wiesbaden: Harrassowitz, 2005, pp. 215–32.

Wu Yakui 吳亞魁, comp.: *Jiangnan daojiao beiji ziliaoji* 江南道教碑記資料集. Shanghai: Shanghai cishu chubanshe, 2007.

Wu Yakui 吳亞魁. *Jiangnan Quanzhen daojiao* 江南全真道教. Hong Kong: Zhonghua shuju, 2006. Expanded edition: Shanghai: Shanghai guji chubanshe, 2012.

Wu Yakui 吳亞魁. "Lun Qingmo Minchu de Jiangnan Quanzhendao 'tan' – yi Haishang 'Jueyun' wei zhongxin 論清末民初的江南全真道壇 – 以海上覺雲為中心," *Paper for the international conference "Quanzhen Daoism in Modern Chinese Society and Culture*," UC Berkeley, November 2–3, 2007.

Xu Dishan (Hsü Ti-shan) 許地山. *Fuji mixin de yanjiu* 扶乩迷信的研究. Changsha: Shangwu yinshuguan, 1941.

Xu Wei 許蔚. "Wenben liuchuan yu keyi pinjie – *Taishang Lingbao Jingming daoyuan zhengyinjing* de zai faxian 文本流傳與科儀拼接——《太上靈寶淨明道元正印經》的再發現," *Quanzhendao yanjiu* 全真道研究, 8, 2019, pp. 151–79.

Yau Chi-on (You Zi'an) 游子安. *Shan yu ren tong: Ming Qing yilai de cishan yu jiaohua* 善與人同: 明清以來的慈善與教化. Beijing: Zhonghua shuju, 2005.

Zhao Jiazhu 趙嘉珠, comp. *Zhongguo huidaomen shiliao jicheng: jinbainian lai huidaomen de zuzhi yu fenbu* 中國會道門史料集成: 近百年來會道門的組織與分布. Beijing: Zhongguo shehui kexue chubanshe, 2004.

Zhou Yangbo 周揚波. *Cong shizu dao shenzu: Tang yihou Wuxing Shen shi zongzu de bianqian* 從士族到紳族: 唐以後吳興沈氏宗族的變遷. Hangzhou: Zhejiang daxue chubanshe, 2009.

Zhu Mingchuan 朱明川. "Qingmo yilai de Guandi shengge yundong – jiantan daojiao Jingmingpai zai jindai de fazhan 清末以來的關帝升格運動 – 兼談道教淨明派在近代的發展," in Wang Chien-ch'uan 王見川, ed., *Lishi, yishu yu Taiwan renwen luncong* 歷史、藝術與台灣人文論叢, vol. 14. Taipei: Boyang, 2016, pp. 209–27.

4   The Dao in the Southern Seas

The diffusion of the Lüzu cult from Meizhou to Bangkok

Yau Chi-on 游子安[1]

During the first half of the twentieth century, many Cantonese people who migrated to Hong Kong, Macau, Thailand, Vietnam, and other places in Southeast Asia brought along with them the Lüzu 呂祖 cult,[2] in which they were initiates as members of spirit-writing halls, *daotang* 道堂 back home.[3] One such case is the Lüdimiao 呂帝廟, founded in 1887 in Meizhou 梅州, northeastern Guangdong. Barely ten years after it was established, Hakka devotees from the temple had already founded a branch in Thailand, thus illustrating the well-known pattern that "even before they set up a community hall, Chinese migrants first build a temple" (未有會館先有神廟). Indeed, the Hakka association in Thailand 客屬總會 was first housed in the Bangkok Lüzu temple before it built its own premises. During the following decades, the Lüzu spirit-writing halls prospered and multiplied in Thailand, while their ancestral temple 祖廟 in Meizhou was falling prey to the revolution, closing down in 1966, only to revive in the mid-1980s with the strong support of the Thai-Chinese and other migrant communities.

This chapter tells the story of this network of temples, based on both fieldwork and a long-term research on the diffusion of the Lüzu cult in Southeast Asia. My attention was first drawn to the Lüzu temple in Meizhou by its photograph inserted in Li Yangzheng's essay on contemporary Daoism.[4] I first visited it in 2000 and published a preliminary field report on the temple.[5] I have since then, through repeated visits, accumulated relevant primary material, including stele inscriptions either copied into local gazetteers[6] and epigraphical collections[7] or still extant on-site, such as the 1897 *Fuyou dijun miao bei* 孚佑帝君廟碑 at Meizhou and the 1992 *Lüdimiao chongjian beiji* 呂帝廟重建碑記 in Bangkok.

I have also collected scriptures and spirit-writing texts produced by the cult, such as the scriptures revealed by Lüzu and other deities and printed by the Bangkok temple: *Lüzu duren zhenjing* 呂祖度人真經, a volume combining *Lüzu zhenjing* 呂祖真經, *Hezu daxian duren zhenjing* 何祖大仙渡人真經, and *Cankui zushi zhenjing* 慚愧祖師真經. Collections of spirit-writing texts include the *Shantou Zanhuagong huixinlu* 汕頭贊化宮回心錄 and *Meixian Zanhuashe baoxun* 梅縣贊化社寶訓, both dating from the 1930s and 1940s, and two collections of texts revealed at the Bangkok temple.[8] The latter are key material for the study of both medical services provided by the Bangkok temple, and the support provided by the Lüzu devotees in Thailand toward the temple in Meizhou. A related source is the oracle slips 籤文 used in both the Meizhou and the Bangkok temples and two print editions of related oracles: the *Baxian zushi lingqian* 八仙祖師靈簽 (printed 1991), and the *Lüzu qian* 呂祖簽.[9] The two temples have also published substantial brochures.[10] Last but not the least, I have done field-work in Bangkok in 2007 and 2010, and conducted extensive field investigations on Daoist temples in the Meizhou area in 2008 and 2009.

The Lüzu temple in Meizhou, 1887–1940

Meizhou 梅州 is located in northeastern Guangdong province, in the Mei river valley 梅江 that is crisscrossed by waterways. It was established as Jingzhou 敬州 under the Han, renamed Meizhou in 971, put under Chaozhou prefecture 潮州府 under the Ming and made the seat of an independent prefecture, named Jiaying 嘉應州, during the Jiaqing period. In 1912, it was renamed Meixian 梅縣, and in 1988, it was upgraded to a municipality 梅州市 with authority over the city itself (called Meijiang ward 梅江區) and six rural counties, with a total population of just over 5 million in 2008. Meizhou is famous for being a Hakka heartland, and was a key point of departure for Hakka out-migration from the Ming onward, hence the nickname of "Land of overseas Chinese." Buddhism is very much present throughout Meizhou, with ancient major mon-asteries such as the Lingguangsi 靈光寺 built in 868; among the 190 places of religious activity officially registered by 1990, 93 were Buddhist and only 1 was Daoist: the Zanhuagong 贊化宮, which was the new name of the Lüdimiao when it was rebuilt in 1985.[11] As of 2011, the Zanhuagong is the largest Daoist temple in the whole municipality and the seat of the Meijiang branch of the Daoist Association.

Spirit-writing altars devoted to the worship of Lüzu 呂祖道壇 appeared in Meizhou as early as the Qianlong period, when locals established an Altar for Immortal Lüzu 呂仙壇 on the Zijinshan 紫金山 hill in downtown Meizhou. There they set up a free clinic, giving drugs to the local poor.[12] During the Guangxu period, a Lüzu temple was built just down the hill. The vibrant Lüzu cult in Meizhou was not limited to this one place, as other altars and temples were built during the same period, including those built by Zhang Gongxia 張公俠 in the city's suburbs (at 大浪口羅屋) and by Zeng Hannan 曾漢南 in Changsha village 長沙堡.[13]

According to the Guangxu-period gazetteer, the Lüdi temple was built in 1887 by the general of the local garrison Li Peng 李鵬 and the prefect Jin Guixin 金桂馨; it was described as located next to the garrison's headquarters and having used disaffected barracks.[14] This gazetteer's map confirms the Lüdimiao's prox-imity to the military headquarters and also to the City God temple 城隍廟, and locates other major temples such as the Wenchang temple to the north and the Guandi temple to the northeast.[15] Nowadays, the temple has a main shrine devoted to Lüzu, and a courtyard to the left with a hall for performing rituals; the wall in front of this hall still has two stele inscriptions, one carrying the temple name 呂帝廟, erected in 1888 by Li Peng, and the other, the *Fuyou dijun miao bei*, composed in 1897 by the Changle county magistrate of Jiang Mingqing 蔣鳴慶.[16] The following extract comes from the stele inscription:

> It is said that while a hero displaying a vast Confucian erudition can be compared to Zhang Liang (Liuhou), an Immortal sharing the same erudition can only be Emperor Lü (Lüdi). ... And public figures in Meizhou have shown exceptional devotion in their worship of Lüdi. In the 13th year of Emperor Guangxu (1887), former prefect Jin Guixin and former general Li Peng led a campaign among the local gentry to rebuild a temple to honor Lüzu at the foot of Zijin Mountain, a project completed within just over a year. ... In the year *yiwei* (1895), a drought had affected the county in the third month of Spring, but prayers for rain had brought gentle downfalls; some other time in Autumn, bandits wrought havoc in the country and this time spirits had been invoked to pacify the region. In the 8th month of the year *bingshen* (1896), panic had struck the area another time but the spirits had once again promptly restored peace. "Absolute sincerity allows us to know things in advance and this is normal and expected." The deity's omnipresent soul can then be invoked, and only sensitiveness is required for communication with it. Prominent worshippers in Meizhou were pious souls deeply grateful for the deity's efforts to ward off evils and calamities. Consequently, as a gesture of acknowledgement of the deity's virtues and achievements, they did not use Tao Hongjing's 陶弘景 swords, neither did they recite Ge Hong 葛洪's alchemical formulae. Instead, it is said that through perfect knowledge of Lüzu's life, they had come to venerate Him. Upon his promotion as prefect, Jiang Mingqing and another Meizhou worthy, Zhai Yiyan, came to the temple for sacrifices and prayers.
>
> Meizhou's worthies requested this message to be engraved on a stele as nothing short of that would have been true to the occasion. Noted with deep devotion.
>
> Composed in the Spring of the 23rd year of Emperor Guangxu's reign by Jiang Mingqing, government sub-prefect and senior provincial government official and Changle County magistrate. [17]

This inscription was thus composed ten years after the temple was established, in response to the deity's help in safeguarding the local population from a disaster.

During the late Qing and early Republican period, Daoism in Guangdong counted a number of prominent temples, such as the monasteries on Luofushan 羅浮山, the Yunquan xianguan 雲泉仙舘 at Xijiaoshan 西樵山, or the Chunyangguan 純陽觀 in downtown Guangzhou, but it was largely dominated, especially in the areas of Guangzhou and Meizhou, by large numbers of lay Daoist charitable halls 善堂 or 善社. Many of them were devoted to the cult of Lüzu, like the Guanghua shantang 廣化善堂 in Guangzhou (founded during the late Qing) or the Zhongguo daojiao Zhibaotai Cishanhui (planned in 1937, established in 1944).[18] A census of 44 Guangdong counties conducted in 1932 listed no less than 228 active charities, 114 of which were primarily medical.[19] According to the 1942 *Guangdong nianjian* 廣東年鑑, the charitable halls were a mainstay of Daoism in the province:

> Daoism in Guangdong is organized along different types of institutions. Besides the monasteries, a major type is the charitable hall. These halls have all the organizational features of a religious group, but take charity and saving the world as their primary goal. Most of them worship deities such as Taishang laojun 太上老君, Lüzu, Guan Yu, or Sun Wukong. Their members are largely middle-class men and women, as well as rich merchants and businessmen. They are bound to engage in both charity and self-cultivation, practicing the Confucian ideal of self-perfection: thus, halls' rules impose on members the eight virtues of filial piety, brotherly love, loyalty, trustworthiness, propriety, sense of justice, honesty and sense of shame. … They also engage in all kinds of charitable endeavors, and print morality books, of which there exist a great many, including *Xiuqiao zhenglu* 修橋整路, *Rude zhimen* 入德之門, *Xuling baofa* 虛靈寶筏, and *Puji jinyu liangyan* 普濟金玉良言. These books circulate in very large numbers among the population, and they impact social life to a considerable extent.[20]

The Lüzu temple in Meizhou and the Zanhuashe 贊化社 (Society for Extolling Moral Improvement) hall that formed around it are an excellent case study of this widespread movement of charities built on the Lüzu cult that developed in the Cantonese world from the late Qing to the present. The Zanhuashe was mostly devoted to medical charity and to giving coffins to the needy; its funds were collected among both local and overseas donors.[21]

The Lüzu temple was first established as a Lüzu spirit-writing hall but after 50 years of gradual development, and under the impetus of temple leaders such as Zhang Gongjian 章公釗, Chen Changsheng 陳暢盛, and Zeng Hannan 曾漢南, it grew into a large, full-fledged charity. In 1940, Zhang and Chen merged the temple and a separate charity, the Guangji shantang 廣濟善堂,[22] and the result of the merger was named Zanhuashe. The following year, they established a primary school 廣濟小學 for poor children on the temple's premises, near the temple's free clinic. Members of the branch temple in Bangkok regularly collected donations to support these charitable projects in their ancestral home. At the same time, the board of the Zanhuashe was collecting and publishing the *Meixian Zanhuashe baoxun*, the anthology of essays and poems revealed by Lüzu and other deities in the temple between 1940 and 1943. The 1943 preface of this work reminded readers how the group was focused on helping society through charity:

> The whole project of the Zanhuashe, in one word, is to cherish and help all human beings, and to humanely dispel ignorance. … In our age, disasters have become increasingly frequent and victims are ever more numerous. The poor and the sick, carrying their old parents and their children, come in ever larger numbers; the corpses of those who died because of famines, draughts and epidemics are all around. We therefore devote all our energy to giving

clothes, medicines, and coffins and to other charitable projects. ... That is why people in all quarters of society have praised our society as the leading charity (in Meizhou) and the one able to complement the state's social work. Besides, our society has established a free school for the benefit of the children from destitute families.[23]

In 1943, under the leadership of Chen Changsheng (president of the board of the Zanhuashe), refugees from areas occupied by the Japanese army came to Meizhou in large numbers, and the Zanhuashe distributed food and clothes. At the height of the crisis, it operated a soup kitchen for 40 days, with some 3 pounds of rice cooked every day for over a thousand refugees.[24]

In 1950, the Lüzu temple was turned by the local government into a school 金山小學校, and in 1958, the Zanhuashe moved to the building of another local charity, the Fuji shantang 福濟善堂, where it continued to offer medical charity until it was disbanded during the "Smash the Four Olds" campaign in 1966.[25] During the subsequent 20 years, the link between the Lüzu temple and its overseas affiliates were severed, but Meizhou Hakkas in Thailand still considered their Lüzu temple as a branch of the "mother temple" in Meizhou,[26] and as early as 1985 lobbied to have the temple rebuilt on a new location. Diplomatic relations were established between the PRC and Thailand in 1975, and the Daoist Association was reestablished in 1979; feeling the possibility of change, as early as 1980, 86 devotees of the Bangkok Lüdimiao formed a delegation to visit Meizhou and set up contact through diplomatic channels to pressure the Meizhou local government to rebuild their ancestral temple in Meizhou.

The foundation of the Lüdimiao in Bangkok, 1902

In 1902, less than 15 years after the Lüdimiao was established in Meizhou, local migrants had brought the cult to Thailand and established a branch Lüdimiao in the heart of the Chinese commercial district in Bangkok, at 砲台縣荳芽廊拍拋猜路.[27] The cult had traveled through the Zanhuagong in Shantou, from where statues were brought to Bangkok by migrants. The story was told by Li Wuyin 李悟因 in a 1958 preface to the *Lüzu tanxun* 呂祖壇訓:

> Chinese migrants to Thailand over the last fifty years have not yet been guided by the gods, but fortunately Zhang Bingkun 張炳堃, a scholar 庠生 then at the Zanhuagong in Shantou obtained to take along with him the statues of the Emperor (Lü) to Bangkok, where He immediately began to make miracles and answer prayers. Mr. Xu Bingzhen 徐秉珍, who had been particularly showered with divine blessings, vowed to build a temple, and raised funds among the local Chinese community, and as a result the Zanhuagong was effectively completed in 1902.[28]

A key stage in that development was thus the Zanhuagong in Shantou. This temple was built in 1899, with Lüzu as its central deity.[29] Shortly thereafter, in 1903, a charity, the Yanshou shantang 延壽善堂, was established very close by (both were on Yanshou street 延壽街, hence the name of the charity) by two brothers, Zhang Rongxuan 張榕軒 (1851–1911) and Zhang Yaoxuan 張耀軒 (1861–1921).[30] The cult flourished and drew devotees from throughout the region, expanding in southern Fujian and Guangdong. The Yanshou shantang thus became one of the five great *shantang* of Shantou.[31] Its spirit-writing revelations were collected and published as *Shantou Zanhuagong huixinlu*,[32] but its best-known feature was its medical oracle slips 藥簽, which were hailed for having cured countless patients.[33] The Bangkok Lüdimiao was built on exactly that model, on Lü's explicit request: "This Palace of mine (in Bangkok) was built by copying the layout of the Shantou Lüdimiao, as I ordered."[34] Such a close relationship was maintained in following years, as is further documented by the printing history of a scripture, the *Zhongwai pudu huangjing* 中外普度皇經, that was printed in 1927 by the Shantou temple with funds from some of its devotees such as Zhang Gongyi 張公益 and Huang Guoqi 黃國琦,[35] and shortly after reprinted by the Bangkok temple using the very same edition.[36] The Yanshou shantang had to close in 1950, but in recent years, along with other *shantang* of the Shantou area, it has been able to start anew. In 1988, the Yanshou shantang obtained from local authorities the permission to register as a charity and build new premises (not on their original location) and to worship Zhenwu and Lüzu.

As Fang Xuejia has demonstrated, the Chaozhou-Shantou area was a transitional place for people in upland Eastern Guangdong (including Meizhou) in their migration routes to Southeast Asia.[37] Hakkas in Thailand, less numerous than the Chaozhou but a sizeable minority among Thai Chinese, mostly hail from places such as Meixian, Fengshun 豐順, Dapu 大埔, Xingning 興寧, and Huizhou 惠州. Professionally, the Meixian migrants originally specialized in retailing imported goods and in clothing and leather goods.[38] One of them, Wen Yuanting 溫淵亭, was one of the founders of the Lüzumiao in Shantou; he was later invited to the Bangkok Zanhuagong as the main medium. After Shantou became a treaty port in 1860, it attracted ever more trade and passing migrants, with steamers and rice boats calling at Shantou being the main artery between mainland Guangdong and the whole of Southeast Asia. In brief, the Zanhuagong in Shantou was the font of the Lüzu cult, which spread over southeast Asia, including the major branch in Bangkok. The three temples, in Meizhou, Shantou, and Bangkok, maintained continuous exchange up to the 1949 revolution.

By the early Republican period, Hakka migrants in Bangkok had already built six temples, including the Lüdimiao, the Guandi temple (built 1915), and the Guanyin temple, all of them owned and managed by the Hakka Association (established 1909). The Lüdimiao was the largest and most active of them[39]; it was particularly active in spreading Daoist texts and practices, having published some 30 different scriptures by Lüzu and other deities over the years. The Hakka Association itself had its first headquarters in the temple, before it built its own office that it still occupies today, on 安南巷（拍柿路）.[40]

The inauguration of the temple took place on 4/1 of 1902. In 1899, Zhang Bingkun had returned from Shantou to Bangkok carrying a statue of Lüzu (a wooden sculpture more than a meter high), which he placed at the 伍廣源隆 warehouse where it attracted many devotees. He looked for a place to build a proper temple, and by 1902 had built the temple that still stands today. This, as a chronicle of the Bangkok Hakka community wrote, "is the largest, and the only Daoist building erected by our Hakka community."[41] The precise location had been decided by Lüzu through spirit-writing. A document entitled "Survey of the temple's upkeep over the past 30 years" details the temple construction process:

> Zhang Bingkun, from Zhangjiawei[42] in Meixian county, had studied at the county school dating back to the early Qing. During Emperor Guangxu's reign, in the year *dingyou* (1897), he sailed to Siam but returned to China in the year *jihai* (1899) only to return to Thailand with a statue of Lüzu in the autumn of that year. In the beginning, the statue was placed inside "Wuguang Yuanlong" warehouse but as the cult developed and prospered, the deity's statue was transferred to a room inside the shop rented by Zhang Bingkun's company. Eventually, people suggested that another site be sought and a new shrine be built as a permanent place of worship. But before this happened, the abbot of Longlian temple 龍蓮寺 (Wat Mangkon Kamalawat),[43] Great master Miao, had sent the former title deeds of the second party, a cereals factory which occupied the present temple location. Master Wu Miao waited a while then bought the property to build the temple and invoked Lüzu to establish the layout and orientation of the temple, a call to which the deity responded in detail. This is why the present temple corresponds to the deity's plans obtained through divination. ... Construction of the main hall of the temple started in 1901, more specifically on the 27th day of the 2nd month of the 27th year of Emperor Guangxu's reign. The temple was completed on the first day of the fourth month of the 28th year of Guangxu's reign (1902). The overall cost of the building amounted to 12,000 baht.[44]

Not only did Zhang Bingkun bring the statue of Lüzu to Siam but he was also a medium himself (for details of spirit-writing, see below). Besides Zhang Bingkun, a number of key figures were involved in the foundation of Lüzu temple: Wu Miaoyuan 伍淼源, Xu Bingzhen 徐秉珍, and Wen Yuanting 溫淵亭. Portraits of Zhang, Wu, and Xu can be seen hanging from a beam above the left altar of the shrine. As for the construction of the temple building itself, major contributors included Wu Miaoyuan (who donated 8,000 baht to start work), Xu Bingzhen, who also contributed 8,000 baht, Hou Youfang 侯有芳, Zhu Qingchu 朱慶初, and Liu Hebo 劉和伯.[45] Some of the disciples were deified on account of their virtues and achievements and, for the members of the cult, joined the ranks of the Immortals. A brief biography of the main protagonists is given below:

(1) Zhang Bingkun: discussed above.
(2) Wu Miaoyuan or the "City God of Siam."[46] The statue of Lüzu mentioned above was first installed at a warehouse Wu had set up in the new harbor of

Bangkok. The Wu clan was originally from Songkoubao in Meixian county but when the port of Shantou was open to trade in 1860, Wu associated with Xu Biji and other people of Chenghai to create a shipping company, "The Red Head Ships,"[47] plying the Southern Seas for a number of years before eventually settling down in Bangkok, where he made a fortune in the lumber trade. His third and fifth sons, Zuonan and Dongbai, were, respectively, chairman and director-general of the Hakka Association in Thailand and made significant contributions toward the foundation of schools, temples, and hospitals. According to spirit-writings records, Wu Miaoyuan multiplied good deeds, and because he had "founded the temple," he was promoted to the status of Siam City God after his demise. In 1925, Cheng Huanghuang, formerly a Shandong province official during the Xianfeng reign, exclaimed during a séance乩示: "God pity me, I was a government official but I did not harm the people and my sense of filial piety made me accept a post of Earth God at the Northern Gate of Chaozhou where I stayed for 8 years and was promoted to the status of City God … Guandi and Lüzu, remembering I was in this place and that I cumulated merits, ensured I was promoted to become the City God of Zhangzhou (Fujian); tomorrow I will leave this position and return. My successor is none other than Wu Miaoyuan, of Jiaying who came to Siam where he became rich through trade. Throughout his life, Wu has displayed a kind and generous heart towards people around him and this was reflected in his efforts to ease people's lives. On the very day he ascended to the Land of the Immortals, this temple was erected and the Great emperor ordered him to succeed me."[48]

(3) Xu Bingzhen: The Xu clan made generous donations and encouraged the Chinese community to support the temple's construction by contributing 8,000 baht.[49] Xu Bingzhen was exceptionally generous and initiated the temple construction project. He asked worthy members of the Chinese community to join in the philanthropic project, as a result of which the construction of Zanhuagong was completed in 1902.[50]

(4) Wen Yuanting or the Immortal Preserving the Void: According to Li Wuyin's notes, "Mediums started with Bingkun who was followed by Wen Yuanting who was himself succeeded by Qin Keyun."[51] "Immortal Preserving the Void" is Wen's posthumous title within the cult: "Immortal Preserving the Void," i.e., the honorable Wen Yuanting, a gentleman from Meixian County and the founder of Lüzu Temple at Shantou, was later asked to serve at Zanhuagong in Siam where he practiced divination for more than 10 years. He eventually passed away in the temple, as a result of which his soul ascended to the Land of the Immortals.[52]

The Hakka Association of Thailand not only presided over the construction of six temples but also oversaw the building of the Jinde School 進德學校 (in 1913), the Asian Trade Institute, along with various charities, cemeteries, and hospitals. In 1927, the association asked the Thai authorities permission to register as a legal

organization, and in 1938, it officially became the "Hakka Association in Thailand."
In the meantime, all the schools, charities, and temples set up by prominent Hakka
members were gradually placed under the jurisdiction of the Hakka association. The
Thai government issued regulations for the custody of the temples and ever since
that date, the Lüdi temple has been administered by supervisors and custodians:

> Concerning the temples built under the auspices of the association, the
> Siamese authorities specified conservation rules in 1920. They ruled that
> temples, as public property, should be maintained by the government and
> protected from trespassers. At first, worthies of our community did not really
> grasp the meaning of these rules and it was not until 1930 that the associa-
> tion named a supervisor and five custodians and asked to be registered with
> the Thai authorities. From then on, the charges of supervisors and custodians
> have been consistently occupied by worthies of our community. In addition,
> custodians are regularly called for meetings to discuss improvements to tem-
> ple buildings.[53]

Custodians 保管 are responsible for temple management and are therefore carefully selected among worthies of the community so as to avoid any power loss to
others:

> After the Chinese Republic was established, the temple started to include med-
> ical facilities in order to combat local calamities and illnesses. The move was
> of course welcome by the Overseas Chinese community! Temple affairs were
> successfully managed by Messrs Xu Ziting 徐子亭, Liang Xinglou 梁星樓,
> Ye Yunfang 葉雲舫, etc. In 1930, Wen Yuanxing 溫醒民 was designated as
> the supervisor while Messrs Xiong Youlin 熊幼霖, Chen Yunsheng 陳雲生,
> Chen Shusun 陳澍蓀 and Jiang Faxiang 江發祥 were named custodians.[54]

Li Guokui 李國奎 was named chairman emeritus of the "preparatory committee for the rebuilding of the ancestral Lüzu temple" in 1980 in Meizhou. He had
previously been appointed as a custodian in Bangkok's Lüzu temple in 1977.[55]

   Lüzu temple's popularity was closely related to the medical prescriptions and
medicines it provided. Charity boxes were placed inside the temple and the pro-
ceeds were used to set up "charities in action" to dispense medicines to the sick.
In 1925, a preface revealed by Divine Lord Wang Lingguan 靈官王天君 reads
as follows:

> I am pleased to write a few words tonight for this preface to celebrate the
> birth of this charity. On this day of the fourth month of the year *yichou*, 14th
> year of the Chinese Republic, as we celebrated the birth and life of Emperor
> Lü, the deity did us the honor of making the following pronouncement: "all
> masters' good deeds are precious and concrete actions and I command you
> disciples to set up active charities and dispense medicines to come to the
> sick's rescue."[56]

In the evening of the 15th day of the 4th month of the year *yiwei* (1955), Immortal Lüzu was invoked for the careful selection of medicinal plants used in decoctions to cure people:

> Why is this temple a cause for joy? Our medical facility can bring a few benefits to people but medicinal herbs in this day and age are often mixed with the wrong kinds of herbs. Therefore, those who prepare medicines must operate with extreme care to avoid harming people with the wrong drugs. Medicinal herbs must be selected among the best varieties and this is why experience is needed and no detail should be overlooked. If this can be done seriously, according to seasons, due merit should be rewarded; old herb collectors should painstakingly cut and weigh their selection, not overlook any detail and avoid thinking that whatever the herbs they have selected, their reward will be the same.[57]

In 1989, at the peak of its popularity, the Lüzu temple was destroyed by fire and was deserted for some time thereafter. The Hakka association in Thailand then encouraged the faithful, the Hakka community and the devotees to rebuild the shrine. The stele *Lüdimiao chongjian beiji* placed inside shrine in 1992 reads as follows:

> Lüzu temple is located in Paipaocai Lane in Bangkok. It was originally built in 1902 and covers a surface of 97 sq. *wa*. Always celebrated for its prestige, the shrine has consistently attracted significant crowds of believers throughout its 90 years' existence.
>
> On February 24th of 1989 (8th day of the first lunar month), the temple was ravaged by fire while in its heyday. In the following year, the 32nd meeting of the council of the Hakka Association in Thailand passed a resolution to rebuild the shrine. The council chairman, Mr. Qiu Pingyuan 丘平遠, donated 1 million baht for the project and the head of the reconstruction committee, Mr. Chen Huasheng, contributed the same amount. Other donators included Ms Wu Liangxiang (2 million baht) and Messrs Luo Guanghua (1 million baht) and Xiao Jianbo (1 million baht). ... Devotees generously contributed and the call for help was heard in all places. The resulting proceeds amounted to more than 20 million baht. Consequently, the reconstruction project was completed in the autumn of 1992.
>
> (Written in the autumn of 1992 by Lu Junyuan and calligraphied by Wen Xianglin)

Among the donators, "Patriarch Dafeng's 大峯祖師 followers contributed 120 000 baht" and "Patriarch Dafeng's followers contributed 450 000 bath towards the temple's lamps." Dafeng (?–1127) had lived during the Northern Song dynasty (Huizong's Xuanhe reign) but in the late Qing period, he was venerated as a Benevolent deity "善神," and numerous charity halls were dedicated to Dafeng's worship, such as the "Preservation of the Heart" charity hall in Shantou. At the end of the nineteenth century, Dafeng's cult spread from Chaoshan to Thailand where, in 1910, overseas Chinese founded the Baode shantang charity in which his "holy portrait" was worshipped. This would later become a major popular charity organization.[58] The popularity of Lüzu temples may be compared to that of Dafeng temples:

> Overseas Chinese in Thailand worship many deities and before the 3rd day of the first month of each lunar year, endless crowds of worshippers flock to temples, the most popular being Zhengwang temples 鄭王廟, Sanbaogong 三保公廟 (Zheng He) temples, Lüzu temples and Dafeng's temples.[59]

According to the author's observations, Bangkok's Zanhuagong temple gates feature a horizontal tablet with the inscription "Lüzu temple" in both Chinese and Thai along with the following couplets: "Walking along the Pure Way, the Yang Enlightens the Honest Heart." Inside the temple, the first story is dedicated to the cults of Guanyin, the God of Wealth and the Buddha of wealth and honors. The second floor includes a Front Hall dedicated to Emperor Lü's worship, with an altar to the left dedicated to Laozi and one to the right, in "Wusheng" Hall, reserved for Jiang Ziya's cult. Wang Lingguan and Zhou Tianjun are found facing Lüzu's statue, while cults to the Three Teachings, Confucius, Buddha and Laozi, the True Immortals, and the Eight Immortals are rendered right and left of Lüzu's statue. On the second floor, the Rear Hall features altars for the worship of the Queen Mother of the West, the Earth God, and the Eighteen Arhats. The third floor is dedicated to the cult of the Ancestral Buddha, while the top floor houses an altar for the worship of the Jade Emperor. Situated to the front and left-hand side of the Front Hall is a pharmacy room featuring a drugs counter and a "List of fame of those devotees who donated money for the medical unit." It is easy to see that all deities are worshipped inside the temple and, as noted in "The annals of Thai Chinese": "if the Hakkas' Lüzu temple is theoretically a Daoist shrine, many other cults are rendered inside it."[60]

The Lüzu temple has consistently played a pivotal role in the promotion of the public good. According to a report in the *Sing Sian Yit Pao* daily, the temple stages yearly ceremonies for the deceased souls' rest during which chants are sung for three days and help is handed out to the poor in the form of white rice donations and distributions of students' equipment to schools and hospitals.[61] Because it had been well managed over a long period and its good actions had been widely praised and recognized, the Lüzu temple was awarded a citation as a "Model temple" by the Thai interior ministry's administrative bureau in 1993.[62] On December 8, 2006, the Thai crown prince and princess "visited" the temple, where they knelt down before Lüzu's statue.[63] The reconstruction of the Lüzu temple in Meixian in the 1980s was further considered as a work of considerable merit.

Medical oracles, spirit-writing and the diffusion of the Lüzu cult

The Lüzu temples in both Meizhou and Bangkok faced similar disasters in their history and had to close down: one was disbanded, while the other was ravaged by fire. But both were restored and their services resumed as before. This renaissance was undoubtedly related to their long-standing traditions of spirit-writing, medical treatment, and benevolent actions – Yanshou charity hall in Shantou was equally restored almost 20 years ago. The 1950s was a period when "crowds came looking for cures and were exceptionally rewarded," a time when "Immortals' potions and medicines healed many who then converted to Daoism, leading more to do likewise," as illustrated in these lines of praise.

In modern China, the role of the Lüzu cult has evolved alongside changes in people's interests and demands but one of the reasons why it has retained such a powerful attraction is the way it places compassion at the center of adepts' self-cultivation, according to Lüzu's vow to reach immortality only after salvation is provided to all living creatures. Close contacts are maintained with the people whenever and wherever possible and the immortals believed to cure devotees with divine drugs are venerated. But why is faith in Lüzu so popular in Guangdong? A major reason is that the "Cinnabar cure saving the world" features prominently among the "efficacious" responses offered in Lüzu temples. Thus, the text *Lüzu jingshiwen* 呂祖警世文, "Lüzu warns the world," mentions the efficacy of Emperor Lü in the Sanyuangong 三元宮, one of the major temples in Canton: "Lüzu's flying phoenix manifests itself, and His pure spirit often pervades the temple; and the Sanyuangong Lüzu temple in Eastern Guangdong is endowed with special efficacy."[64] According to what the English missionary John Henry Gray, a long-time resident in Canton, said in 1870, "the Lüzu hall within the Sanyuangong temple features, in a central position, a large vat filled with water and it is said that herbal medicine teas obtained using water from this vat are especially effective."[65] As for Macao's Lüzu temple, whose construction was completed in 1891, a horizontal inscription placed inside the building proclaims "Heal Our Chronic Diseases," a powerful indicator of the protection offered by the deity to the people.[66] The Lüzu cult in and around Guangzhou has been especially vibrant since the mid-Qing and this can only be related to the fame the Lüzu temples gained as providers of medical prescription slips. Among these temples, the Yunquan Hall of the Immortals in Xiqiaoshan is famous for its medical oracles whose "effect is constant" and "rarely failing":

Among those who pray to the Immortals and ask for medicine, many choose to request favors from the Patriarch Lü Chunyang and Baiyundong 白雲洞 Temple in Xijiaoshan is especially famous in this respect. In Huadai, in the provincial capital, a cult is rendered to a sole divinity, i.e. Wang Fangping 王方平 (or rather Huang Chuping 黃初平), the Great Immortal Wang implored by all those who wish to be cured and whose effectiveness is often remarkable. Therefore, this temple has also attracted a great number of officials and doctors. The medical prescription slips offered in Baiyundong temple are quite "stable": each prescription includes 1 / 2 to 4/5 measures with each measure limited to 4/5 *fen* (1/2 grams) to 4/5 *qian* (5 grams). The medical slips also involve a number of specialties: andrology, gynecology, pediatrics and ophthalmology. Prescriptions do not depart from tradition and medical doses are measured: as a result, illnesses are gradually cured and the medicines only very rarely fail to have an effect. People will sometimes ask for three slips in advance but no quack remedy recommending "cold" or "hot" treatment is given here. The oracles prove effective and are by no means accidentally operative. [67]

The temple of the Great Immortal Huang in Huadai (Canton) has locally gained fame because of the medical slips provided by the immortal.[68] The popularity of Lüzu's places of worship is not restricted to Canton or Fujian: it also concerns temples in northeastern China and this general phenomenon cannot be separated from the efficacious prescriptions offered by the Immortal. The Taiqinggong 太清宫 temple in Shenyang (Liaoning province) was first built under Kangxi's reign (the place changed its name in 1779) and the medical oracle slips performed by Lüzu there are equally famous. It was in the 1930s that a cult to Emperor Lü was introduced in the upper floor of the eastern building of the temple and the practice was known as "Taiqinggong temple's Lüzu oracle slips." There worshippers would be guided and eventually stood waiting to get access to the upper floor for a "medical consultation." Separate inquiries and medical prescription slips would then be offered among one of the following specialties: andrology, gynecology, pediatrics, surgery, and ophthalmology.[69]

(1) Medical prescription slips and the cult in Lüzu temples

Zanhuagong temples in Meizhou, Shantou, and Bangkok all offer facilities for Lüzu's medical oracles, a practice inherited from a tradition prevailing in Lüzu temples since the Qing dynasty. Medical prescription slips are divided into five major departments, i.e., andrology, gynecology, pediatrics, ophthalmology, and surgery. A total of 100 slips are reserved for the first three specialties, 73 for ophthalmology, and 50 for surgery. Besides offering believers the possibility of drawing divination sticks for the five medical specialties, Bangkok's Lüzu temple also features "Lüzu miraculous slips" written in both Chinese and Thai. In 1985, the Zanhuagong reopened in Meizhou as a major center of religious activities. A room inside the temple is again dedicated to the manufacture of drugs and its own pills, which are freely distributed to devotees. The manual listing medical slip prescriptions has been sent over from Bangkok, and it is said that this book had originally been in use at Meizhou temple, so that it has now "returned home." Besides offering medical oracle slips, Meizhou's Zanhuagong also has doctors giving consultations on its premises. In recent years, a doctor, Xiao, was posted to the health station of Dongxiang, close to Lüzu temple, where he had practiced for some time: therefore, believers asking for Lüzu's immortal prescriptions on the temple premises may then head toward the health station to get their prescription.

The popularity of the Lüzu temple in Meizhou is due to its famous medical oracle slips: since the Qing dynasty, the shrine has offered devotees the possibility of drawing medical prescription slips, asking medical advice and taking medicinal herbs. A Republican-period poem offers the following description:

> Prescriptions are kept ordinary and never purposely uncanny,
> "cold" or "hot" treatment is only suited to people's needs.
> North of the city, requests made to Emperor Lü are answered,
> not a penny is spent there though the cure is better than at the doctor's.

The commentary notes that at Lüzu's altar on the upper floor of the temple north of the city, it is said that the statue of the Immortal was brought back from abroad by Mr. Xiao, a man from Guanjingtou 官井頭 district in town and he adds that the cult is thriving. The altar features three baskets for medical slips, one for surgery, another one for internal medicine and the last one for ophthalmology. The sick go there to seek prescriptions and they are regularly satisfied.

All prescriptions are kept simple and harsh medicines are excluded: even if they may be wrong, they are never harmful. Many superstitious souls flock there to pray and make requests.[70]

It is worth noting here that this passage mentions that there are only three medical departments, i.e., surgery, internal medicine, and ophthalmology. In addition, the passage alludes to the reliable medical properties of the "Immortal's prescriptions."

The Bangkok temple operated along the same lines. The predecessor of Chongzheng Hospital currently managed by the Hakka Association in Thailand was the free medical facility of Lüzu temple. In 1924, Emperor Lü's temple in Bangkok established a unit offering free medical advice and dispensing medicines, which was later named "Emperor Lü's pharmacy 呂大帝藥方"[71]:

> Among the six temples (managed by the Hakka association), the Lüzu temple is the largest and includes facilities for spirit-writing. In 1924, Lüzu expressed His will, through spirit-writing, to have a facility for medical oracles and the distribution of medicines established on the temple premises. Devotees cursed by incurable diseases could therefore go and seek medical advice at the Lüzu temple: they took drugs according to the prescription slips and the effects were magical. This explains why attendance at the temple was ever growing and the average number of prescribed doses reached more than 10,000 annually.[72]

For 1958 alone, Lüzu temple dispensed a total of 16,342 medical doses and in 1966, the number totaled 13,655 doses.[73] In 1977, the annual number of medical doses distributed reached 16,705. Concerning the establishment, within Lüzu temple, of an "active charity" designed to dispense drugs and cure believers, the Medicine King Immortal 藥王仙師 was conjured up in the evening of 4/14, 1925, and offered the following revelation:

Emperor Lü has urged me to offer free prescriptions to be used by the "active charity" to help those in need. Today, I gathered ingredients for a prescription to cure stomach ache. I fried 2 *liang* (50 g) of 紫香, 1 *liang* of rhizoma acori graminei, 3 *qian* of costus root, 1 *liang* of white peony root and I ground the whole into powder. 1 *qian* of the medicine is to be taken each time. I deeply wish that this charity be set up as scholars would leap for joy and this would amount to a most tangible charitable gesture. The ensuing merits would not be small indeed![74]

Besides medical prescription slips, before 1990, Lüzu immortals frequently transmitted to their disciples personal prescriptions via spirit-writing. In 1984, Liu the Perfected 柳真人 thus proclaimed:

Rao Chunhua 饒春華 (female disciple), you are affected by exogenous typhoid fever. I, the Immortal, give you this prescription (gynecology, #38) and you will soon be cured.

Luo Mojia 羅莫家 (devotee), your ailment is due to a renal calculus. I, the Immortal, give you this prescription (andrology, #28). First take a cup of boiled water with Lysimachia Christinae, mix it with honey and wait for an hour before taking the prescribed medicine. You will soon be cured.[75]

It was in 1939 that on the basis of the Lüzu temple experience the Hakka Association in Thailand decided to offer free medical services in other locations and this is how it founded a hospital under its management in 1949.

Among Lüzu's various sets of medical prescription slips, the *Boji xianfang* 博濟仙方 or "Extensive Help Divine recipes" are highly representative prescriptions which are included in Sakai Tadao's compilation of divination and medical oracle slips.[76] The present version of *Boji xiangfang* is mostly based on the 1918 edition of the Shoujingtang 守經堂 in Guangzhou.[77] The book contains a preface "respectfully written by the disciple Li Qixiu 黎琦修" and the name of the contributor to its publication, Chen Shaoxiu, disciple of the Great Harmony Grotto 太和洞弟子陳紹修. In its foreword, Li Qixiu says:

Emperor Lü's spirit descended on the Western Accumulated Benevolence Altar in Guangdong's eastern city. Having once consigned His recipes (for five medical specialties) to the northern provinces, He brought 300 slips to Southern China. Since the eastern Guangdong province is closely linked to the Dipper and Ox constellations, it is unique among Chinese provinces and this is why the preparation and use of prescriptions is also different: caution is needed when using drugs, as if armies were to be positioned. ... It was Lüzu who, using His teachings of deities and spirits, wished people to exert self-restrain and cultivate morality, set out together on the road to benevolence, leaving suffering behind, saving the world, His succoring heart reaching all places, however small, His saving virtue extending to each and all.

Indeed, as far as Emperor Lü's prescriptions are concerned, variations are observed according to geography and medicinal plant selection and applications obey to local customs and medical traditions.[78] My opinion is that variations in medical prescription slips according to book versions and compilation dates cannot be overlooked either.[79] In Taiwan, the work is often known under the title "Lüzu's immortal prescriptions." Song Jinxiu has provided the Sanxing Baoangong temple 三星保安宮 (built around 1890 and dedicated to Baosheng dadi's 保生大帝 cult) in the Yilan area in Taiwan with an appendix of prescription slips (gynecology) and proclaims that it had the same origins as the *Boji xianfang*. Furthermore, he considers that Lüzu's immortal prescriptions "must be a widespread and long-standing system of prescription slips in Guangdong, Hong-Kong and Taiwan."[80] I have ascertained the existence of the following versions of "Lüzu's prescriptions" in Guangdong province.

Table 4.1 shows that the Andrology, Gynecology, and Pediatrics sections include 100 prescriptions; Surgery has either 100 or 50 prescriptions, whereas Ophthalmology includes 20–53 to 73 prescriptions.

Besides Thailand, Lüzu's divine prescriptions spread to Taiwan and Vietnam, among other places. In Hanoi, Jade Mountain temple was built in 1843 and is dedicated to three cults: Wenchang, Guandi, and Lüzu. This old Vietnamese temple originally printed an edition of "Lüzu's divination slips" along with 370 prescriptions covering five medical specialties.[81] In 1918, Jade Mountain temple published the *Lüzu quanshu* 呂祖全書 in 66 *juan* with an additional volume including 370 prescriptions in five departments (andrology, gynecology, pediatrics, ophthalmology, and surgery).[82] It is then clear that Lüzu's prescriptions and their associated beliefs traveled to the whole of South East Asia.

（2）*Spirit-writing and Lüzu temple cults*

From the late Qing period to the late 1940s, spirit-writing was actively pursued at Lüzu temple in Meixian county. Indeed, the phrase "assistance sought at Lüzu temple north of the city is effective" was often heard in Meixian: Lüzu temple was not only well known for its medical oracles, it was also celebrated for its invocations to the deity which, just as in the case of Lingguang temple, had helped dispel severe droughts on several occasions:

> To the Southeast of our city, on the Five Fingers Mountains 五指峯, stands the Lingguang temple 靈光寺, the first pagoda ever built in Meizhou. It was during the Tianbao era (742–756) in the Tang dynasty that Master Cankui founded the Buddhist monastery. … Whenever a drought affected the area, prayers were said to Buddha for rain and the desired effects soon came afterwards. In the summer of the *jiawu* year, just after grains had been sown, many days had passed without any rain. Expectations ran high and everyone in the county remembered with emotion and admiration the Master's efficacy. … And it was precisely on the third day of the fourth month that an altar was built to welcome the Buddha's statue: countless devotees gathered around the altar, everyone fervently praying and pleading. Another three days

Table 4.1 Simplified Representative Table of Lüzu's Divine Prescriptions in Guangdong and Southeast Asia

title	Andrology	Gynecology	Pediatrics	Surgery	Ophthalmology	Publisher/Year/Status
博濟仙方	100	100	100	100	53	香港五經印刷所, 1918
呂祖簽 (cover:博濟仙方)	100	100	100	100	53	香港陳湘記書局, n.d.
呂大帝藥方	100	100	100	50	73	Stored at Lüzu temple in Bangkok
呂祖大仙仙方	100	100	100	50	73	Stored at Lüzu temple in Meizhou
呂祖靈簽(附五科藥方)	100	100	100	50	20	Printed in Hanoi Jade Mountain temple 玉山祠, stored at the Vietnam Han-nom Institute Library[a]
呂祖藥簽	100	100	100	50	20	Collected by Rong Zhao in Guangzhou[b]

[a] Identical to the version kept at Meizhou Lüzu temple, except for the missing sections on ophthalmology, 21–73.
[b] Rong Zhaozu, "Zhanbu de yuanliu," 42–43.

elapsed but still no rain. It was then that Zeng Zaixi and others conjured up the deity through spirit-writing in the Lüzu temple in the city. Lüzu eventually revealed that "as long as you pray in earnest, it is no use to make fruit or vegetable offerings but it is appropriate to recite and study sutras. After three days, an abundant and timely rain will come and if sutras are frequently recited, natural disasters shall recede and happiness will prevail."[83]

Master Cankui 慚愧祖師 (817–866) was originally named Pan Liaoquan 潘了拳. After his demise, he came to be revered as the founder of Lingguang temple on Mount Yinna and was popularly known as Master Cankui. The *jiawu* year, i.e., 1894, mentioned in the scriptures, is only seven years after the Lüzu temple's foundation and according to the *Meixian Zanhuashe baoxun* compiled by the board of the Zanhuashe, it contains a written record of the 1940–1943 period when Lüzu and all immortals and True men descended to offer their instructions in literary form.[84] In the fourth month (lunar calendar) of 1943, the Daoists in the Zanhuashe prayed for rain and the Altar's protecting god inspired the following instructions: "All living creatures shall congregate and recite sutras in the first nine days, … and if they sincerely thank the gods, they may obtain rain."[85] Even though spirit-writing has now been interrupted for many years in Meizhou's Zanhuagong, a "special spirit-writing session from Thailand took place at the Zanhuagong" in 2007. Verses of poetry appeared in Lüzu's temple front hall, stressing that the temple's popularity and fame resulted from the availability of medical prescriptions:

> Magical hands bring the dying back to life,
> whatever is asked for shall be granted,
> The heart of the Dao succors the world,
> no prayer shall remain unanswered.[86]

It is said that 20 years went by in Bangkok's Lüzu temple without any spirit-writing session, with the last recorded séance taking place in the *dingmao* year (1987).[87] In 1988, the temple was ravaged by fire and burnt down to ashes, causing spirit-writing to be totally interrupted. Two compilations of spirit-writing recordings are still extant: *Lüzu tanxun*, 1st and 2nd volume and *Taiguo Zanhuagong xingben shanlu*, 1st and 2nd volume, containing parts of spirit-writing records. The 1931 edition of the latter includes three prefaces by Lüzu and one by Wang Lingguan.
    Preface dictated by Fuyou dijun 孚佑帝君 (Lü Dongbin):

> In the *xinwei* year, on the first day of the fourth month, the Sages decided to print out spirit-writing records: they asked me to write a preface, for which I was extremely pleased. I therefore took my pen and wrote a few words. Books urging readers to benevolence have been numerous but versions have always differed according to regional habits, their authors' faiths (Daoist, Buddhist or Confucian), local customs and teaching materials. Education and moral teaching require the Immortal saints' painstaking efforts.

Preface by Daoist Hui 回道人 (a common self-reference of Lüzu) written at the Zanhuagong in Siam, 22nd year of the Chinese Republic.

Lüzu spoke again: even though they are but simple words, their meaning reaches far and wide. They are the produce of the Sages' exhortations to thought and this is why this classic can rightfully bear the name of "Human nature is good."[88]

The compilations of spirit-writing records were collated by Chen Liangyu 陳亮予 from 1928 to 1931, and they were edited and rectified by Zhou Xianqian 周象乾. In 1931, Zhou uttered the following words:

Preface dictated by Fuyou dijun
In the autumn of the *wuchen* year, Chen Ziliang gave me a volume containing Lüzu's spirit-writing records and recommended that I should put them in good order and publish them. I therefore washed my hands, opened the precious volume and set out to read it. I realized that the text, though plain, contained profound truths. If one can put it in practice in one's body, then one could model one's behavior on that of the Sages and Saints, either to become a Saint or a Buddha ... and this was what these revelations are all about. As for the general meaning of the volume, only a venerable scholar could correct it and restore its benevolent flavor. ... And only with the purpose of embracing goodness with the rest of humankind.
Zhou Xiangqian in Gu Mei, May 8th (Gregorian calendar), *gengwu* year.[89]

Lüzu's spirit-writing records were published to "promote exhortations to do good as explained in the revealed words" and the collator, Yang Zhuoru 楊卓如, said that:

Preface dictated by Fuyou dijun
In the summer of the *xinyou* year, as I approached once again the city of Bangkok, I became acquainted with Chen Liangyu. In the course of our discussions, he told me that the Zanhuagong was an imposing temple and a place for good and happiness, and he invited me to go there with him. The humility and worship prevailing in the temple brought about an atmosphere of deep veneration which fostered benevolence in the hearts of the faithful. It was amazing to see how the Sages' footprints could move and inspire believers in this way! At the end of the year, Mr. Chen returned with a volume of Lüzu's spirit-writing records and said he wished it to be printed out so as to advertise and promote the good deeds contained in it. He urged me to collate them and I respectfully heeded his command.
Preface by Yang Zhuoru – once cured in the capital city of Siam – in Gumei, in the autumn of 1931.[90]

The list of spirit-writing practitioners from the 1920s to the 1980s is not complete due to faulty records: only such early practitioners as Zhang Bingkun, Wen

Yuanting, Qin Keyun, Li Wuyin, and Huang Zhishan were recorded. At some point, spirit-writing stopped altogether and the only name listed for the 1980s is Liu Liangqing.[91] According to Li Wuyin's notes, spirit-writing was a key factor determining Lüzu temples' popularity and attendance records:

> The first spirit-writing practitioners included Zhang Bingkun, Wen Yuanting and Qin Keyun. After the latter returned home, spirit-writing stopped for a number of years and Liang Xinglou became the general administrator of the temple. He grew aware that attendance had declined and wished spirit-writing and requests be resumed. Regretting the absence of qualified practitioners, he discussed the issue with Chen Liangyu who suggested I should take up the practice and set up an altar. From then on, the temple regained great popularity.[92]

From 1924 to 1948, Li Wuyin and Huang Zhishan took over as spirit-writing assistants:

> [F]rom the summer of the *wuzi* year, as I was seeking another assistant, Huang Zhishan took over the charge but in the twinkling of an eye, spirit-writing was discontinued once again. It was not until the *wuzi* year that the practice was resumed with Huang as the main practitioner. As the number of worshippers requesting prescriptions gradually grew due to unusually high effectiveness rates, the main practitioner secured the help of an assistant.[93] In the 1920s, Huang Zhishan was thus assisted by Chen Shiyin, the latter having been "appointed" by Lüzu Himself: "the student will learn the practice and as soon as he fully masters his art, he may take on the role of assistant."[94] In the early years, students were numerous and in 1923, Lüzu could profess that "students are eager to study the art and this gives me great joy! First there was Huang Zhishan, then Wen Zunde and then again He Guozhen."[95]

Huang Zhishan and Wen Yuanting studied spirit-writing, but they also benefited from the guidance of Zhentan Wang tianjun 鎮壇王天君, the temple's protecting god, Yiqing Daoren 一清道人, and all accomplished saints.[96] An example of this is illustrated by the séance, which took place on the evening of the 22nd day of the first month of the *jiazi* year (1924) when

> as shown by Zhentan Wang tianjun, if things can be reported, Wen Zunde will report while his disciples, still learning the art, are not yet proficient but can be sent to other places to complete their studies. Once they are fully proficient, they may disperse and civilize the world.[97]

In the early years of its foundation, Bangkok's Lüzu temple had already set up a spirit-writing unit which attracted numerous people seeking prescriptions, making it a prosperous place of worship. On the 29th day of the 11th month of the *renxu* year (1982), Lüzu's spirit alighted on the shrine: "the temple's present prosperity relies mostly on all disciples' achievements and meritorious actions in terms of spirit-writing. If not for these, the place would not look the way it does today."[98] And, according to Xu Zhizhen's records:

> The former sages founded the Zanhuagong (Lüzu temple) in Bangkok and the shrine first enjoyed a period of great prosperity. A spirit-writing unit was then set up to meet the requirements of a growing number of worshippers. On the 9th day of the month, or fasting days, deities were invited to descend on the shrine and offer help to the faithful through spirit-writing, a practice commonly known as "stylus writing." Unfortunately, in 1988, the temple was destroyed by fire and reduced to ashes, stopping the practice of spirit-writing altogether. Spirit-writing records suffered in the process and were left incomplete. Luckily thanks to the unrelenting efforts of dedicated believers, the remaining records were gathered and edited into books.[99]

For a long time, the Lüzu temple conducted charitable activities, and in the 1950s, it was regarded as the most popular shrine in Bangkok due to the many signs left by the gods:

> Lüzu temple's popularity placed it at the top of the Thai capital's shrines. Numerous worshippers benefited from the Immortals' prescriptions and medical treatments and this led to many conversions among those beneficiaries who then joined a growing number of disciples. Could it not be possible that with so many real spirits invoked and delivering a constant flow of earnest enjoinders, resources would not be forthcoming?[100]

Among the deities and holies most frequently invoked besides Lüzu and the eight immortals, Guandi was often called upon, along with Zhang Huanhou 張桓侯, Buddha the savior, Master Cankui, Wang tianguan, Hezu daxian 何祖大仙,[101] and the temple's Earth God.[102] All sages reminded the temple's worshippers that the purpose of spirit-writing resided in encouraging the faithful to do good and to improve themselves through education. As Hezu Yuanjun once declared:

> "Bear in mind that this temple's disciples are fully aware that spirit-writing equals to a transformation through education and that would-be disciples respect the master's words."[103] "My personal view is that the influence exerted by deities exhorts people to do good and thus transforms them and if ceremonies rely on the "sand tray" and "the wood stylus" as motivators, what is really needed is honesty among practitioners for effective results, the very source of the appearance and incarnation of the flying phoenix."

(3) *Lüzu cult's propagation through printing and dissemination of scriptures*

The Zanhuagong has often printed out and distributed scriptures on the occasion of Lüzu's birthday on the 14th day of the 4th month. Publications include the

Table 4.2 Lüzu Scriptures Printed in/Sent from Bangkok's Zanhuagong

Title	Printed in	Observations
Lüzu zhenjing 呂祖真經 + *Hezu daxian duren zhenjing* 何祖大仙渡人真經 + *Cankui zuzhi zhenjing* 慚愧祖師真經	1987	
Eight Immortals' medical slips 八仙祖師靈簽	1991	
Lüzu sanshi yingguo shuo 呂帝三世因果說	1995	
Lüzu's complete book 呂祖全書	1999	Eleven chapters
Lüzu duren zhenjing 呂祖度人真經	2001	
Daozu Lüshi duji duren sizi zhenwen 道祖呂師度己度人四字真文		
Lüzu and Hanxian: master and disciple's questions and answers 呂祖韓仙師弟問答	2002	Reprinted from Shanghai Mingshan Press 明善書局
Fuyou dijun bapin zhenjing 孚佑帝君八品真經 (in Thai, with Chaozhou pronounciation)	2004	

newly issued Daoist Scripture of Universal Salvation" printed in 1993, a joint edition of the *Taishang Qingjingjing* and the Jade Emperor's Scripture printed in 1993, Lüzu's complete book printed in 1999, the *Lüzu duren zhenjing* printed in 2001, etc. Some of Lüzu's scriptures were also brought back to Meizhou from Thailand, such as the *Lüzu duren zhenjing*, printed in 1992 by "disciples and worshippers from Bangkok's Zanhuagong" or the *Lüzu zhenjing* cum *Hezu daxian duren zhenjing* cum *Cankui zushi zhenjing*, printed jointly in 1987.[104] Over the past 20 years, the Zanhuagong has printed a great variety of scriptures related to Lüzu, as shown in Table 4.2.

The Bangkok temples and the 1985 revival of the Meizhou temple

In 1982, 21 religious buildings were officially designated by the PRC government as key Daoist temples; and in 1984, the White cloud temple in Beijing was reopened as a center of religious activities, welcoming pilgrims and visitors, an example quickly followed by other Daoist temples in the provinces.[105] But what few people observed was that the Meizhou Lüzu temple in northeastern Guangdong also resumed services in 1985. In fact, the Lüzu temple in Meizhou had taken a clearly distinct path from that followed by other Daoist temples in Guangdong because of its historical traditions and close links to overseas Chinese in Southeast Asia. Indeed, Lüzu devotees from Meixian county and Shantou had emigrated to every port of Southeast Asia, especially Thailand. Devotees frequently raised funds to support charitable causes in their "home country." In August 2009, I visited the Yanshou charity hall in Shantou and discovered abandoned steles, which I surmised were reminders of past donations. Indeed, the inscriptions he found on the steles were the names of contributors

Wu Guangyuan and Liu Guangzong, founders of the Lüzu temple in Bangkok and belonging to the overseas Chinese community. Similarly, the Guangji elementary school in the 1940s fully depended on the voluntary contributions of overseas Chinese and rich benefactors. The present abbot of Zanhuagong, Zhong Biaofa 鍾標發, wrote an article about the relations established between Daoist figures in Guangdong and Hong Kong, Macao, and Southeast Asia, and their advantages:

> Guangdong province has assumed a unique and unprecedented historical mission ever since the new period of reform and development was launched in China. With the intensification of reform and development, links between the Daoist community of the province and the outside world have been steadily increasing. In our contacts, we fully take advantage of the regional and human advantages of Guangdong province as we multiply exchanges and contacts with Daoist circles in Hong-Kong, Macao, Taiwan and various countries and areas of Southeast Asia. This implies that growing numbers of our Daoist friends in these parts of the world are increasingly aware of the Party's religious policy: these relations help foster bonds of mutual understanding and friendship while gaining our friends' support. Thus, the development of the Chongxu guguan temple in Boluo (Guangdong) could not be achieved without the vital support it received from the Yuanxuan Institute in Hong-Kong: the latter funded the renovation of the temple, restoring the ancient building to its original condition, its gold and jade in glorious splendor. Equally, the full resumption of religious services in Meizhou Zanhuagong was clearly related to the support and pilgrimages of Thai overseas Chinese returning to their ancestral home.[106]

Just as Huaguang dadi had inspired through spirit-writing "disciples from the Zanhuagong in Thailand to initiate" the rebuilding of Lüzu temple, the plan of the construction had been directed by Patriarch Lü in Thailand. As early as 1980, Lüzu devotees in Thailand set up a party of 86 people and headed for Meizhou, calling themselves "a party of Lüzu disciples returning "home" to visit their families and worship their deity." They asked the authorities to rebuild the Lüzu temple and obtained permission to do so in 1983. They immediately set up a "Preparatory committee for the revival of the Lüzu temple." Committee members elected Hou Jinhua, an overseas Chinese from Thailand, as committee head while Li Guokui was named emeritus chairman of the board. Chen Changsheng and Zhong Baiquan were also among the seven committee members. A site was chosen for the temple reconstruction: Baizigang in the eastern suburb.[107] The Meizhou city gazetteer described the whole process as follows:

> In 1980, a party of Thai disciples of Lüzu returned to their ancestral homeland, Meizhou, asking for the reconstruction of Lüzu temple. They had written letters to the Chinese embassy in Thailand which had then sent a report to the provincial authorities via the United Front Department of the regional

Party committee. Eventually permission to rebuild the temple was granted. More than a million Yuan was raised in 1985 for the reconstruction of the temple buildings in the Baizigang hill, in an eastern suburb. The temple extends on more than 2,500 m² in surface and its interior features five halls: one hall dedicated to Lüzu, one for worship, another housing the Three Pure Ones, a cabinet for the Scriptures and auxiliary facilities. The temple officially resumed its services during the Autumn festival of the same year. In 1988, the compound received the official name of "Daoist Zanhuagong in Meizhou, Meijiang district." [108]

The record of the revelations in *Lüzu tanxun* and *Taiguo Zanhuagong xingben shanlu* emphasizes the fact that for the reconstruction of the temple in Meizhou, support from Thai Lüzu devotees had been highly anticipated and as "indicated" by Lüzu and Wang Lingguan, it was "Good news for the restoration of the Daoist faith" and "a great achievement indeed." In the *jiazi* year (1984), on the 15th day of the 5th month, Huaguang Dadi's spirit manifested itself:

My presence here tonight is to congratulate all disciples and devotees for coming together and assisting in the reconstruction of the holy Lüzu temple on Chinese soil. Thanks to the initiative of the Zanhuagong disciples in Thailand, the temple located on Baizigang Hill in Sancunxiang in Meizhou City now sits on prosperous ground. In the past, Dingguang gufo 定光古佛 had come to the Longyan area near Fuzhou to "trace the dragon's steps" and when he arrived in Baizigang in Meizhou, he called the place "Live Dragon's Mouth," indicating that instructions for a planned construction in the area in future times should be reported in this hall.[109]

Originally, the committee contemplated building the Lüzu temple on its former site, but since the latter was then occupied by school buildings, they eventually decided to build the new shrine at Baizigang Hill in the eastern suburb, somewhat to the north of the former construction.[110] Today, the following rhyming couplets may be seen on the entrance gate to the Zanhuagong:

贊參天地 化育生靈
Assistance and participation in worldly affairs helps refine the human soul

And the following couplet is inscribed on the outside pillars of Lüzu Hall in the Bangkok temple:

贊參宇宙 化育華洋
Assistance and participation in cosmic affairs helps refine China and the outside
    world

The reason why Baizigang was selected for the temple reconstruction is that, according to folklore, the place is shaped like a "butcher's knife" (rainbow irrigation) and is considered as geomantically auspicious.[111] Outside the front hall, a couplet alludes to the shape of the place:

羨一脈千里龍蟠形號屠刀正合仙家開廟宇
喜四圍諸峰鳳起崗稱百子允宜香火結因緣

Admire the veins of the coiling dragons over a thousand *li*, shaped as a butcher's knife, a perfect residence for the Immortals and for the construction of a temple;
Joyous are the rising phoenixes surrounding the place, hills by the name of Baizi, a fitting name for a place predestined to welcome worshippers.

In its present location in the eastern suburb of Meizhou, the Zanhuagong faces two tombs of great antiquity: those of Yang Yunxiu 楊雲岫 and Dingguang Gufo. Yang Yunxiu, titled "Great Master of Court Attendance" under the Southern Tang is the ancestral founder of Meizhou in Guangdong. Dingguang Gufo, lay name Zheng Dingguang 鄭定光, was conferred the title of "Gu Fo" (Old Buddha) by Li Houzhu 李後主 of the Southern Tang.[112] Zheng buried Yang Yunxiu in the eastern suburb of Meizhou and placed his fingernails to the left of the tomb, as a sign of friendship.[113]

Spirit-writing records explain how all immortals had placed great hopes in the temple's reconstruction. On the 15th day of the 5th month of the *yichou* year (1985), Wang tianjun's spirit's was conjured:

> His Sanctity Lüzu has graced us with the honor to come this morning with His immortal friends on an inspection tour of Meizhou. He paced the ground selected for the temple's reconstruction and said it could be a major achievement.[114]

The "Eye opening ceremony" was fixed and attended by the Eight Immortals and on the 15th day of the 5th month of the *yichou* year, spirit-writing revealed that:

> The opening date has been debated and fixed by the Eight Immortals and it was decided that the "Eye opening" ceremony would be held on the 15th day of the 8th month: elevation of the throne in the first quarter of the *ji* hour and Eye opening during the *wu* hour.

On the first day of the eighth month of the *yichou* year (1985), Lüzu manifested Himself in a spirit-writing proclamation entitled "I dispatch the Protectors of the Law to Meizhou":

> I was presented with a memorial today by the Celestial Lord, a list of the names of the worshipping party bound for their ancestral homeland. The present Immortal has exceptionally sent today the Protectors of the Law to the city of Meizhou and has learnt that they travelled safely. On the fifteenth day of this month, the opening ceremony of Lüzu temple in Meizhou will be

held in great solemnity and pomp and it may be said that the attendants and worshippers back to their ancestral homeland for this occasion will be graced with "fortune in three lifetimes."[115]

According to a senior custodian of the Lüzu temple, M. Xu Jiangtao 許江濤, "the Lüzu temple in Meizhou was built based on the model erected in Thailand's Chinatown."[116] The influence of Bangkok's Lüzu temple in the reconstruction of the "ancestral shrine" essentially appears in the design and configuration of the interior architecture and the representations of the deities. As intimated by Zhentan Wang tianjun:

> Disciple Hou Jinhua 侯金華, considering all expedients as the best policy, chose the fifth day of this month as an auspicious day for the congregation of Man, Heaven, and deities, a perfect day for the contract. As for the gilded statue of the Great Emperor, the statues of the two Celestial Lords and of the Immortal Lads, right and left, their dimensions could not be different from those of the original temple. They were cast in Foshan near Canton, incense wood could be used and gold leaves could be applied onto bamboo structures, with pure gold as a background. Metals came from Germany and were bought through Thailand.[117]

For instance, the design for the Three Teachings Hall was firmly advocated by the Lüzu devotees in Thailand and the images of the deities also came from this country. The main buildings of Meizhou Zanhuagong are the front and rear halls. The front hall is a simple 11 m high one-storied building and is known as "Lüzu precious hall." This room houses a statue of Lüzu in military attire which is very similar to the statue of the god in Bangkok. The rear hall is an 18-m high three-storied building: the ground floor consists of the God of Wealth hall, the Zhenwu hall, and the Guandi hall. The first floor houses the Guanyin hall, the Female Immortal hall (containing a representation of He Xiangu), the Jade Emperor hall, the Three Teachings hall, and the Eight Immortals hall. The second floor houses the Three Purities hall. Courtyards situated right and left include small reception rooms, a pharmacy, a cabinet room for scriptures and a prayers hall, among others. The character *hui* 回 (a pun on Lüzu's name) appears everywhere in the temple and the various halls are closely interconnected. The internal architecture and inner configuration of the building differ somewhat from the traditional forms observed in China and they feature specific characteristics: besides Lüzu, the Immortals and Buddha, Liuren Xianshi 六壬仙師 was equally instrumental in establishing a blueprint for the temple, and they all warned of the problems to be encountered during fundraising and the gathering of building materials and suggested ways to avert those difficulties. On the 15th day of the 11th month of the *jiazi* year (1984), Lüzu's spirit manifested itself:

> Tonight I invited all Immortals and deities to grace this altar with their holy presence. Disciple Jinhua (Hou Jinhua, a Thai overseas Chinese who chaired

the Preparatory committee for the reconstruction of Lüzu temple) submitted his project to the Meizhou county authorities and obtained their permission, bringing with it the good news of the restoration of our Daoist faith. I hope that all disciples join their efforts in this sacred mission to rebuild this temple, and that reconstruction be promptly completed. Liuren Xianshi will shortly provide His instructions.

Liuren Xianshi's spirit has descended and disciples pay homage to the deity with wine and tea offerings. This place is graced with joy and happiness as Lüzu has invited all the deities to convene for the reconstruction of His temple in Meizhou. Drawings have been sent to the relevant authorities. … This temple has a history more than eighty years long and it stands on vigorous ground. The original building blueprint was based on that of the Lüzu temple at Shantou city, according to my instructions. However, the construction of the Lüzu temple in Meizhou was marred with problems of funds and materials and was completed in several stages. First the front hall was built at the northwest: 56 metres long with 9 metres left at the rear of the erection of the main hall. The building width of 26 metres includes two spaces to the right and left, both 13 metres wide, the central part being reserved for the main hall. The latter is 8 meters wide and 9 meters long and it also includes four pillars, just like the temple along with a central 人-shaped 14 metres high hall. When the model of the shrine was first drawn, clear indications were given through spirit-writing as to its dimensions. The rear building and both aisles to the right and left were designed in a second stage through spirit-writing. Construction work began at an auspicious time of day set between 5 and 7 pm on 21st day of the 3rd month of the *yichou* year (1985). As the front hall had been completed at an earlier date, the Great Emperor's image was raised and it was at that time that overseas Chinese returned to the Motherland to visit relatives and raised money for the temple's reconstruction, which solved the financial problem. The future completion of the shrine will be largely owed to the meritorious efforts of Lüzu's disciples and believers and the support of the Immortals and Pure Ones to strengthen our glorious Daoist faith.[118]

The temple construction funds were raised by Thai disciples of Lüzu, who sent delegations to Zanhuagong at various stages.[119] As previously indicated, the money raised for the reconstruction came mostly from overseas Chinese in Thailand and Indonesia. In 1981, for example, Zhong Baiquan, an Indonesian Chinese donated more than 200,000 yuan to help rebuild Lüzu's temple. In addition, the list of donors inscribed on the stele outside the Lüzu's Throne Hall mentions that "the whole Guhuangdeng Zhengu family were happy to donate 307 000 bath."[120] Then, a managing committee was set up based on the principle of the three autonomies: self-propagation, self-rule, and self-support.[121] In 1985, the 2,500 m² Zanhuagong temple building was completed at a cost of more than 1 million yuan, and as it officially resumed services during the autumn festival of that year, its anniversary is celebrated every year on the 15th day of the 8th lunar month. From 1985 to

1995, on the temple anniversary date, the "Thailand Overseas Chinese Association" prompted disciples to organize "parties of Lüzu worshippers" returning to Meizhou, as reported in a local periodical, the "Meizhou Overseas Chinese Monthly":

> The 9th anniversary of the Lüzu temple's reconstruction and official reopening: a party of more than 200 disciples left Thailand on 20 September and headed towards Meizhou to pay homage to their deity, thus marking the 9th anniversary of the temple's reconstruction and resumption of services. The delegation was headed by Messrs Hou Jinhua, Li Guokui and Ye Zhixin, among others. Contributions from the pious men and women belonging to Thailand's Lüzu worshippers have helped rebuild the temple, return it to service and organize yearly trips for the deity's faithful believers. On the present occasion, Thai worshippers have journeyed together and provided generous funds to support the erection of the temple gates and the printing of Daoist scriptures, among other actions.[122]

Thailand's Lüzu worshippers' support for the temple reconstruction also contributed to the "propagation to a large extent of our (Bangkok) temple's liturgy to the deity's homeland." On the 28th day of the 8th lunar month of the *yichou* year (1985), Lüzu's spirit manifested itself in writing:

> The completion of Lüzu's main temple in Meizhou is an event that devout worshippers will fondly remember for a thousand years. ... It is the greatest achievement ever in terms of benevolent action and accumulated virtue and it will be instrumental in propagating the cult ceremonies to the deity's home county. This temple in Meizhou will not only reintroduce long-standing rites but it will equally give disciples and their descendants a unique occasion to celebrate the Nine Emperors festival. This gives ample food for thought and proves that good actions are graced with good consequences.[123]

> The "eye opening" celebration and the ceremony of Lüzu's elevation held on the inauguration of the new temple followed the Daoist ritual: an altar was set up, offerings were made, incense was burnt, the altar was raised, ritual incantations were chanted to invoke and greet the deity, incense burned were lighted, prayers were said to the deity, and all the rituals took place in a dedicated area for two days.[124]

Lüzu worshippers from Thailand returned to China to assist in the restoration of the temple and a few scholars went on to say that "Lüzu's cult had been reintroduced from Thailand."[125] Meizhou Lüzu temple's reconstruction by Thai disciples was a major achievement as far as charitable and good deeds go and the spirit of Linghou Guan Dataizi 靈侯關大太子 made the following pronouncement: "Guandi's return to the temple along with that of disciples from the Southern Zanhuagong several years in a row amounted to a dazzling feast and a meritorious achievement for our ancestral land."[126]

Due to the vicissitudes of human affairs, the organization of trips to Meizhou by Thai disciples has declined over the recent years and it would appear that the latest such trip to Lüzu temple took place in 1995.

The Zanhuagong and Daoism in contemporary Meizhou

The number of registered Daoist temples in Meizhou increased from 1 in 1990 to 8 in 2002, and 13 in 2006. These include Holy Mother temple 聖母宮, White Crane temple 白鶴宮, Queen Mother temple 王母宮, Wuxian temple 五顯宮, Shigu Dawang temple 石古大王廟, Qixingniang temple 七星娘宮, and Three Pures temple 三清宮 in Xingning. Other shrines are located in Pingyuan county such as Zhenwu temple[127] and Tianhou temple. Other temples still include Chenghuang temple in Wuhua and Gongwang temple 公王廟 in Pankeng county.[128] Even though all these temples are managed by the Daoist association, they also clearly reflect the numerous popular beliefs prevailing in the Meizhou area since the Qing dynasty with cults to Zhenwu, Wenchang, Guandi, Wuxian Dadi, and Sanshan Guowang, among other deities. Among these shrines, Meicheng Sandi temple 三帝廟 was established under Kangxi's reign by Hong Tuguang 洪圖光, a county head magistrate, and was dedicated to the cults of Zhenwu, Wenchang, and Guandi.[129] The Meijiang Daoist association was founded on January 6, 1990, and placed under the supervision of Yang Jueqian 楊爵謙, with Wu Baokang 吳保康 and Zhong Biaofa acting as his deputies.[130] In recent years, the association has been headed by Zhong Biaofa, who has been assisted by Huang Rengui 黃壬貴, head of the Zanhuagong and Hou Gangping 侯鋼平, Pankeng Gongwang temple's supervisor.

Upon Lüzu temple's restoration in 1985, long-standing traditions were equally restored and "one year after restoration, spending for the distribution of free coffins and medicine among other charitable actions reached 13,300 yuan."[131] In recent years, a pavilion for the souls' rest was built within the Zanhuagong to allow believers to pay homage to departed spirits. The Zanhuagong's grand celebrations and festivals include:

玉皇大帝聖誕	The Jade Emperor's birthday on 1/9
本宮許福	Prayers for benedictions on 2/8
太上老君聖誕	Taishang laojun's birthday on 2/15
真武大帝聖誕	Zhenwu's birthday on 3/3
呂祖大仙聖誕	Lüzu's birthday on 4/14
靈寶天尊聖誕	The Heavenly Worthy of the Numinous Treasure's birthday on the Summer Solstice
關聖帝聖誕	Guandi's birthday on 6/24
本宮暖福（盂蘭法會）	Ghost Festival on 7/21–22
本宮復宮紀念	The temple's restoration anniversary date on 8/15
本宮完福	Thanksgiving for benedictions received on 11/8
元始天尊聖誕	The Heavenly Worthy of Original Beginning's birthday on the Winter Solstice
玉皇大帝巡天之日	Jade Emperor's Celestial Journey on 12/25[132]

As far as the Zanhuagong's management is concerned, a managing committee was set up in the 1980s and first headed by Chen Changsheng 陳暢盛 (Chen was named director general of the Zanhuashe – Society for Assistance and Education – in 1983; then, in 1985, he became a member of the Preparatory Committed for Lüzu temple's reconstruction; so it can be argued that he was naturally bound to carry on as the head manager). Chen's successors included Zhong Boquan and Yang Jueqian. The management committee is now known as the "management board" and the board director is referred to either as the "manager" or the "abbot." The present manager is Zhong Biaofa, whose religious name is Xinyang or "Propagation of the faith." Zhong embraced Daoism in 1983, and in 1988, he went to Beijing's White Cloud temple to study management techniques for Daoist temples. Recently, Zhong asked old Daoist masters from Zhejiang province to come to the Zanhuagong to teach Daoist rituals for the benefit of young Daoist practitioners.[133] Eleven Daoist priests were present in 1998 when the Zanhuagong was officially registered as a Daoist temple in Meizhou. According to statistics, the temple's total number of believers and worshippers now reaches 3,000, including those in Hong Kong and Thailand.[134] As the Zanhuagong was officially restored as a religious center in 1985, and since it is equipped with all that is necessary to help out other Daoist temples, the place serves as a center for short training periods for newly opened temples in Meizhou. The Zanhuagong offers them opportunities to acquire Daoist knowledge and learn the rituals along with experience in temple management.[135] Over the years, the Zanhuagong has thus provided assistance to temples in such places as Wuhua, Pingyuan, and Xingning, "standardizing the development of the temples and training temple staff."[136] Concrete examples of this help are listed below:

Training Clerics Teaching and administrative staff are essential to religious centers and activities. At present all managing staff in Meizhou temples became Daoist monks at the Zanhuagong, becoming disciples of the priest Zhong Biaofa of the Quanzhen School and spawning a new branch of the Longmen lineage in the *chong* 崇-character generation.

Teaching Daoist Liturgy The Zanhuagong places emphasis on the transmission of the orthodox Daoist liturgy and has regularly invited eminent Daoist priests from Zhejiang to come to Meizhou to teach Daoist rituals for the benefit of young disciples. The practices and rituals now prevailing in the temples are mostly based on liturgical manuals from places such as Cangnan in Zhejiang province. The present *gaogong*, Daoist master Zhong Zengguang 鍾增光 (Zhong was awarded an official ordination to become a Daoist monk in 2005 at the age of 37 under the name of Chongguang 崇光), once studied the Quanzhen ritual with Daoist master Lei Zongnan from Changchun temple in Wuhan (Hubei province). Besides teaching rituals to staff from a large number of temples, the Zanhuagong also seconds its own Daoist masters to other temples to perform grand offerings 醮 when needed.

Assistance Provided to Restore Regular Religious Services The Zanhuagong actively assists all temples asking for a restoration of regular religious services. For instance, it had provided help in ceremonies for sacrifices to the City God temple in Huacheng 華城 and had copies of the scripture *Chenghuang ganying xiaozai jifu miaojing* 城隍感應消災集福妙經, especially sent from Zhejiang province.

Master Zhong Biaofa has underlined the major development axes of the Zanhuagong over recent years: improving disciples' standards to promote Daoism, housing the headquarters of the Daoist association of the Meijiang area within the Zanhuagong on account of its good management record (the Zanhuagong's ultimate goal is to share its experience for the sake of the promotion of Daoism in the Meizhou area), supporting social activities (handing out free medicines to combat heat strokes and belly aches, dedicated education, help for the elderly and disaster relief), standardizing and transmitting scriptures and rituals, and the reconstruction of the Halls for the Three Pure Ones and the Jade emperor in the rear hall, among others.[137]

Conclusion

In the early twentieth century, Daoist temples originally found in Guangdong province were set up in other parts of Southeast Asia as Daoist priests and monks emigrated to Hong Kong, Thailand, and Vietnam, spreading the Lüzu cult to these areas. An example of this was the introduction of Lüzu's worship in Thailand in 1902 with the construction of the Zanhuagong and the establishment of a *shantang* in Bangkok in 1914 by Xiantiandao adepts.[138] By the early 1940s, the Dejiao had reached Hong Kong, Thailand, Singapore, and Malaysia. All the temples built in these areas endeavored to set up and develop charities: disaster relief, help for the poor, free medical help and medicines, setting up of free schools, etc. As years went by, Daoist temples in Hong Kong and Thailand kept the spirit alive and developed it so much so that some of the Lüzu shrines built in the areas had outgrown their models in Guangdong province. Some of them also retained long-standing traditions such as keeping scriptures and documents, following rituals and distributing potions prescribed by immortals. An illustration of this is the Patriarch Dafeng cult introduced to Thailand from Chaoshan: the charity structure initially set up has now become a famous and popular charitable organization and a nursing institution, the Overseas Chinese Chongsheng University 泰國華僑崇聖大學 was founded in Thailand.[139] In the mid-1980s, Lüzu temple was "restored" in Meizhou, thanks to the efforts and support provided by Thai Lüzu disciples and overseas Chinese. Today the Zanhuagong is the most impressive Daoist temple in Meizhou. Lüzu temples in both China and Thailand suffered the same woes and had to stop functioning for a while but both were restored and regained their former popularity among the faithful. This rebirth was no doubt related to their traditions of spirit-writing and free medical services. And these temples' promotion of Lüzu's cult, the help they extend to the poor, and their charitable aims are implemented wherever the deity is worshipped.

Notes

1 The author would like to thank Pascal Herbelot and Vincent Goossaert for helping with the English version. A previous version was published in Chinese as "Qingmo yilai Lüzu xinyang de chuanbo."

2 In our sources, Lüzu is called by various titles, including Emperor Lü 呂帝, but I shall consistently refer to him as Lüzu for the sake of clarity.

3 For instance, the Qingyun nanyuan 慶雲南院 in Ho Chi Minh Ville, Vietnam, is a branch of the Qingyundong 慶雲洞, a Lüzu hall in Chashan 茶山 (Nanhai county, Guangdong) established in 1899 that spawned branches first in Hong Kong (the Tongshantan 通善壇, in 1938) and then Vietnam (the Qingyun nanyuan, in 1942): Yau Chi-on, "Daomai nanchuan," "Hatachi seiki."

4 Li Yangzheng, comp. *Dangdai Zhongguo daojiao*, picture in prefatory material.

5 Yau Chi-on, "Meizhou daoguan Zanhuagong."

6 Notably in *(Qianlong) Jiaying zhouzhi, (Guangxu) Jiaying zhouzhi, Meixian zhi*, and *Meizhou shizhi*.

7 *Taiguo huawen mingke huibian.*

8 The *Lüzu tanxun* 呂祖壇訓 was published in 1992 (vol. 1, comprising revelations dating 1923–1957) and 1995 (vol. 2, comprising revelations dating 1960–1987), and the *Taiguo Zanhuagong xingben shanlu* 泰國贊化宮性本善錄, also in two volumes, in 1992 (vol. 1, comprising revelations dating 1923–1925) and 1996 (vol. 2, comprising revelations dating 1981–1987).

9 Cover title: *Boji xianfang* 博濟仙方, Hong Kong, Chenxiangji shuju, s.d.

10 *Taiguo huaqiao keshu zonghui sanshi zhounian jiniankan* 泰國華僑客屬總會三十週年紀念刊 (1957), *Taiguo keshu zonghui wushi zhounian jinian tekan* 泰國客屬總會五十週年紀念特刊 (1977) and *Taiguo kejiaren: Taiguo kejia zonghui chengli bashi zhounian huiqing tekan* 泰國客家人：泰國客家總會成立80週年會慶特刊 (2007).

11 *Meizhou shizhi*, 1764.

12 In the 1980s, devotees rebuilt "the old Altar of Immortal Lüzu" at 22, Jiangbei Jinshanding Dongcang Lane in Meicheng using funds provided by Overseas Chinese. The old city of Meicheng is the political and cultural center of Meixian county and includes active popular temples dedicated to the worship of Wenchang, Guandi, and Lüzu. According to a stele embedded in a wall of the latter temple on the 12th day of the 4th lunar month of 1988, the shrine "is an altar commemorating Lüzu and the City God." The stele bears the following inscription: "Seven benefactors (names listed) from Hong-Kong, Indonesia and Taiwan" donated money for a place nearby. This temple is an example of commonplace vernacular architecture; it is located on a hillock, including an altar and 12 deities arranged as follows (from left to right): Lüzu, Cankui, the God of wealth, Laozi, the Jade Emperor, the City God, the City Goddess, Bao Zheng, Gong Wang, the Northern Emperor, the Five Manifestations 五顯大帝, and Guandi.

13 *Meizhou kejia fengsu*, 87.

14 *(Guangxu) Jiaying zhouzhi, juan* 17, "Cisi 祠祀," 7.

15 *(Guangxu) Jiaying zhouzhi, juan* 1, "Tushuo 圖説," 15.

16 Jiang Mingqing, a man from Jurong 句容 (Jiangsu), was a *juren* from the 1867 promotion, and was promoted to Changle magistrate in 1888.

17 The text of the *Fuyou dijun miao bei* follows my own transcription on site in 2000. It was published in *Guangdong beikeji*, 880–81, but with many errors and omissions.

18 Li Weiyun, *Guangzhou zongjiaozhi*, 111.

19 *Guangdong shengzhi – Minzhengzhi*, 124.

20 *Guangdong nianjian*, section 25, "Shehui shiye 社會事業," 167.

21 *Meixian zhi*, 816.

22 The Guangji shantang was established in 1902 by Ceng Tingyao 曾廷輝 and his wife. It was located just outside the city's north gate, and specialized in medical charity: Li Bolin, *Meizhou shiji conglan*, 60.

23 *Meixian Zanhuashe baoxun*, vol. 1, 4, 46.

24 *Guangdong shengzhi – Zongjiaozhi*, 138; Yu Xinchang & Yang Jueqian, "Meizhoushi daojiao Zanhuagong," 50.

25 Yang Jueqian, Zhong Biaofa & Huang Yinggu, *Daoguan shengdi*; Yu Xinchang & Yang Jueqian, "Meizhoushi daojiao Zanhuagong"; *Meixian zhi*, 816.

26 "Zhua guanli," 8.

27 Bangkok's Lüzu temple was built in 1902, but its construction date is often wrongly indicated as either 1905 or 1908. For example, *Guangdong shengzhi – Zongjiaozhi*, 186 that cites 1905 and Liu Lifang and Mai Liufang, "Mangu yu Xinjiapo," 19, that cites 1908. The stele commemorating the reconstruction of Lüzu temple inside Bangkok's temple main inner hall (erected in 1992) states that "the temple was originally built in the year 1902."

28 *Lüzu tanxun*, 3.

29 Xie Xueying, *Shantou zhinan*, chapter "Temples 祠廟," 185. I am grateful to Chen Jingxi 陳景熙 for sharing this material with me.

30 The two brothers hailed from Songkouzhen 松口鎮 in Meixian. They have run a plantation in Medan, Indonesia, and then the Chaozhou-Shantou railway (completed in 1906), the first entirely private railway managed by Overseas Chinese.

31 On the Yanshou shantang, see Ma Ximin & Chen Yun, *Chao-Shan shantang daguan*, 93 and Hu Xingrong, *Chao-Shan wenhua baogao*, "Shantang daoyuan 善堂道緣," 1–5.

32 *Shantou Zanhuagong huixinlu*, vol. 10.

33 As I could observe during fieldwork at the Yanshou shantang on August 21, 2009, this temple currently uses the medical oracle slips and divine drug recipes printed as an appendix to the *Fuyou dijun jueshijing* 孚佑帝君覺世經; this edition was reprinted from a Hong Kong 1976 edition.

34 *Taiguo Zanhuagong xingben shanlu*, vol. 2, 137–38.

35 Shantou's Zanhuagong, originators – Corrected and verified by Zhang Gongyi 張公益, altar affairs managed by Huang Hehui 黃和輝, constant supervision: Huang Guoqi 黃國琦. *Xinban Zhongwai pudu huangjing*, 42.

36 On this scripture, see Yau, "Ming zhongye yilai de Guandi xinyang," 36–40. It was reprinted in 1927 by the Bangkok branch of the World Red Swastika Society 世界紅卍字會暹京寄修所. The 1993 reprint by the Bangkok Zanhuagong carries a photograph of that temple's chief medium 乩生, named Liu Liangqing 劉良青: *Zhongwai pudu huangjing*, 17–18.

37 Fang Xuejia, "Yuedong Meizhou de Tianhou xinyang," 292.

38 Later on, members of a Meixian family, the Wu 伍, established the Sino-Thai Agricultural Bank 泰華農民銀行 that became one of the five large Thai banks.

39 "Huiwu baogao 會務報告," *Taiguo keshu zonghui wushi zhounian jinian tekan*, 9.

40 The forerunner to the Hakka association in Thailand, the Jixianguan 集賢館, was founded in 1870, while the Hakka Association in Thailand itself was established in 1909. In 1916, the association converted the Guandi temple into a three-storey shrine: the third floor was dedicated to Guandi's worship, the second floor was used by the Hakka association, while the first floor became a school. Eventually, because of an ever larger number of pupils at the school, the Hakka association's bureau was transferred to the Lüzu temple. The Hakka association obtained permission from the Thai authorities to be registered as a legal association. In 1936, the Siam Overseas Chinese Hakka Association changed its name to "Thailand Overseas Hakka Association." In 1972 and in 2001, it changed names again to finally become the "Hakka Association of Thailand." For details, see the association's website at www.hakkathailand.com/home/default_Chaina.php?lang=Chaina (accessed 2010/10/17).

41 Xiao Ganru 蕭皸儒, "Benhui huishi 本會會史," *Taiguo huaqiao keshu zonghui san-shi zhounian jiniankan*, 4.

42 The Zhang clan lived in Zhangjiawei 張家圍, i.e., an administrative unit located in the Eastern suburb (East Street). Baizigang hill in the Eastern suburb was the site selected in 1985 for the temple reconstruction.

43 The Longlian temple is located in the Chinese district in Bangkok and was built in 1871 by the abbot Xuxing 續行法師, a man from Chaozhou.

44 Li Xunlin 李訓粦, "Sanshi nianlai benhui shenmiao baoguan gaikuang 三十年來本會神廟保管概況" *Taiguo huaqiao keshu zonghui sanshi zhounian jiniankan*, 18.

45 Li Xunlin, op. cit.

46 For a brief biography of Wu Miaoyuan, see details in *Taiguo kejiaren: Taiguo kejia zonghui chengli bashi zhounian huiqing tekan*, 99–100, 305–6; for Wu Zuonan and Wu Dongbai, see pp. 105–8.

47 In the second half of the Qing dynasty, tradesmen were allowed to sail to Siam to purchase rice. As a result, Chaozhou set up a sailing company, commonly referred to as "the Red head shipping Co." 紅頭船 to develop the rice trade between China and Siam.

48 *Taiguo Zanhuagong xingben shanlu*, vol. 1, 總頁253–54.

49 Lüzu once acclaimed Xu Bingzhen as the most devout disciple in the temple's development over more than 20 years, during a spirit-writing session dated 1923: *Taiguo Zanhuagong xingben shanlu*, vol. 1, 總頁9–10. Xu Bingzhen, his brother Binghu and other members of his family were also major donors for the construction of the Bangkok Guandi temple in 1915: *Taiguo huawen mingke huibian*, 119–20.

50 *Lüzu tanxun*, vol. 1, 2.

51 *Lüzu tanxun*, vol. 1, 2.

52 *Taiguo Zanhuagong xingben shanlu*, vol. 1, 128–29（總頁255–56）.

53 "Benhui huishi 本會會史," *Taiguo huaqiao keshu zonghui sanshi zhounian jiniankan*, 5.

54 Li Xunlin, "Sanshinianlai," *Taiguo huaqiao keshu zonghui sanshi zhounian jiniankan*, 18.

55 "Liu shenmiao gaikuang baogao 六神廟概況報告," *Taiguo keshu zonghui wushi zhounian jinian tekan*, 2/9.

56 *Taiguo Zanhuagong xingben shanlu*, vol. 1, 總頁3.

57 *Lüzu tanxun*, vol. 1, 163.

58 Lin Wushu, *Taiguo Dafeng zushi chongbai*.

59 *Taiguo huaqiao zhi*, 142.

60 *Taiguo huaqiao zhi*, 146.

61 *Sing Sian Yit Pao*, 2010/10/28. I am grateful to M. Huang Weihong of the Hakka Association in Thailand for the information.

62 *Taiguo kejiaren*, 211.

63 *Sing Sian Yit Pao*, 2006/12/9. In the eyes of Lüzu temple members, this was "the most brilliantly propitious day in the history of the temple since its construction and marked the glory of overseas Chinese temples in Thailand."

64 *Lüzu jingshiwen*, postface by Zhuang Wengui and others (1864), 38. The text written on a beam in the Lüzu hall in the Sanyuangong were restored in 1862, see the section on Sanyuangong in *Guangzhoushi wenwuzhi*, 191.

65 Gray, *Walks in the City of Canton*, 382–85, quoted from Shiga Ichiko, "Jindai Lingnan daojiaoshi."

66 For information on Lüzu spirit-writing halls in Macao, see Yau, "Aomen diqu daotang."

67 *(Xuantong) Nanhai xianzhi*, juan 26, "zalu 雜錄," 49.

68 Concerning the Huangxian temple in Huadai 花埭 (Canton), see Yau, *Xiangjiang xianji*, 21–30.

69 Igarashi Kenryū, *Dōkyō sōrin*, 229–36.

70 *Meixian fengtu erbaiyong*.

71 "客總崇正醫院簡史," *Taiguo kejiaren*, 212.

72 Qiu Ruoxu 丘若虛, "Sanshinian lai benhui shiyao zengyi ji yiyuan gaikuang 卅年來本會施藥贈醫及醫院概況," *Taiguo huaqiao keshu zonghui sanshi zhounian jiniankan*, 13.

73 *Taiguo kejiaren*, 208.

74 *Taiguo Zanhuagong xingben shanlu*, vol. 1, 總頁208.

75 *Taiguo Zanhuagong xingben shanlu*, vol. 2, 128.

76 Sakai Tadao et al., *Chūgoku no reisen*, 417–27.

77 *Boji xianfang*. See also Xue Qinglu, comp., *Quanguo zhongyi tushu lianhe mulu*, 515–16.

78 Lin Guoping, "Fujian chuantong shehui de minsu liaofa," 69–70.

79 The *Zhongguo yiji dacidian*, 515 entry on the *Boji xianfang* wrongly says that it was compiled by Chen Shao 陳紹 in 1919. Chen Shao compiled and published the book but he was not the author of the work which had had several editions before 1918.

80 Song Jinxiu, "Taiwan simiao yaoqian huibian," 16, 21–25.

81 Wang Xiaodun, et al., *Yuenan hannan wenxian mulu tiyao*, 487.

82 Yau, "*Boji xianfang*."

83 *Lüzu zhenjing – Hezu daxian duren zhenjing – Cankui zushi zhenjing*, 59–61. The "True Scripture Scriptures of Master Cankui" also includes a section on "Incantations to stop opium smoking, spirit-writing session held in the name of Master Cankui of Yinna Mountain, on the 25th day of the 3rd month of the year *jiayin* (1914)," 69–72.

84 *Meixian Zanhuashe baoxun*, vol. 1, 73–74. I am very grateful to Shiga Ichiko 志賀市子 for sharing a copy of this source with me.

85 *Meixian Zanhuashe baoxun*, vol. 1, 73–74.

86 Information gathered during interviews at Zishenge temple in Bangkok, August 2007.

87 Interview with Lu Junyuan 盧均元, director the Thailand Hakka Association, 2010/8/2.

88 *Taiguo Zanhuagong xingben shanlu*, vol. 1, 總頁1–2.

89 *Taiguo Zanhuagong xingben shanlu*, vol. 1, 總頁5.

90 *Taiguo Zanhuagong xingben shanlu*, vol. 1, 總頁6–7.

91 See a picture of Liu Liangqing practicing spirit-writing, note 34 above.

92 *Lüzu tanxun*, vol. 1, 2.

93 *Lüzu tanxun*, vol. 1, 3.

94 *Taiguo Zanhuagong xingben shanlu*, vol. 1, 180–181.

95 *Taiguo Zanhuagong xingben shanlu*, vol. 1, 54–55.

96 *Taiguo Zanhuagong xingben shanlu*, vol. 1, 64–66, 69, 73.

97 *Taiguo Zanhuagong xingben shanlu*, vol. 1, 64.

98 *Taiguo Zanhuagong xingben shanlu*, vol. 2, 41–42.

99 Xu Zhizhen's preface, *Lüzu tanxun*, vol. 2, 1.

100 Zhang Daming's preface (1957), *Lüzu tanxun*, vol. 1, 1.

101 On the identity of Hezu xianshi 何祖仙師, a.k.a. Hezu yuanjun 何祖元君, Jinque puhua yuanjun 金闕普化元君, see *Lüzu zhenjing – Hezu daxian duren zhenjing – Cankui zushi zhenjing*, 41–53.

102 The Zanhuagong's Earth God was reputed to have been a palace graduate during Emperor Wanli's reign in the Ming dynasty, and then a City God after his death: see *Taiguo Zanhuagong xingben shanlu*, vol. 1, 55.

103 *Taiguo Zanhuagong xingben shanlu*, vol. 2, 35.

104 The *Lüzu duren zhenjing* was published separately but also in a compilation, including *Hezu daxian duren zhenjing* 何祖大仙渡人真經 and *Cankui zushi zhenjing* 慚愧祖師真經.

105 For details, see Li Yangzheng, *Dangdai daojiao*, 85.

106 Zhong Bioafa, "Guangdong daojiao ershinian huigu."

107 *Meixian zhi*, 1049.

108 *Meizhou shizhi*, 1765.

109 *Taiguo Zanhuagong xingben shanlu*, vol. 2, 84.

110 The expression *zanhua* 贊化 originates from the "Doctrine of the Mean" 中庸.

111 *Daojiao Zanhuagong.*
112 Lagerwey, "Dingguang gufo."
113 "Yangxing Dashizu Yunxiugong jianjie."
114 *Lüzu tanxun*, vol. 2, 125.
115 *Taiguo Zanhuagong xingben shanlu*, vol. 2, 176.
116 Interview with Xu Jiangtao 許江濤, August 2, 2010, Bangkok Lüzu temple. For details on Xu Jiangtao, a senior member of Lüzu temple supervision committee, see *Taiguo kejiaren*, 211.
117 *Taiguo Zanhuagong xingben shanlu*, vol. 2, 149.
118 *Taiguo Zanhuagong xingben shanlu*, vol. 2, 137–38.
119 Yang Jueqian, Zhong Biaofa, Huang Yinggu, *Daoguan shengdi Meizhou Zanhuagong*, 4–5.
120 Manuscript copy of the Meizhou Zanhuagong, August 6, 2000. On revelations of Liu zhenren to Huang Dengzhen, see *Taiguo Zanhuagong xingben shanlu*, vol. 2, 134, 136.
121 *Meizhou kejia fengsu*, 88.
122 "Taiguo Lüzu tongmen chaobai Meizhou Lüdimiao," 46.
123 *Lüzu tanxun*, vol. 2, 136–37. Another version, with some variants, in *Taiguo Zanhuagong xingben shanlu*, vol. 2, 182.
124 Fang Xuejia, "Meizhou de xigong," 146.
125 Fang Xuejia, "Meizhou de xigong," 146.
126 *Taiguo Zanhuagong xingben shanlu*, vol. 2, 282–83.
127 Local gazetteers record that the Zhenwugong in Pingyuan county was "built in the 47th year of Wanli's reign, beyond the Southern Gate bridge": *(Qianlong) Jiaying zhouzhi*, juan 8, "temples 寺廟," 467. In 1993, the temple was rebuilt on the same premises and open to the public: *Guangdong shengzhi – Zongjiaozhi*, 187.
128 The Bankang Gongwangmiao was built under the Ming and was devoted to the Sanshan guowang 三山國王.
129 *(Qianlong) Jiaying zhouzhi*, juan 8, "temples 寺廟," 373.
130 *Meizhou shizhi*, 1764–65.
131 *Meixian zhi*, 1050.
132 Besides the four major events celebrated each year at Bangkok's Lüzu temple, i.e., the Jade Emperor's birthday, Lüzu's birthday, Guandi's birthday, and Ullambana (7/15), particular emphasis is placed on the three last days of the Nine Emperors festival (9/7–9).
133 In the early period of the Zanhuagong, Lai Chengyou, a Daoist master from Cangnan, Zhejiang, was invited to teach Daoist liturgy.
134 *Guangdong shengzhi – Zongjiaozhi*, 186, 195.
135 Zhong Biaofa, "Guangdongsheng Daoxie."
136 "Zhua guanli," 10; Zhong Biaofa, "Guangdongsheng Daoxie."
137 Interview with Zhong Biaofa, 2006/8/17.
138 Lin Wanchuan has showed that the Thai branch of Xiantiandao was attached to the Wanquantang 萬全堂 religious district in Guangdong province. In 1871, Lin Fashan 林法善 founded the Cangxiadong 藏霞洞 temple in Qingyuan, Guangdong province. In 1914, Zhu Cunyuan 朱存元 founded the Fuyangtang 復陽堂 as a branch in Bangkok: Lin Wanchuan, "Taiguo Xiantiandao yuanliu," 140–41.
139 Lin Wushu, *Taiguo Dafeng zushi chongbai*, "Introduction."

Bibliography

Sources

Boji xianfang 博濟仙方. Hong Kong: Xianggang wujing yinshuaisuo, 1918.
Chenghuang ganying xiaozai jifu miaojing 城隍感應消災集福妙經. 1998 reprint by the Wuhua Chenhuangmiao 五華城隍廟.

Daojiao Zanhuagong xuyan 道教贊化宮序言. Leaflet edited and printed at the Zanhuagong in 1997.

Guangdong beikeji 廣東碑刻集. Tan Dihua 譚棣華 et al., comp. Guangzhou: Guangdong jiaoyu chubanshe, 2001.

Guangdong nianjian 廣東年鑑. Qujiang: Guangdong Sheng zheng fu mi shu chu, 1942.

(Qianlong) Jiaying zhouzhi (乾隆)嘉應州志. 1750. In *Gugong zhenben congkan* 故宮珍本叢刊, Haikou: Hainan chubanshe, 2001, vol. 174.

(Guangxu) Jiaying zhouzhi (光緒)嘉應州志. 1898. Taipei: Chengwen, 1968.

Lüzu jingshiwen 呂祖警世文. Guangzhou: Zhengwentang 正文堂, 1864.

Lüzu tanxun 呂祖壇訓. Bangkok: Zanhuagong, 1992 (vol. 1), 1995 (vol. 2).

Lüzu zhenjing – Hezu daxian duren zhenjing – Cankui zushi zhenjing 呂祖真經・何祖大仙渡人真經・慚愧祖師真經（合刊）. Bangkok: Zanhuagong, 1987.

Meixian fengtu erbaiyong 梅縣風土二百詠. Liang Bocong 梁伯聰 (1871–1946). Hong Kong: St John's English Publications, 1944.

Meixian Zanhuashe baoxun 梅縣贊化社寶訓. Meizhou: Zanhuashe lishihui 贊化社理事會, 1943.

Meixian zhi 梅縣志. Meixian difangzhi bianzuan weiyuanhui 梅縣地方志編纂委員會, comp. Guangzhou: Guangdong renmin chubanshe, 1994.

Meizhou shizhi 梅州市志. Meizhoushi difangzhi bianzuan weiyuanhui 梅州市地方志編纂委員會, comp. Guangzhou: Guangdong renmin chubanshe, 1999.

(Xuantong) Nanhai xianzhi 宣統南海縣志, 1911.

Shantou Zanhuagong huixinlu 汕頭贊化宮回心錄. Shantou: Yanshou shantang, 1935.

Sing Sian Yit Pao 星暹日報. Bangkok: Daily, 1950.

Taiguo huaqiao keshu zonghui sanshi zhounian jiniankan 泰國華僑客屬總會三十週年紀念刊. 1957.

Taiguo huaqiao zhi 泰國華僑志. Taipei: Huaqiao zhi bianzuan weiyuanhui, 1959.

Taiguo huawen mingke huibian 泰國華文銘刻彙編. Fu Wukang 傅吾康, Liu Lifang 劉麗芳, comp. Taipei: Xinwenfeng, 1998.

Taiguo kejiaren: *Taiguo kejia zonghui chengli bashi zhounian huiqing tekan* 泰國客家人: 泰國客家總會成立80週年會慶特刊. 2007.

Taiguo keshu zonghui wushi zhounian jinian tekan 泰國客屬總會五十週年紀念特刊. 1977.

"Taiguo Lüzu tongmen chaobai Meizhou Lüdimiao 泰國呂祖同門朝拜梅州呂帝廟," *Meizhou qiaoxiang yuebao* 梅州僑鄉月報, 11, 1994.

Taiguo Zanhuagong xingben shanlu 泰國贊化宮性本善錄. vol. 1, 1992; vol. 2, 1996.

Xinban Zhongwai pudu huangjing 新頒中外普度皇經. Hong Kong: Nanyang shangwu yinshuguan 南洋商務印書館, reprint of Shantou Zanhuagong edition, 1927.

"Yangxing Dashizu Yunxiugong jianjie 楊姓大始祖雲岫公簡介," Yangjiaci gongyuan zhouweiyuanhui 楊家祠公園籌委會編, comp., *Jianbao* 簡報, 2005.

Zhongwai pudu huangjing 中外普度皇經. Bangkok: Zanhuagong, 1993.

Secondary

Fang Xuejia 房學嘉. "Meizhou de xigong, xianghua foshi jiqi keyi 梅州的覡公、香花佛事及其科儀," in Zheng Zhiming 鄭志明, comp., *Daojiao wenhua de chuanbo* 道教文化的傳播. Jiayi: Nanhua daxue zongjiao wenhua yanjiu zhongxin, 2000, pp. 143–74.

Fang Xuejia 房學嘉. "Yuedong Meizhou de Tianhou xinyang 粵東梅州的天后信仰," in Lin Meirong 林美容 et al., comp., *Mazu xinyang de fazhan yu bianqian* 媽祖信仰的發展與變遷. Taiwan zongjiao xuehui 台灣宗教學會: Beigang Chaotiangong 北港朝天宮, 2003, pp. 285–308.

Gray, John H. *Walks in the City of Canton.* London: De Souza and Co., 1980.

Guangdong shengzhi – Minzhengzhi 廣東省志 - 民政志. 1993.

Guangdong shengzhi – Zongjiaozhi 廣東省志. 宗教志. Guangzhou: Guangdong renmin chubanshe, 2002.

Guangzhoushi wenwuzhi 廣州市文物志. Guangzhou: Lingnan meishu chubanshe, 1990.

Hu Xingrong 胡興榮, comp. *Chao-Shan wenhua baogao* 潮汕文化報告. Shantou: Shantou daxue chubanshe, 2004.

Igarashi Kenryū 五十嵐賢隆. *Dōkyō sōrin -Taiseikyū shi* 道教叢林-太清宮志. Tokyo: Kokusho Kankōkai, 1986 [1935].

Lagerwey, John. "Dingguang Gufo: Oral and Written Sources in the Study of a Saint," *Cahiers d'Extrême-Asie*, 10, 1998, pp. 77–129.

Li Bolin 李柏林. *Meizhou shiji conglan* 梅州史迹縱覽. Guangzhou: Guangdong renmin chubanshe, 1989.

Li Weiyun 李偉雲, comp. *Guangzhou zongjiaozhi* 廣州宗教志. Guangzhou: Guangdong renmin chubanshe, 1996.

Li Yangzheng 李養正, comp. *Dangdai Zhongguo daojiao* 當代中國道教. Beijing: Shehui kexue chubanshe, 1993.

Li Yangzheng 李養正, comp. *Dangdai daojiao* 當代道教. Beijing: Dongfang chubanshe, 2000.

Lin Guoping 林國平. "Fujian chuantong shehui de minsu liaofa he simiao yaoqian 福建傳統社會的民俗療法和寺廟藥簽," *Yilan wenxian zazhi* 宜蘭文獻雜誌, 37, 1999, pp. 47–89.

Lin Wanchuan 林萬傳. "Taiguo Xiantiandao yuanliu ji fangwen jishi 泰國先天道源流暨訪問記實," *Minjian zongjiao* 民間宗教, 1, 1995, pp. 139–52.

Lin Wushu 林悟殊. *Taiguo Dafeng zushi chongbai yu Huaqiao Baode shantang yanjiu* 泰國大峰祖師崇拜與華僑報德善堂研究. Taipei: Shuxin chubanshe, 1997.

Liu Lifang 劉麗芳 & Mai Liufang 麥留芳. "Mangu yu Xinjiapo huaren miaoyu ji zongjiao xisu de diaocha 曼谷與新加坡華人廟宇及宗教習俗的調查," *Minzuxue yanjiusuo ziliao huibian* 民族學研究所資料彙編, 9. Taipei: Academia Sinica, 1994, pp. 1–187.

Ma Ximin 馬希民, Chen Yun 陳雲, comp., *Chao-Shan shantang daguan* 潮汕善堂大觀. Shantou: Shantou daxue chubanshe, 2001.

Meizhou kejia fengsu 梅州客家風俗. Meizhou difangzhi bianwei bangongshi 梅州市地方志編委辦公室, comp., Guangzhou: Jinan daxue chubanshe, 1992.

Rong Zhaozu 容肇祖. "Zhanbu de yuanliu 占卜的源流," in *Rong Zhaozu ji* 容肇祖集. Jinan: Qilu shushe, 1989, pp. 1–65.

Sakai Tadao 酒井忠夫, Imai Usaburō 今井宇三郎 & Yoshimoto Shōji 吉元昭治, comp., *Chūgoku no reisen, yakusen shūsei* 中国の霊簽・薬簽集成. Tōkyō: Fūkyōsha, 1992.

Shiga Ichiko 志賀市子. "Jindai Lingnan daojiaoshi shang de 'xianguan' chutan 近代嶺南道教史上的「仙館」初探," *Taiwan zongjiao yanjiu tongxun* 臺灣宗教研究通訊, 7, 2005, pp. 93–122.

Song Jinxiu 宋錦秀. "Taiwan simiao yaoqian huibian: Yilan 'Yiyaoshen' de xitong 臺灣寺廟藥簽彙編: 宜蘭「醫藥神」的系統," *Yilan wenxian zazhi* 宜蘭文獻雜誌, 37, 1999, pp. 3–46.

Wang Xiaodun 王小盾, Liu Chunyin 劉春銀 & Chen Yi 陳義, comp., *Yuenan hannan wenxian mulu tiyao* 越南漢喃文獻目錄提要. Taipei: Zhongyang yanjiuyuan Zhongguo wenzhe yanjiusuo, 2002.

Xie Xueying 謝雪影, comp., *Shantou zhinan* 汕頭指南. Shantou: Shishi tongxunshe, 1933.

Xue Qinglu 薛清錄, comp., *Quanguo zhongyi tushu lianhe mulu* 全國中醫圖書聯合目錄. Beijing: Zhongyi guji chubanshe, 1991.

Yang Jueqian 楊爵謙, Zhong Biaofa 鍾標發 & Huang Yinggu 黃鶯谷. *Daoguan shengdi Meizhou Zanhuagong* 道觀聖地梅州贊化宮. Zanhuagong, 1994.

Yau Chi-on 游子安. "Aomen diqu daotang zeji 澳門地區道堂側記," *Taiwan zongjiao yanjiu tongxun* 臺灣宗教研究通訊, 3, 2002, pp. 85–88.

Yau Chi-on 游子安. "Boji xianfang — Qingmo yilai Lingnan diqu xianfang, shanshu yu Lüzu xinyang 博濟仙方——清末以來嶺南地區仙方、善書與呂祖信仰," *Zhongguo kejishi zazhi* 中國科技史雜誌, 32(supplement), 2011, pp. 47–63.

Yau Chi-on 游子安. "Daomai nanchuan: Ershi shiji cong Lingnan dao Yuenan Xiantiandao de chuancheng yu bianqian 道脈南傳:二十世紀從嶺南到越南先天道的傳承與變遷," in Jin Ze 金澤 & Chen Jingguo 陳進國, comp., *Zongjiao renleixue* 宗教人類學, 2. Beijing: Shehui kexue wenxian chubanshe, 2010, pp. 232–56.

Yau Chi-on 游子安. "Hatachi seiki, Sentendô no Kôtô, Honkon kara betonamuhe no denpa to henyô 二〇世紀、先天道の広東・香港からベトナムへの伝播と変容," Takeuchi Fusaji 武内房司, comp., *Ekkyô suru kindai Ajia no minshû shukyô* 越境する近代東アジアの民衆宗教. Tokyo: Akashi Shoten, 2011, pp. 47–81.

Yau Chi-on 游子安. "Meizhou daoguan Zanhuagong kaocha ji 梅州道觀贊化宮考察記," *Taiwan zongjiao yanjiu tongxun* 台灣宗教研究通訊, 2, 2000, pp. 137–43.

Yau Chi-on 游子安. "Ming zhongye yilai de Guandi xinyang: yi shanshu wei tantao zhongxin 明中葉以來的關帝信仰:以善書為探討中心," in Wang Jianchuan 王見川, Su Qinghua 蘇慶華 & Liu Wenxing 劉文星, comp., *Jindai de Guandi xinyang yu jingdian: jiantan qi zai Xin, Ma de fazhan* 近代的關帝信仰與經典:兼談其在新、馬的發展. Taipei: Boyang wenhua, 2010, pp. 4–46.

Yau Chi-on 游子安. "Qingmo yilai Lüzu xinyang de chuanbo: cong Guangdong Meizhou Lüdimiao dao Taiguo Mangu Zanhuagong 清末以來呂祖信仰的傳播:從廣東梅州呂帝廟到泰國曼谷贊化宮," in Yau Chi-on, ed. *Shanshu yu Zhongguo zongjiao. You Zian zixuanji* 善書與中國宗教.游子安自選集. Taipei: Boyang, 2012, pp. 335–69.

Yau Chi-on 游子安, comp. *Xiangjiang xianji – Jiangseyuan lishi yu Huang daxian xinyang* 香江顯跡——嗇色園歷史與黃大仙信仰. Hong Kong: Sik Sik Yuen, 2006.

Yu Xinchang 余信昌 & Yang Jueqian 楊爵謙. "Meizhoushi daojiao Zanhuagong 梅州市道教贊化宮," *Zhongguo daojiao* 中國道教, 2, 1990, pp. 50–51.

Zhong Biaofa 鍾標發. "Guangdongsheng Daoxie erjie erci lishihui gongzuo baogao 廣東省道協二屆二次理事會工作報告," *Guangdong daojiao* 廣東道教, 1, 2002, p. 7.

Zhong Biaofa 鍾標發. "Guangdong daojiao ershinian huigu 廣東道教二十年回顧," *Zhongguo daojiao* 中國道教, 5, 1999, pp. 13–15.

Zhongguo yiji dacidian 中國醫籍大辭典. Qiu Peiran 裘沛然, ed. Shanghai: Shanghai kexue jishu chubanshe, 2002.

"Zhua guanli, cu fazhan, shiying xiandai shehui – Meizhou Zanhuagong guanli jingyan tan 抓管理・促發展・適應現代社會—梅州贊化宮管理經驗談," *Guangdong daojiao* 廣東道教, 1, 2003, pp. 8–10.

Part III
Householder urban Daoists

5 The modern transformations of the Old Eastern Peak temple in Hangzhou

Fang Ling

Translated by Catherine Seidner

The cult of the Eastern Peak (Dongyue 東嶽) has gone through many major evolutions. Since antiquity, the Eastern Peak, also known as Taishan 泰山 and one of China's Five Peaks, located on the Shandong peninsula, has been perceived as possessing the power of life over living people, and revered as the god of long life and immortality. Under the Eastern Han period (AD 25–220), Taishan had already assumed jurisdiction over the dead souls, as testified in both official and Daoist ancient and medieval documents. But the most radical development occurred at the beginning of the Northern Song dynasty (960–1127). In 1008, Emperor Zhenzong himself went to Mount Taishan to offer sacrifice and bestowed the title of "King of Benevolence," 仁聖王, on Taishan. Three years later, he added the rank of "Emperor of Benevolence equal to Heaven of Mount Taishan," 東嶽天齊仁聖帝 citing as the reason for the promotion that "his benevolence equals heaven." Of this series of events, the most important one occurred in 1010 when the emperor promulgated a decree to encourage people to build, as they wished,[1] Dongyue temples, thus setting up the cult of Dongyue as a public institution. Prior to that, according to Confucian ritual, the emperor was formally the only being entitled to worship heaven, earth, mountains, and rivers. Dongyue temples built by the people were indeed very few. But after 1010, the people were integrated into the cult of Taishan in a legal way, as the state now more or less acknowledged their spiritual needs. Therefore, the Imperial Court and the ordinary people now shared a common cult. From then on, Dongyue temples began to spread all over China. The main temple was located on Mount Taishan in Shandong, while all the temples located elsewhere were regarded as the God's travel palaces (*xinggong* 行宮, *xingci* 行祠, *biemiao* 別廟).

In 1127, after being driven from their capital Kaifeng by the invading Jurchens, the Southern Song court (1127–1279) fled south and established Hangzhou as their new capital. There the first place of worship of Dongyue was set up in 1159,[2] on the premises of a former hall built in 1107–1110 on Wushan 吳山 hill, in the center of the city. More Dongyue temples soon appeared. The *Mengliang lu*

夢梁錄 (written in 1274) mentioned that "there are five Dongyue travel palaces in and around Hangzhou[3]: Wushan, Fahuashan 法華山 in Xixi 西谿, Jingxing Daoist temple 景星觀 in Linping 臨平, Shunji Daoist temple 順濟宮 in Tangzhen 湯鎮, and Tanshan Buddhist temple 壜山 in Yangcun 楊村."[4] This figure includes four temples located in the outskirts of Hangzhou, in both Qiantang 錢塘 and Renhe 仁和 districts. The Hangzhou prefecture had jurisdiction over nine districts, and each district had its own Dongyue temple. Qiantang and Renhe districts, whose administration was located in the capital, were considered as part of Hangzhou; this is the reason why the author inventoried these five temples. Except for Mount Fahua temple, which seems to have been a new building, the other four places of worship were established in existing Daoist and Buddhist temples. They were of different sizes. The temple at Tangzhen was erected under imperial orders. During the Qiandao reign (1165–1173), the Xiaozong Emperor financed the construction of the hall dedicated to the Five Peaks – a large comprehensive temple located next to the Shunji temple.[5] In addition, three Dongyue temples were located in Xixi, Linping, and Tangzhen, which were suburban market towns and parts of the market system of Hangzhou as well as new economic centers.[6] Scholars have noted the crucial role of religion in the formation of networks of market towns in the Jiangnan area, as town temples periodically attracted farmers from rural areas.[7] However, Hangzhou during the Southern Song era was a wealthy metropolis with a very large population; it probably was the largest city in the world at that time. The suburban Dongyue temples attracted the emperor as well as ordinary people because of their space:

> In the capital, there were many territorial associations (*shemo* 社陌), therefore, it was difficult for only one temple to welcome the offering of all associations, [this is the reason why they used to go] either to Wushan temple [inside the city] or to Tanshan temple in the southern part of the city, or to Linping temple in the north, or to Tangzhen in the east, or to Mount Fahua in the west.[8]

The last temple was later colloquially named Lao Dongyue 老東嶽 (Old Dongyue temple) to show its seniority. In Hangzhou today, it is one of several community temples that have managed to rebuild and exist on the outskirts of the city after a long period of disappearance. It is also the only Dongyue temple in this area functioning as a place of worship. This chapter is devoted to a study of the history and transformation of this temple. It adopts historical and anthropological approaches, and it relies on historical sources, published or manuscript surveys, and my own materials and field data (2001, 2007–2012). I will briefly review the history of the temple, including the context and the process of its contemporary reconstruction. I will then study the role that the Daoist masters of the Zheng clan played before the destruction of the temple and the violent repression they suffered, as well as the return of the Daoist liturgical services. Finally, I will review the organization of communities of worship and their activities in the past and examine the renewal of associations of pilgrims who are reforming again.

Birth and rebirth

The most majestic Dongyue temple of Hangzhou

The Old Dongyue temple is located in Dongyue village, north of Fahua hill in the west of Hangzhou; the village was named after the temple. Since the Southern Song dynasty, this ancient village has been successively subordinated to Qiantang and Hangxian districts, and then integrated into Hangzhou city in 1958. As part of a rampant urbanization, since 2004 the Dongyue village is no longer an administrative entity, but it lies within the jurisdiction of the new commune of Dongyue which encompasses nine natural villages.

The temple was founded in 1167.[9] Apart from this date, we have no other information about its construction. Half a century later, it was restored and expanded. The stele inscription dedicated to the restoration of the Dongyue temple on Fahua hill (*Fahuashan chongxiu Dongyue miao ji* 法華山重修東嶽廟記, 1227) states that this temple is located 30 *lis* (15 km) from the capital.[10] Despite the fact that, over the years, it greatly deteriorated and fell eventually into disrepair, the local officials and the people (*shimin* 士民) still continued to patronize it.[11] However, Wang, a local scholar, collected money, which enabled him to restore the beams of the main hall. Later, Song Nian 松年, the temple manager, donated the statue of Dongyue and restored the alleys. However, due to sickness, he was confined to bed for a long time and his family secretly prayed for him in the temple. One night, Song Nian had a dream in which he was in the temple and a divine being made him promise to collect more money for the expansion and restoration of the temple. When he woke up, his illness was cured. He told this story to Marquis Li and Mi. In turn, they told this story to Minister Shi Miyuan 史彌遠 (1164–1233), who not only made a significant donation amounting to 300,000 *liang* 兩 but also launched a fundraiser to which many people contributed. The renovation work started during the tenth lunar month of 1224 and ended during the third lunar month of 1227. Every single piece was restored, from the roof to the basement, the access road was paved and inside, the altars were completed. Four new halls for secondary cults (*suisi* 隨祀) were also built. A well was dug to draw healing water for sick people. We can therefore understand that the temple, though it was located 15 km away from the city, was a common place of worship for the whole society, from the ranking officials to ordinary people. Song Nian's dream about the divine will thus became a foundation myth of which we will later survey the enduring influence and transformation.

In 1276, the Mongol army captured the capital, ending the Southern Song dynasty. Though the Yuan dynasty was a foreign power, they worshipped nature deities and continued to revere the Chinese sacred mountains like their predecessors. In 1291, Khubilai, the first emperor of the Yuan dynasty, bestowed a new title upon the Eastern Peak by adding two characters to the title already bestowed in 1011.[12] We lack historical data about the Fahua Dongyue temple during the Yuan dynasty, but according to a stele discussed below, it seems that the temple continued to develop. In addition, as the Yuan court forbade the repair of urban fortifications, the walls of Hangzhou were gradually dismantled and traffic between the city and suburbs became much easier, inadvertently facilitating the pilgrims' travels to the Eastern Peak temples there.

After the fall of the Yuan dynasty, under the influence of Confucians, who were always fiercely opposed to the expansion of the Dongyue cult all over the country, rejected the anthropomorphic representation of Taishan in official rituals, and advocated a return to the classical tradition, Zhu Yuanzhang, the first emperor of the newly founded Ming dynasty, removed in 1370 all the names conferred on sacred mountains and rivers by the previous dynasties. However, this did not stop or hamper the development of Dongyue temples under the Ming, because, on the one hand, the imperial state implemented a policy of relative religious tolerance and the Dongyue temples continued to be officially recognized[13]; and on the other hand, the development of the Dongyue cult under the preceding two dynasties had become both ubiquitous[14] and essential in the religious life of society.

By the late Ming, during the Wanli era (1572–1619), Qin Maoguang 秦懋觀, a provincial administration commissioner (*buzhengshi* 布政使), had the Dazhonggong 大中宮, Great Centrality temple, built.[15] It became the central hall of the Dongyue temple at Fahuashan. From a description written during this period, we can see that the temple included two pavilions for the empress (Dongyue's spouse), one for her clothing and the other for her makeup, and, on both sides of the two alleys, the 72 judges of hell were placed under the authority of the Dongyue Emperor.[16] Lang Ying 郎瑛 (1487–1566), a renowned scholar, commemorated the temple in his "Inscription on the restoration of the Dongyue temple" (1565):

> [Hangzhou] has three temples, one is Wushan, in the centre of city, another is Bapanling, in the outskirts of the city, and the third is in Fahuashan which is located 30 *li* from the city. This [last] is the place dearest to the people's heart. 人心趨向以此為最.
>
> Of these three temples, only Fahuashan is greatly honoured. Why? My opinion is that this is a divine manifestation: Let us note the temple's source that has the power to heal diseases, and Song Nian's dream and his promise to collect money, details of which were mentioned in the stele inscription [1227]. From the Song until today, more than 500 years have elapsed. The temple looks more and more prosperous, and one wonders how human strength alone could have achieved such a thing.[17]

According to this account, in Hangzhou during the Ming dynasty, there were three famous Dongyue temples. Among them, the one at Fahuashan, after 500 years of development, had become the most popular not only in size but also in terms of number of pilgrims. Besides, the author emphasizes the founding myth and the divine will from which the temple originated. Wushan, the most ancient Dongyue temple, lacked space for expansion, and was destroyed at the end of the Yuan dynasty; it was rebuilt during the Jingtai era (1450–1456), burnt down in 1474, and rebuilt again only in 1532. This might be one of the reasons why many pilgrims turned to patronize the Fahuashan temple instead.

The Qing dynasty marks the apex of the temple's further development, as it thrived to become the "most majestic of all Dongyue temples in Hangzhou" (*Hangjun Yuemiao zhiguan* 杭郡嶽廟之冠)[18] and become a very important center for the Taishan cult in the whole Jiangnan region. During the autumn festival, named "Audience and Judgment [by the Great Emperor Dongyue]" (Chaoshen 朝審), the number of pilgrims used to reach about 100,000 people. Three subordinate temples (*xiayuan* 下院) were built, two in Hangzhou (at Caoying xiang 草營巷 and Tianshui qiao 天水橋) and one in Tonglu 桐廬 district, southwest of Hangzhou,[19] and the designation "Old Dongyue" appears for the first time in the records.[20] Under the Qing dynasty, the temple endured many disasters (floods, fires), but, thanks to the powerful pilgrim associations, it was restored or rebuilt each time. For instance, a fire broke out on August 11, 1875, burning the temple to the ground with only 13 statues being spared;[21] but the temple was entirely rebuilt the following year. In the middle of the nineteenth century, like many other temples, the Old Dongyue temple faced a period of instability and political repression. First, the Taiping army caused major destruction to Hangzhou. In 1860 and 1861, the army besieged Hangzhou twice within a short period, and eventually breached and occupied the city, which caused many deaths – estimated at about 1 million people who were either slaughtered during and after the siege or succumbed to diseases and starvation. Most of the temples located in the city were destroyed, including the Dongyue temple on Wushan.

The good fortune of the Old Dongyue temple was due partly to its location outside the city. This explains that though plundered by the iconoclast Taipings, the temple's buildings and the statues were spared. Second, though under Qing law festive processions were forbidden, this kind of ban was very rarely enforced in Hangzhou till the advent of the Taiping occupation. Some temples that had been destroyed during the Taiping era were rebuilt just afterward, and festive processions gradually resumed. However, the policy of the local authorities in this matter became more and more restrictive. From 1898, local religious politics radically changed with the onset of the "Expropriation of the temples for schools" (*feimiao banxue* 廢廟辦學) and the "anti-superstition" (*pochu mixin* 破除迷信) campaigns.

During the early Republican era (1911–1949), the anti-religious movement became even more violent, as the Republican government issued and enforced more anti-superstition decrees. A significant number of temples and festive processions were suppressed.[22] In December 1928, a decree was issued by the Home Minister with specific criteria whereby to determine which temples were to be destroyed and which to be preserved (*Shenci cunfei biaozhunling* 神祠存廢標準令). An official list of these temples was also edited. Some Daoist institutions – or temples narrowly linked to Daoism – appeared in this list which included the Dongyue cult. As a result, suppression of Daoism was therefore legalized,[23] and, in the case of the Old Dongyue temple, the procession celebrating its anniversary was discontinued for more than 20 years. By the end of the Qing dynasty, the "Audience and Judgment" festival, which attracted a significant number of people, had become a permanent target of the religious reform movements. During the Republican era, this festival was targeted by the "anti-superstition" policies and was repeatedly banned. Besides, from the 1930s to 1949, wars and economic recession also hampered the Old Dongyue temple festivals. In 1937, after the Japanese army marched into Hangzhou and occupied the city, it established one of its headquarters in Dongyue village, and till the end of the war in 1945, all the festivities were suspended. After the war, in 1946 and 1947, the festivities were permitted to resume. But then, as war broke out between Communists and Nationalists, festivities were suspended again.[24] Despite worsening political, social, and economic conditions before these wars, the Old Dongyue temple was able to maintain its majesty and was even completely renovated from 1923 to 1925 – these were the only works undertaken during the Republican era. At that time, the temple occupied a surface of about 1 ha, included over 100 rooms, and housed over 300 statues[25]; it was organized around the first and second great gates, the main entrance, the lateral galleries that sheltered the 76 Judges of Hell (a list expanded from the 72 judges mentioned in an earlier source), the main hall of the Dongyue Emperor and many other halls, such as those for Hell and the Blood Lake.[26] However, at the end of the Republican era, due to a lack of maintenance, some halls were in ruins (Figure 5.1).[27]

Destruction and reconstruction

As early as May 3, 1949, Hangzhou came under the authority of the Communist regime. The temples were declining rapidly: according to a survey conducted in 1932, the city of Hangzhou had 280 Daoist temples, but by 1950, only 78 temples were left and by 1958 there were only 46. These were merged into five, but they were then occupied during the Cultural Revolution.[28] In the list of temple names established in 1950, there are four Dongyue temples, including one Old Dongyue's subordinate, but the Old Dongyue temple itself was not included in the statistics. This was because at that time, it was under the administration of the Hangxian district.[29] According to the memories of Daoist masters, the temple activities were maintained until the spring pilgrimage (*chunxiang* 春香) of 1958. However, during the summer of that year, the Public Security Bureau declared the Community of the Dongyue's worship (Dongyuehui 東嶽會) as one of the "reactionary secret societies" (*fandong huidaomen* 反動會道門), and so the temple was closed.[30] The following year, as building materials were needed for other civic construction projects, the temple was demolished. Over a period of three months from June to September, the Old Dongyue temple was entirely pulled down, and only the foundations of the temple were left behind. The nearly 800-year-old Daoist temple and major center of both official and popular worship of Jiangnan was razed to the ground.

Although the Old Dongyue temple was entirely demolished, the cult did not totally disappear. Local devotees claimed that the Great Dongyue Emperor had entered the body of a local old lady and demanded a shelter. Therefore, the people installed his statue in the Sanfang temple 三方廟, a nearby local shrine dedicated to the God of earth and cereals (*tugu shen* 土穀神). However, all the statues of that

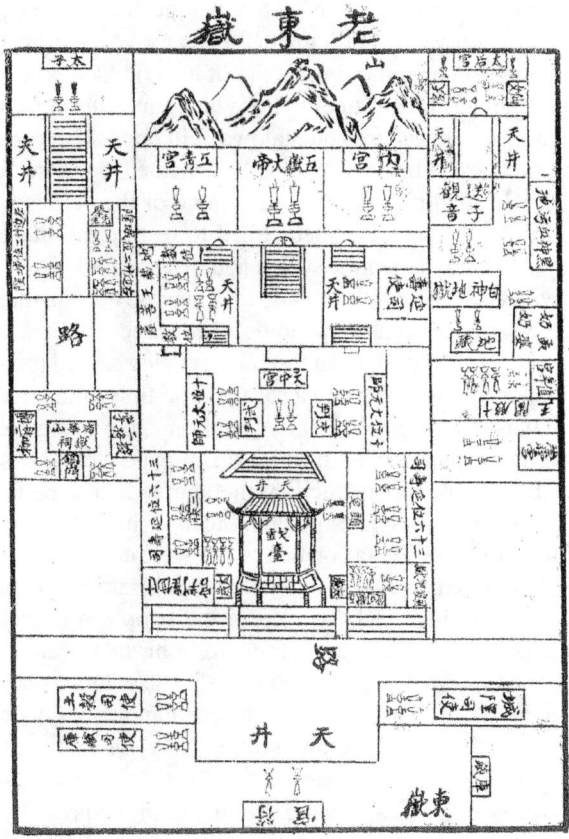

Figure 5.1 Old Dongyue temple layout in *Wulin jinxiang xuzhi*, p. 563. This map does not show the entrance hall Jianing baodian built in 1809, destroyed in 1929, and later restored; it was thus likely drawn before 1809.

temple were soon destroyed and crushed to bits in order to make fertilizer. The ruined site of the Old Dongyue temple became the headquarters of the Zhejiang provincial police canine training department and, later, a detention center was also created in the vicinity. However, despite such conditions, pilgrims continued to travel inconspicuously to the former site of the temple to burn incense. Even at the height of the Cultural Revolution, people continued to secretly go to the old temple site on the hill for worship.

During the late 1970s, the CCP Central Committee began to implement more liberal religious policies, "in order to resolve as soon as possible the question raised by the needs of religious people to practice their religion: a place for worship, the supply of religious objects, and a clergy in charge of religious activities."[31] In 1983, China's State Council approved the opening of a first list of Daoist temples, among which one was located in Hangzhou, the Baopu Daoist

Monastery (Baopu daoyuan 抱朴道院). Despite many initial difficulties, since it had neither a hall nor an altar,[32] it restored hope for the Hangzhou Daoists in what had become known as the "major disaster area" for their religion. As more and more people went to the former site of the Old Dongyue temple to burn incense, the management committee of the village met during the first half of 1993 and decided then to have three bungalows built opposite the detention center at the foot of the hill. At the beginning, the place, named "incense burning point," *xianghuodian* 香火點, had no statue and the name of the deities was written on red paper. The Daoist priests were then called to restore the liturgical services. This is how the Old Dongyue temple which had disappeared for 34 years by then first began its revival. In the next few years, the "incense burning point" expanded to the extent that a two-story house had to be built to accommodate pilgrims. The expansion included a dining hall and a room for reciting sacred texts on the lower floor, and additional rooms on the upper floor. The first time I went to the Old Dongyue temple was in September 2002. At that time, the village committee was already planning the reconstruction of the Old Dongyue temple. As there was no more land available for the reconstruction, the temple had to be built in accordance with the mountain topography. In 2006, the main hall, the Dongyue baodian 東嶽寶殿, and the storied buildings on both sides were completed. Then, in 2008, the Dizang 地藏 Hall dedicated to Ksitigarbha bodhisattva was built, the three bungalows were demolished, and the gate to the temple was erected. In April 2009, when I investigated the Dongyue Emperor's birthday celebration, the Old Dongyue temple had a new look and, although its size could not compare with that of its former counterpart, it still looked as great and magnificent as it used to be. I also note that in the main hall, around the Dongyue Emperor, the ancillary cult is that of the emperor's ten generals. The 76 Judges of Hell, including the very popular Judge Bao 包公, who were prominent in the pre-1949 temples and in the popular cult, are not present anymore.

"A point for the people's belief" (minjian xinyang dian 民間信仰點*)*

Fifteen years elapsed from the erection of the simple and basic "incense burning point" to the completion of the brand new, magnificent Old Dongyue temple, the gate, and the pilgrims' house. The fact that this temple, initially condemned to disappear, could be rebuilt and developed is primarily due to the courage and perseverance of the village leader and the villagers. The Dongyue village is an area of 3 km², comprising of cultivated land and mountain forest which, in the early 1990s, was still an economically backward place. In 1993, Hu Jianmin 胡建民, the head of the village committee, dared to launch a project that took advantage of the good location on the suburban border. The whole village, which co-financed the construction of factories and the development of industry, made a profit as early as the end of that same year.[33] By 2000, the total output value of agriculture and industry of this village of 350 inhabitants amounted to 330 million yuans, with available funds exceeding 23.6 million yuans. The Dongyue village after obtaining the honorary titles of "Zhejiang economically powerful village," and "civilized village of the Province"[34] was also the subject of a report on the CCTV. In September of that same year,[35] Hu Jianmin, who aimed to provide free education to the children of the village, was dismissed from his position as party secretary because he had established a private college without official authorization.[36] However, he was rehabilitated very soon. He had served as village head, village party branch secretary, and CCP secretary, and had also been rated as an outstanding member of the West Lake District branch ever since.

In 1993, when Hu was appointed as a supervisor, the village committee was concerned by the fact that "pilgrims were burning incense everywhere on the former site of the Old Dongyue temple, creating a fire hazard." It had therefore set up an "incense burning point." Later, Hu requested from the West Lake municipality the authorization to restore the Old Dongyue temple and the nearby Fahuasi 法華寺 Buddhist monastery, stating that it would boost tourist resources which, in turn, would develop the economic and social development of the Dongyue village.[37] He also set up the Fahuashan Management Committee (Fahuashan guanli weiyuanhui 法華山管理委員會), with his brother put in charge of the reconstruction of the two temples. The history of the Fahuasi can be traced back to the Eastern Jin dynasty (317–420). However, after the modern political upheavals, only the main hall had survived. As his applications for restoring and rebuilding the temples produced no results for several years, Hu Jianmin personally went to Beijing to visit the Chinese Buddhist Association and solicited help from its head Zhao Puchu 趙樸初 (1907–2000), vice-chairman of the Chinese People's Political Consultative Conference. Thanks to Zhao's support,[38] the request was eventually approved by the Hangzhou Municipal Government which also approved of the reconstructed Fahuasi as a place for religious activities. The formal foundation stone laying ceremony for the reconstruction of the Fahua Monastery took place on August 28, 2000, and three years later, the reconstruction was completed. The inauguration ceremony of the Fahua temple was held on October 30, 2003.[39] The newly reconstructed temple, which covers an area of about 7 ha was financed by Hangzhou Huatai Industrial Company 杭州法華實業公司, a collective enterprise of the Dongyue village founded by Hu Jianmin, who also served as its general manager. The total cost of reconstruction amounted to 40 million yuans. The temple management authority derives from the village committee.

All the previous requests for the reconstruction for the Old Dongyue temple had failed repeatedly because in 1958, the Dongyue association was officially labeled as "a reactionary secret society." According to the concerned parties, due to this "historical issue," all the former requests were then perceived by the Hangzhou municipality as "slightly thorny." Though I went there many times, I could never secure authorization to consult the reconstruction plan. I was eventually told not to make any further requests. This temple was in the end rebuilt under circumstances of tacit consent. Therefore, we can easily understand why the wealthy Dongyue village could have the Fahuasi built within three years, whereas 15 years were needed to build the Old Dongyue temple. We have here one village with two temples, each with a different status. The Old Dongyue temple is like most temples in China: without any legal status for hosting "religious activities," but possessing only a "point for people's belief," the new official term for the "incense burning points." Numerous reports and interviews are devoted to the Dongyue village and Hu Jianmin in the media; while they make references to the Fahuasi, they never even mention the Old Dongyue temple.

The contrast extends to the management of both temples. Regarding the Fahuasi, Hu Jianmin had initially approached the Zhejiang Buddhist Association in order to have a monk of renown appointed as temple manager (*zhuchi* 住持), but his request had not been successful. During the first years of operation, management was challenging because of general confusion, as the local administrative authorities declared themselves "powerless" to act faced with recurring complaints related to some clerics of the temple who used to make visitors pay whatever they felt like charging. In 2006, Ge Deju 葛德鉅, who was both a contractor and a lay Buddhist who had several companies to his name, had volunteered to manage the temple and the Dongyue Administrative Committee had then signed an agreement with him by appointing him as the Director of the Management Committee of the monastery. According to this agreement, 30% of the temple income was allocated to the local community and the remaining 70% to the temple, which was to assume all the expenses, including maintenance and renovation. After taking up the post, he created an academy (*shuyuan* 書院) and a company named after the temple. He also planned to use "Fahuasi" as a trademark. In 2011, he auctioned the name of Fahuasi academy and one of the institutes of his company in order to publicize it and attract investors. This kind of auction was the very first experience of this kind in China and the advertisement in the media had provoked indignant reactions. Both the Minorities and Religious Affairs Bureau of West Lake municipality and the Dongyue Administrative Committee intervened and requested the auction to be stopped. At that time, local authorities decided that, concerning the registration of Fahuasi with the administration, the supervisor of Fahuasi was Hu Jianmin and that regulations regarding the management of the places of worship in Hangzhou strictly prohibited all forms of rentals and contracts.

The management of the Old Dongyue temple is supervised by the Fahuashan Management Committee and especially Hu Jianmin's sister who is in charge of the temple. The committee hired Daoist masters who provided the liturgical services in conjunction with local persons in charge of both the maintenance of the temple and accommodation of pilgrims (canteen, dormitory). Mrs Hu keeps a very close eye on the sources of income of the temple: worshippers' gifts, liturgical and accommodation services, sale of entrance tickets, and cult supplies. In 2006, the Committee leased a side hall to a couple with the proviso that they arrange a "Buddha's room" (*fotang* 佛堂) and a service of interpretation of oracles (*lingqian* 靈籤). This couple hired a "grand master" and "eminent monk," argued that this *fotang* was an annex of the famous Lingyin monastery 靈隱寺 which is located on the other side of the mountain. They also hired touts to attract tourists to this *fotang* and charged them exorbitant prices. This fraud, which lasted more than a year and resulted in many people being duped, was brought to an end by the arrest of the group by the Hangzhou police. Yet, would there be a divination service run by genuine specialists, it would be very successful.

Therefore, in spite of the wealth of the village, the main concern of the temple's management committee is the generation of and control over income. The Zheng clan, a great local lineage which used to manage the temple and includes many Daoist masters of the Zhengyi school, is not represented in the committee. The Zhengs challenge and openly criticize the management of the temple by using terms such as "they only want to earn money" or "they lack any knowledge of the cult." Behind the palpable tension with the Hu family, that holds power, the shadow of the political repression of the past lingers on. By the early 2000s, the Zheng clan contacted the Hangzhou Daoist Association and expressed the wish that it could take over the management of the Old Dongyue temple, so that it could be recognized by the state as a "place of religious activity." But the Hangzhou Daoist Association is presently controlled by Quanzhen Daoists, in contrast to the Zhengyi Daoist lineage to which the Zheng clan belongs. The chairman of the Hangzhou Daoist Association once stated: "The temple should be managed by Daoist masters [of our association], only then will the Daoist Association recognize its status." No agreement was ever found. What underlies the rift between the Daoist Association and the so-called people's temples are vital and genuine economic benefits at stake. Indeed these economic interests have led the village committee to take up a simple position on this matter:

> Since the total cost of our temple reconstruction amounted to 20 million yuans, therefore, if the Bureau of Religious Affairs and the Hangzhou Daoist Association wish to manage this temple, they will have to refund our expenditure incurred for its reconstruction.

At the moment I learned the position of the local community, the political categories for the management of religions were already part of a relatively open political debate on the part of the central authorities.[40] Until then, the Hangzhou Daoist Association owned and managed only five affiliated temples, the last of which had been restored in 2011 by the municipality, which planned to make this temple dedicated to Zhang Xian 張憲, a hero of the Southern Song, a base for patriotic education. However, the so-called places of popular beliefs are infinitely more numerous and a majority of them are dedicated to the local gods.[41] In 2004, the State Administration of Religious Affairs 國家宗教事務局 began to conduct investigations and studies on the religious situation on the ground, among which "popular beliefs" that go far beyond the officially recorded religions. In the meantime however, the threat to ban community temples was gradually diminishing. Yet, many of them were still seeking to position themselves within an administratively recognized framework. The rigid position of the Hangzhou Daoist Association regarding community temples being well-known, some have turned to the Hangzhou Buddhist Association, but very few have managed to be affiliated to it, and at what cost! Indeed, they must accept to be, on the administrative level, a mere component of a Buddhist monastery located in the vicinity of their temple. This is how a major temple, the Lüshamiao 綠沙廟, became the Hall of the Earth God 土地殿 of a Buddhist monastery while keeping its management autonomy, for a lump-sum contribution to the Buddhist Association. The members of its management committee I have met have repeatedly insisted on the fact that "our temple is Daoist, their [monastery] is Buddhist."

Under the terms of the registration, on an experimental basis, of the "sites for practices of popular beliefs" in a few provinces, in 2014, a document issued by the State Administration of Religious Affairs requests that "on the basis of the existing investigations and reviews, measures should be surveyed and established for the management of matters regarding popular beliefs." By the end of that same year, "Regulations relating to the registration and identification of places of activities of popular beliefs in the province of Zhejiang" 浙江省民間信仰活動場所登記編號管理辦法 were released and, by the following year, the municipality of Hangzhou began their implementation. After its revival, the Old Dongyue temple will eventually be administratively recognized. However, will this be enough to erase the stigma of the past?

The Daoist masters of Old Dongyue temple

"The Zheng altar of this temple"

Until its destruction in 1958, the temple had been managed by the Zheng clan over a long period. The Daoist masters in the village have been, and still are, exclusively members of this clan, and they are respectfully called "Old Dongyue (temple) Daoist Masters." Zheng is the dominant family name in the village. At the present, the clan has approximately 600 members coming from a hundred families; they belong to the Ming, Fa, You, and Ben generations in the Zheng genealogy.[42] Many members of the clan live in other villages. According to the ancients, the Zheng clan originates from the Pujiang district in Zhejiang. But because the genealogy was lost, the Zhengs had neither textual proof nor knowledge of their early history. However, in 2002, the clan founded a small research group which included some old Daoist masters in order to find its origins and to know their ancestors (*xungen renzu* 尋根認祖). The research project was launched a year later in 2003. According to the findings of this survey, the Zhengs' ancestors originate from Yongyang, a place located in Henan province. During the wars that took place during the Yongjia reign (AD 307–313) of the Western Jin dynasty, the Zhengs emigrated southward, to the region of Pujiang. During the Jiading reign (1208–1224) of the Southern Song dynasty, in order to escape from famine and despair, Zheng Mao 鄭茂 resettled in Xixi, at the foot of Fahuashan. He became the founder ancestor of the Zheng clan. Zheng Mao had four sons, who founded four branches: Yongqing tang 永慶堂, Yanqing tang 衍慶堂, Yuqing tang 餘慶堂, and Rongqing tang 榮慶堂. All these four branches' names are still in use. On February 12, 2012, the Association for Friendship among the Descendants of the First Fraternal Zheng Clan of Jiangnan and the Association for Study of Culture & History of the first Zheng Family of Jiangnan declared in a joint statement that they agreed that the Zheng clan of Xixi in Hangzhou does descend from the Zheng ancestral clan; and that they would integrate the Xixi Zhengs in their meta-lineage. On April 4, 2012, on the day of the Qingming festival, in front of the Old

Dongyue temple, the Zheng clan held a ceremony to celebrate the fact that they were acknowledged and reintegrated with their origins.[43]

This choice of venue for the ceremony says a lot about the complex history of the connection between the Zheng clan and the Old Dongyue temple. According to a survey conducted in 1936, the various buildings of the Old Dongyue temple were the properties of the associations of devotees because they had financed their construction. In addition, each of the associations was responsible for the maintenance of its own buildings.

> However, the land on which these buildings are erected and their surroundings are the property of the Zheng clan. That explains why descendants of the Zheng clan have lived at and managed the temple for so long. Therefore, when descendants became more and more numerous, the Old Dongyue temple became a small market town and the Zheng Daoists also attained the status of native people. As a result, the temple had since been managed by the Zheng clan and all the Daoist masters at the temple have been descendants of the Zheng clan.[44]

When and how was the Zheng clan's real estate established? And when and in what manner did the Zheng clan start to manage the temple? We still lack evidence to provide any definitive answers to these questions. However, according to their own legends, the Zheng clan members themselves assert that "when our ancestor Zheng Mao fled his home country's misery, he first built a shed in the Fahua valley and opened up land for agriculture. Later, he built a small temple there." The Zhengs nowadays are convinced that this little temple later evolved to become the Old Dongyue temple.[45] Later, during their survey completed between 2003 and 2012 to trace back their origins, the Zhengs gained knowledge of the stele inscription dated 1227 about the restoration of the Dongyue temple. They therefore thought that their ancestor arrived in Hangzhou before 1224, the date of the beginning of the restoration, and that the extension of the temple took part of the land of their ancestor. They thus used and further developed the foundation myth of the Zheng clan.

We must remember that the 1227 stele celebrating the restoration of the temple makes no mention of any Zheng as donor or as manager. In the historical documents at our disposal, the earliest mention of a Zheng is recorded in the 1565 stele inscription mentioned above, where the temple manager is named Zheng Shicheng 鄭仕成. All this proves that the management of the temple by the Zheng clan may have been an historical process and the result of their gradual development and possession of land. Based on available evidence, the Zhengs' management of the temple can be firmly dated to only around the sixteenth century. Later the clan installed "the Zheng Altar of this temple" 本廟香火案鄭 among the statues of the Judges of Hell in the Old Dongyue temple.[46] During New Year, the clan members came to the temple for presenting it an offering.[47] But despite the privileges of the Zheng clan, the Old Dongyue temple is neither a family nor a clan temple as some people let it believe.[48] It has long been a community temple, and its activities have always been maintained, thanks to the various voluntary associations of devotees. Therefore, we can reasonably assume that these associations were the employers of the Zheng families and their Daoist masters.

As temple managers, members of the Zheng clan enjoyed a monopoly on the temple revenue which was shared among their four branches. Each of these four branches had a branch head (*fangzhang* 房長), and the clan head (*zuzhang* 族長) usually came from the first branch. In the 1920s, the four branches had a total of 48 families (*fang* 房), and by the 1940s, the number of families had grown to 52.[49] The foundation of a family is dependent on its financial independence. This means that its own income must proceed from both liturgical services and accommodation of pilgrims, which implies that it must be able to draw and retain pilgrims in the temple. In addition, among the people named Zheng, some were initially surnamed Kang 康, Zhu 朱, or Yuan 袁 and later were allowed to adopt the surname,[50] because they contributed to the protection of the temple when disasters occurred. However, these families were not allowed a share of the revenue generated from and at the temple.

The Zheng clan was prosperous and renowned, thanks to its Daoist masters. However, we lack information to determine the identity of their first Daoist master, and the origin of their ritual tradition. According to their founding myth, after the construction of the temple, their ancestor Zheng Mao "converted to Daoism and studied the Zhengyi School."[51] The current Daoist masters of the Old Dongyue temple often insist on the fact that, like the Daoist masters of the former Chenghuang temple, they belong to the Zhengyi school of the Zhang Heavenly Masters 張天師 on Longhushan 龍虎山 in Jiangxi province. They also insist on the close connection between the two temples that used to house the largest number of Daoist masters in Hangzhou until 1949. Their management system was similar: the Chenghuang temple was managed by Daoist masters who were initially divided into 15 families and, during the Qing era, there still were 11 families with 40 ordained masters (*shoudu zhe* 受度者) in total. During the seventeenth and eighteenth centuries, some Daoist masters from Chenghuang temple were sent to Longhushan for liturgical services and carried out some functions there. Among them, some of them were chosen to serve at the court in Beijing.[52] However, regarding the Daoist masters of the Old Dongyue temple, the Daoist families' legends and the survivors' memories contain no information concerning the ordination, or the total number, or even a famous figure in the lineage.

These appellations of "Daoist masters family" and "Daoist masters of the Zheng clan" first appear in historical sources only by the middle of the Qing dynasty,[53] which means that the Zheng clan's Daoist masters were by then known and rather numerous. A newspaper article of the early Republican era about the autumn festival of the "Audience and Judgment" mentioned "a total of 300 Daoist masters who did not live on the premises of the temple. However, all these Daoist masters' families lived around the temple and were all named Zheng."[54] This number seems quite exaggerated because, during that festival, the whole clan was mobilized and, in addition, many guest Daoist masters (*keshi* 客師) attended, as well as the other families of the village. The reporter undoubtedly created some confusion by mixing all these people. Both the prosperity of the Old Dongyue temple and the demand of local society for Daoist rituals imply that a good number of the Zheng's descendants became Daoist masters. However, despite the advantage granted by the Daoist family in-house transmission, one needs not only to be hardworking but also tenacious to become a good Daoist master. For instance, Zheng Youwen 鄭有文 officially started an apprenticeship at the age of 16 when he was accepted by a master who also was a relative. His master was very strict, and, during his apprenticeship he endured bullying and physical punishment. Among the 52 Zheng families, not all of them had a Daoist master. However, due to incomplete historical data and genealogical information, we still as of now do not have an exact total number of the Zheng Daoist masters for the pre-1949 period.

The Zheng clan Daoist masters are the cornerstone and elite of the clan. The clan head and the branch heads are all Daoist masters. The profession of Daoist master is handed down within the clan and, apart from individual transmissions from a master to his disciple, young clansmen are trained in Daoism as acolytes (*xiaodaoshi* 小道士). Senior Daoist masters teach them the fundamental principles of Daoism and train them to recite sacred texts, as well as ritual skills.

All the Zheng Daoist masters live in their houses and not at the temple. Minor rituals are held at the altar, which is located in the master's house and bears a specific name. For instance, the altar of Fuqing erfang 福慶二房 family is named Yuanbaodian 元寶殿. Major rituals are usually held in the temple. Funerary rituals are held either in the home of the dead person in the case of a natural death, or, in the case of premature death (by accident or disease) or in the case of a salvation (*chaodu* 超度) ritual for the souls of ancestors, at the temple. In ordinary times, each family takes turns in serving at the temple. The spring and autumn pilgrimages are the busiest periods of the year for the Daoist masters. The first runs from the 1st day of the 2nd lunar month to the 8th day of the 4th lunar month; the second, from the 30th day of the 6th lunar month to 15th day of 7th lunar month. For the latter, the Zheng Daoist masters all wear their ritual robes when entering the temple whatever the reason, arrangement, management, or ritual services. They also ritually welcome the tablets of the deceased (*paiwei* 牌位) who had signed in their lifetime a commitment (*touwen* 投文) to serve the Dongyue Emperor. The tablet may then be deposited in the temple; it also can be deposited in an office of the deceased (*yingongsuo* 陰公所) at the Daoist master's house.[55] To face the strong demand for rituals, all the houses must therefore hire "guest masters," the number of which may be as many as a dozen, from the Chenghuang temple of Hangzhou or from surrounding villages.

Accommodating pilgrims is another major duty of Daoist masters during the spring and autumn pilgrimages. "As a small market town, the Old Dongyue temple has a lot of shops but no hotels,"[56] so wealthy associations of devotees erected buildings on site with office and dormitory facilities for their members. Other pilgrims are put up at the Zheng families' houses. All the families are then very busy and have to hire extra staff such as cooks. This is an important source of income for them. For instance, Fuqing erfang's house included 16 rooms and could accommodate many pilgrims. On the occasion of the spring festival, Zengrong erfang's 增榮二房 patrons come from Jiaxing 嘉興, Jiashan 嘉善, and Shanghai, whereas the autumn festival patrons mostly come from the surroundings of Hangzhou. Each group is accommodated for two to three days. Zheng Youwen, an old Daoist master, used to travel with his relatives every year during the sixth lunar month, rowing their boat to Jiaxing, Tangqi 塘栖, and Lin'an 臨安 to "fetch the pilgrims" (*jie xiangke* 接香客), that is, to make an advance call on the leaders of the associations (*xiangtou* 香頭). It then took about a fortnight for the round voyage. Daoist masters would bring quality goods – such as towels, soap, scissors – as gifts to the leaders of associations. Zheng Youwen used to say that if "you didn't pay advance calls on them, and if you were not kind to pilgrims, they would switch to another family to provide their accommodation." This is a good example of the competition within the Zheng clan. Pilgrims living in the countryside pay for their accommodation with rice at the time of the harvest. Therefore, the Daoist master would pay another call on the leaders of the associations during the 11th lunar month. That is the time when they would collect the rice from each of the pilgrim's family and bring it back by boat to Hangzhou.

An old Daoist master summed up to me their lives by saying that "we relied entirely upon the income of the temple." As the networks of pilgrims are quite extended and the Zheng clan depended upon the direct or indirect income produced by the temple, Daoist masters never waited for pilgrims to come, but rather would reach out to them. Daoist masters of each family had no monopolistic relationship with the pilgrims, and long-term relationships would depend on the quality of the service provided.[57] Let us quote, for instance, old Daoist master Zheng Fazhen 鄭發振 whose father knew traditional Chinese medicine very well. In addition to conducting liturgical services, he also used to provide treatment to pilgrims; poor pilgrims were treated for free. When pilgrims felt comforted by the action of a Daoist master, their relationship would then become a long-term, sometimes even a life-time and trans-generational relationship, and they would come to the temple whenever necessary.

From the Taiping war to the Republican era, many temples in Hangzhou were either destroyed or damaged because of floods, fires, war, and political repression.[58] However, the Old Dongyue temple was able to survive, thanks not only to its location and the action of the very powerful pilgrim associations but also to the efficient management of the Zheng clan. Though all the temple halls were financed and maintained, thanks to worship associations, the temple management could step in at critical moments. For instance, a devastating fire occurred during the autumn festival of 1875 and almost burnt the whole temple to the ground. The next morning the site was cleaned up, the temple employed workers to cover the structure and shelter the pilgrims. The festival could therefore continue.[59] After this disaster, the reconstruction was urgent for the next spring pilgrimage and its cost was enormous, but the associations could not find the necessary money in such a short time. At this critical juncture, the temple manager made a fundraising appeal by engraving a text on a wooden board. Despite the fact that this action was criticized by a journalist who suspected that by publicizing this announcement, the temple management compelled and forced people to make a donation,[60] the temple was fully restored to its former grandeur by the following year.[61]

During the Republican era, the Zheng clan members held positions in the local administrations and political organizations. Their positions in government probably provided protection for their temple. According to our sources, during the 1920s, members of the Zheng clan were already among the executives of the local Guomindang (KMT) party committee, and two Daoist masters of the Old Dongyue temple were members of the Hangxian KMT committee and the Zhejiang Union of the Daoist Associations 浙江道教聯合會 founded in 1927.[62] For the Zheng clan, the Japanese occupation (1937–1945) was one of the most difficult periods. The troops were stationed in the Dongyue village and some houses of the Zheng clan were requisitioned by the Japanese army. It seems that the reputation of the Old Dongyue temple as a branch of Hell prevented the Japanese troops from occupying the temple itself, unlike what happened at other temples in the region. However, the festivals were suspended. For their survival, seven families of the Zheng clan had to flee to Shexian in the neighboring Anhui province.[63] In the aftermath of the war, when the autumn festival was held in 1947, the number of Daoist families was reduced to 48 from 52 in the prewar era. In his report about the festival, a reporter who was impressed by the atmosphere, the number of pilgrims, and the amount of their expenses, made the following statement:

> Though the pilgrims who want to spend a lot of money are the best ones for Daoist masters, the reaction of Daoist Zheng (the clan head) is unexpected. What pilgrims treasure most is "the communication between the world of yin and that of yang (*yin yang heban* 陰陽合辦)" and other rituals, but he thinks that these are a toxic legacy of feudalism. This reporter asked him several times about this topic but he would elude the matter by saying that the subject was not worth debating. He would declare that "we live from our work, and all the members of our clan who are educated have gone elsewhere to earn their living. For instance, one of my own nephews studies in a school of the Chinese Air Force." His assertion clearly shows the reality of the gradual decline of the Daoist masters. Naturally, this is also a good sign of social progress.[64]

Yet the reaction of the Zheng clan head and the commentary of the journalist also reveal some of the tactics that the Zheng Daoists were using as they tried to survive in a difficult political environment. Like the clan head, during the Republican era, many Zhengs were engaged in other occupations such as Chinese medicine and teaching in Hangzhou or other places. But we also know that local administrative and political authority was held by members of the Zheng clan. All the political and social resources at the disposal of the Zheng clan undoubtedly contributed to the maintaining of the festival of Audience and Jugdement held at the Old Dongyue temple, in spite of the Republican government's bans on pilgrimages and festivals.[65] In 1936, both the neighborhood head (*baozhang* 保長) and the township mayor (*xiangzhang* 鄉長) of Dongyue were members of the Zheng clan. Zheng Mingji 鄭明濟, a neighborhood head eventually became the mayor of Liuxia borough 留下區, and Zheng Mingzheng 鄭明徵 became the head of Hangxian district, secretary of the KMT Hangxian branch, chairman of Hangxian Bank, and concurrently served as a senator of Zhejiang province and a member of the Supervisory Committee of the Zhejiang Bank.[66] From the 1920s to the 1940s, many Zhengs joined the KMT and Sanqingtuan 三青團 (the People's Three Principles) Youth parties, because they were called upon by their relatives who were already executives and officials of these parties. According to what several old Daoist masters told me, "as we are all from the same clan, when they solicited me, I used to accept their request," even though most of the members had no actual political activity.

In any case, the deep local embedding, the religious influence, and the political power of the Zheng clan within local society inevitably made it a target of pitiless suppression when the CCP came to power.

Repression

The People's Republic was founded in October 1949. In order to strengthen its political authority and destroy all real and potential resistance, as early as March 1950, the regime launched the campaign to suppress counterrevolutionaries (*zhenya fangeming* 鎮壓反革命). In 1951, Zheng Mingzheng, who was then the Hangxian district head and the KMT Hangxian branch secretary among other titles, was sentenced to death and publicly executed at the Sanfang temple; his crime was being a special agent of the Zhongtong 中統, one of the main KMT intelligence offices.[67] This execution was only the beginning of a long tragedy for the Zheng clan who had thought that Zheng Mingzheng's condemnation only concerned him.

Indeed, after the death of Zheng Mingzheng, although the atmosphere was tense, life continued in the clan. It was only in the summer of 1958 that the Dongyue association (Dongyuehui 東嶽會) was condemned as one of the "reactionary secret sects and societies" (*fandong huidaomen* 反動會道門) and suppressed. This category of condemnation was hitherto applied essentially to redemptive societies like Yiguandao 一貫道; by contrast, Daoism was officially one of the "religions" to be protected under the principle of religious freedom. Before the founding of the People's Republic, the communist authorities had already engaged in a campaign to destroy redemptive societies that continued after 1949, and reached its climax in 1953 and 1954.[68] But in 1958, what was the argument used to accuse a Daoist clan and a Dongyue association as *fandong huidaomen* in order to destroy entirely? It is impossible to access the archives of the Public Security Bureau in Hangzhou, and our only available source for the sketch below is oral history with living Daoist masters.

According to them, after 1958, the life of Daoist masters and their families was suddenly completely disrupted. All sacerdotal vestments, texts, and objects pertaining to rituals were burnt. All the fittings for accommodating pilgrims were confiscated on the grounds that they had not been acquired on a legal basis. All the family heads were summoned by the local police and grouped into a "class for legal education" (*xuexi ban* 學習班).[69] All the former members of the KMT party and Sanqingtuan as well as the family heads were condemned to either harsh sentences of imprisonment or "lighter" sentences of being "ordinary counterrevolutionaries" (*putong fangeming* 普通反革命).[70] "All Zheng Daoist masters were given labels" (*dai maozi* 戴帽子), that is, convicted as criminals or counterrevolutionaries without incarceration, as several Daoist masters confirmed to me. Due to this total ban, the Daoist masters lost all of their sources of income, and in order to live, all, old and young, had to look for jobs elsewhere. Many of the elderly masters especially suffered from such difficulties.

However, new sanctions were imposed during political purges in urban areas. In the so-called *chengqian* 城遷, that is, the forceful resettling of politically unreliable persons and their families to the countryside, all the members of the Zheng clan who had been convicted were sent with their families to the Canton production brigades (1958–1986). In the process, their urban residential household registration (*jumin hukou* 居民戶口) and all the related benefits and rights were cancelled, and they were re-designated as "rural household residents" (*nongye hukou* 農業戶口). It should be remembered that, behind this binary system of residency, there was enormous inequalities in the supply of daily essentials, employment, education, health, and welfare benefits. Daoist masters who were accustomed to making a living from their rituals all of a sudden had to live by working the farmland.[71] Some elder Daoist masters in poor health could not endure the double punishment and died. Their children's education, employment, and future life were all hindered by the punishment of their parents.

After the Cultural Revolution, a political measure was implemented, enabling the children of the convicts to return to town and reclaim their urban residence status. In addition, those who were sent to the countryside before 1961 were allowed to receive a pension, so the older Daoist masters had a small income. But for the elder Daoist masters and their families, the trauma is deep. "The sentences inflicted in 1958 to Daoist masters gave them a most execrable notoriety (*gaochoule* 搞臭了), rendering them completely scared," one of their descendants told us. Born during the 1930s, he thinks that the condemnation of clan Zheng was unfair, he is now endeavoring to understand what happened at that time, and yet he declares that Zheng Mingzheng "contaminated" the Zheng clan. He also says that many in the younger generation share the idea that the clan's disaster is due to the religion, and they no longer want to speak or hear about that anymore.

The renewal of liturgical services

In 1993, the village committee erected an "incense burning point" at the request of the Daoist masters to provide liturgical services in response to increasing popular demand. At that time, the Zheng clan still had a few elder Daoist masters. However, among those who were still in fair health to perform rituals, some were really traumatized and did not want to resume their service, while others agreed to perform but their families totally disagreed. This explains that the number of Daoist masters who resumed liturgical services was rather small.

Among them was Zheng Fazhen. He told us that having been convicted as an anti-revolutionary, he had to work as a painter on an assembly line in a factory in Hangzhou. This profound life change had been really very hard for him. In 1982, he learned that the party would implement the policy of religious opening,[72] which gave him hope for the restoration of Daoism and his vocation as a Daoist master. As early as 1983, when the Baopu Daoist monastery reopened in Hangzhou, he had been preparing to return to his life as a Daoist ritualist. As all the ritual manuscripts and objects had been burnt in 1958, he had to tackle the key task of reproducing and reconstituting them according to the memories of the elder Daoist masters from his family; he also visited other Daoist masters outside of Hangzhou in order to copy their manuscripts. By 1993, when the village committee asked him to resume ritual work, he had actually been preparing for ten years. He then made all the necessary arrangements, such as the installation of altar tables and lamps, and the formation of a ritual group by contacting several Daoist masters so that the service of rituals could be restored. When I met him, he recounted the following anecdote:

> On the 20th day of the 7th lunar month, a pilgrim from Hangzhou who was possessed by a god (*pusa shangshen* 菩薩上身, in this case, the Dongyue Emperor)[73] was running all over the hall. He stopped right in front of me, knelt down while crying and declared that he was the Dongyue Emperor. He kept on holding my hands and calling me "son and grandson of the Buddha" (*fozi fosun* 佛子佛孫), he was saying that life was very hard for him, wandering from place to place as he had no home. I only replied: "Now, I have become a Daoist master again" and then, he stopped crying.[74]

This anecdote reflects the conviction of these old masters that gods and people need their service. However, the return of Daoist masters to the temple has not been easy. First of all, they were challenged by a relationship rooted in mutual mistrust with the powerful temple management committee which was now the employer of the Zheng Daoist masters. In order to guarantee an income for the temple, the committee had stipulated that the Daoist masters were not allowed to perform rituals in their home. However, they were free to perform outside the village. In the beginning, they refused to follow the rules and practiced rituals at home as before 1958. Soon the committee found out, and the local police were informed and descended on them at their homes. Their ritual implements were confiscated and their practice forcefully stopped. Such violence reminded them of what had happened in the past and the harsh reality of the balance of power between themselves and the local authorities.

The village committee first proposed to share the income generated by rituals at the ratio of 65% for the temple and 35% for the Daoist masters, but the latter did not agree, so their cut was then raised to 40%. Though Daoists still thought this new ratio was unfair, they eventually accepted it because the large demand for rituals in the temple made it still more profitable than the profit they could generate in places outside the village through self-employment. At that time, the retirement pension was very low, and earning more money was one of the reasons for their return to the temple. All requests for rituals are managed by a temple employee who transmits them to a representative of the group of Daoist masters. When the ritual performance is over, the lead Daoist goes and collects the payment from this employee and shares it between the members of the group of Daoists, according to the hierarchy. Should the head of the temple committee think there is any concern, she summons this representative Daoist master for questioning. Despite their palpable tension with the temple management committee head, the Zheng Daoists still have a great desire to maintain their presence in the temple.

Second, after an interruption that lasted 35 years, the Zheng Daoist masters had to face a harsh reality: ageing and the lack of successors. Their group is composed of seven Daoist masters, which is the minimum required to hold any ritual. From 2002 to 2011, its members were Zheng Youwen (b.1918), Zheng Fasen 鄭發森 (b.1927), Zheng Fatang 鄭發棠 (b.1930), Zheng Mingzhao 鄭明昭 (b.1933), Zheng Fazhen (b.1937), Zheng Shuigen 鄭水根 (b.1946), and Zheng Jiankang 鄭健康 (b.1956). Their respective birthdates speak for themselves (Figure 5.2).

Figure 5.2 Old Dongyue temple Daoists burning spirit money, 2009. At the end of the ritual of merit for the Dongyue Emperor's birthday, the Daoists send him their pledges of faith, in the form of spirit money. © Fang Ling.

The oldest, Zheng Youwen, started apprenticeship when he was 16. Having passed through rigorous training, he was the most experienced of this group as he was well-versed in calligraphy and psalmodies. He was the only one who could draw talismans. In 2011, when he reached the age of 93, he ceased to perform rituals. Before he retired, he had trained the other Zheng Daoists. He also accepted some disciples from outside the Zheng clan. He was called "transmitter of Daoism" (*daojiao chuanren* 道教傳人). He told us that now the procedure for accepting disciples was much simpler than it used to be. The disciples just bring a present (money) and the master gives him Daoist texts to copy. The disciple recorded the ritual performed by the masters, and then he trains to chant rituals by listening to the cassettes. As for himself, after the Cultural Revolution, he was proposed twice to receive his registers (*shoulu* 授籙), the ordination of Daoist masters at the headquarters of the Heavenly Masters at Longhushan in Jiangxi.[75] However, the first time, he could not afford the fees, which amounted to 720 yuans, so he declined. The second time, he was already very old and found it unnecessary. He was also invited to join the Hangzhou Daoist Association; he applied but his request came to naught.[76]

Two other younger Zhengs also became Daoist masters. After his retirement from the factory at the age of 60, Zheng Shuigen decided to become a Daoist master when there was a vacancy in the Daoist group. He started by playing music for the group. His father was a Daoist master and said that from the age of 10, he was a jack of all trades and used to lend a hand in the temple. Despite this early and limited experience from his youth, he is serious and assiduous and, above all, has a presence. His progression turns out to be fast. Old Zheng Youwen does appreciate him and finds him very intelligent. He has gradually earned his place and knows how to take care of elder Daoist masters.[77]

As for the youngest one, Zheng Jiankang, his grandfather was a Daoist master. Since his father was an only child, he did not want to be a Daoist master, and instead chose to be a doctor in Chinese traditional medicine. When the temple was destroyed, he was only 2 years old and he spent his life as a factory worker. He loved to play the music and, by 2000 or so when someone was needed in the Zheng Daoist group, he was requested to join them to play the music. His wages amounted to about 400–500 yuan when he worked at the factory. In 2002, in the group, he then earned about 1,000 yuans per month performing rituals for only seven or eight days. But he insisted that "I do not want to be a Daoist for the money, but because I am interested in Daoism." He has no master, and learned the ritual skills by practice. He felt that it was difficult for him to be integrated with the group because, as he said, "they do not want to teach me." But according to a Daoist master, they reproached him for not being assiduous. When the Daoist group of the Jiangcun village (some 6 km away) needed someone, he then left the Old Dongyue temple group to join the Jiangcun group. But in 2011, he went back to the Old Dongyue temple.

The return of Zheng Jiankang at that time was no coincidence. Indeed, 2011 was a challenging year: Zheng Youwen was then 93 years old, and Zheng Fatang was 81. Both masters had ceased their professional activities during that year. In 2012, Zheng Fatang's two sons, who were sexagenarians, were then integrated into the Daoist group. One was retired, while the other had an unstable occupation that he quitted. But both of them were novices. One grandson also became a novice. Should we then conclude that, despite the traumas of the past, the Zheng clan's descendants were eager not to allow the traditional Daoist priestly vocation disappear from the family?

In the mid-2000s, there were only six Zheng Daoist masters active. This means that they were always short of one or more outside Daoist masters as "guests." Li Zhangyu 李樟餘 and Daoist masters from Jiangcun used to fill in as guest ritualists. Li Zhangyu, one of Zheng Youwen's disciples, was initially a regular substitute and eventually became a permanent member of the Old Dongyue temple group. However, in 2011, he was injured in a traffic accident and was no longer able to come to the temple. As he lived in a village located in the western part of Yuhang district, relatively far from the temple, he used to drive a scooter to go to the Old Dongyue temple while carrying his Chinese two-string fiddle (*erhu* 二胡) and his ritual clothes, quite a long journey compared those Zheng masters living on-site. During his military service, he was assigned to an army propaganda troupe (*xuanchuan dui* 宣傳隊), and could play and compose music as an amateur. After leaving the service, he was hired by the provincial Geological Bureau. When he retired, he chose to become a Daoist master. In 2008, when I met him for the first time at the Old Dongyue temple, he had been a Daoist master for five or six years, and was particularly interested in Daoist ritual music. His initiation master (*xueyi shifu* 學藝師傅) was Xu Jinshui 徐金水 of Hangzhou who had been ordained at Longhushan, and was part of the "da 大" generation of the Longhushan Zhengyi lineage. In order to learn the Daoist rituals of the Old Dongyue temple, notably their music, he eventually chose Zheng Youwen as his "internship supervisor" (*guotang shifu* 過堂師傅).[78] He stated that "since Daoist ritual and its music are transmitted from generation to generation in an oral tradition, it is therefore very difficult for someone from the outside to access them." In the Old Dongyue temple, he is very discreet as a "guest," but when the Daoist masters in the villages of Jiangcun and Wuchangcun 五常村 need Zheng Youwen's teaching and consulting, it is often Li who stands in for the old master.

Finally, let us evoke the restoration of the liturgical services. In 1958, as all the liturgical manuscripts and texts of the Zheng Daoist masters had been destroyed, one part of those currently in use were transcribed according to the memories of the elder Daoist masters, the other part was copied or bought from other Daoist masters or temples. According to Table 5.1 established in 2012, we can see the proposed liturgical services.

From Table 5.1, it is clear that most of the 27 services which are proposed consist of reciting litanies (*baichan* 拜懺), except for 18, 24, and 25–27. Then *gongde*, a word initially meaning "merit" which is given to services for the salvation of deceased souls, here also includes the services for prolonging life (*yansheng* 延生). The *Yuanshi tianzun shuo Dongyue jieyuan xiezui fachan* 元始天尊說東嶽解冤謝罪法懺 ("Litany for Delivery from Enmity and Forgiveness by the (Emperor of) the Eastern Peak, Preached by the Heavenly Worthy of the Primordial Beginning"), the first one on the list, is called by the

Table 5.1 List of Rituals Offered at the Temple in 2012, with Price (in Yuan) and complete name as per the temple's liturgical manuals

東嶽廟功德價格表

東嶽懺 (元始天尊說東嶽解冤謝罪法懺)	650 (元)	玉皇懺 (玉皇宥罪錫福寶懺)	760
南斗懺 (太上南斗六司注生延生寶懺)	900 九員 1,200	觀音懺 (度世觀音寶懺)	760
北斗懺 (太上北斗七元消災度厄延生寶懺)	760	九幽懺 (太上慈悲九幽拔罪法懺)	1,600 九員 2,100
財神懺 (財神福德寶懺)	760	地藏懺 (幽冥教主地藏慈尊法懺)	760
純陽懺 (九天大羅玉祖呂聖真君無極寶懺)	640	太歲懺 (太上歲德延生去祛災度厄靈華寶懺)	900
水懺 (三元滅罪水懺)	760	土地懺	560
大血湖懺 (太乙救苦天尊說拔度血湖寶懺)	900	土谷懺 (天下土穀尊神消災解厄錫福寶懺)	640
小血湖懺 (太乙救苦天尊說拔度血湖寶懺)	760	朱天懺 (朱天寶懺)	1,200
大十王懺 (太上慈悲戒非釋過救苦拔罪十王寶懺)	1,400	解冤釋結	360
小十王懺 (太上慈悲戒非釋過救苦拔罪十王寶懺)	560	報恩懺 (玄武靈真報恩法懺)	1,600
庚申懺 (廣設路頭庚申寶懺)	1,200	路頭懺 (太上慈悲廣設路頭寶懺)	1,400
關帝懺 (無極大帝護國救民錫福關帝寶懺)	760	禮燈 (燃燈度亡)	460
青華煉 (太極仙翁青華冶煉)	550	上供	360
祭煉 (太極仙翁水火祭煉)	60		

Daoist masters of the Old Dongyue temple as "Home litany" (*benjia chan* 本家懺). It is used for both the services for prolonging life and the salvation. The *Yuhuang youzui xifu baochan* 玉皇宥罪錫福寶懺 ("Precious Litany of Repentance That Moves the Jade Emperor to Grant Absolution from Guilt and the Allotment of Blessings") and eight other litanies are performed only for salvation. Among these nine litanies, the *Taishang cibei jiuyou bazui fachan* 太上慈悲九幽拔罪法懺 ("Litany for the Mercy of the Most High for Deliverance from the Nine Realms of Darkness and the Remission of Sin," henceforth *Jiuyouchan*), the longest litany for the salvation ritual, is also the "heaviest" or "most important" according to the Daoist masters.

The prices of rituals are fixed according to both the length of litanies and the number of officiants. Some of the rituals can use either full-length or abbreviated litanies. For instance, the *Taiyi jiuku tianzun shuo badu xuehu baochan* 太乙救苦天尊說拔度血湖寶懺 ("Precious Litany for Deliverance from the Lake of Blood, Preached by the Great One Heavenly Worthy who Saves from Distress") and *Taishang cibei jiefei shiguo jiuku bazui shiwang baochan* 太上慈悲戒非釋過救苦拔罪十王寶懺 ("Precious Litany of the Ten

Kings for the Mercy of the Most High for Deliverance from Transgression of Precepts, Save from Distress and the Remission of Sin") each have both complete (*da* 大) and abbreviated versions (*xiao* 小). The rituals are performed by seven officiants. For the *Taishang Nandou liusi zhusheng yansheng baochan* 太上南斗六司注生延生寶懺 ("Precious Litany of the Most High for Recording Births and Prolonging Life by the Six Arbitrators of the Southern Dipper") and *Jiuyouchan*, if a grander scale is required, they may be performed by nine officiants. Though the fixed rates for services, either in the temple or in a private house, are the same, the people who live in the Old Dongyue village enjoy a special discounted rate. Rates charged by the Old Dongyue temple group are higher than those charged by other Daoist groups of the region. As a comparison, in 2008, *Jiuyouchan* (when the ritual is performed by nine Daoist masters) would cost 2,000 yuans with the Old Dongyue temple group, whereas the same litany would cost only 1,000 yuan when performed by a group of Daoist masters from Jiangcun in 2010. However, these 1,000 yuans were exclusively paid to Daoist masters themselves because they officiate in temples such as Sanfang temple where they do not share their revenue with the temple management committee.

As to the choice of services, some are designated by the patron (*zhaizhu* 齋主). For instance, in April 2009, some persons who succeeded in their business gave thanks to the gods *(huanyuan* 還願) by requesting 11 services of litanies to the God of Wealth, *Caishen fude baochan* 財神福德寶懺 ("Precious Litany of the God of Wealth of Blessings and Virtue"). Some are requests by divinities, meaning that divinities order the service through dreams or mediums. In most cases, the Daoist masters design the services according to the patron's reasons and circumstances as well as their budget. As we have observed, only one litany is requested for a service for prolonging life, *Dongyuechan*, *Xuehuchan* (for women), and *Guanyinchan*, for instance. Should a service including two litanies be held, it will combine *Dongyuechan* and *Yanshengchan* or another litany, according to the circumstances.

For the service of the salvation, *chaodu*, patrons often request a service of litanies by choosing *Yuhuangchan* for two or three generations of ancestors. Within the frame of a single litany, we also note that *Jiuyouchan*, or the *lideng* 禮燈 ritual, "worshiping with lamps" is often held. However, in case of problems of accusations from beyond the grave (through a dream or medium), services to pacify the soul of the dead are more substantial. As shown in a case we observed in October 2008, the service in this particular kind of circumstances consisted of three litanies: on the first day, *Dongyuechan* and *Shiyanwang chan*, and on the second day *Jiuyouchan*.

As for *chaodu* rituals for the funeral service, the Daoist masters are invited into the family to hold the service. The first one, in Hangzhou, is named "collecting the soul of the deceased on the third day after his death" (*sanchao jiesha* 三朝接煞),[79] which takes place before the body is placed in a coffin (*dalian* 大殮). According to the local belief, on the third day after death, the dead is on the road to the Yellow sources, and has not yet arrived in the dark world. His future has not been decided yet 在黃泉路上, 冥府未到, 吉凶未卜.[80] But through the rituals, divinities may be summoned to come to him and guide him on his underworld journey. For instance, on the third day after the death of an inhabitant at the Old Dongyue village, the Daoist masters went to the dead person's home to hold the *chaodu* service, which lasted one full day.[81] The main rituals involved are as follows: invitation of the deities using *Taishang cibei guangshe lutou baochan* 太上慈悲廣設路頭寶懺 ("Precious Litany of the Mercy of the Most High for Opening the (Dark) Road"), *Shiwangchan*, and *Taiji xianweng qinghua yelian* 太極仙翁青華冶煉 ("Qinghua [Method] of Old Immortal Taiji for Sublimating [the Souls of the Deceased]"). Eventually, the funeral ritual ends with the *shishi* 施食 rite of "feeding other hungry spirits," a ritual that is usually called by its Buddhist term *Fangyankou* 放焰口 by the Old Dongyue temple Daoist masters.[82] On the following day of funeral services, the dead is placed in a coffin and then cremated.

As for the second one, the *chaodu* ritual is held during the funeral period of seven-seven. In the local tradition, the family of the deceased must accomplish the seven funeral ceremonies (every seven days from death, *zuoqi* 做七).[83] According to their financial means, the family decides whether they invite the Daoist priests for the rituals and on which moment. So far, according to what we could observe, the rituals are almost always requested to be performed during the sixth period when the *Jiuyouchan* is performed.

Besides, the Daoist masters also hold the *chaodu* rituals for abnormal death, this time within the temple. According to tradition, a victim of accidents, suicides, and many other premature deaths must not return to his/her home. In most cases, the remains are deposited either in a temple or in a provisional place where the funerary ritual would be held.[84] Since temples had disappeared for a long period, and with the implementation of the funeral reforms,[85] the zones of compulsory cremation have expanded ever more widely. Now many of the prematurely dead are held at the hospital or at the morgue. Some families of the prematurely dead will travel to the Old Dongyue temple to request *chaodu* rituals no matter how far away from it they live, because of the temple's reputation for this kind of service. For instance, on August 24, 2009, the Daoist masters of the Old Dongyue temple held a *chaodu* ritual for a man who died at the age of 45 and used to live in Liangzhu, which is over 20 km away. He had died over one month before at the hospital, but the doctors could not say why. He left behind his young wife of 45 years and a son aged 15. His widow was devastated with the painful loss. But at his service, the Daoist masters who usually remain fairly distant expressed their compassion for the dead through their chants and music.

The Old Dongyue temple Daoist group's repertoire of liturgical services are the same as those of the other Daoist groups of the region, but their music is specific. They call their ritual music "the Dongyue style" (*Dongyue pai* 東嶽派). According to the Zheng and the other Daoist masters, the difference consists in the tone of music. First, the Old Dongyue Daoist style of ritual music feature very diverse tones (*jiuqiang shiba diao* 九腔十八調), and it is very difficult to learn. Second, the music for the *liandu* 煉度 ritual (alchemical salvation of the dead) is based on what is known as the *yindiao* 陰調 (also *xiaogong diao* 小宮調, A note), the lowest note, because the Old Dongyue temple is considered a *yin* place, a temple of hell. But in the other places of the western parts of Hangzhou, the same ritual uses the *yangdiao* 陽調 (also *dagongdiao* 大宮調, C note). The specificity and the origin of the ritual music of the Old Dongyue temple are still a subject to be studied by the specialists in this field.

After 35 years of interruption, the ritual services offered by the Zheng Daoist masters mainly consist of the *chan* 懺 (litanies). This doubtlessly explains why, on the proclamations (*bang* 榜) on yellow paper posted on the site of rituals, the Daoist masters call themselves "masters of litanies" (*lichan shi* 禮懺師). As all the ritual manuscripts were burnt in 1958, and the ritual practice was discontinued for so long, there is no means to know precisely the extent of loss, but through some of the remarks by Daoist priests from outside the Old Dongyue village, we can see the extent of the damage: "Nobody in the Old Dongyue temple knows how to perform such rites as Shangchao 上朝 (Audience), Shangtianbiao 上天表 (Presenting a Memorial to Heaven), or the *bugang* 步罡 (Pacing the Mainstay) anymore." As for myself, I can also attest to the disappearance of the talismans writing at the Old Dongyue temple after the retirement of Zheng Youwen.

Besides, in the current rituals, we can note some omissions and simplifications which have drawn criticism by outside Daoist masters. For instance, the Zheng Daoists are criticized for no longer performing the *raotan* 繞壇 rite of circumambulating the altar. These truncated rituals can be explained, on the one hand, by the physical condition and advanced age of the Daoist masters. But on the other hand, the regulations of the temple forbid the Daoists from declining any demand for a ritual. Due to the prestige of the temple, they are also victims of their own success. In addition to many advanced bookings of rituals, many pilgrims also make requests for ritual service only after they arrive at the temple. As a result, during the pilgrimage seasons, it is not rare for the Zheng masters to hold as many as 10 rituals per day, their record was a total of 17 rituals over one day and night. Such an overpacked ritual schedule also may have led to simplified or truncated services at the Old Dongyue temple.

So to say the essentials, the extremely brutal repression of 1958 completely broke the Daoist tradition and the local dominance of the Zheng clan. After 35 years of interruption, some old surviving Zheng Daoists tried to restore the local ritual tradition as well as they could, but the clergy remaining in small numbers no longer has the influence and power it had before. Within the clan, the dominant Daoist profession was stigmatized, few people among the younger generations want to take over and engage in hard and difficult learning. So far, the Zheng Daoist masters are still the majority in the group, but for how long? Within the rebuilt temple, the Daoist clergy no longer has its place in the management, it is only by its ritual function that it holds its legitimacy within local society.

The Eastern Peak Congregation (Dongyuehui 東嶽會)

Dongyue's Divine Birthday Celebration, "Audience and Judgment"

The main festivals held at the Old Dongyue temple are the celebrations of the Dongyue Emperor's birthday and his Audience and Judgment. They appeared and developed during different periods. With the apparition of the Dongyue temples in the capital, in the middle of the thirteenth century, the birthday celebration – on the 28th day of the 3rd lunar month – was already one of the most vibrant festivals held in Hangzhou. The *Mengliang lu* notes that:

> The elites and the common people of the capital compete in the expression of their devotion, starting as early as the second decade of the month, either just by burning incense; or by putting on an outfit of a penitent while wearing a cangue, flagellating themselves; or, in the case of shopkeepers, by bringing offerings such rare fruits and flowers, and refined foods made from wheat flour; or, in the case of Buddhist and Daoist monks, by reciting sacred texts or by undertaking rituals in the temples for the celebration of [the Dongyue Emperor]'s birthday. Worshippers come either by boat, carriage or on foot without stopping. This is the way it is, every single day of the festival. There are also the [association of] beggars who offer banners made with coloured ribbons threaded with metal coins (*qianfan* 錢幡) intended be suspended before the hall of the Dongyue temple on Wushan. The procession of this association is very impressive.[86]

Noteworthy here is the participation of the Buddhist monks and Daoist masters at the festival – one of the places of cult was located in a Buddhist temple –along with a large number of associations. The first pilgrims arrived as early as on the 20th day (of the 3rd lunar month) though the apex of the festivities was on the 28th day. Among the five temples, it was Wushan's which used to welcome the most remarkable festivities. It seems that his most emblematic association was the Qianfan association.

In the middle of the sixteenth century, the Old Dongyue temple outshone the Wushan temple and became the most popular and important place of the cult. According to the 1565 stele, its visitors came to obtain longevity, chase epidemics, call back the frightened souls of the sick, and obtain salvation for their ancestors (*zhuiyuan* 追遠). At the time of the Dongyue Emperor's birthday celebration, the associations organized a procession in his honor. On the road, days and nights, there was a large influx of pilgrims from Hangzhou. Countering the criticism of the Confucians who opposed the Dongyue cult as improper, the author approved the pilgrims by quoting the classics: "The Dongyue temple is the place where the souls of the dead and the evil spirits appear. This is the reason why people are hitherto bound to beg for help from Emperor Dongyue."[87] In a mid-seventeenth-century poem about the temple, we notice that the author describes only two festivals: the Dongyue Emperor's birthday and Qingming (April 4 or 5), with most attention given to the latter: at Qingming, apart from sweeping the graves, men come also to the temple with their wives to lodge complaints with the dead and the gods.[88]

As early as the beginning of Qing dynasty, the birthday festivities at the Old Dongyue temple were on the increase, thanks to the extension of the number of pilgrims coming from the provinces of Zhejiang and Jiangsu.[89] A local gazetteer dating back to the eighteenth century states that, on the birthday, about 100 different associations used to gather and play different parts: theatre, music, acrobatics, martial arts, etc.[90] There were so many performances to be watched that the spectators were baffled and filled with wonder.

During the seventeenth century, the ritual of "Paying the Heavenly Taxes" (*jietianxiang* 解天餉) began to appear and spread in the Jiangnan region. During the festival, the villages or neighborhood associations had to carry their Earth God in a palanquin to the Dongyue temple of their city or market town with the spirit money collected by them, and to pay the taxes to the divine authority. This ritual practice of "Paying the Heavenly Taxes" reminds us of the above-mentioned association of beggars in thirteenth-century Hangzhou as they used to offer banners made with metal coins, *qianfan*. We note that the Qianfan associations in the Dongyue's birthday festival still existed in the seventeenth century in the Songjiang area, near Shanghai, and the processions could last for several days.[91] In the nineteenth century, the combination of two rituals appeared: "Paying the Heavenly Taxes" to the Dongyue Emperor and "universal salvation" during the Zhongyuan 中元 festival for the salvation of the dead, held on the 15th day of the 7th lunar month. The Dongyue Emperor then redistributed the spirit money that had been collected to all the provinces of the netherworld. Combining with yet another ritual, the judgment of the insane, also held at that time, these festivals of universal salvation and paying heavenly taxes became the Audience and Judgment of the Dongyue Emperor.

This festival named "Audience and Judgment [of the Dongyue Emperor]" (Chaoshen) was initiated during the first half of the nineteenth century[92] and developed until the Taiping war. It used to last 16 days and attract up to 100,000 pilgrims.[93] From the 1936 ethnographic description,[94] we know that sessions would start during the night, after the Dongyue Emperor's desk had been installed in the hall and his statue put on the throne behind his desk. Members of the dedicated association would then play the administrative and penal parts of the court. The Chaoshen included three main acts: audience (*chaocan* 朝參), hearing and judgment (*tingshen* 聽審), and distribution of spirit money (*faxiang* 發餉). During the audience, inferior deities, represented by two members of the association who moved back and forth on the stage, would appear each in turn before the Dongyue Emperor. Distribution of spirit money was the final act of this ritual. According to the Dongyue Emperor's edict, it consisted in allotting the offerings collected among the wandering souls of each province. The hearing and judgment of insane people (*shen fengdian* 審瘋癲) was the second and most spectacular act of the ritual.

According to traditional etiology, insanity is due to possession by spirits of the dead (*guihun* 鬼魂). For the patient to be cured, the spirits should be forced out. In the literature of the eighteenth century, a story describes a young boy living in Qiantang (Hangzhou) who was aged about 15 and who, all of a sudden, went insane because of possession by a spirit. A neighbor who worshipped Dongyue and noticed his condition advised his father:

> [Y]ou should bring your son before the Dongyue Emperor on the Emperor's birthday, all the service people will be there, you should burn your indictment in the incense burner while I'll be beating the drum and ring the bell to advance your claim. You'll ask assistance from someone to hold your son in the hall and wait for the sentence, the spirit may be expelled out of your son.

In the morning, on Dongyue's birthday, the father followed the advice, held his son in the temple hall but the boy fainted, and when he regained consciousness, he was brought back home though he still could not speak. Only during the middle of the night, he said that, in the Dongyue temple, the judge of the Swift retribution office (Subaosi shen 速報司神) arrested the spirit who was following him and brought it before the Dongyue Emperor. The latter carefully read the indictment and pronounced his verdict: the possessing spirit was put in the cangue as a punishment. The young boy was then cured and sent back to the world of the living.[95] This story does not disclose if this temple in Qiantang was the Old Dongyue temple, but it shows that the ritual of the judgment of the insane was already practiced by laymen engaged in the service of the divine administration.

In the nineteenth century, the ritual of judgment of the insane in the Old Dongyue temple grew more elaborate and longer. The patient would be brought by his family before the temple door, where a formal complaint in writing would be lodged. The court clerk would then duly register the complaint and the patient and his/her family would be confined in a dedicated room named "hell" while waiting for the audience. During the night, the patient was tied to a straw mannequin (substitute body) and brought before the court. The court clerk would ask the patient "tell us what injustice did you endure and what sin did you commit?" If the patient would keep quiet, the court clerk would demand the straw mannequin to be severely beaten and would repeat his question twice. Then, the patient would relate in place of the spirit the injustice he had endured. The court clerk would then pronounce the Dongyue Emperor's judgment, explain his decision, and untie the knot of hatred. According to reports written in the eighteenth century, we can note that, on the one hand, the ritual of the judgment of the insane held in Old Dongyue temple became more and more theatrical and elaborate. On the other hand, according to the current theological concept of wandering and deprived souls (*guhun* 孤魂),[96] should a spirit possess a living, it was understood to be for revenge of some injustice caused by this living. This is why the ritual was not only an exorcism as it also aimed at listening to his/her grievance and negotiating with him/her in order to untie the situation.

For example, according to a 1897 report from Hangzhou, a lady Gu of sound mind became insane and was brought before the Dongyue Emperor. During the audience, the possessing spirit explained that she used to be that lady's maid and was wrongly accused of a theft but as she claimed her innocence in vain, killed herself by drowning. However, as the maid would not resign herself to this injustice, she wanted to seize her mistress's life. The Dongyue Emperor's judgment was that the wandering soul had endured injustice while she was alive. However, as she took her own life, she was not entitled to seize her mistress's life. However, while taking into account her grievance, the Dongyue Emperor prescribed that lady Gu should recite more sutras and burn large amounts of spirit money in order that the souls of her former maid be delivered from the state of suffering, and added, telling the maid: "all the sins of your anterior life are now pardoned, you must no longer cause disorder, harass and accuse her." After the ritual was over, when the patient went back home after sunrise, she was no longer insane.[97]

After the Taiping war, in the late nineteenth century, festivities could again be held at Old Dongyue temple but very soon they were faced with changes in local politics regarding religious festivals. So far, the imperial law which banned the religious festivals was rarely enforced. One of the most popular festivals in Hangzhou used to be the procession held in honor of Marshal Wen (Wen yuanshuai 溫元帥), a deity of epidemics, on the 16th day of the 5th lunar month, a cult based at Jingde temple 旌德觀. However, in 1868, it was banned by Zhejiang Governor Yang Changjun 楊昌濬 (1825–1897),

> because in our province, many former soldiers are still on the run and might cause disorders. Besides, the local economy is still quite weak as it has not yet recovered its normal level. So how can this kind of event be authorized as it exhausts the people and is a waste of money?

The text of this ban was engraved on a stele erected in the temple, meaning that this was an everlasting ban.

During a period that lasted over 30 years, the other Marshal Wen temple kept on holding the processions while reducing their size. From 1876, the local elites and shopkeepers would regularly request the lifting of the ban and, indeed, under the pressure of both episodes of epidemics and the public opinion, the local prefect would sometimes agree to lift the ban, but would also restore the ban again very quickly.[98] Within this historical context, the procession of the Old Dongyue temple held in honor of the Dongyue Emperor's birthday was interrupted during about 20 years, till 1894 when they were resumed but only for a three days duration.[99] However, about two months later, while a procession in honor of Marshal Wen was planned at Jingde temple, the prefect heard of it and immediately put a ban on associations.[100] In 1895, as epidemics had been raging for three years, the inhabitants, through their elites, demanded the procession of the Dongyue Emperor to be held again in order to contain the epidemic, but the authorities maintained the ban. However, the inhabitants nonetheless held the procession for a few days during the seventh lunar month, going both inside and outside Hangzhou city.[101] The reporter did not state the name of the temple that organized this procession, but according to the description it is very likely that it was the Old Dongyue temple.

From the beginning of the Republican period in 1912, the Dongyue Emperor procession was still being held but the itinerary was very limited. The palanquin used to be carried from the temple to Xinliangting pavilion 新涼亭, located on Xixi Road, in the immediate surroundings. The statue would then be placed and hosted there for a little while, so that pilgrims could make offerings and the statue would then be brought back to the temple.[102] During the civil war (1926–1928), probably after February 1927, when the KMT army occupied Hangxian and, later, the whole Zhejiang province, processions were no longer held.

Was the Chaoshen festival, which used to be even more important than the processions in terms of scale and number of participants, banned by the end of the empire? On that issue, the *Shenbao* 申報 newspaper quotes two sources. An editorial, which dates back to the second day of the seventh lunar month in 1879, reported that "yesterday a friend from Hangzhou said that the prefect strictly banned the Chaoshen for this year," although adding that this information had not been checked.[103] The second source is an editorial dated the 14th day of the 6th lunar month in 1880, that is during the period of collection of spirit money, a fortnight before the beginning of the Chaoshen festival, reporting that the Zhejiang governor Tan Zhonglin 譚鍾麟 (1822–1905) banned the Chaoshen forever.[104] However, afterward, neither this newspaper nor any other document ever confirmed that these two bans were actually enforced. Therefore, it is very difficult to assert that in 1879 and 1880, the Chaoshen was entirely banned. In 1881, the Old Dongyue temple not only held the Chaoshen once, but, because that year there was a second, intercalary seventh lunar month, the associations jointly decided to hold Chaoshen a second time, as well as birthday festivities. The second Chaoshen was also held during 16 days.[105] That year, the prefect Tan Zhonglin was promoted and relocated to another province and, from that moment till the end of Qing era, notably during the New Policy era (1901–1911), even though the Chaoshen was still the target of propaganda and reforms,[106] there was no formal ban on it.

In 1878, while relating that Audience and Judgment was not banned, the *Shenbao* had the following comment:

> [A]s the great mandarin and local officials consider that these rituals do not much harm to the people, no ban is announced. Besides, pretending to follow the way of the gods, and actually confusing the people is a traditional practice and this is the reason why no public figure would take the initiative to ask for a ban as it would anger the Dongyue Emperor. Moreover, all the members of local administration, who belonged to cult associations, covered up. Although the local officials had actually heard about it, they could not determine what happened and would not therefore dare publicly making obstructions.[107]

During the following 30 years, these factors did not significantly change, unlike the situation of the Dongyue procession. Although participants in the Chaoshen were ever more numerous and festivities lasted much longer, ritual activities were held within the temple, public order was not threatened, and therefore, the local officials did not seek to ban festivities.

At the beginning of the Republican period, the government launched a major anti-superstition campaign. In May 1913, due to anti-Yuan Shikai movements, curfew was imposed in Hangzhou and later, the Zhejiang governor Zhu Rui 朱瑞 (1883–1916) proclaimed a ban on the festivities during the Zhongyuan period:

The festivities held during the 7th lunar month – such as Chaoshen and sacrifices to deprived souls in the Old Dongyue temple – are unavoidable superstitions forming part of the customs of Hangzhou. But, curfew is in force as the prefect feared that gangs of ruffians would mix up with the crowd and provoke public disorder. Therefore, he gave special orders both to the commanding officer of the garrison, to the local police and to all the districts of the areas of Jia(xing) and Hu(zhou) to announce an anticipated ban [of the Chaoshen festivities]. Also, as early as the first days of the 7th lunar month, he planned to send police forces and the army respectively to Fahuashan and the quay [of the river Yuhangtang] in Gongshu 拱墅 to cordon off the routes, in order to prevent pilgrims from arriving in Hangzhou.[108]

We can note that the local government, faced with the importance of the Chaoshen and its influence on social life in Hangzhou and beyond, named it as "unavoidable superstitions." However, with the motive of gangs causing "public disorder," they put an anticipated ban on Chaoshen festivities. We have no reports on what actually happened, however; this ban probably did not last. In 1924, during the Chaoshen period, in order to avoid the gangs, the local authorities did not put a ban on festivities but instead sent troops and police forces for night and day surveillance.[109]

With the national revolution at the end of the 1920s and the strengthening of the nationalist regime (1927–1949), a new anti-superstition campaign was launched.[110] In July 1927, the government of Zhejiang province, in the name of "the eradication of superstitions," proclaimed in advance a ban on Chaoshen festivities on the Old Dongyue temple and that of Santaishan 三台山, among others.[111] However, the actual situation was as follows:

> This year, due to men and women, as well as good and bad people indiscriminately mixing in temples, Hangzhou Municipality banned festivals. But local habits are deep rooted, and eradication is no simple and easy matter. Following a request from several parts to maintain festivities, Public Security Commissioner and Municipal Authorities allow only incense burning, but do not allow Audience and Judgment rituals. Therefore, only daily activities are maintained in the temples, when they are lively, but the nights are very quiet.[112]

Therefore, the hearing and court trial (of the insane people) was discontinued at the Old Dongyue temple, but the other rituals soon resumed, as we know from Lin Yongzhong and Zhang Songtao's 1936 survey report. In 1937, the Japanese army occupied Hangzhou and was stationed in Dongyue village; although incense burning continued, the Audience and Judgment festival was suspended for eight years. After the war, in 1946, even though the livelihood of the people was very difficult, the Audience and Judgment resumed. The *Shenbao* reports that some people from out of town came to fetch their dead to come back home, some local people came to send wandering souls back to their home, and all these procedures were submitted to the Dongyue Emperor for approval. In this ritual of "sending approval " (*songpi* 送批) the Dongyue Emperor assesses the souls wandering in foreign territories, judging whether they are innocent souls, and distributes them spirit money so that they can return to their native place. He also orders them not to disturb the good people on their way home.[113] Apparently the associations had replaced the forbidden judgment of insane people with the new ritual "Judgment of souls victims of injustice" (*wuyou yuangui* 無由冤鬼). Although there is no specific description of this ritual, the (new) ceremony for reviewing the foreign wandering souls reflects a real need: with the development of cities and transportation, the migrant population in Hangzhou had considerably increased, yet, according to tradition "Fallen leaves return to the roots" (migrants eventually return to their homeland), but wars and turmoil have prevented many of the dead from returning to their homeland. In 1947, the number of pilgrims was back to half of its prewar level; however, according to concordant memories of Old Dongyue village people, it was the last time in history this festival took place.

Why did the Old Dongyue temple stop holding Audience and Judgment in 1948? The archives relating to the Dongyue temple in Santaishan provide us with information on the control of festivals by the Hangzhou municipality after the war. The Audience and Judgment held at Santaishan used to take place after the Old Dongyue temple's own festival, and its fame and the number of pilgrims were much less important. During three years, in 1946, 1947, and 1948, arguing that the local security had to be maintained, for sanitary reasons and others, several local public figures, the head of the *bao* 保長, and the mayor of the district submitted a request to the municipality of Hangzhou for the ban of the Audience and Judgment festival in the Dongyue temple in Santaishan. The first two years, the city municipality responded that it should be banned, but in fact, the festival was held as usual. But on August 16, 1948, as the civil war was turning against the KMT, the mayor declared: "[D]uring this period of turmoil, Audience and Judgment must obviously be strictly prohibited, however, incense burning may be maintained." He also instructed the Provincial Police Department to send troops to enforce the ban and maintain order.[114] On the one hand, these archival materials confirm that the Old Dongyue temple was not the only one where the Audience and Judgment was discontinued in 1948; on the other hand, we also note that, although the festival in the Old Dongyue temple has always been the most important in Hangzhou, and it was the first target in the 1927 provincial government ban, it seems like, unlike the situation at Santaishan, there was no public denunciation and elite request for a ban at Old Dongyue during the 1940s.[115] Undoubtedly, that temple benefited from the Zheng family members' power in the local party at all levels in Hangzhou and Hang district; furthermore, the direct impact of the Old Dongyue temple's Audience and Judgment on the local economy was a factor against any opposition before the overall political situation makes it untenable.[116]

After the 1948 ban on the Audience and Judgment festival, the practice of incense burning survived for a few years under the new regime; then, in the summer of 1958 it in turn disappeared with the closure and then the destruction of the temple.

The Return of Incense Communities

The mass return of pilgrims on the premises of the destroyed monument to burn incense started in the early 1990s. As the majority of them would come in groups, incense communities were reborn and developed over the years, which, as early as 1993, prompted the village authorities to set up, without official authorization, an "incense burning point" which would be replaced, in 2006, by a newly erected temple. Inscriptions on donation steles (*lezhu* 樂助) as well as various objects in the temple provide valuable information on the contributions of worshippers and their communities, e.g., a stele dated the 4th day of the 11th month of 1992 includes the names of 208 inhabitants of Wubao and Liubao villages (Hangzhou) who raised 11,380 yuans (minimum amount 50 yuans, maximum 100 yuans) for the construction of the future place of worship (江幹區彭埠鎮五堡村六堡村募捐修廟樂助名單), a large incense burner offered by a translocal community in 1993, long, narrow tables donated by a community located in Wangjiangmen district 望江門 (Hangzhou) in 1994, and a magnificent horizontal tablet (*bian* 匾) bearing the name of the temple, donated by the Dongyue Congregation in Shaoxing, Shaoxing yuehui 紹興嶽會, in 1998. We note, however, that these are only part of the donations for the "incense burning point" that I could spot, because many other objects could not be stored by the temple while it was under construction.

As for the other ten steles carved by the temple authorities, these are lists of donations received during the period between the third month of 2006 and the third month of 2008 for the reconstruction of the temple; they list about 30 groups, including the names of several thousand donors. A vast majority of donations dates back to 2006 and was intended for the construction of the great hall and the unveiling ceremony of the statue of Dongyue; donations dating back to 2007 and 2008 were intended for the Dizang hall and its statues.

As in 1992, the minimum amount was 50 yuans (imposing a minimum amount on donors so that their names are carved on a stele is a common practice in Jiangnan temples). We notice a group of 255 people among whom each and every person donated precisely this amount. For reference, retired people in Dongyue village then earned only 800 yuans, of which 600 were paid by the village and 200 by the municipality of Hangzhou; therefore, donating 50 yuans was a real effort for people with low income. On the other hand, there were major donors whose highest donations amounted to 60,000 yuans, the majority of them offering between 100 and 1,000 yuans.

The increase in donations between the two phases of the temple rebuilding process is quite impressive and clearly emphasizes the development of religious societies, both in number and financial resources. The economic reform, the rise in power of rural businesses, and urbanization have led to both the enrichment of a small minority and the income increase of a large part of the population.

The part played by worshippers in the rebirth and development of the temple also reflects the fact that the traditionally close relationship maintained with the divine has not changed: after carrying out the devotional rites – lighting candles and burning incense sticks – they communicate to the Great Emperor of the

Eastern Peak the reason for their visit and their request, and they promise to come back in order to thank him if their wish is granted. Donating money to support works in the temple is one possible thanksgiving action. Let us add that pilgrims also support the temple each time they visit: entrance ticket, liturgical services, canteen, dormitory, incense ash and candle butts, all this, according to a village official, pays off between 20,000 and 30,000 yuans a year.[117]

However, the return of incense communities also reflects many changes. Traditionally, two types of associations were hosted by the temple: the *banhu* 班戶, devotional congregations, and the *xianghui* 香會, incense associations. There were about a hundred *banhu* and most pilgrims were part of them. However, nowadays, the situation is the opposite as, among the few dozen communities, there is only one *banhu*, which I will come to later. Besides, very few associations have a name such as "Dongyue Congregation in Shaoxing" or *foban* 佛班, "Group for chanting Sutras" appended to the name of their district.

The vast majority of groups display the name of their locality only when necessary: residential district 社區, street 巷, sector 組, city 市, village 村, town 鎮, etc. as can be seen on donation steles, e.g., "good men and women of great faith from Jinjiang district, outer side sector of Hangzhou Wangjiang Gate" 杭州望江門外近江段善男信女. When I asked several groups about their name, they were surprised by my question and most of them would simply answer "*fuhui* 福會," i.e., Association for Blessings.

It seems to me that this situation is partly linked to the decline of the *banhu* tradition. Let us recall that in the past, each *banhu* used to have a name which, in many cases, referred to the tasks it was assigned to in the temple. For instance, Dazhonggong chahui 大中宮茶會, the Tea Association of the Dazhonggong, was in charge of both maintaining this temple hall and providing food and drinks to pilgrims.[118] The loss of a certain religious practice, the ban on great assemblies like *miaohui* 廟會, "temple congregation," that implied some competition for representation, and the fact that associations no longer play a part in the management of the temple do not incite these groups to pay more attention to their denomination.

The other remarkable change is that although the geographic origin of pilgrims and societies are roughly the same as in the past: Hangzhou, Jiaxing, Huzhou, Shaoxing, Shanghai, Ningbo, Zhoushan, etc., the periods of pilgrimage are no longer limited to the spring (from the 1st day of the 2nd month to the 8th day of the 4th month) and autumn (from the 30th day of the 6th month to the 15th day of the 7th month[119]). As an old Daoist master says: "now, people have money, so they come all year round" (Map 5.1).

According to my observations, farmers and silkworm raisers as well as those who know and stick to tradition,[120] still continue making the pilgrimage in the same period as in the past, while the others choose their date more freely. In the temple, I noted diverse frequencies, such as once or three times a year. The most assiduous group is an incense society from the district of Guangfu 廣福 (Hangzhou), whose members have been going to the temple almost every month since 2008, although not on a specific day.

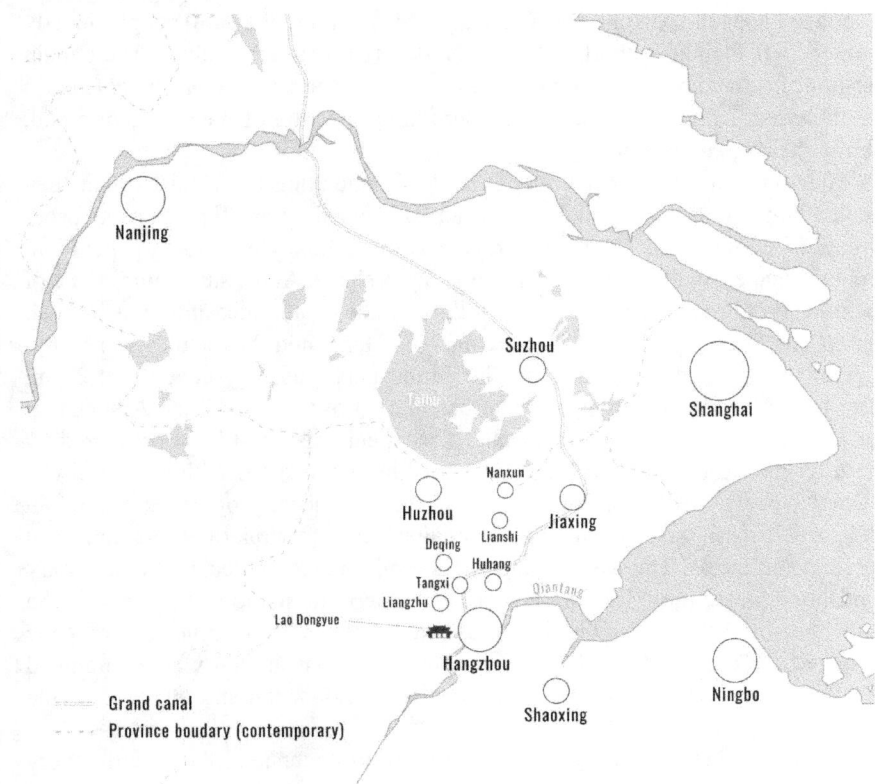

Map 5.1 Location of the Dongyue associations.

In order to better illustrate the present situation of the pilgrim societies, I will hereunder make a quick presentation of the pilgrimage performed by the Association for Blessings of the Xinsheng village 新生村 then, I will present the *banhu* in a more extensive way.

Xinsheng, a village of 2,300 souls (as reported by the leader of pilgrims) located in the district of Puyan 浦沿, south of Hangzhou, near the seventh Qiantang Bridge, once belonged to the city of Xiaoshan 蕭山. In 1996, as part of the economic and urban development and the expansion strategy of Hangzhou city across the Qiantang River (*guojiang fazhan* 過江發展), the three districts of Xiaoshan, including Puyan, formed the new district of Binjiang 濱江 of the provincial capital dedicated to new technology industrial development. Since then, more and more land has been requisitioned by the municipality for various constructions. Urbanization and modernization have deeply changed the environment and diversified the occupations of the villagers. Those who hold to religious tradition have more time to live their faith.

The Association for Blessings of this village makes a pilgrimage almost every month to a different temple. The pilgrimage to the Old Dongyue temple takes place every year on the 29th day of the 4th month. In 2008, this pilgrimage corresponded to Monday, June 2. On that day, at 5 am, more than 130 people, mostly women, left their neighborhood and boarded two chartered buses. Their main program for the day was to request from Daoist masters a *baichan* ritual (litany) for the Great Dongyue Emperor to ensure the protection of their neighborhood, family, health, and businesses.

After performing their devotional rites and attending the Daoist ritual, they moved into one of the pilgrims' rooms and displayed a *bang*, i.e., "a ritual proclamation" on the wall. The women prepared spirit money by folding papers into an ingot shape and assembling them into a lotus shape. At the same time, some of them began to recite sacred texts by following the beaten measure on a wooden fish. It is a *foban* group, like there are many in Hangzhou. While they were singing, a woman went into a trance. The atmosphere was very devout. At 2 pm, after burning spirit money and the "proclamation of the ritual," the Association for Blessings went back home by bus. This special day had been organized by the pilgrims' leader, a local scholar. Everything had started with a person who wished to host a ritual to prolong life and to ensure peace; the others agreed to join and participate in the costs of this pilgrimage: transportation, offerings, liturgical service, and meals. The leader budgeted the pilgrimage, collected the necessary funds, and wrote the "ritual proclamation," where the name of the person who made the initial request for the ritual was listed as the main *zhaizhu*, preceding the names of the other 260 participants, and the total contribution which amounted to 3,040 yuans. According to the pilgrims' leader, this sum entirely covered the expense of the day.

That particular day gave us the opportunity to understand the way this very active society works to organize pilgrimages. A total of 130 pilgrims also represent their families on the "proclamation of the ritual" and, among the names of the 260 attendees, we can easily identify several families with multiple members. The fact that everyone contributed to the best of their ability enabled the society to pool the costs and allowed all the worshippers, even those with lower incomes, to attend the pilgrimage and join the ritual performance.

The Zongtong yiban 總統一班

The Zongtong yiban – literally the first congregation of the president, but *(da) zongtong* 大總統 is likely a mistake for Dazhonggong, the name of the former temple's main hall – is the only association founded according to the tradition of the *banhu*. This means that its members take a vow to be the servants of the Dongyue Emperor during their life on earth and in the hereafter. Actually, this congregation results from the merger of two former groups. Nowadays, it has over a thousand members. The two heads of this association, S and N, were born in 1949. S, the first one, is a fish farmer from Nanxun 南潯. He is a spirit medium and a lay member (*jushi* 居士) of the Daoist Association of Nanxun. N, the second one, was a factory worker in Hangzhou. They did not know each other and had never attended a festival in Old Dongyue temple. So, how did they meet and how did they both happen to serve the *banhu*?

S had decided to found a *banhu*, the Association of the Great President 大總統班, to serve the Dongyue Emperor, according to his own expression, "through spiritual transmission" (*xinchuan* 心傳), that is, after he had been possessed by the Dongyue Emperor. On the other hand, N is descended from families of fishermen, his father used to row his boat to Tangqi 塘棲 while his mother used to fish. Before he began working in a factory at the age of 17, he used to fish with his parents. When he was 19, he was sent off to Shandong for his military service in the air force for five years. He was then sent back to Hangzhou and resumed his work in the factory. Though his mother's grandfather and his wife's father were both heads of an Old Dongyue temple *banhu*, he would keep on declaring that he was not a "strong believer" himself. When he was 7, and again at age 13, he nearly died because of severe illnesses and, shortly after he returned from the army, he was very sick for the third time. His father was scared and, as this happened during the Cultural Revolution, discreetly went to the Dongyue village and consulted the Daoist master he knew well. The master told him: "[Y]our son must come and visit Old Dongyue temple as often as possible." Once more, N recovered, which made him say: "I am now on my third life" (*sanshi ren* 三世人). As a consequence of this, he decided to continue the familial tradition, that is, to be a servant of the Dongyue Emperor. After the reconstruction of the temple, he decided to found a *banhu* association, the First Association of Dongyue 東嶽一班, in the same way as the ancients of his family had done before and was introduced to S through the elder Daoist master (now deceased). As they got on well together, they decided to merge the Association of the Great President and the First Association of Dongyue and the new association was named the First Congregation of the President, both S and N being heads of this new congregation.

Since the beginning of the 1990s, through both the networks (family and descendants of the former *banhu* members), they managed to gather over a thousand people. The greatest part of the members of the Zongtong yiban are the descendants of the former members of various *banhu* that existed before 1949. Some have a family relationship.

Their parents and grandparents were members of about ten of these former *banhu*, for instance the Eunuchs of Qiantang (Qiantang taijian ban 錢塘太監班), the Imperial Guard of Xiaoshan (Xiaoshan Yulin jun 蕭山御林軍), the Vehicles fleet (*jiayi* 駕役), the Audience group (*shangchao* 上朝), etc. All of them were fishermen. These groups of fishermen used to be in charge of the maintenance of the halls of Dazhonggong, Shangqinggong 上清宮, and Neigong 內宮, which were parts of the former Old Dongyue temple. The Daoist masters of Old Dongyue temple and the *xiangtou* S told me the following legend:

During the Taiping movement (1860 and 1861) Old Dongyue temple was totally ransacked. One day, a fisherman found a large seal in his net and realized that it was the stolen seal of the Dongyue Emperor. The seal was given back to the Old Dongyue temple and the cult of the Dongyue Emperor then spread among the fishermen.

The *banhu* of fishermen blossomed from that time onward. Freshwater fish markets used to extend from Wulin gate to Hushu, that is, about 1.6 km. In the dead of night, the boats would arrive from Tangqi and Deqing 德清 at the Maiyu bridge 賣魚橋 and the fish would be unloaded and weighed. During the autumn Audience and Judgment festival, the pilgrims' boats used to berth on the quays from the bridge of Gongchen 拱宸 to Maiyu bridge, as a consequence of which this market place would be even busier. However, a major change occurred with the development of both railways and roads and freshwater fish farming. The fishermen changed their profession, they moved to the mainland and all lived in the same buildings. They were regrouped by the authorities in districts such as in Yuye xincun 漁業新村, the new village of aquaculture located in the district of Gongshu, or Shuichan cun 水產村, another such village located in Yuhang. However, the past history of the *banhu* association of fishermen and their belief in the Dongyue Emperor are still the strongest factor in their current cohesion.

Joining a *banhu* association means to make the vow of being the servant of the Dongyue Emperor during one's life on earth as a *sheshen ren* 捨身人 (he/she who gives one's body), as well as in the hereafter. The 1936 ethnographic survey describes the related processes that were stated in three documents.[121] The first one was the "declaration of registration" (*touwen* 投文), a personal commitment addressed to Taishan qingfu 泰山青府 (Green Palace of the Dongyue Emperor): "while I am alive, I commit myself to doing good in serving the public interest and after my death, I shall be your servant and take orders from you." The second one, *mingping* 冥憑, is a travel permit to pass into the hereafter. The third one, *zhizhao* 執照, is a certificate, proving that one is enrolled on the register of the Green Palace. "When, on a regular basis, the time comes for you to deliver the service to which you are committed, you have to go to the temple and fulfill your commitment with a pure heart and great sincerity." After the fees are duly paid, these three documents are wrapped in a yellow paper and handed to the believer who would then keep them at home. When the believer died, the *mingping* would be burnt before his/her bed, the *touwen* and the *zhizhao* would be brought with his/her funerary tablet (*paivwei* 牌位) to the Old Dongyue temple and burnt in front of the Dongyue Emperor. Nowadays, the *zhizhao* is the only document in the *banhu*'s possession. The models for the first two documents have been lost forever. The *zhizhao* still exists, thanks to the elder Zheng Daoist master who introduced it to N and S, because he had taken the risk of burying his own *zhizhao* in the ground in 1958. The document could therefore be saved, and in 2001, it could be used as a model and be reproduced by the Zongtong yiban to be awarded to its members. As dragons have been drawn on the *zhizhao*, they call it "Dragon sheet" (*longpian* 龍片); the first part, on the right side, is printed in red, and the second part, larger, is printed in yellow. These two colors symbolize the world before and after death (Figure 5.3).

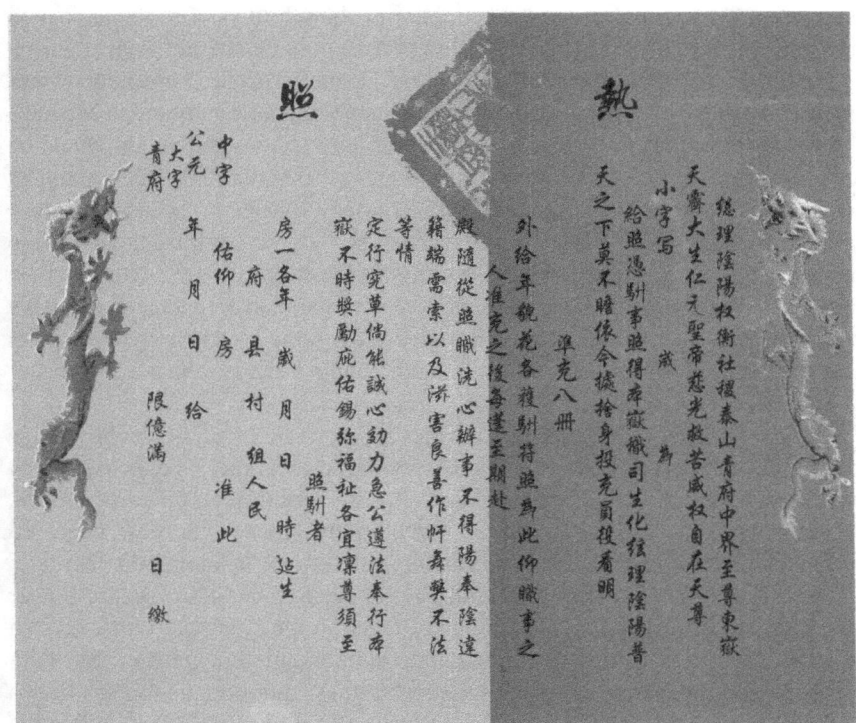

Figure 5.3 Certificate (*zhizhao*) issued at the Old Dongyue temple. © Fang Ling.

The *banhu* is autonomous and managed by its heads (*xiangtou*). It is divided into four smaller groups, split according to the places of residence of the members: Liuxia,[122] Gongshu (Qingshitou 青石頭, Yuye xincun), Yuhang (Dongtang 東塘, Zhangshan 獐山, Chongxian 崇賢) and Huzhou (Xinshi 新市, Lianshi 練市, Deqing). N and S are each responsible for one smaller group in addition to them both supervising the greater group of 1,000 members. The other two groups have their own head; Liuxia group's head is a retired woman. "A *banhu* is represented by its heads" 一個班戶就是香頭, S told me, meaning by this, that assuming all the group's moral commitments is his duty. In the past, for organizational needs, "all the *banhu* and associations used to have their own head, who was in charge for all the necessary bookings for the accommodation of pilgrims. They would also decide in a discussion with other *xiangtou* the dates of the pilgrimage, and be on-site on the D-day whatever weather conditions might have been. In case the members could not come, the heads should all be present."[123] Nowadays, the heads of the Zongtong yiban still comply with this traditional rule.

It goes without saying that members should comply with their commitments, meaning that they should join their group at the planned dates to go the temple.

Should a member not be able to come, he/she should ask for time off from the *xiangtou*, and should also pay his/her share of the offerings. The *xiangtou* will then burn incense on his/her behalf. However, should he/she not join in during three years in a row, he/she would be excluded from the group. The entrance fees for membership amount to 320 yuans per family. Should substantial expenditure be incurred, materials for processions, for instance, a subscription would be launched. The *xiangtou* is often one of the biggest contributors. The amount of cash advance due for the next pilgrimage (money offerings, incense, entrance tickets to the temple, cigarettes, tips, red envelopes, etc.) is fixed from one time to the next and money is given when the current pilgrimage is over. After the next pilgrimage, members will either be paid back (for overpaid amounts) or will have to compensate. The amount of cash advance is the same for everybody, which is a very egalitarian process. The *banhu*'s funds cannot be used to make presents or invite guests at a restaurant.

The *banhu* actually started its activities as early as 1993, when the village committee had the incense burning point erected. At that time, it collected money and commissioned a large incense burner. This ritual object, made of bronze, was brought to the village during the seventh lunar month. On it are engraved the names of the five places the contributors came from, including the fish farm of Yuhang and the temple of the Earth God of Zhangshan. This incense burner is the symbol of the birth of a community revering the Dongyue Emperor.[124] It expresses their commitment to continue the tradition of the *banhu* and their faith in the revival of the temple. As the incense burning point became too small, this incense burner was moved to a place located on the hill until 2006. When the Old Dongyue temple was entirely rebuilt, it was installed before the main hall, the Dongyue baodian. The Zongtong yiban performs three pilgrimages per year to the Old Dongyue temple, following the lunar calendar: 27th day of the 3rd month, 13th day of the 7th month, and 16th day of the 9th month. The *xiangtou* explained that for the *banhu*, the first two dates are the most important. The birthday of the Dongyue Emperor is on the 28th day of the 3rd lunar month. In the past, the procession organized by the *banhu* used to last three days, from the 26th to the 28th.[125] Nowadays, the *banhu* choose to celebrate this birthday during one single day, on the 27th. The procession is subject to an authorization delivered by the Public Security Bureau and the Civil Affairs Bureau but, due to current circumstances, this authorization is impossible to obtain, and the *banhu* decided to have the festivities celebrated in its own way. All the equipment necessary for the processions of the *banhu* were confiscated during the 1950s and they therefore had to go to Suzhou and buy a dragon robe (the imperial robe) as well as an imperial canopy, ceremonial arms, etc. From 2001 on, they started to organize a yearly procession on the Dongyue Emperor's birthday. In the past, a wooden statue in the Great Hall, the Dazhonggong, especially dedicated to that purpose, would be placed on a palanquin and taken out for the procession. Nowadays, as processions are no longer allowed, the Dongyue Emperor possesses (*shangshen* 上身)[126] a medium that walks instead of sitting on the palanquin; the route is about 1 km long.

In 2009, on the 27th of the 3rd lunar month, very early in the morning, the members of the *banhu* gathered before the former main gate (*shanmen* 山門), gongs, and drums began to play and the procession then started. N, who was at the head of the procession, held an "imperial" banner. He was followed by members holding a streamer on which were embroidered characters celebrating the Dongyue Emperor's birthday and naming the *banhu*. S, impersonating the Dongyue Emperor and wearing the dragon robe, came next. They were followed by a dozen people who held the canopy and the theatrical arms, performing the role of the imperial guard. Next walked the other members of the *banhu*, among whom octogenarians and babies carried by their parents: most members came with their family. As many pilgrims joined the procession and as it passed through a very narrow street, the cortege walked very slowly. When it approached the temple, the crowd of believers who were standing before the temple knelt down and when the Dongyue Emperor passed before them, they bowed down. This was the climax of the procession. The cortege entered the temple and the crowd followed it to burn incense and present their offerings in the temple. It lasted for a whole morning. When it was over, the procession equipment was taken away by several members of the Liuxia group who keep it in their homes while awaiting the celebration of the following year.

The tradition of the judgment of the Dongyue Emperor, held in the seventh lunar month, has not been reestablished yet. *Xiangtou* S explains that this ritual is very expensive and the *banhu* cannot afford it: "the problem is that those who know the tradition do not have money, those who have a lot of money are very ignorant of the tradition." What the *banhu* does is to come on the 13th day of the 7th lunar month to hold *jiemingxiang* 解冥餉, that is, to pay for the taxes of the hereafter. As the *xiangtou* explained to us: "we come and bring to the Dongyue Emperor *yuanbao* 元寶 (ingot-shaped spirit money), so that he can distribute it in each province of the netherworld." At the same time, each family also brings *xibo* 錫箔, that is, spirit money for the *daren* 大人 (ancestors). The rituals for dispatching *yuanbao* (for all suffering souls) and *xibo* (for one's own ancestors) are not only codified and differentiated but also held separately. The spirit money itself (*yuanbao* and *xibo*) is bought in advance: each family contributes according to their means to the head of the smaller group to which it belongs. In turn, when each head has collected the total amount paid by his/her group, a global order is made on behalf of the *banhu*. A bulk order enables the *banhu* to get the best value and have the spirit money delivered directly to the temple, instead of having it carried there by each pilgrim. Regarding the *jiemingxiang* held in 2011, the two smaller groups from Hangzhou came to the temple; the other two smaller groups were just represented by their respective *xiangtou*. On that day, at 7 am, the pilgrims gathered and entered the temple, each member carrying a pilgrimage basket containing incense and candles. In the hall reserved for pilgrims, everyone put *yuanbao* into a large bag made of red paper on which was written "to the attention of the Great King Judge of the terrestrial palace of Dongyue temple" (東嶽地府大判王) as well as the name of the taxpayers. Regarding *xibo*, they were put into yellow, pre-printed paper bags on which each family had written the name of their deceased kin and their own. Then, the accountant of each group arranged all the bags of *yuanbao* before the altar and placed on the altar of the Dongyue Emperor the list of the names of the taxpayers and the amount they paid, written on a large-sized red paper. For instance, on the list of the Liuxia group, the total amounted to 40 families and 300 piles of *yuanbao*. After all the members had bowed down and prayed, each group burnt the list on red paper and the *yuanbao* in a dedicated stove, thereby completing the *jiemingxiang*. All the *xibo* for the ancestors was then placed in a heap on the ground and burnt. For the Liuxia group, the *jiemingxiang* ceremony involved an average expense of 76 yuans per family, whereas for Gongshu group, it amounted to 133 yuans.

At the time of pilgrimage, *xiangtou* S would also organize rituals in the temple for families who needed them. The above-mentioned *chaodu* ritual held in October 2008 was one such case. The global amount of travel expenses, accommodation and meal in the temple, fees for ritual services, and offerings reached 20,000 yuans and was therefore unaffordable for a single family as they all are employees with modest income. "This is the reason why I grouped seven families so that they all could perform *chaodu* to benefit the souls of their ancestors."

After a first contact with these families in the temple, I went to visit one of them, family G in Xinshi, about 60 km from Hangzhou, a young couple with a toddler. They told me the reason why they had this ritual performed. For some time, the housewife had been often dreaming of her father who had died ten years before. Her husband had concerns with his family business as well as health problems, which led his wife to consult S, the spirit medium, who knew his late father. His diagnosis was that the dead soul was causing trouble and therefore, a *chaodu* ritual was needed to soothe him. *Xiangtou* S therefore proposed to have it performed in the Old Dongyue temple, a place renowned for holding this kind of ritual. Within a very short period of time, *xiangtou* S managed to organize both their travel and the preparation of the ritual. Offerings for the dead father included clothes and, as winter was near, clothes specially stuffed with silk floss were needed. Therefore, S took the families to shops selling such fabrics and hired two dressmakers specialized in the making of that kind of clothes. They both came to the temple and sew the clothes on the premises so that everything was in order, not only before, but also during and after the ceremony. Mr G and his wife were born during the 1980's, they had no knowledge of the Dongyue cult, but after this *chaodu* ritual, he, his family, and his brother-in-law all became members of the *banhu*. The following year, I met them again during the processions and the "Payment of the taxes of the hereafter" held in the Old Dongyue temple.

When the congregation was reestablished in the 1990s, over 40 years after the demise of the old *banhu*, the pre-1949 *xiangtou* were not there anymore. Yet, the Zongtong yiban proved able to adapt to a difficult situation and with limited resources; they developed and perpetuated the *banhu* tradition as much as possible. The *xiangtou* S and N have different personalities and competences complement each other; their collaboration allowed them to create a trans-local congregation based on multiple networks and to pool their human and financial resources to organize the procession for the Dongyue Emperor's birthday. Even though this procession is staged on a limited scale and remains inconspicuous, it has great importance for the devotees: on the procession day in 2009, not counting groups which pay separate entrance fees, the temple sold over 800 tickets to individual visitors (*sanke* 散客) who came to join in the procession. The following day, which was the birthday proper, only some 200 tickets were sold.

Conclusion

I would like to briefly conclude my study of the Old Dongyue temple's historical transformation. It was founded in 1167 during the expansion of this cult encouraged by the first Song emperors. Over the following periods, the critical and contemptuous discourse of Confucian conservatives towards this official and popular cult often turned into hostility or a source of bans. Therefore, when in 1959 the total destruction of the temple was finally achieved, it was generally taken for granted that it would never raise from its ruins and become once more a major place of worship for the people.

Today we see how the present renaissance has been achieved in the face of considerable difficulties, and that these obstacles remain. They are due not only to the present political environment, but also to the fact that so many aspects of the Eastern Peak cult and its age-old liturgy have been lost.

And yet the old religion of the Chinese people does stage an impressive comeback. As Kenneth Dean and and Zheng Zhenman have written in their detailed study of the return of the gods in the region of Putian in central Fujian province, it can be presumed that in the year 2010 "more than a million village temples have been rebuilt or restored across China and ritual traditions long thought lost are now being celebrated in many of these temples."[127] This estimate does not include towns and urban centers. And yet, returning to Hangzhou, we can also see that a great many shrines that formerly adorned the city have not been restored and for many different reasons must be believed to be gone forever. This also obtains for the different temples of the Eastern Peak. Only our "Old Dongyue" has seen a renaissance, not only as a building, but for its different liturgical functions as well, although, as we have seen, the latter are far from having recovered their former vitality. This brings us to the question of why, among a great number of former places of worship, it is this old temple of the Eastern Peak that has witnessed such a revival.

The answer is that the Taishan, Eastern Peak, is since high antiquity the foremost place where the souls of the dead go and their retribution is administered. This is not only the case for the "regular souls" (*zhenghun* 正魂) of those who left this world on their allotted time, but also for all those that for any reason and by any means had suffered an untimely death. These souls know no peace and manifest their cruel fate by disrupting the lives of the living. The latter turn therefore to the Lord of the Taishan and his extensive administration for protection and healing, and hold *chaodu* services and, if necessary, exorcisms in his name.

The history of China during the last two centuries speaks for itself if we need to understand why there is a great return to these religious observances. Thanks to the resurrection of the Old Eastern Peak Temple, these demands can, at least in the Hangzhou region and only to a certain measure, be met in a meaningful way. Peace and dignity may thus finally be restored. This achievement, obtained through great difficulties, is something for which everybody can be grateful.

Notes

1   Fang Ling, "Hokusō Tōgakubyōshi no denpa."
2   Wu Guan 吳琯, *Chongjian Dongyue xinggong ji* 重建東嶽行宮記: the text of this inscription is lost but is quoted in *Wulin fangxiang zhi*, vol. 2, pp. 446–447.
3   After the writing of the *Mengliang lu*, during the Xianchun era (1265–1279), a new Dongyue temple was built at Santaishan 三台山, so there were at least six Dongyue temples in Hangzhou at the end of the Song dynasty: *Xihu youlan zhi, juan* 4, p. 7.
4   *Mengliang lu, juan* 14, p. 127.
5   *Xianchun Lin'an zhi, juan* 75, p. 11; *Yunlu manchao, juan* 6, p. 4.
6   On the development of the Dongyue cult in Song-period Jiangnan, see Kanai Noriyuki, "Nansō jidai"; Hansen, *Changing Gods in Medieval China, 1127–1276*, pp. 184–94; von Glahn, "Towns and Temples."
7   von Glahn, "Towns and Temples."
8   *Xihu laoren fansheng lu*, p. 12.
9   *Xianchun Lin'an zhi, juan* 30, p. 11, *juan* 73, p. 10.
10 *Xixi fanyin zhi, juan* 4, pp. 7–8.
11 About the duality of the Dongyue's cult, cf. Schipper, "Note sur l'histoire du Dongyue miao de Pékin."
12 On the Dongyue cult under the Yuan, cf. Goossaert, "Portait épigraphique d'un culte."
13 The Emperor Yingzong (1427–1464) reversed Taizu's decision. He also restored the Dongyue temple of Beijing built in 1323.
14 Zhou Ying, "Dongyuemiao zai quanguo de chuanbo yu fenbu."
15 Cf. *Chongxiu Dongyue xinggong beiji* 重修東嶽行宮碑記 (1925): this damaged inscription is still visible within the Lao Dongyue village.
16 *Xixi baiyong, juan* 1, p. 18.
17 *Xixi fanyin zhi, juan* 4, p. 9.
18 *Xihu zhi* (1735), *juan* 15, p. 47.
19 *Shenbao* 申報, 1894/4/27; and oral testimonies of the Daoist masters.
20 *(Qianlong) Hangzhou fuzhi, juan* 9, p. 14; *Shenbao*, 1873/10/15.
21 "Yuemiao beifen xiangshu 嶽廟被焚詳述," *Shenbao*, 1875/8/26.
22 Goossaert, "The Local Politics of Festivals: Hangzhou, 1850–1950."
23 Shi Zhouren, "Daojiao zai jindai zhongguo de bianqian"; Goossaert, "1898: The Beginning of the End for Chinese Religion?"
24 Fang Ling, "Minguo shidai de Hangzhou Lao Dongyuemiao."
25 Lin Yongzhong & Zhang Songtao, *Lao Dongyue miaohui diaocha baogao*, p. 4.
26 Zhong Yulong, *Shuo Hangzhou*, pp. 663–64.
27 *Shenbao*, 1947/9/5.
28 *Hangzhoushi zhi*, pp. 439–42.
29 On May 1, 1958 the Hangxian district was abolished and integrated into Hangzhou municipality.
30 The relevant archives remain inaccessible as this chapter is being published.
31 Jin Yifeng, "Cong dangde wenxian kan xinshiqi zongjiao zhengce 30 nian."
32 Cao Benye & Xu Hongtu, *Hangzhou Baopu daoyuan daojiao yinyue*, p. 121.
33 Shan Jinfa, "Ta shi xiandaihua nongcun jianshe de daitouren."
34 Bulletin board of Dongyue village, seen on 2002/9/9. On the economic development of Dongyue village, cf. Song Kejie et al., "Fazhan cunzhen jingji yu chuangjian wen-ming cunzhen huwei dongli."

35 Jiang Xiaobin, "Hangzhou Huatai gongsi suozai de Dongyue cun liangxiang zhong-yang dianshitai."

36 "Dongfang zhongxue weifa gongcheng youle jieguo 東方中學違法工程有了結果," *Zhongguo jianshe bao* 中國建設報, 2001/9/13.

37 Song Kezhu 宋克主 & Xiong Changwu 熊昌武, "Fu er sijin chuang daye 富而思進創大業," *Dangdai jingji* 當代經濟, 2000.6.

38 Hu Jianmin 胡建民, "Zhao Puchu yu Hangzhou Fahuasi 趙朴初與杭州法華寺," *Zhongguo tongyi zhanxian* 中國統一戰線, 2013/11/14.

39 http://www.yjue.com/caishuifagui/200807/21-97452.shtml, accessed 2010/9/10.

40 Goossaert & Palmer, *The Religious Question in Modern China*, pp. 346–50.

41 According to the 2015 figure, there were 980 places of activities of popular belief in Hangzhou, http://www.qxzh.zj.cn/mobile/magazine/article/1708.

42 The currently used genealogical poem giving a name for each generation was initiated during the Qianlong era (1736–1795): Zong 宗, Ting 廷, Jia (Guan) 嘉 (觀), Jing 景, De 德, Sheng 勝, Ming 明, Fa 發, You 友, Ben 本, Zhong 忠, Liang 良, Ke 克, Xiu (Yun) 秀 (允). Cf. Zheng Fachu 鄭發楚, *Hangzhou Xixi Zhengshi xungen renzu de diaocha baogao*, unpublished document, 2011, p. 3. All the above-mentioned information about the Zheng clan come from this document that was handed to me by the author, to whom I express my gratitude.

43 I attended this ceremony where the letter of the Association and the "Golden Text for the happiness of returning to the origin" (*Guiyuan jinxi shu* 歸源金禧書) were posted.

44 Lin Yongzhong & Zhang Songtao, *Lao Dongyue miaohui diaocha baogao*, p. 7.

45 Zheng Fachu, *Hangzhou Xixi Zhengshi xungen renzu de diaocha baogao*.

46 Lin Yongzhong & Zhang Songtao, *Lao Dongyue miaohui diaocha baogao*. This shows the increase in the number of statues in the Old Dongyue temple.

47 Zheng Fachu, *Hangzhou Xixi Zhengshi xungen renzu de diaocha baogao*.

48 Ōtsu Taniyama 大津瀾山, "Hangzhou de foji diaocha." From the Song to the Qing, because of the laws banning and, later, restricting the commoners from building domestic temples, it was frequent that the major families worshiped their ancestors in the temples: Wang Jian, *Lihai xiangguan*, 146–51.

49 *Shenbao*, 1927/8/11. Lin Yongzhong & Zhang Songtao, *Lao Dongyue miaohui diaocha baogao*, p. 17.

50 Information supplied by the Zheng clan Daoists. See also Zheng Fachu, *Hangzhou Xixi Zhengshi xungen renzu de diaocha baogao*, pp. 9–10.

51 Zheng Fachu, *Hangzhou Xixi Zhengshi xungen renzu de diaocha baogao*.

52 This figure does not include unordained Daoist Masters (*weijing pidai zhe* 未經批戴者): *Wushan Chenghuang miao zhi, juan* 5, pp. 828–30, 833–34, 837.

53 Ding Licheng, "Wulin zashi shi"; *Shenbao*, 1883/12/3.

54 *Shenbao*, 1947/9/5.

55 Lin Yongzhong & Zhang Songtao, *Lao Dongyue miaohui diaocha baogao*, p. 9. During my field survey, the Zheng Daoist masters confirmed the reality of the *yin-gongsuo* in the past.

56 Lin Yongzhong & Zhang Songtao, *Lao Dongyue miaohui diaocha baogao*, p. 16.

57 This situation is very different from the Daoist masters' parishes, *mentu* 門徒 or *menjuan* 門眷, composed of families for which the master had a monopolistic right to perform. See Goossaert, "A Question of Control."

58 For example, before the Sino-Japanese War, in less than 20 years, ten temples came under the tutelage of the Fuxingguan 福星觀 because of financial difficulties and to benefit from the Fuxingguan's influence in order to recover their real estate. See Lai Yuxun, *Hangzhou Yuhuangshan zhi, juan* 18.

59 *Shenbao*, 1875/8/26.

60 *Shenbao*, 1875/10/29.

61 By way of comparison, in Hangzhou, many communal temples were struggling to restore their buildings and activities due to a lack of money, such as the Chenghuang temple.

62 Hangzhou difangzhi bianzuan weiyuanhui, *Hangzhou minzu zongjiaozhi*, p. 249.

63 Zheng Fachu, *Hangzhou Xixi Zhengshi xungen renzu de diaocha baogao*, p. 8.

64 *Shenbao*, 1947/9/5.

65 Fang Ling, "Minguo shidai de Hangzhou Lao Dongyuemiao," pp. 117–22.

66 http://auction.socang.com/collection/2600315.html

67 This information is provided by one of the leaders of the Zheng clan.

68 Goossaert & Palmer, *The Religious Question*, pp. 146–52.

69 Another administrative detention system.

70 Imported from Soviet Russia, the term "counterrevolution" appears in China after the movement of May 4, 1919. The first "Regulation on the crime of counterrevolution" (*Fangeming zui tiaoli* 反革命罪條例) was promulgated by the KMP-CCP government. Since then, "counterrevolution" has been rather randomly used to impose political stigma, sometimes resulting in the death penalty. Cf. Wang Qisheng, "Fangeming zui zai Zhongguo de yuanqi." *Putong fangeming* implied a counterrevolutionary conviction without incarceration.

71 According to the survey report, at that time, more than 140 families in the neighborhood (*bao*) lived only from activities related to the Old Dongyue temple: Lin Yongzhong & Zhang Songtao, *Lao Dongyue miaohui diaocha baogao*, p. 18.

72 This is the official document *Guanyu woguo shehui zhuyi shiqi zongjiao wenti de jiben guandian he jiben zhengce* 關於我國社會主義時期宗教問題的基本觀點和基本政策.

73 In Hangzhou, *pusa* and *fo* are generic terms for divinities.

74 My field notes.

75 The ordination of Zhengyi Daoist masters was interrupted in 1946 and resumed for masters from Mainland China for the first time in 1995. Since 2000, it takes place every year at the Xiayuan holiday, the 15th day of the 10th lunar month. The ordinations are conducted by the Chinese Daoist Association.

76 My field notes.

77 Remoiville, "Le renouveau religieux en Chine urbaine contemporaine," pp. 233–35.

78 *Guotang* is a customary practice in technical jobs: after an initial apprenticeship, the person takes a renowned master for a practical training.

79 On funeral customs in Hangzhou, see *Hangsu yifeng*, pp. 76–77.

80 About the *Kaitong minglu cibei yinjie* 開通冥路慈悲引接 ritual proclamation to summon the dead as practiced in the Old Dongyue temple, see Julie Remoiville, "Le renouveau religieux en Chine urbaine contemporaine," p. 193.

81 On the description of this day, see Remoiville, "Le renouveau religieux en Chine urbaine contemporaine," pp. 185–98.

82 According to the funeral regulations of the Hangzhou municipality, promulgated in 1995, the whole municipality is henceforth a zone of compulsory cremation; crematoriums must proceed with cremation within 24 hours of receiving a body.

83 *Hangsu yifeng*, pp. 77–79.

84 Chang Renchun, *Hongbai xishi*, p. 259.

85 Goossaert & Fang Ling, "Les réformes funéraires et la politique religieuse de l'État chinois, 1900–2008."

86 *Mengliang lu*, juan 2, pp. 13–14.

87 Lang Ying 郎瑛, "Chongxiu Dongyue xinggong beiji 重修東嶽行宮碑記" (1565), in *Xixi fanyin zhi*, juan 4, pp. 13–14.

88 *Xixi baiyong*, juan 1, p. 18.

89 Wang Jian, "Ming Qing yilai Hangzhou jinxiangshi chutan."

90 (*Kangxi*) *Qiantang xianzhi*, juan 14; (*Qianlong*) *Hangzhou fuzhi*.

91   (*Zhengde*) *Songjiang fuzhi*, juan 4; (*Chongzhen*) *Songjiang xianzhi*, juan 7; Fan Ying, *Shanghai minjian xinyang yanjiu*, p. 189, 307.

92   "Fengdao shiting 風倒石亭," *Shenbao*, 1881/8/10.

93   *Hangsu yifeng*, p. 10.

94   Lin Yongzhong & Zhang Songtao, *Lao Dongyue miaohui diaocha baogao*, pp. 9–11.

95   "Maijiang zhe er 賣漿者兒," *Zi buyu quanji*, juan 10.

96   Schipper, *Le corps taoïste*, pp. 51–56.

97   "Dongyue shenfeng 東嶽審瘋," *Shenbao*, 1897/10/13.

98   Goossaert, "The Local Politics of Festivals: Hangzhou, 1850–1950."

99   "Hangyan 杭諺," *Shenbao*, 1894/4/27.

100 "Santan yuese 三潭月色," *Shenbao*, 1894/6/19.

101 "Sanzhu zhongsheng 三竺鍾聲," *Shenbao*, 1895/9/20.

102 Zheng Fachu: *Xixi minsu wenhua suoying: Laodongyue miaohui kaozheng baogao*, p. 18.

103 "Lun jianjiao jiexiang zhiwu 論建醮解餉之誣," *Shenbao*, 1879/8/19.

104 "Jinzhi Hangzhou Dongyuemiao chaoshen yi 禁止杭州東嶽廟朝審議," *Shenbao*, 1880/7/20.

105 "Chongxing chaoshen 重行朝審," *Shenbao*, 1881/9/2.

106 *Zhejiang fengsu gailiang qianshuo*, p. 18.

107 "Lun Dongyue chaoshen 論東嶽朝審," *Shenbao*, 1878/8/8.

108 "Jinzhi zhongyuan saihui 禁止中元賽會," *Shenbao*, 1913/8/2.

109 "Hangzhou kuaixin 杭州快信," *Shenbao*, 1924/9/9.

110 Li Xuechang & Dong Jianbo, "Ershi shiji shangbanye Hangxian yingshen saihui shuailuo yinsu qianxi."

111 "Shizhengfu jinzhi dajiao 市政府禁止打醮," *Shenbao*, 1927/7/22; "Hangzhou kuaixin 杭州快信," *Shenbao*, 1927/7/27.

112 "Yanyun liaorao Fahua xiang 煙雲繚繞法華香," *Shenbao*, 1927/8/11.

113 "Hangzhou Dongyuemiao guishijie xianxingji 杭州東嶽廟"鬼世界"現形記," *Shenbao*, 1947/9/5.

114 He Shanmeng, "Yingshen saihui haishi putong shaoxiang?," and *Mingguo Hangzhou minjian xinyang*, pp. 91–97.

115 In 1926, a citizen named Gu Bingnan wrote to the Hangzhou Public Security Bureau calling for a ban on meat in meals for pilgrims for hygienic reasons. His request was successful, and since then the pilgrims have been eating vegetarian food during the festival. See Lin Yongzhong & Zhang Songtao, *Lao Dongyue miaohui diaocha baogao*, p. 16.

116 Ibid., p. 18.

117 Interview held on December 2, 2009.

118 Lin Yongzhong & Zhang Songtao, *Lao Dongyue miaohui diaocha baogao*, pp. 13–14.

119 Ibid., p. 8.

120 *Hangsu yifeng*, p. 9.

121 Lin Yongzhong & Zhang Songtao, *Lao Dongyue miaohui diaocha baogao*, pp. 14–15.

122 The Old Dongyue temple is in the Liuxia residential district.

123 Lin Yongzhong & Zhang Songtao, *Lao Dongyue miaohui diaocha baogao*, p. 17.

124 Schipper, *Le corps taoïste*, pp. 36–37.

125 See *Shenbao*, 1894/4/27.

126 We see the same kind of practice in "Cangshen futi" 倉神附體, *Dianshizhai huabao*, volume Yin, p. 19.

127 Dean & Zheng, *Ritual Alliances of the Putian Plain : Historical Introduction to the Return of the Gods*, vol. 1, p. 5. For a justification of this estimate, see the long footnote on the same page.

References

Cao Benye 曹本冶 & Xu Hongtu 徐宏圖. *Hangzhou Baopu daoyuan daojiao yinyue* 杭州抱朴道院道教音樂. Taipei: Xinwenfeng, 2000.

Chang Renchun 常人春. *Hongbai xishi* 紅白喜事. Beijing: Yanshang chubanshe, 1998.

Dean, Kenneth & Zhenman Zheng. *Ritual Alliances of the Putian Plain: Historical Introduction to the Return of the Gods*. Leiden: Brill, 2009.

Dianshizhai huabao 點石齋畫報. Shanghai: Shenbaoguan, every ten days, 1882–1898. Rpt. Guangzhou: Guangdong renmin chubanshe, 1983.

Ding Licheng 丁立誠. "Wulin zashi shi 武林雜事詩," *Wulin zhanggu congbian* 武林掌故叢編. Yangzhou: Jiangsu Guangling guji keyinshe, 1985.

Fan Ying 范燨. *Shanghai minjian xinyang yanjiu* 上海民間信仰研究. Shanghai: Renmin chubanshe, 2006.

Fang Ling. "Hokusō Tōgakubyōshi no denpa — *Shanxi Dingxiang Dongyuemiao bei* shotan 北宋東岳廟祀の伝播 — 山西定襄東岳廟碑初探," in Tsuchiya Masaaki 土屋昌明 & Vincent Goossaert (eds.), *Dōkyō no seichi to chihōshin* 道教の聖地と地方神. Tokyo: Toho shoten, 2016, pp. 213–24.

Fang Ling 方玲. "Minguo shidai de Hangzhou Lao Dongyuemiao 民國時代的杭州老東岳廟," in Kong Linghong 孔令宏 & Han Songtao 韓松濤 (eds.), *Minguo Hangzhou daojiao* 民國杭州道教. Hangzhou: Hangzhou chubanshe, 2013, pp. 117–22.

Goossaert, Vincent & David A. Palmer. *The Religious Question in Modern China*. Chicago: University of Chicago Press, 2011.

Goossaert, Vincent & Fang Ling. "Les réformes funéraires et la politique religieuse de l'État chinois, 1900–2008," *Archives des Sciences Sociales des Religions*, 144, 2008, pp. 51–73.

Goossaert, Vincent. "1898: The Beginning of the End for Chinese Religion?," *Journal of Asian Studies*, 65(2), 2006, pp. 307–36.

Goossaert, Vincent "A Question of Control: Licensing Local Ritual Specialists in Jiangnan, 1850–1950," in Liu Shufen & Paul R. Katz (eds.), *Xinyang, shijian yu wenhua tiaoshi. Proceeding of the Fourth International Sinology Conference* 信仰、實踐與文化調適. 第四屆國際漢學會議論文集. Taipei: Academia Sinica, 2013, pp. 569–604.

Goossaert, Vincent. "Portait épigraphique d'un culte. Inscriptions des dynasties Jin et Yuan de temples du Pic de l'Est," *Sanjiao wenxian. Matériaux pour l'étude de la religion chinoise*, 2, 1998, pp. 41–63.

Goossaert, Vincent. "The Local Politics of Festivals: Hangzhou, 1850–1950," *Daoism: Religion, History & Society*, 5, 2013, pp. 57–80.

Hangsu yifeng 杭俗遺風 (Prefaces 1863, 1864, Fan Zushu 范祖述, with additional notes by Hong Yueru 洪岳如, 1920s). Shanghai: Shanghai wenyi chubanshe, 1989.

Hangzhou difangzhi bianzuan weiyuanhui, *Hangzhou minzu zongjiaozhi* 杭州民族宗教志. Hangzhou: Hangzhou chubanshe, 2010.

(Qianlong) Hangzhou fuzhi (乾隆) 杭州府志.

Hangzhoushi zhi 杭州市志. Beijing: Zhonghua shuju, 1997.

Hansen, Valerie. *Changing Gods in Medieval China, 1127–1276*. Princeton: Princeton University Press, 1990.

He Shanmeng 何善蒙. "Yingshen saihui haishi putong shaoxiang? Cong Minguo Hangzhou Santaishan Dongyuemiao hui shijian kan Zhongguo zhengzhi shehui bianqian zhong de minjian xinyang 迎神賽會還是普通燒香? 從民國杭州三台山東嶽廟會事件看中國政治社會變遷中的民間信仰," *Paper for the "Religion and State in Local*

Society in Late Imperial and Modern China 中國近世地方社會中的宗教與國家" international workshop, 16–17 October 2013, Fudan University, Shanghai.

He Shanmeng 何善蒙. *Minguo Hangzhou minjian xinyang* 民國杭州民間信仰. Hangzhou: Hangzhou chubanshe, 2012.

Jiang Xiaobin 蔣小斌. "Hangzhou Huatai gongsi suozai de Dongyue cun liangxiang zhongyang dianshitai 杭州華泰公司所在的東嶽村亮相中央電視臺," *Dangdai jingji* 當代經濟, 5, 2001, p. 31.

Jin Yifeng 金以楓. "Cong dangde wenxian kan xinshiqi zongjiao zhengce 30 nian 從黨的文獻看新時期宗教政策30年," *Dangshi yanjiu yu jiaoxue* 黨史研究與教學, 6, 2008, pp. 13–14.

Kanai Noriyuki 金井德幸. "Nansō jidai no shichin to Tōgakubyō 南宋時代の市鎮と東嶽廟," *Risshō shigaku* 立正史學, 61, 1987, pp. 21–39.

(Qianlong) Hangzhou fuzhi 乾隆杭州府志.

Hangzhou Yuhuangshan zhi 杭州玉皇山志 (1945). Lai Yuxun 來裕恂, comp. Hangzhou: Hangzhou tushuguan, 1985.

Li Xuechang 李學昌 & Dong Jianbo 董建波, "Ershi shiji shangbanye Hangxian yingshen saihui shuailuo yinsu qianxi 二十世紀上半葉杭縣迎神賽會衰落因素淺析," *Huadong shifan daxue xuebao* 華東師範大學學報, 30(5), 2007, pp. 49–53.

Lin Yongzhong 林用中 & Zhang Songtao 章松壽. *Lao Dongyue miaohui diaocha baogao* 老東嶽廟會調查報告. Hangzhou: Zhejiangsheng Limin jiaoyue shiyan xuexiao, 1936.

(Xianchun) Lin'an zhi 咸淳臨安志.

Mengliang lu 夢梁錄 (1274), Wu Zimu 吳自牧. *Congshu jicheng chubian*. Shanghai: Shangwu yinshuguan, 1939.

Ōtsu Taniyama 大津潤山. "Hangzhou de foji diaocha 杭州の佛蹟調查," (in Chinese), *Zhejiang wenhua yanjiu* 浙江文化研究, 39, 1944.

(Kangxi) Qiantang xianzhi (康熙)錢塘縣志. In *Zhejiang fuzhi* 浙江府志 vol. 4, *Zhongguo difangzhi jicheng*. Shanghai: Shanghai shudian, 1993.

Remoiville, Julie. "Le renouveau religieux en Chine urbaine contemporaine : Le rôle social de la relation dans la vie quotidienne à Hangzhou," PhD dissertation, EPHE, 2013.

Schipper, Kristofer. "Note sur l'histoire du Dongyue miao de Pékin," in Jean-Pierre Dieny (ed.), *Hommage à Kwong Hing Foon, Etudes d'histoire culturelle de la Chine*. Paris: Collège de France, Institut des Hautes Etudes Chinoises, 1995, pp. 255–69.

Schipper, Kristofer. *Le corps taoïste*. Paris: Fayard, 1982.

Shan Jinfa 單金發. "Ta shi xiandaihua nongcun jianshe de daitouren 他是現代化農村建設的帶頭人," *Jingcai rensheng* 精采人生. Beijing: Zhongguo jingji chubanshe, 2010.

Shenbao 申報. Daily. Shanghai: Shenbaoguan, 1872–1949.

Shi Zhouren 施舟人 (Kristofer Schipper). "Daojiao zai jindai zhongguo de bianqian 道教在近代中國的變遷," Shi Zhouren, *Zhongguo wenhua jiyinku* 中國文化基因庫. Beijing: Beijing daxue chubanshe, 2002, pp. 146–62.

Song Kejie 宋克杰, et al. "Fazhan cunzhen jingji yu chuangjian wenming cunzhen huwei dongli 發展村鎮經濟與創建文明村鎮互為動力," *Dangdai jingji* 當代經濟, 3, 2001, pp. 8–10.

Song Kezhu 宋克主 & Xiong Changwu 熊昌武. "Fu er si jin chuang daye 富而思進創大業," *Dangdai jingji* 當代經濟, 2000.

(Zhengde) Songjiang fuzhi 正德松江府志.

(Chongzhen) Songjiang xianzhi 崇真松江府志.

von Glahn, Richard. "Towns and Temples: Urban Growth and Decline in the Yangzi Delta, 1100–1400," in P. J. Smith and von Glahn (eds.), *The Song-Yuan-Ming Transition in Chinese History*. Cambridge: Harvard University Asia Center, 2003, pp. 177–211.

Wang Jian 王健. *Lihai xiangguan. Ming Qing yilai Jiangnan Su Song diqu minjian xinyang yanjiu* 利害相關. 明清以來江南蘇松地區民間信仰研究. Shanghai: Renmin chubanshe, 2010.

Wang Jian 王健. "Ming Qing yilai Hangzhou jinxiangshi chutan 明清以來杭州進香史初探," *Shilin* 史林, 4, 2012, pp. 89–97.

Wang Qisheng 王奇生. "Fangeming zui zai Zhongguo de yuanqi 反革命罪在中國的緣起," *Jindaishi yanjiu* 近代史研究, 1, 2010, pp. 28–39.

Wulin fangxiang zhi 武林坊巷志 (preface 1896). Ding Bing 丁丙, comp. Hangzhou: Zhejiang renmin chubanshe, 1984.

Wulin jinxiang xuzhi 武林進香需知 (ca. 1924–1927), in Wang Jianchuan 王見川 & al. (eds.), *Minjian sizang: Zhongguo minjian xinyang minjian wenhua ziliao huibian* 民間私藏: 中國民間信仰民間文化資料彙編. Taipei: Boyang, 2011, vol. 1.

Wushan Chenghuang miao zhi 吳山城隍廟志 (1879), Zhu Wencao 朱文藻 (1735–1806), in *Xihu wenxian jicheng*. Hangzhou: Hangzhou chubanshe, 2004, vol. 25.

Xihu laoren fansheng lu 西湖老人繁盛錄. Naide Weng 耐得翁 (époque Song), in *Xihu wenxian jicheng* 西湖文獻集成. Hangzhou: Hangzhou chubanshe, 2004, vol. 2.

Xihu youlan zhi 西湖遊覽志 (1547), Tian Rucheng 田汝成, 1896 edition in *Zhongguo fangzhi congshu* 中國方志叢書, Huazhong n° 487. Taipei: Chengwen chubanshe, 1975.

Xixi baiyong 西溪百詠 (Preface 1640). Shi Dashan 釋大善. *Siku quanshu cunmu congshu* 四庫全書存目叢書 edition.

Xixi fanyin zhi 西谿梵隱志. Wu Bentai 吳本泰, comp., in *Zhongguo fosi ji* 中國佛寺集, vol. 1. Taipei: Mingwen shuju, 1980.

Yunlu manchao 雲麓漫抄 (1206), Zhao Yanwei 趙彥衛, *Siku quanshu* edition.

Zhejiang fengsu gailiang qianshuo 浙江風俗改良淺說. Hangzhou: Zhejiang Provincial Government, 1910.

Zheng Fachu 鄭發楚. *Hangzhou Xixi Zhengshi xungen renzu de diaocha baogao* 杭州西溪鄭氏尋根認祖的調查報告, unpublished document, 2011.

Zheng Fachu 鄭發楚. *Xixi minsu wenhua suoying: Laodongyue miaohui kaozheng baogao* 西谿民俗文化縮影 —— 老東嶽廟會考證報告, unpublished document, 2007.

Zhong Yulong 鍾毓龍 (1880–1970), *Shuo Hangzhou* 說杭州, in *Xihu wenxian jicheng* 西湖文獻集成. Hangzhou: Hangzhou chubanshe, 2005, vol. 11.

Zhou Ying 周郢, "Dongyuemiao zai quanguo de chuanbo yu fenbu 東嶽廟在全國的傳播與分佈," *Taishan xueyuan xuebao* 泰山學院學報, 30(2), 2008, pp. 17–29.

Zi buyu quanji 子不語全集. Yuan Mei 袁枚 (1716–1798). Shijiazhuang: Hebei renmin chubanshe, 1997.

6 Zhengyi Daoists and the Baoqing Pier neighborhood in modern Hankou

Mei Li 梅莉 *and Xun Liu* 劉迅

Introduction

The Baoqing Pier 寶慶碼頭 is located in Hankou, one of the tri-cities that make up the modern Wuhan metropolis. It lies on the north bank of the Yangzi River and to the east of the confluence of the Yangzi and the Han Rivers. From the mid-nineteenth century on, the Baoqing Pier was one of the main docks and moorings for the timber rafts and coal cargo boats from central Hunan. It was first established during the mid-eighteenth century by the merchants, timber rafters, and coal transport boat owners from the five counties: Shaoyang 邵陽, Wugang 武崗, Xinning 新寧, Chengbu 城步, and Xinhua 新化 of the Baoqing prefecture in central Hunan. Located in central Hunan, the Baoqing region is a crossroad of the imperial pony express routes southward to the Yunnan-Guizhou highlands, and the waterway of the torrential Zi River 資水 winding northward first into Lake Dongting 洞庭 and then further eastward to major cities like Hankou downstream along the Yangzi River.

With the rapid commercial expansion and urban development in Hankou from the eighteenth century onward, merchants, coal and timber transporters, laborers, and other immigrants from many different parts of China, including those from the Baoqing region, came to do business and settle in the busy bustling commercial city.[1] There the Baoqing settlers, like many other immigrants to the city, began to build their own port on the northwestern bank at the confluence of the Yangzi and Han Rivers. The streets and alleys around the port became over time the exclusive cargo distribution and storage center for goods from central and western Hunan, and many of them also evolved into a residential neighborhood where merchants, laborers, and other sojourners from the Baoqing region congregated. Along with the flow of trade and migration out of the Baoqing region also came the Zhengyi Daoists 正一道士 and local ritualists who began to settle and serve their fellow sojourners in Hankou. From around the mid-Qing period onward, generations of these Daoist ritualists from Baoqing have lived and practiced in the Baoqing Pier community in Hankou.

Their experience affords us a unique opportunity to investigate the social history of Zhengyi Daoism in the context of the commercial expansion, immigration, and urban development in Hankou since the late Qing up to the present. For over two centuries, they have been providing a variety of ritual services, from funerary services to geomantic adjustments, and from managing seasonal temple festivities in the city to organizing pilgrimages to the sacred Southern Peak (Nanyue南嶽) of Hengshan 衡山 and to home temples in the Baoqing region. Their ritual services to fellow immigrants not only provided practical solutions to the crises in their lives, but they also played pivotal roles in helping shape their fellow immigrants' cultural identity and maintain their social network and communal solidarity in their newly settled city of Wuhan. Yet as Wuhan underwent the Republican and Communist social revolutions and urban transformations from the early twentieth century onward, the Baoqing immigrant community in the city has also experienced deep social and economic change. Beginning in the early 1980s, the "reform and opening" policies created both new opportunities and challenges to the Daoist ritual masters in the Baoqing Pier district. Just as the new reforms set forth more tolerant religious policies and generated more political and social space for the Daoists to practice, they also unleashed deeply transformative social and economic processes which have had a lasting impact on the Baoqing Daoist ritual masters and their communities. With the new economic liberties, loosened social control, and market-driven entrepreneurship and mobility, the more educated and better trained younger children of the old immigrant families began to leave the traditional enclaves and neighborhoods. Even the new immigrants from Baoqing to Wuhan now settle and live in diffused patterns in streets and alleys where they follow their own trade and professional niches, often far away from the traditional immigrant enclaves and neighborhoods in Hankou. As elsewhere in China, the market-driven real estate boom and urban development plan in Wuhan has also threatened to disrupt and even uproot the traditional Baoqing immigrant enclaves near the confluence of the Han and the Yangtze Rivers, creating further havoc to the Daoist ritual masters living and practicing their crafts in the community there.

How have these transformative social, political, and economic processes impacted the Daoist ritual masters and their community? How have they dealt with these challenges and changes brought on by the new market economy and urbanization? Can and will they perish or survive as they are confronted with the arguably most daunting obstacles as well as opportunities in the history of modern Daoism? This chapter hopes to answer these questions and others by examining the history of a small group of Daoist ritual masters from Xinhua county of the Baoqing region in Hunan. By examining the group's early migration to Wuhan, its transmission and growth as a distinct Daoist tradition and organization amidst the increasing social and political upheavals, economic development, and urbanization in the city of Wuhan from the pre-1949 years to the present, we hope to shed light on the social history of the Zhengyi Daoist ritual masters in the urban setting, and to gain some insights in its future. To accomplish this goal, we have relied on a combination of different materials: the local gazetteers of both Baoqing and Wuhan, memoirs and archival materials about the Baoqing Daoists, oral history interviews with the Baoqing Daoist masters and field observations of their ritual services in Wuhan conducted between 2007 and 2011, and a body of ritual scriptures collected from the Daoists during the same period.[2]

The rise of Hankou and the emergence of the Baoqing Pier

Hankou only rose to become a major river port and trading center on the Yangzi River during the late seventeenth and early eighteenth centuries. Throughout the Hongwu reign (1368–1398), the area remained largely an uninhabited collection of dry lands, sandbars, and marshes thick with reed growth. Under the Tianshun 天順 reign (1457–1464), the area began to be reclaimed and inhabited by a few settlers. In the Chenghua 成化 reign (1465–1488) that followed, as the Han River changed its course, its former multiple branch streams combined into a single drain into the Yangzi River. The new channel now divided the Hanyang 漢陽 region north of the Yangzi River into two areas: the Hanyang town to the southeast of the Han River, and the new region now known as Hankou lying northwest of the Han River and its confluence with the mighty Yangzi River. Together with the old administrative town of Wuchang 武昌 on the southern bank of the Yangzi River, the new tri-cities' geography both divided and connected by the Han and the Yangzi Rivers was thus formed for the first time. As the new Han River at the confluence with the Yangzi River flew slow, smooth, and deep, the nearby riverfront of Hankou not only offered wide-open and easily accessible landing ports and piers, but it also served as an ideal mooring place and sanctuary for cargo ships and passenger boats from the windy Yangzi River. During the Chenghua reign, a long embankment was built along the two rivers' confluence and extending upstream along the Han River and downstream along the Yangzi River. The new dyke not only protected Hankou from floods of both rivers, but it also rendered the city a suitable place for both human habitation and riverborne commercial traffic and landing. Hankou thus gradually evolved to become a major port of call on the Yangzi River. Under the Qing, between the Kangxi and the Qianlong reigns (1662–1795), Hankou had already become one of the "Four Towns of Gathering Commerce" in the realm.[3]

According to the extant records, Hankou's earliest commercial port, the Pier of the Heavenly Treasures (Tianbao matou 天寶碼頭) was built on the city's Han riverfront upstream from the confluence in 1736. In the following three years, 14 additional piers and ports were built further downstream along the north bank of the Han River. By 1868, a total of 35 docks and ports had been built along Hankou's southern quarters facing the Han River. Starting from the upstream Pier of Heavenly Treasures down to the Dragon King Temple Pier 龍王廟碼頭 at the mouth of the confluence, these docks and ports contributed to Hankou's growing wealth and prosperity. By contrast, the southern Hanyang side of the Han River saw construction of only a few small landings, which functioned as temporary docking and mooring places for the arriving cargo boats and merchant cargo ships that congregated on the northern bank (Figure 6.1).

Though little is known about how these piers and landings operated in their early days, we do know that by the mid-seventeenth century, merchants' cargo boats arriving at Hankou from various provinces all called at their own proprietary piers or dockings. For instance, cargo junks from Jiangxi province and other parts of Hubei province all docked at the piers and landings on the north bank of Hankou, whereas the smaller local boats all moored near the auxiliary landings on the Hanyang side. Additionally, the powerful "downstreamer (*xiajiangren* 下江人)," merchants, and traders from Jiangnan and Anhui who formed the core of the Hankou commercial elite all docked their transport ships at their ports and piers on premium waterfronts of the city.

These geographically based proprietary ports and landings seem to have formed over time, most of them originally sponsored and paid for by native place-bound trade guilds or native place associations which had settled in Hankou. These guilds and associations did so in order to secure both ownership and operational rights over their commercial piers and landings. As a result, not only the richest and most powerful guilds owned their ports, but even small trade gangs such as the river transporters and boatmen from Pingxiang 萍鄉 and Liling 禮陵 counties on the Jiangxi-Hunan border tried to have their own landings built.[4] Native place associations also built their own ports, but non-member merchants could also rent access to them.[5] Because of their proximity to the bustling markets, businesses, and stores which spread along the Hanzheng 漢正 Street near the riverfront in Hankou, these piers became favorite places for loading and unloading cargoes, and temporary moorings. These piers and docks were thus also objects of intensive competition and even armed feuds among various gangs of merchants, bargemen, and dockhands as they struggled for survival and dominance in local markets. Feuding factions often resorted to bribing local government offices, and even getting high-ranking court officials and provincial governors to intervene on their behalves. These intense rivalries have evolved into high drama in the local lore of Hankou. Around 1881, the Shanxi and Shaanxi Merchant Guild in Hankou acquired their own port, the Horse King Temple Pier (Mawangmiao 馬王廟).[6] According to William Rowe, the Horse King Temple Pier came with animal corrals and stockyards, and additional buildings that housed the livestock markets. The pier was originally managed by Daoist keepers. But by the late 1870s, the local magistrate confiscated the pier together with its affiliated buildings from its original owner, citing Daoist clerical venality and corruption as the reason, and entrusted it with the Shanxi and Shaanxi Merchant Guild for its daily operations. His rationale for the decision was that since the guild members were the most frequent users of the pier and its facilities, their management of the pier and its facilities best accorded with the public interest.[7]

As the piers alongside the Han riverfront provided easy access to river transport and travel, commerce and trade flourished in Hankou. Main streets such as the Long Dyke (Changti 長堤) and the Hanzheng streets were lined with retailers and distributors who traded herbs, cotton cloth, grains, and other merchandises. Hotels, restaurants, and entertainment quarters spread throughout the streets and alleys of Hankou. The long and arrow shape of Hankou was defined largely by the streets and lanes that had access to the piers and docks on the Han riverfront.[8]

By contrast, the piers and docks on Hankou's Yangzi riverfront were built after the second Opium War. In 1858, Hankou was stipulated as one of the inland treaty ports in the Tientsin Treaty. As the British, French, and Russian trading firms and merchants began to open banks, factories, and warehouses in their respective concessions in Hankou, they also soon built their own "foreign docks" (*yang matou* 洋碼頭) on the Yangzi riverfront. In its efforts to break into the foreign-dominated yet highly profitable market of inland river transport and commerce, the Qing government established its own China Merchant Shipping Ltd (Zhaoshangju 招商局). In 1874, a branch of the CMS was set up in Hankou. Soon after, privately owned and run Chinese shipping companies such as Minsheng 民生 and Ningshao 寧紹 were also established to compete with foreign commercial and passenger shipping lines that plied the Yangzi Rivers. In addition, the new arsenals and industries launched in the aftermath of the Taiping Uprising by Qing regional leaders such as Governor General Zhang Zhidong 張之洞 (1837–1909) in Hubei also drove the need for expanded inland river transport and new ports along the Yangzi River. As a result, the city of Hankou saw a spatter of new piers and ports being opened along the city's Yangzi riverfront.[9]

The Hunan immigrants to Hankou and the Baoqing Pier

Hankou thrived because of the growing commerce, and especially in the post-Taiping reconstruction and recovery. Migrants and sojourners made up the bulk of the city's resident population. According to an early Republican source, Hankou never had any native residents. While 90% of the city's residents were involved in business, immigrants outnumbered locals.[10] According to a study, throughout the nineteenth century, immigrant households constituted 70–80% of the total number of the households in Hankou. By contrast, those households that were registered as Hanyang local residents barely made up 20% of the total.[11] In his study of the city's history of commerce and immigration, Rowe divided the city's population into five categories: (1) the natives of Hankou and Hanyang; (2) those who came from Wuchang and surrounding areas; (3) those who were from the surrounding regions marginalized by Hankou's urbanization; (4) those who were from market towns in central and southern Hubei; and (5) those who were from Hunan.[12] The majority of the Hunan immigrants in Hankou came from the major trade towns such as Changsha, Hengzhou 衡州, Xiangtan 湘潭, in the Xiang River valley and Shaoyang, Xinhua, and Yiyang 益陽 in the Zi River valley.

With numerous rivers and lakes in its territory, Hunan enjoyed a well-developed inland river transportation system. Many of the local population in Hunan made a living by engaging in river transportation and shipping of logs from their province. The lumber and bamboo market in Hankou initially started at the end of the Ming dynasty. It began to thrive toward the end of the Kangxi reign in the 1720s. The market was by then dominated by the so-called Huang Gang (Huang bang 黃幫), i.e., the Jiangxi lumber and bamboo merchants who had migrated to Huangzhou 黃州 prefecture in eastern Hubei province. From the 1720s onward, demand for lumber and bamboo rose sharply around the country. Lumber merchants upstream in Hunan began to ship timber logs from their home province to Hankou. To reduce their operation costs, the Hunanese lumber merchants built rafts of timber logs instead of barges for downstream sailing only. After their timber rafts reached the Hankou lumber yards, the rafts of timber logs were then taken apart and processed as wood planks to be sold at the local lumber market in Hankou. Their rather unique ways of shipping the timbers downstream also earned the Hunanese lumber merchants and their crews the unsavory nickname "raft-hicks (*fangpai lao* 放簰佬)" in Hankou. But their cost-cutting method gave them a competitive advantage against their rivals, the Huang gang and other merchants, and contributed to their gradual ascension as the dominant merchant group in the Hankou market. An early Republican era gazetteer of Xiakou 夏口, a town near Wuchang, makes a note of the Hunanese-dominated river transport and shipping business, stating:

> The thriving Hankou market does not only attract merchants from Hubei province proper. Merchants and businessmen from other provinces all opened their own firms and branch firms here without an exception. … The Hunan gang dominated the river transport here. They were most numerous in the shipping and navigation business.

In addition to timber, the merchants from Hunan also transported rice, coal, bamboo, paper, iron, and other products to Hankou. Though the Hunanese merchants did not necessarily stand out in terms of wealth, they did wrest full control of the lumber and wood business in Hankou from the once dominant Jiangxi and the local Huangzhou lumber merchants. By the mid-nineteenth century, with the rise of the Hunan militia army during the anti-Taiping campaign, the Hunan lumber merchants' dominance and control over the Hankou lumber market were complete.[13]

A recent historical demographic study shows that at the height of the migration from the Hu-Guang region, the Yongzhou and Baoqing prefectures of Hunan provided the second largest source of outbound immigrants to other provinces such as Sichuan. In addition, major commercial centers in the Yangzi River valley such as Hankou, Changsha, and Nanjing also counted among the most favored destinations for Baoqing immigrants and sojourners.[14] Indeed, such familiar expressions as "risking it on the rivers and lakes (*zou jianghu* 走江湖)" and "striking out at the pier (*chuang matou* 闖碼頭)" are expressive of the laborers, peddlers, and small businessmen from Baoqing, who risked it all by moving with their families to faraway booming towns like Hankou in the hope of striking it rich there.[15]

At the time, commodities such as coal, timber, tobacco leaves, stibium ingots, paper, dried bamboo shoot slices, tea, and lime produced in Baoqing were exported in large quantities to Hankou. Of these, tobacco leaves, stibium ingots, paper, dried bamboo shoot slices, tea, and lime were transported primarily by small boats which were built structurally solid. Because of their relative small displacement and light tonnage, they did not have to wait for the river water to rise, and could navigate well in shallow waters, and ply back and forth easily between Baoqing and Hankou. But the transportation of timber and coal required special handling. The timber produced in Xinning, Wugang, Shaoyang, and Xinhua was often assembled and bound into small rafts. These timber rafts were then floated along the Zi River 資水 down to Yiyang 益陽, where they were reassembled into large rafts and floated downstream northwestward and then eastward over a distance of nearly 800 km to the Parrot Shoal (Yingwu zhou 鸚鵡洲), and White Sand Shoal (Baisha zhou 白沙洲) near Hankou. The rich coal deposits located in Shaoyang, Xinhua, and Wugang yielded high-quality coal. Most of the coal mines are located along the Zi River with easy access to river transportation. Coal used to be transported in small barges known as "small lake barges (*xiaodong bo* 小洞駁)," or "autumn boats (*qiuchuan* 秋船)," which typically carried only 2–3 tons of cargo. Each year, the number of small coal barges that sailed to Hankou numbered in the thousands. After off-loading their cargo, the coal barges would return to Hunan. Another kind of barge was much larger and known as the "Pure River (*qingjiang* 清江)." These large barges could carry as much as 20–50 tons of cargo, but their operation required many deck hands, and moved slowly on the water. While they could be reused, their initial cost remained high with small returns. During the early 1820s, coal began to be transported by the so-called rough plank boats (*maobanchuan* 毛板船).[16] This type of large barges costed very little, but was capable of carrying large weight. Though it was difficult to maneuver, its operation could fetch tenfold profit. In addition, these rough plank barges could be sold to the scrapyards and taken apart as wood planks for local markets in Hankou. On average, a barge bought at 500 silver dollars in Shaoyang could earn just as much when sold in Hankou for its planks. The Planks Lane (Bancai xiang 板材巷) along the Moonlake Dyke (Yuehu ti 月湖堤) in Hanyang and the Hanzheng Street in Hankou were lined with scrapyards devoted for taking apart the rough plank boats during the 19th century.[17]

The operations and all affairs aboard a rough plank barge were overseen by a supervisor (*changshou* 長守) who was entrusted by the timber merchants. Upon arrival in Hankou, he would return home to Hunan to supervise the operations of the next barge. But since most of his deckhands and sailors were hired temps, they would often seek other employments once they arrived in Hankou. Most of them ended up settling down in the city and becoming part of its low-level yet skilled labor force. These rafts-men took up residence largely on the Parrots Shoal and the White Sands Shoal off the Hankou and the Hanyang riverfronts. On the Parrots Shoal alone, the number of the lumber transport and processing workers reached 4,000 by 1912. On the eve of the People's Republic in 1949, they numbered over 10,000. Most of them were of Hunan origin, and known to the locals as "Southern (Hunan) Gang laborers (*Nanbang gongren* 南幫工人)," as opposed to the "Northern Gang," which refers to the laborers from Hubei.[18] These Hunan lumber laborers were initially sojourners in Hankou: they lived and worked in the city after their timber rafts were disassembled for sale in Hankou, and then returned to their hometowns in Hunan as the New Year approached. But over time, many began to take roots in Hankou, moving from their sheds on the shoals to settle with their families in the neighborhoods along the Han and Yangzi riverfronts.[19]

Native place ties played an important role among most trades and professions in imperial China. The Hunan lumber and dock yards in Hankou were no exception.

After securing their exclusive rights in lumber transportation and loading business in Hankou, most lumber yard and dock operators preferred to hire workers from among their compatriots.[20] The sailors, barge hands, and dockyard workers from the same counties tended to form their own barge crews and dock gangs.

The Baoqing immigrants set up four docks: the main Baoqing dockyard near the Hanzheng street in Hankou for all kinds of boats and barges; the Moonlake Pier in Hanyang for docking the rough plank boats and for taking them apart for sale; the two other ports on the Parrots Shoal and the White Sands Shoal where bamboo and timber rafts moored before being disassembled. These docks also became the neighborhoods where the Baoqing immigrants, sailors, raft hands, and merchants settled. The White Sands Shoal port and the Moon Lake Pier were located in remote areas along the Yangzi River, and the Parrots Shoal port was inhabited by mixed settlers from both Anhua and Yiyang counties, as well as Baoqing prefecture. Since these three port neighborhoods were built much later, the main Baoqing dock in Hankou remained the largest neighborhood of Baoqing immigrants in the city.

There is little record left of the Baoqing Pier in local gazetteers and official sources. Much of its history can only be reconstructed from stories passed down for generations among elderly Baoqing settlers and residents. In the 1980s, a local scholar interviewed more than 20 Baoqing elders. Corroborating their accounts and memories against available relevant textual sources, Li Shu compiled a history of the Baoqing Pier and the Baoqing Guild in Hankou.[21]

According to Li's study, the Baoqing Pier used to be a marshland known to the locals as "the Bay of Circling Water (Huishuiwan 迴水灣)." It had long been used as a shared landing where local fishermen and boatmen stored their sails. But as Hankou's commerce and trade flourished, more and more boats, barges, and rafts began to dock and moor along the bay. By the late 1890s, immigrants from Baoqing had taken over the pier along the bay. But prior to that time, the Baoqing immigrants' hold on the territory was at best tenuous. On one occasion when the Baoqing Pier was left unattended, the Huizhou gang (Huizhou bang 徽州幫) in Hankou moved in and took over the pier. The seizure sparked off a long-running feud between the Baoqing and the Huizhou gangs. At the beginning, the Baoqing dockhands and bargemen were at a disadvantage. But around 1808, a Baoqing bargeman by the name of He Yuanlun 何元侖 allegedly lobbied Liu Guangnan 劉光南 (1736–?), an imperial academician and reader-in-waiting (*shidu xueshi* 侍讀學士) to the Jiaqing Emperor to intervene. Academician Liu used his power and prestige to redraw the boundaries of the Baoqing Pier neighborhood and ordered all non-Baoqing boatmen and settlers expelled out of the redrawn district. At the height of the Qing court's anti-Taiping campaign in 1853, the now elderly He Yuanlun invited two top literati generals of the ascendant Hunan militia forces, Liu Changyou 劉長佑 (1818–1887) and Zeng Guoquan 曾國荃 (1824–1890) to visit the Baoqing Pier in Hankou. During the visit there, He, his fellow Baoqing merchants, dockhands, and bargemen gave their distinguished Hunan literati generals a warm welcome and reception that deeply impressed Liu and Zeng. Now with the clear backing by their compatriot Hunan militia officials, the Baoqing settlers and workers' morale was greatly uplifted. In a major armed conflict with the Huizhou gang over the rights of the pier that year, the Baoqing gang finally prevailed.[22] They now not only took back the pier but also greatly expanded their territory by gaining control over new territories that extended northward to the Highwater Lane (Dashui xiang 大水巷) and the Shen Lineage Shrine (Shenjia miao 沈家廟), and eastward to Broad Fortune Lane (Guangfu xiang 廣福巷). The expansion also set the boundaries of the modern Baoqing Pier neighborhood in Hankou.[23]

The population of the Baoqing Pier neighborhood varied in number over time. From 1820 to 1845, the Baoqing residents numbered in several thousands. By 1921, the neighborhood consisted of six streets and eight lanes, all lined with houses and flats. By 1937, the population rose to between 40,000 and 50,000. At the time, residents living in the Xinhua county seat back in Hunan numbered around only 30,000. As a result, many people from Hunan called Baoqing Pier as the first city of all Xinhua. A ballad popular among the Baoqing immigrants in Hankou goes:

Hold my head up to the Sun;
Cast my eyes down on Shaoyang.
Stomp my feet on Yiyang;
Land my body in Hanyang.
As my boat's tail turns to churn up huge waves in the Chang River,
I traverse to the four corners of the realm with my hands on the oars.

The ballad reflects the confidence and bravado of the early Baoqing settlers and bargemen in Hankou. The fact that they were able to take roots in Hankou also has a lot to do with the support and protection by their compatriot patrons and officials in Wuhan. In addition, they benefited from their own martial tradition. Local gazetteers are full of such descriptions of their character traits in terms such as "Baoqing is closely adjacent to many mountain brooks and streams; and its residents are simple yet brave," and "Its people worship righteousness and fidelity, and they like the straightforward, and detest the fraud. They are simple, economical and eschew luxury. They are honest and benevolent, and dislike frivolity." Xinhua was also a land where martial arts were widely popular.[24] A widely circulating saying among the local residents of Wuhan vividly captures the ferocity of the Baoqing immigrant: "The Hubei folk may be as smart as the Nine-headed Bird in the sky; but even ten Hubei bros can't match up to one bro from Baoqing!"[25]

From Baoqing Pier to Baoqing neighborhood

Based on the presently available primary sources, the Baoqing district first took shape sometime around the 1770s. The neighborhood became a fully established district of Hankou by mid-nineteenth century, and marked by the formal establishment in 1847 of the Baoqing Guild (Baoqing huiguan 寶慶會館). Like many other guilds in imperial China, the Baoqing Guild was a self-governing social organization based on shared native place ties. Its primary function was to provide a range of basic services to and governance over the migrant population from Baoqing in Hankou.[26] The founding of the guild signaled that the Baoqing migrants had firmly established their foothold in the docking business in Hankou.

The origin of the Baoqing Guild dates back to the Baoqing Inn 寶慶客棧, which was first built by He Yuanlun. The inn was a major converging point for Baoqing migrants in Hankou. In 1848, led by He and others, the old inn was demolished to give way to a much expanded new building, which now housed the Baoqing Guild established under He's sponsorship. Along the streets on each side of the guild's entrance were shops and stores owned or operated by the guild. Passing the entrance was an open space used for staging the guild's ritual activities such as dragon-lantern dance, and theatrical plays for the public. Beyond the square was an array of the guild's administrative halls and offices. At the center was the Main Hall (*dating* 大廳) flanked on both sides by a two-storied wood-structure building that housed the guild's offices and storage rooms on the first floor, and bedrooms on the second floor. Behind the administrative office building was an atrium covered with glass roof. Behind the atrium was the guild school, which was set up to provide basic education to children of the guild members in Hankou. The guild school was a finely built wood structure supported by an array of massive posts nearly a yard in diameter. In 1892, the guild erected a shrine dedicated to the memory of Peng Fengquan 彭灃泉 and another early emigrant bargeman, who lost their lives during a feud for control of the piers in Hankou. Like many other guild shrines, the construction of the Lord Peng Shrine (Penggong ci 彭公祠) celebrated those who had made major contribution to the Baoqing migrant community in Hankou, and served to strengthen the cohesion and unity of the community.[27]

During each Bright Pure Festival (Qingming jie 清明節), the Baoqing immigrants would come to the Lord Peng Shrine where they rendered ritual worship of the Baoqing martyrs by staging dragon dances and lighting up firecrackers. Regrettably, the Lord Peng Shrine was destroyed during a Japanese air bombing raid of Hankou. In addition to its ritual functions, the Baoqing Guild also instituted several offices to provide a range of services such as managing the Baoqing Pier properties, conducting business negotiations, operating the guild school, providing financial aids to Baoqing compatriots in need, and handling burial services for the dead.[28] But unfortunately, the Baoqing Guild building was located in one of the low-lying districts of Hankou and was often vulnerable to floods by rain. During the 1931 flood, the district was inundated in 2–3 m deep standing water. As a result, the foundation of the guild building was soaked and weakened, and the building risked collapsing. In 1953, this landmark building was taken down.

In addition to its self-identity, the Baoqing Ward's public recognition is just as crucial. Its popular name, the Baoqing Pier, took some time before it gained its present stable form and full official acceptance. On the 1918 Comprehensive Map of Hankou Streets (*Hankou shijie quantu* 漢口市街全圖), the Baoqing Guild was identified by its other more generic name: the Baoqing Association

(Baoqing gongsuo 寶慶公所).[29] In 1933, while the location of the Baoqing Pier was clearly marked on the New Hankou City Survey Map (*Xin Hankoushi shice xiangtu* 新漢口市實測詳圖), it was casually identified as the Pier of the Bao(qing) Prefecture (Baojun matou 寶郡碼頭). But by 1938, the Detailed Map of Hankou City Streets (*Hankoushi jiedao xiangtu* 漢口市街道詳圖) identified the ward as the Baoqing Pier.[30] This widely used name had since then gained further official recognition. For instance, a municipal government study in 1949 unequivocally and consistently referred to the ward as the Baoqing Pier, and even the municipal police station in the ward was identified by the now popular name. The Republican era naming practice was continued after 1949 by the new regime for its municipal public security branch station and the neighborhood office in the ward.[31] By then, all government agencies, cartographers, and city map makers, as well as private sectors in Wuhan, had given full recognition of both the ward's popular name and territory as the Baoqing Pier.

Since 1949, the physical boundaries of the Baoqing district have remained largely unchanged. The same cannot be said of other Baoqing immigrant settlements in the Wuhan tri-cities. Because of recent decades of urban renovation in Wuhan since the 1990s, the Baoqing residents in the Moonlake Dyke and Planks Lane neighborhoods have all been relocated to different districts of the Wuhan tri-cities, whereas the Baoqing resident neighborhoods on the Parrots and the White Sands Shoals have continually dwindled. So, the Baoqing Pier district remains the largest enclave of the Baoqing residents in the Wuhan tri-cities.

Figure 6.1 A view of a harbour landing. Baidu.com open source image, accessed on Sept 12, 2020

The present Baoqing Main Street (Baoqing zhengjie 寶慶正街) is located in the southeast corner of the Qiaokou district of Hankou. Starting from the Riverside Boulevard (Yanhe dadao 沿河大道) to the southeast, the Main Street is a paved concrete road. It is about 4 m wide, and extends for about 188 m to enjoin with the Baoqing Second Street (Baoqing erjie 寶慶二街) to the northwest. After 1949, especially after a major fire that destroyed most of the wooden houses in the 1950s, most of the housing structure had been rebuilt and renovated. According to the statistics from the 1990s, the population of the Baoqing neighborhood was about 90,000. Most of the residents are Hunanese, with a majority of them coming from the Baoqing region. The neighborhood is also inhabited by residents of Hubei and Jiangxi provinces. But because of the squalid living conditions of the neighborhood, many of the Baoqing residents have opted to relocate to other parts of Wuhan, and chosen to lease their flats to the businessmen and street vendors who have come to do business en masse in the nearby Hanzheng Small Business district since the 1980s. But the influence of the Hunan Baoqing settlers remains visible: most of the municipal district officials and the community leaders are of Hunan extraction. The residents in the district are either descendants from earlier immigrants or the new small business and labor migrants from Baoqing region themselves. Generally speaking, they are not a highly educated lot, and very few have attained high political or influential government positions, but they form a socially and culturally cohesive community. They bind tightly together, and are

Figure 6.2 A sketch of Baoqing neighborhood location marked; Map prepared by Mei Li in Sept. 2017.

slow to integrate with the local Wuhan culture and civic life. Instead, they have chosen to preserve and continue their native customs and practices among themselves, resulting in a cultural and social "enclave" in Hankou (Figure 6.2).

The Zhengyi Daoists of the Baoqing Pier neighborhood in Republican era

Hunan was exposed to early Daoist dissemination during the late Han era when the new religion was just beginning to expand from northwestern China. As the people from North China and Sichuan began their southward migration, many ended in Hunan region, bringing with them the early seeds of Daoism. By the Wei-Jin period, the core of the Meishan 梅山 region such as the later Xinhua and Anhua area already witnessed activities of early Daoism.[32] From the tenth century onward, as the immigrants from neighboring Jiangxi moved in and settled en masse in the Xinhua region, Zhengyi Daoism centered on Mount Longhu and near Nanchang 南昌 in Jiangxi also began to spread to Hunan.[33]

The Zhengyi Daoists from Xinhua arrived in the Baoqing Pier community in Hankou most likely together with the timber rafts men and transport boat hands from the hometown by way of the Zi River. The river which originates from Ziyuan 資源 county of Guangxi 廣西 province merges with the Hao Stream that originates from Chengbu county in southwestern Hunan and flows through Shaoyang, Xinhua, Anhua, Taojiang, and Yiyang counties before draining into the expansive Lake Dongting and the Yangzi River in northern Hunan. The segment of the Zi River from Baoqing to Yiyang is about 400 km in length and known as the Inner River (Neihe 內河), whereas the segment of Zi River from Yiyang to Hankou is about equally long and known as the Outer River (Waihe 外河). But by comparison, the Inner River is much more dangerous to navigate, as its course is filled with more than 100 rapids, shallows, and sharp falls.

A local ballad familiar among the raftsmen and transport boatmen captures the speed of the rising Zi River in the torrential spring season:

> So rapid and ferocious are the currents of Zi River in the spring;
> And in merely three days and nights, they reach Yiyang.[34]

Boatmen and rafters were particularly wary of their voyage through this segment of the Zi River, as any oversight or careless move would likely result in their boats or rafts being overturned or dashed to pieces on the submerged rocks and rapids. While Baoqing boatmen and rafters possessed bravado, they also made every ritual effort to ensure their safe passage through the Inner River as they plied back and forth between their hometown and bustling Hankou (Figure 6.3).

Before setting sail from places such as Shaoyang or Xinhua, boat merchants and sailors would hold a solemn ritual to honor the Lord the Water Administration Shrine (Shuifu miao 水府廟), also known as the Boddhisattva of the Water Administration (Shuifu pusa 水府菩薩) who was believed to reign over the treacherous river.

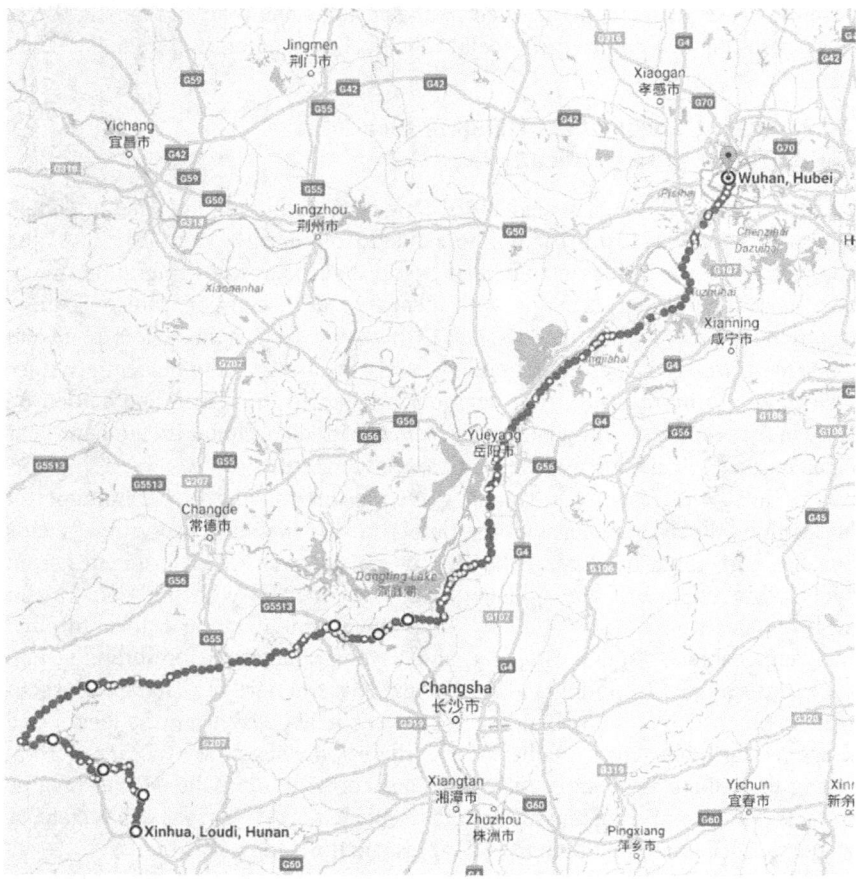

Figure 6.3 Water route from Xinhua to Hankou via Zi and Yangzi Rivers (Google Maps with watery route marked by Mei Li and Xun Liu, Sept, 2017). For a recent study of the commercial navigation on the Zi and other major waterways in Hunan, see Huang Juan, "Hunan jindai hangyunye yanjiu."

The ritual took place aboard the boats with the bows all tied with a piece of red cloth as a sign of good fortune. With incense, candles, and paper money, the boat merchants and their crew placed on board their offer of the Three Great Sacrifices of the cow, the pig, and the lamb to the Water Lord. At the beginning of the ritual, as the merchants and their crew stood in reverence and offered their prayers, a rooster was slit of its neck on the spot, and its blood was scattered onto the bow and into the river. At the conclusion of the ritual, the master sailor or the helmsman would shout out, "Set sail!" to his crew. At that, the sailors would wield their poles and push off their respective boats to get under way. Along the way, the deck crew would continue to pray to the Water Lord for protection as their boats passed by the various treacherous sections of the river voyage. For instance, as the boat arrived at the Bronze Pillar Shoal (Tongzhutan 銅柱灘), the crew would perform worship to Lord Grandpa Zhi (Zhigong yeye 志公爺爺). Passing by the Shrine of the Territorial Lord (Xiashen miao 轄神廟) in northern Shaoyang, the sailors would render homage to the Territorial Lord Grandpa. When their boats sailed by the Mud Shoal, they would pray to Lord Grandpa Nanmu (Nanmu yeye 楠木爺爺). As the fleet sailed through the treacherous segments of the voyage, sailors would also scatter cups of rice into the river so that the water gods and ghosts would enjoy. The fleet typically took three to four days and nights to sail through the most dangerous segment of their voyage to reach Yiyang, a river port town in northern Hunan, and the half point on their voyage to Hankou.

Upon their safe arrival at Yiyang, they would no longer worry about the rising tides or treacherous shoals for the rest of their voyage. For that, they would moor their boats or rafts at Bianyu Bay (Bianyu kou 鯿魚口) and go ashore to join their boat owners who would typically take the straight shortcut land routes to arrive there a day or two earlier. There the owners of the boats and rafts would stage a major ritual to honor Lord Grandpa Wei at his shrine on the Yangzi River to thank the god for his protection of the safe voyage to Yiyang. The owners would have already prepared in advance the Three Sacrifices together with incense and candles. Again a rooster would be sacrificed at the ritual staged inside the river bank shrine. The shrine witnessed the peak seasons of such rites of worship during the spring and summer floods.[35] A ballad sung by deckhands from western Hunan, "The Zi River Shoal Song," not only depicts the various scenes of the Zi River and the boat crewmen's sufferings and joy, but it also captures their acts of ritual worship to ensure their own safety on the choppy and dangerous waterway. One ballad entitled "Going down the shoals (*Xiatan ge* 下灘歌)" goes like this:

> Sailing from Baoqing, our boat heads to Hankou … .
> A chain of zigzag turns below the Shrine of the Territorial Lord … .
> (We moor at) the Lotus Flower Shrine after the Patriarch Master's (shrine) … .
> Inside the Temple of Lord Yangsi, we pray and divine for the Lord's will
> By casting divinatory slips thrice before sailing through the Triple Gate Shoal … .
> With paper money falling to ground, the diviner aligns the Eight Trigrams signs,
> And he sees us off at the Temple's gate.
> After going ashore to render our homage at Lord Grandpa's Shine,
> We brothers then feel more relaxed in our minds.
> Sailing from Yiyang, our boats head to Hankou,
> Upon seeing the Carp's Hill,
> We pay homage to the god in the Shrine of Lord Wei.
> At the Shrine of Oranges, we request a divination before sailing further … .
> Inside the Temple of the Fishbone, we light a candle for protection.[36]

Another ballad is entitled "Going up the shoals" and goes:

> Leaving Hankou, my boat sail upstream,
> At the Eight Trigrams Shoal, I cast a divinatory lot.
> In the Shrine of the Water Lord located at the Su's Rapids,
> Boatmen up and down the River all burn incense for protection.[37]

As the river voyage was always risky, even dangerous for the boatmen and rafts-men, they sought divine protection by performing various rites of worship and sacrifice, and by observing taboos. Though Daoist ritualists or clerics are not men-tioned in these old ballads sung by the Baoqing boatmen and barge sailors, it is clear that the boatmen were familiar and even performed the necessary rituals and sacrifices before and during their dangerous voyage from Xinhua to Hankou. Though the source of their ritual knowledge and practice was never attributed expressly to Zhengyi Daoists, it is highly likely that the Baoqing boatmen and barge owners may well have hired Daoists or local ritualists to perform these ritu-als. Indeed, the earliest Baoqing Daoists may have arrived in Hankou shortly after the first Hunanese timber raftsmen and barge sailors did, if not at the same time. As an increasing number of western Hunanese immigrants, sailors, merchants, and laborers came to settle in the Baoqing Pier neighborhood, many Daoist cler-ics followed them and took up residence in Hankou's riverfront neighborhood to serve the ritual needs of their compatriots. In the early days in the Baoqing Pier neighborhood, these Daoists seem to have met intense competition from some of their ritually self-reliant clients among the boatmen and deckhands. Indeed, con-temporary memories of how Baoqing Daoists first settled and survived in Hankou were preserved and passed down by many elder residents and surviving Daoists in the neighborhood.[38]

Today, at all Daoist ritual altars and activities officiated by Xinhua Daoist cler-ics, they invariably invoke divine blessing by incanting the plea: "Reverence to Lord Zeng Rushou 曾如壽 of the Jade Void Palace 玉虛宮!" This is due to the fact that the Jade Void Palace once served as the Daoist ritual center for Zhengyi Daoists in Xinhua region. Managed by Daoist clerics of the region, the tem-ple's prominence lasted for several centuries dating back to the end of the Yuan dynasty, if not earlier. The temple remained under the care of Daoist clerics until 1950s, when it gradually fell into disrepair.[39] Based on a scripture thrice-com-piled during the Qing dynasty and provided by Chen Zhuquan 陳祝泉 of Xinhua Daoist Association, the temple's origin can be traced to Lord Zeng Rushou, who descended from a long lineage of Daoist migrants from Jiangxi. According to *A Thrice-compiled Genealogy of Wen Jin's Daoism* 文斤道教三修宗譜, Lord Zeng belonged to a Daoist lineage which traced its origin to the magistrate-turned-Dao-ist Wen Jin 文斤 of the Eastern Jin era. He served as the magistrate of Gaoping 高平 county of the old Shaoling 邵陵 prefecture during the Xiankang 咸康 reign (335–342), but he later gave up his post and withdrew to a mountain wherein he lived as a recluse and allegedly attained immortalhood. The mountain was later named after him by the locals as the Mount of Immortal Wen (Wenxian shan 文仙山) and a shrine in his honor was constructed there. Throughout the Tang and the Song periods, Wen was reported to have been particularly responsive to requests for rain by those who came to pray on the mountain. Several officials of the Tang and Song periods left stele inscriptions there eternalizing him for his efficacious responses to their pleas for rain in the region. On the fourth moon of 1159, Emperor Gaozong of Southern Song bestowed upon Wen the title of "Perfected Man of Wondrous Response" (Miaogan zhenren 妙感真人).[40] The local Daoist lineage in Xinhua to which Zeng belonged claimed direct transmission from this efficacious immortal.

The local Daoist lineage first flourished under the reign of the Song founder Zhao Kuanyin 趙匡胤 (927–976) after his troops first conquered and unified the central Hunan region in the 960s. The Song founder was alleged to have donated a thousand taels of silver and ordered that Daoist residences, belvederes and yards be built (chuanxiu daoshi, guan, chang 創修道室觀場) in the region. At the time, Lord Tan Guanmiao 譚觀妙, the founding patriarch of a local Daoist lineage, was active at the Temple of Immortal Wen (Wenxian guan 文仙觀), which honored the memory of Wen Jin 文斤, who served as the magistrate of Gaoping but later went to live as a hermit and ascended as a transcendent. The temple was located in Xinshao 新邵 county upstream on the Zi River south of Xinhua. There, Lord Tan transmitted the lineage to Lord Wang Guilin 王桂林, who later founded three derivative subbranches (yanpai sanfang 衍派三房). These sublineages were, respectively, headed by Lord Deng Yuanshou 鄧元壽, Lord Li Zhizhen 李志真, and Lord Zeng Rushou. Lord Deng in turn set up four separate houses under his sublineage (paiyan sifang 派衍四房) and pioneered Daoism in Shaoyang county. Lord Li's sublineage created a total of three houses and flourished in Xinhua, where he and his disciples opened up 28 mountains and built Daoist residences on each of them. Lord Zeng took up residence at the Jade Void Palace in Xinhua. Later he returned to the secular world, but continued to practice Daoist teachings (fansu xingjiao 返俗行教). His sublineage transmitted from father to son (父子相繼) and came to be known as the Jade Void Sublineage (Yuxu pai 玉虛派), which was also known as the sublineage of Hosting Fire (Zhuhuo pai 主火派), an allusion to Zeng's continued Daoist ritual practice as a lay householder.[41]

Another account places the founding of the Jade Void Palace sometime in the late Yuan dynasty, and describes Zeng Rushou as a disciple who started his Daoist training first at the Temple of Immortal Wen but later traveled to the Dragon and Tiger Mountain in Jiangxi where he stayed to study with the Heavenly Master in Daoist liturgy for eight years before returning to Xinhua, where he founded the Jade Void Palace. According to this account, Lord Zeng established six branches of Daoist disciples (liufang dizi 六房弟子) who later dominated the Zhengyi Daoist ritual practice in Xinhua.[42] As a result, Daoist clerics in Xinhua today continued to revere him as the founding patriarch of the Zhengyi Daoism in the region. But we still know very little about the origins and the course of development of Daoism in Xinhua. But accurate knowledge of the genealogical transmission and lineage identification of the present Baoqing Daoist clerics in Hankou have been made much more difficult, since many of the Baoqing Daoist clerics have adopted for themselves the Quanzhen Daoist lineage naming system, which first emerged in the late Yuan or the early Ming dynasty in Baoqing area.[43] Further complicating the situation is the fact that the Baoqing Zhengyi clerics have since modified their adopted genealogical names which differed from the regular Quanzhen genealogy naming system. For instance, the characters for the Quanzhen genealogy names from the 18th to the 20th generations are "Yong-Yuan-Ming 永-圓-明," but the Baoqing Daoists have modified these characters to "Yong-Chuang-Yang 永-傳-揚." Additionally, some Baoqing Daoists have also further modified their adopted Quanzhen genealogical names in recent years. For instance, the Zhengyi Daoists at the Baoqing Pier neighborhood and their counterparts back home in Yangxi 洋溪 district in Xinhua used to adopt the Quanzhen 15th-generation lineage character "He 合" as their genealogy names, but many of the Baoqing Daoists of that generation now further modified the adopted lineage character to "Kuan 寬" as their generational identification names. As a result, two contemporary Baoqing Daoists in Hankou with lineage roots to the Jade Void Palace in Xinhua, Zeng Hezhu 曾合鑄, and Song Hecheng 宋合烖 now identify themselves, respectively, as Zeng Kuanzhu 曾寬鑄 and Song Kuancheng 宋寬烖.[44] This change by the sublineage of the Jade Void Palace in Hankou remains an unresolved mystery.

In Xinhua, the Jade Void Palace also served as the venue for staging a variety of personal and communal rites from the salvation of the dead to the petition for longevity and fortune. By contrast, the Eastern Peak Temple 東嶽廟 there served as the site for ritual events staged by vernacular priests (*shigong* 師公) of Meishan Daoism (Meishan jiao 梅山教) in Xinhua. Also known as the Masters' Teachings (*shijiao* 師教), Meishan Daoism had its roots in local shamanism and has its own unique liturgical scriptures, and masters, or ritualists who engage themselves primarily in exorcism and ritual healing. The Zhengyi Daoist clerics and the vernacular Meishan ritualists used to have a clear division of ritual services, each administering their respective ritual functions for the locals. But as time went by, their ritual division became blurred, as their local patrons often had multiple ritual needs. To increase their ritual repertoire to meet the demands, both Zhengyi clerics and the vernacular priests began to offer ritual services beyond their traditional repertoires. As a result, the shamanistic priests of the Meishan Teachings came to offer the Zhengyi Daoist ritual services, whereas the Zhengyi ritualists also learned and performed the shamanistic rites in modern times. In some cases, the Zhengyi and the vernacular priests even offered Buddhist rites to expand their ritual service.[45]

The main rituals of the Zhengyi Daoists

As an immigrant community in a bustling commercial hub, the Baoqing people struggled to preserve their native traditions, and their religious beliefs and practices. Indeed, their indigenous Daoist beliefs and ritual traditions which they brought from their hometown played a key role in sustaining their identity in Hankou for several generations. Indeed, of the 100,000 Baoqing residents living in Xiaban 下板, Yanhe 沿河, and Baoqing neighborhoods, the majority have continued their Daoist beliefs and practices. They participated in a variety of Daoist religious activities such as Daoist-officiated funerals, marital celebrations, communal rituals, and the annual pilgrimage to the Southern Peak (more on this pilgrimage below). Their daily life is inseparably connected with Daoism.

Because of scarcity and loss of primary sources, we have very little data about the ritual activities carried out in Hankou by early Zhengyi Daoists from Baoqing. Our knowledge is largely limited to the period starting in the 1930s onward. We owe our limited understanding to the memories and interview accounts provided by the living Daoist ritualists in the Baoqing Pier community.

In the late 1930s, Wu Fabao 伍法寶 and Wang Laifu 王來復, two Baoqing Daoist masters arrived in Hankou by boat from Xinhua to take refuge from the Japanese invasion of central and western Hunan. They soon became the heads of two major Daoist ritual altars at the Baoqing Pier community because of their ritual prowess and renown. As outsiders to Hankou, Xinhua settlers usually had a hard time establishing their practices or business in the city. As a result, they tended to bind together and even provided mutual support across trade or business lines within the community in order to make it in the city. Within the Zhengyi Daoist circles, the territorial lines among various Daoist ritual altars were not strictly demarcated or enforced. Indeed, they even collaborated by combining their own altars in rendering ritual service. Many Daoists could set up and operated their ritual altars in different Hunanese neighborhoods. The more skilled they were in their ritual performance, the more ritual business they would generate from their clients.

After their arrival in Hankou, Wu Fabao, Cai Zizheng 蔡子政, and Wang Laifu, respectively, adopted many disciples among the Hunanese immigrants in the city, such as Luo Guangwan 羅光萬, Luo Congdao 羅從道, Wang Hengshan 王衡山, and Cai Dongsheng 蔡東昇 (son of Cai Zizheng). Each of these disciples excelled in their chosen specialized ritual crafts: Luo Guangwan was adept in calligraphy for writing talisman and flute-playing; Luo Congdao was well-versed in talismans and hand-mudra, and was particularly skilled in drumming. Wang Hengshan specialized in drafting ritual petitions and practiced ritual healing and medicine, whereas Cai Dongsheng was initially an adept in vernacular shamanistic ritual (*shijiao*), but he later studied Zhengyi Daoist rites with his father-in-law Xie Yihui. All these disciples themselves have since transmitted their respective teachings and ritual crafts by adopting their own disciples.[46]

Based on available government registration records preserved in the Wuhan municipal archives, the Baoqing Daoists did not seem to have been ever brought under the scrutiny and regulation by the various state governments in the first half of the twentieth century. Indeed, they seem to have intentionally stayed out of several major Republican state registrations of all religious personnel of the period. For instance, the Hankou Republican Government carried out a recertification of all Zhengyi Daoist clerics in the city in mid-May of 1936. The goal was to register and license all Daoists, especially the Zhengyi ritualists who practiced their crafts in the city. It is not clear what initially inspired the Hankou government to conduct this licensing campaign. Nor was it clear if such a drive was mandatory or voluntary and if it carried any adverse political and economic implications for the targeted religious, including the Daoist practitioners. In any event, the existent archival records show that only 147 Daoist practitioners were issued a new license for their ritual practice in the city. Of the 147 recertified Daoists, none of them were from the Baoqing port neighborhood. Shortly after the end of the Sino-Japanese War in 1946, the Hankou government conducted another relicensing drive. Of the 84 cases involving Daoist relicensing, none came from the Baoqing port community. In both cases, those Daoist practitioners who participated in the relicensing programs tended to be indigenous Daoist ritualists from the surrounding countries around Hankou, such as Huangpi.[47]

The absence of the otherwise active Baoqing neighborhood Daoist ritualists from the Hankou municipal records suggests at least two plausible explanations. One is that the Hankou government took a rather laissez faire approach to its management of religious affairs, leaving the Baoqing port neighborhood's Daoists free to ply their ritual business in their enclave. Another more plausible explanation may have much to do with the identity of the Baoqing ritualists. First, many of the Baoqing Daoists were by no means full-time ritualists who depended for their livelihood entirely and exclusively on their ritual practice. Indeed, most of them were often full-time small business owners, tradesmen, or skilled workers, and lived at home much like an ordinary lay person. While they did perform rituals to generate additional income for themselves, their ritual services in funerals, weddings, healing, business operations, and family settings were often viewed as fulfilling a social function for their fellow compatriots. In addition, the Baoqing Daoists' ritual services were largely confined to clients within the Baoqing Pier neighborhoods. Another important fact is that the Baoqing Daoists were all at-home practitioners, and they never owned or operated any temples like the Quanzhen monastic Daoists at the Changchun Monastery across the Yangzi River in Wuchang. All this combined to make them both feel and look much less like an average Daoist ritualist or cleric, especially in the eyes of the Republican state officials in Hankou.

Not bound by the strict precepts and monastic rules of their Quanzhen Daoist counterparts, the Zhengyi Daoist ritualists or householders of Baoqing Pier neighborhood do not observe vegetarian diet except on days when they perform rituals. They provide their clients with services such as the retreats, rites of sacrifice to, and salvation of the dead. Though their service concentrates in the Baoqing Pier neighborhood, they are not strictly territorially bound, and often offer services at clients' homes beyond the Baoqing Pier neighborhood. Most of the Baoqing ritualists reside in the neighborhood. They take on most of their disciples from within the community and transmit their ritual craft and secrets only to Hunanese disciples. Most of them are from Xinhua county. Though most of them do not receive registers (*shoulu* 受錄) from the Heavenly Master based in Jiangxi, they insist that their Xinhua Daoist tradition originated from the Dragon and Tiger Mountain in Jiangxi. They regard the Jade Void Palace in their native Xinhua as their ancestral temple and have continued to maintain special ties with it even today.

Indeed, there may be some truth to the Baoqing Daoist clerics' claim to their historical connection with the Dragon and Tiger Mount in Jiangxi. They normally hold their ritual service at Baoqing Plaza, an open and shared flat ground within the Baoqing Pier neighborhood. During the early Republican era from the 1910s to the 1940s, the Baoqing Daoists typically performed for their clients a variety of rites for longevity (*shoujiao* 壽醮), grand peace (*taiping jiao* 太平醮), fire prevention (*huojiao* 火醮/*qingshui jiao* 清火醮), rain (*qiyu jiao* 祈雨醮), and sun (*qiqingjiao* 祈晴醮). They also staged the thunder rites for expelling epidemic or illness (*leijiao* 雷醮), the Universal Heaven rite for peace and prosperity (Luotian dajiao 羅天大醮), the Duchang litanies 都猖懺, the Jade Emperor Retreat (*Yuhuang jiao* 玉皇醮), and other major communal rites.

These communal rites often come in direct response to the natural consequences of Hankou's unique geography and ecology. Situated at the confluence of two major rivers, Hankou's easy watery and land accesses to all parts of the realm have undoubtedly contributed to its rise as a major market town. But the city also suffered constant threat of floods and fire. When it first began, Hankou was built on a low alluvial delta region, with the Han River flowing along its southern edge, large lakes encircling its northern boundary, and the Yangtze River raging to its eastern shore. Every summer and fall when the water level rose in the rivers and the lakes, the city would be flooded from all sides, especially on the lakefront to the south. The city's expansion was also greatly hampered as a result, since it had very little high ground to grow. But when a major dyke was constructed along the southern edge of the city by the great statesman and general Yuan Chonghuan 袁崇煥 in 1635, Hankou was finally able to find security from floods from its southern border. The city and its trade soon grew rapidly. But Hankou's much needed river dyke construction and consolidation projects lagged far behind the city's commercial expansion. Except for the Lord Yuan Embankment and the Lord Zhang Embankment, the city had no other flood prevention measures worth mentioning for the Ming and Qing dynasties (1368–1911). Indeed, even Hankou's pride, the Lord Yuan Embankment was far from being a stalwart against the annual floods, as it had to be repaired and consolidated each year. When faced with swelling water, people in the city quickly became anxious over a potential major flood.[48] For several centuries, Hankou never fully escaped the threat and ravage of floods. Further, as the city's physical expansion was driven and shaped largely by the merchants and guilds, there was hardly any state planning or regulations for the city, except for the international settlements established after the second Opium War (1865). As most of the city's commercial and residential buildings were constructed with woods and bamboo, and tightly grouped in close range with each other, fires often spread quickly, jumping from one building to another without hindrance. With winds blowing into the city from the rivers, even isolated fires could quickly expand and engulf much larger inhabited quarters and business districts, resulting in massive casualties and disasters. As Wang Baoxin 王葆心, a long-time resident and a local literatus, observed, "Hankou's markets started and thrived during the Ming era. Its numerous fires with massive damages and casualties also first appeared during the Ming." Having listed a score or so major fires between the late 1550s and the late 1790s, Wang expressed a sense of helpless resignation over the ubiquity and frequency of these fires in his hometown by writing, "In the recent hundred years, whether we lived under chaotic times, or during lasting peace, fire disasters have been such a regular occurrence that they are beyond enumeration."[49]

Besides the frequent floods, Hankou also faced constant fire hazards. Situated in the city's low-lying riverfront area, and with most of its houses, huts, stock-yards built with timber and bamboo, the Baoqing Pier neighborhood bore the brunt of these frequently occurring floods and fires. These disasters often required ritual interventions by the Baoqing Daoists. In addition, the commercial activities which carried on at the Baoqing riverfront docks were also a major source of demand from the Daoist ritual services. The large coal barges and timber rafts arriving safely from central and western Hunan all required their owners to offer sacrifices, thanks to the gods who had ensured safe passage to their precious cargo on a long and treacherous river journey. After the large piles of coal and mountains of timbers were off-loaded from the barges into the storage yards along the Han River, it was also customary for the coal and timber owners to hire the Baoqing Daoists to perform fire-prevention rites to ensure safe storage for their cargos.

Further, deaths, whether natural or incurred during a fire or flood, also required proper ritual service for the deceased souls to ensure their salvation. When deaths occurred, Baoqing migrants routinely relied upon the Daoist clerics and vernacular ritualists to handle the funerary services for their dead relatives, staging a ritual altar by hanging up the ritual gods' paintings, writing talismans and drafting petitions to gods, and performing rites of cleansing, sacrifices, and salvation to ensure a safe journey for the dead to the yonder realm. Thus, funerary rites were the stable of Baoqing Daoists' services, enabling many to make a living out of it in the pre-Socialist era.

Through their roles as ritual specialists, Baoqing Daoists also exerted influence on the daily life of the residents in the Baoqing Pier neighborhood. The loss of the Baoqing Guild's archival materials no longer permits us to ascertain the details of the Daoist activities in the community during the late Qing and early Republican periods. But studies of Daoist ritualists active in guilds in other parts of China have shown that the Daoists and guild shrine keepers typically played an important role in integrating local communities through their ritual performance whereby they not only render sacrifices to repay the blessings of gods, but they also strengthen compatriotic ties and promote public philanthropic work among their fellow countrymen.[50] Like many other societies based on shared native places and trade, the Baoqing Guild also attached primary importance to worshipping their native patriarchs and gods whom they believed to have bound them together as immigrants in Hankou. It was this divine common bound that enabled the Baoqing Build to engage in joint enterprises, public philanthropy, and communal regulations among its members.[51] Indeed, guilds were the venue of numerous ritual events in a given year. Based on Tinglong Guild Gazetteer compiled during the Tongzhi reign (1862–1874), a typical guild with membership from a whole county would hold as many as 26 ritual worships of native and patron gods within a 12-month period. Given such a high frequency of ritual events, it would be quite inconceivable for any guild to manage entirely on its own without the assistance and participation by ritual specialists. A more common practice was for a guild to hire either Buddhist or Daoist priests as its shrine or temple keepers who handled its daily ritual affairs. For instance, the Shanxi-Shaanxi Merchants Guild at the Sheqi 社旗 Township in Nanyang 南陽 of Henan consisted of a Daoist temple whose clerics not only acted as its keepers, but they also served as the hosts to officials and visitors who came to call on the guild.[52] With its thriving Daoist-centered ritual activities such as the worship of native and patron gods and sacrificial rites at the Shrine of Lord Peng, the Baoqing Guild in Hankou would have certainly involved regular and active Daoist clerical participation.

Zhengyi Daoists in the post-1949 Baoqing Pier community

After 1949, the PRC state policies and regulations, including social control measures such as work unit affiliation and household registration systems, exerted a great impact on the Baoqing Zhengyi Daoists' livelihood, and their daily activities.

The Baoqing neighborhood in Hankou used to be part of the Hanyang County under the Ming dynasty. During the Qing period, the neighborhood fell under the jurisdiction of the Inspection Circuit Agency of Hankou of the Xiakou subprefecture (Xiakou ting Hankou xunjian si 夏口聽漢口巡檢司). In the early Republican era (1912–1949), it was part of the Hanzheng Ward of Hankou Municipality (Hankou si Hanzheng qu 漢口市漢正區). After 1949, the PRC Wuhan government retained the name of Baoqing for its representative branch office at the city's grassroots level for social control and management. In 1952, it first established the Baoqing Neighborhood People's Government (Baoqing jiedao renmin zhengfu 寶慶街道人民政府) under the Qiaokou Ward. By 1954, the name of the government office was changed to Baoqing Neighborhood Office (Baoqing jiedao banshichu 寶慶街道辦事處), under the Wuhan Municipal Government. Between 1957 and 1959, the Baoqing district under the new administrative office was enlarged to include two additional adjacent neighborhoods of the Plank Yard Street (Banchang jie 板廠街) and the Quarry Port (Shimatou 石碼頭), making it one of the largest of the nine neighborhoods of the Qiaokou Ward Hankou. But the old Baoqing Pier Neighborhood populated largely by the immigrants from central Hunan continued nonetheless as the core of the newly reorganized administrative district. For a brief interlude from 1960 to 1961, the Baoqing neighborhood was reorganized as a commune (*gongshe* 公社), probably due to the presence of many vegetable farmers and agricultural laborers in its newly expanded territory.[53]

The Baoqing Neighborhood Office oversees a total of ten street blocks. Based on the record of the residents' native places collected in the 1960s, while the Baoqing Pier neighborhood consisted primarily of Hunanese settlers, especially those from Xinhua prefecture, it was also home to migrants from ten prefectures and counties of Hubei province. Additionally, many migrants from Jiangxi, Henan, Anhui, and other provinces also called it home. The migrants from Hunan settled mostly in the Shangban, Xiaban, Yanhe, Zhengjie, and Sanjie street blocks.[54] In September of 2009, the Hanzheng Ward Office changed its name to Chongren Ward Office. Its affiliated Liji, Sanshu, Xin'an, and Baoqing neighborhood offices were merged into a large ward office and renamed as the Hanzheng

Ward Office 漢正街辦事處. The original Baoqing Neighborhood Office as a grassroots administrative unit was thus abolished.

The host of socialist reforms carried out in the 1950s against private industries and businesses gradually integrated many of the residents into the state-owned or collectively owned enterprises. Individuals became now affiliated under their work units. Then, through household registration and management system, the residents were placed under strict control. The flow of migrants, especially the movement of rural migrants from the rural regions into the cities and towns, was also greatly limited. This restriction was kept in place until well after 1978.

After 1949, ritual activities were greatly reduced because they were regarded as "superstitions." As a result, a great majority of the Zhengyi Daoist clerics abandoned their ritual practice as a profession and began to engage themselves in other economic activities and production. Only a small minority of them continued to perform occasional funerary salvational rites for the dead upon request. Before 1949, the Baoqing Pier neighborhood largely escaped the brunt of state control and regulations, giving rise to a robust presence of the Zhengyi Daoist clerics in the community. In the early years after 1949, though the neighborhood was subject to waves of the "anti-superstitions" campaign, the Zhengyi Daoists were nonetheless able to survive. This was mainly due to the fact that the neighborhood was a culturally homogeneous and geographically insular enclave within Hankou, where residents remained predominantly migrants, for many of whom Daoist rituals had a structuring role in their daily life. As a result, the Zhengyi Daoist clerics in the neighborhood may have been driven underground, but they were never completely eradicated. The clients of the Zhengyi ritualists consisted of the residents of the Baoqing neighborhood and Hunan residents living throughout the Wuhan tri-cities. Based on the official record in 1964, the Baoqing Pier neighborhood had two "practitioners of superstitions (*mixin zhiye*)," and 107 "participants in superstitions (*mixin huodong canjiazhe*)." Of these, 3 were male and 104 were female. Given the anti-religion and anti-superstition context of the 1960s, the so-called practitioners and participants of superstition no doubt refer to the Zhengyi clerics and their followers in the neighborhood. At the time, the Baoqing neighborhood had a total of 5,334 registered households and a population of 21,379.[55] At first glance, the total number of participants in the Daoist Zhengyi rituals neighborhood appears rather low. But it should be pointed out that the record was compiled in the eve of the approaching Great Proletariat Cultural Revolution, and those who were entered in the record were generally considered to be "hardcore (*wangu* 頑固)" cases: those who had persistently resisted the post-1949 socialist education campaigns aimed at reforming them. It is reasonable to believe that the actual number of the Zhengyi ritual participants would have been far greater in number than those shown in the 1964 record. During this period, Xinhua Zhengyi ritualists, Zeng Yongxi and Zhou Hansheng, both disciples of the senior Daoist Zeng Qiushun, were active on the Parrots Shoal.

During the course of the ensuing Cultural Revolution (1966–1976), all religions suffered devastating attack. The Daoist ritualists within the Baoqing neighborhood were not spared, either. Zhengyi ritual masters Luo Congdao, Luo Guangshan, and Wang Hengshan each suffered varying degrees of devastation, with their residences ransacked, and their Daoist ritual instruments, images, and scriptures seized and burnt. But some Baoqing residents persisted in burning incense and worshipping deities in secret. Zhengyi ritualists Zeng Yongxi and Zhou Hansheng also carried out secret salvational rites for their clients who had deaths in their families in Hanyang, even though they often had to downsize their ritual procedures in order to minimize the risk of discovery. For instance, when they performed the salvation rites for the deceased at their client's residential quarters, Luo and Zhou would use bicycle bells in place of their usual percussion instruments so as to avoid being found out by the neighbors and passersby in the neighborhood. But the situation was much harsher in the Baoqing Pier neighborhood in Hankou. Once, the Red Guards found the ritual master Wang Hengshan silently shedding tears during a public burning of his ritual scriptures. He was immediately condemned for holding onto a "problematic position," and ordered to parade himself barefoot in his Daoist garb along the Yangzi River Boulevard for public ridicule and criticism. Despite such occasional incidents, the Daoist ritualists continued to take risks in preserving and transmitting their ritual implements and canonical scriptures to their disciples. For instance, Wang managed to pass on to his disciples such ritual implements as the Dark Baleful Constellation Seal (*Heisha yin* 黑煞印), the Celestial Awning Marshal's Ruler (*Tianpeng chi* 天蓬尺), and the Command Tablets (*lingpai* 令牌), and such ritual scriptures as Scrolls of the Equinox (*Huangdao huajuan* 黃道畫卷) and the Dharma Treasures of Orthodox One Earth Administration (*Zhengyi disi fabao* 正一地司法寶), and the Dharma Treasure of Knotting the Flags (*Jiefan fabao* 結幡法寶).[56]

With the end of the Cultural Revolution, the Baoqing Zhengyi Daoists gradually revived their ritual activities, and the religious practices also became gradually open. According to the statistics of the 1998 Qiaokou District Gazetteer, there were a total of 5,000 practicing religious residents in the district, including Catholics, Protestants, Buddhists, Muslims, and Daoists. Of these, 3,000 were Christians with one legally registered church named the Salvation Hall (Jiushi tang 救世堂). There were also a total of over 1,000 followers of the Zhengyi Daoism in the district. Most of the Daoist followers were concentrated in the streets and neighborhoods of the Baoqing Ward.[57]

The Baoqing Daoist lineages and transmission in the post-1970s Hankou

Beginning from the late 1970s, with the relaxed religious policies, the Daoist clerical ranks in the Baoqing neighborhood began to swell. Elderly Zhengyi clerics of the neighborhood all started to adopt disciples to further their lineages. Master Luo Guangwan 羅光萬 adopted Luo Shangjin 羅尚金 as his disciple, while Master Luo Congdao 羅從道 took on Xie Hansheng 謝漢生. Master Cai Dongsheng 蔡東昇, one of the most senior Zhengyi ritualist accepted Feng Songwen 封宋文, Zeng Mengxiong 曾夢熊, Wu Jihe 伍基河, and Zeng Liqiang 曾利強 as his disciples. Another master Zhao Yangwang 趙陽旺 had Wang Songsheng 王松生 as his chief disciple. Drawing on their native ties in Xinhua, some of the new rural immigrants from Xinhua to Wuhan such as Zou Changzhang 鄒長章 also joined the Hankou Baoqing Daoist lineages.

These newly initiated Zhengyi ritualists all received rigorous clerical and ritual training under their teachers, and many of them also underwent a formal ordination (more on this below). Of these disciples, Xie Hansheng, Wang Songsheng, and Luo Shangjin underwent their ordination in Xinhua, while Zeng Mengxiong, Feng Songwen, and Wu Jihe received their ordination at Baoqing neighborhood in 1994. Feng Songwen, Zeng Mengxiong, and Wang Songsheng traveled to the Heavenly Masters' headquarters on the Longhu Mount in Jiangxi to receive their Zhengyi registers. Aside from their professional liturgical training and scriptural studies, many of the senior and young Zhengyi ritualists from the Baoqing neighborhood also began to participate in the post-Cultural Revolution religious revival and Daoist self-organization at the municipal and local level.

At the fifth congress of the Wuhan Daoist Association in 1989, Luo Congdao was elected into the Association's prestigious presidium (zhuxi tuan 主席團), while his son Luo Changsong was appointed as the deputy secretary general of the presidium. Their positions in the fifth Wuhan Daoist congress mark for the first time the formal entry of the Baoqing Zhengyi ritualists into the Daoist organization in Wuhan. A year later in 1990, the Baoqing ritualists' extensive cooperation with the Quanzhen Daoist Changchun Monastery in Wuhang was cited at a national Daoist Association in Hangzhou as a successful pilot model for peaceful and mutually beneficial cooperation and development between Zhengyi and Quanzhen Daoism throughout the country. As a result of this public presentation of the Baoqing Daoists' dilemma and efforts, the Chinese State Religious Affairs Bureau and the China Daoist Association both called for more attention to the healthy development of Zhengyi Daoism throughout the country.[58]

One of the direct results of the 1990 Daoist affairs conference in Hangzhou is the establishment of the Zhengyi Daoist Management Council of the Wuhan Daoist Association in 1992. The council was clearly an acknowledgement of and accommodation with the robust Zhengyi Daoist revival in the Baoqing neighborhood. Made up of more than 30 ritualists representing various Zhengyi lineages and altars in Wuhan, the council was headed by the Baoqing senior ritualist Cai Dongsheng, with Zeng Mengxiong and Wang Ping serving as his deputies. Throughout the 1990s and 2000s, the Zhengyi Daoist council affiliated with the Wuhan Daoist Association achieved prominence throughout the Daoist circles by staging a host of ritual performances by participating in major regional temple fairs throughout the country. At the same time, their liturgical services to clients in the Baoqing neighborhood and beyond have also gained wider recognition and acceptance. Many of the active Baoqing ritualists were elected into the local and regional representative and governance bodies in Hankou. For instance, Feng Songwen was elected a member of the Qiaokou District Political Consultative Assembly in 1998. Cai Dongsheng was appointed as the deputy secretary general of Wuhan Daoist Association in 2000, and later an executive member of the Hubei Provincial Daoist Association. Eight years later in 2008, Zeng Mengxiong was elected to the same positions as Cai Dongsheng.[59]

Today two Zhengyi lineages with roots traced to Xinhua continue to be active in the Baoqing neighborhood. These two lineages are headed by Wu Fabao and Cai Zizheng. At present, these two lineages have a total of six ritualists active within the Baoqing neighborhood. All of them are of Xinhua origin and have been certified by the Wuhan Daoist Association. Two of the six Daoist ritualists came from families with a legacy of Zhengyi liturgical practice for a living. For instance, Wang Songsheng's father and elder brother were all Zhengyi clerics. He began his liturgical training and study with his father in his childhood. Zeng Mengxiong, who is the deputy director of the Zhengyi Daoist council of Wuhan Daoist Association also hails from a family with a long genealogy of Zhengyi ritualists in Xinhua. His great grandfather Zeng Faqi 曾法奇 established the family altar, the Palace of Universal Salvation (Pudu gong 普渡宮) in Xinhua. It had been passed down within the Zeng family for generations. Zeng Mengxiong was the 31st generation at-home cleric of the Zeng household altar. As Zeng's father did not learn the liturgical craft and take up the family altar transmission, Zeng's grandfather decided to transmit the family altar to a nephew and Zeng's cousin Chen Chunfang 陳春芳 (aka. Chen Demei 陳德美, the famous Xinhua Zhengyi ritualist studied by Patrice Fava, Edward Davis, and others).[60]

Zeng began his own liturgical training with his grandfather, but his training was disrupted when his family was classified as religious landlord class (*zongjiao dizhi* 宗教地主) during the land reforms in the early 1950s. Consequently, Zeng abandoned his training and moved in 1959 to the Baoqing neighborhood in Hankou where he made a living as a construction worker, and only occasionally participated with the Zhengyi ritualists in their liturgical services in the neighborhood. By the 1970s, he moved with his work unit to Puqi 蒲蘄 southeast of Wuhan where he worked as a construction worker until his retirement in 1999 when he moved back to the Baoqing neighborhood. But even before his retirement, Zeng had resumed liturgical training. He traveled back and forth between Hankou and Xinhua and studied the Zhengyi rites under the guidance of Chen Demei, his cousin and now the master of the Pudu Altar in Xinhua. He later also became a disciple to Master Cai Dongsheng, the son of Cai Zizheng 蔡子政 based in the Baoqing neighborhood.

Genealogy of the Wu and Cai lineages

There are two major master lineages at the Hankou Baoqing Pier neighborhood, namely those led, respectively, by Masters Wu Fabao and Cai Zizheng, with a most recent lineage transmission by Chen Demei of Xinhua. Presently available materials and oral histories allow us to trace the history of the Baoqing Zhengyi ritualist lineages to the early Republican era (From left to right):

(1) Wu Fabao 伍法寶 – Luo Guangwan 羅光萬 – Luo Shangjin 羅尚金;
    Wang Hengshang 王衡山 (father) – Wang Songshen 王松山 (son)
(2) Cai Zizheng 蔡子政 – Luo Congdao 羅從道 (brother to Luo Guangwan) –
    Xie Hansheng 謝漢生

(3) Cai Dongsheng 蔡東昇 (son of Zizheng) – Feng Songwen 封宋文 – Zeng Mengxiong 曾夢熊
(4) Chen Demei 陳德美 (Xinhua) – Zeng Mengxiong 曾夢熊 – Zou Changzhang 鄒長章

As both the senior Cai and Wu came originally from Xinhua, the Baoqing Zhengyi ritualists thus inherited the liturgical traditions of their hometown. This is evident not only in terms of ordination and genealogy, but also in scriptural transmission. All the liturgical scriptures used by the Baoqing ritualists originate from Xinhua. For instance, the liturgical texts owned by Zeng Qiushun, grandfather of Zeng Mengxiong, weathered the anti-religious storms of the Land Reforms and the Cultural Revolution, with some of it confiscated and destroyed. The remainder was further divided among his disciples. Only a few survived and were bequeathed to Zeng's nephew Chen Demei. These few scriptures consist of what has survived of the Zeng collection. Beginning from the early 1990s, Zeng Mengxiong traveled to Xinhua each year to manually copy these remaining scriptures. In total, he has managed to have copied over a hundred or so titles from the collection. These manuscript copies have formed the core textual basis for the Baoqing Zhengyi ritualists' liturgical practices in Hankou.

Discipleship and ordination

The transmission of the Zhengyi Daoism among the Baoqing ritualists follows two patterns: (1) family or ancestral transmission (*zuchuan* 祖傳); and (2) master-disciple transmission (*shichuan* 師傳). The family transmission takes place within the same surname lineage or household. Having already established the lineage or household's ritual altar, the ancestors-masters then transmit the family ritual expertise to the younger generation disciples of the same surname. The master-disciple transmission takes place when a ritual altar master passes his ritual expertise and skills to a disciple of a different surname. Among the Baoqing Zhengyi ritualists in Hankou, Zeng Mengxiong, Wang Songsheng, and Zhou Changzhang all received their ritual craft through the family transmission, whereas Luo Shangjin, Feng Songwen, and Xie Hansheng acquired their ritual expertise by undergoing the master-disciple transmission. Regardless of modes of transmission, ritual masters require that their disciples must have a certain level of education, as they will be reading a large number of scriptures, and recite and commit to memory "internally transmitted oral secrets (*neichuan koujue* 內傳口訣)." They are expected to be able to compose ritual memorials, petitions, and other official documents. In addition, each of the disciples will also learn from their masters a host of skills of "singing and chanting, blowing (flute, cow-horn, and other wind instruments), striking (drums, cymbals, and other percussion instruments), reciting (scriptures, etc.), performing (ritual dance and steps), and composing (petitions, commands, and writs, etc)." Since full or adequate proficiency in all these skills take three to five years, it usually takes an equal number of years for a disciple to become a ritualist.

Luo Shangjin, a Zhengyi cleric based in the Baoqing neighborhood recalls his own experience of discipleship toward a ritualist:

It was in the mid-fall of 1979 when I was still in middle school. One night I noticed there was quite a ruckus going on in the house of a street neighbor who had just lost their elderly parent. There were drum beats, clanging cymbals accompanied by a lingering tune on the flute. At the time, I did not know what really was going on. After some asking, I learned that they were staging a Daoist rite (*zuo daochang* 作道場) for their dead parent. There, several old masters and a young cleric were performing the ritual (*zuo fashi* 作法事). After that, whenever there was a Daoist rite in the neighborhood, I would go and watch. I was quite naughty, and occasionally I would strike a beat on the drum or hit the gong. Gradually, I became very attracted by the rhythm and music of the drum and cymbals, especially the flute that was performed at the Daoist rite. One of the old masters of the ritualist crew saw that I frequently showed up at their ritual service, and asked me if I was interested in doing what they do. After careful deliberation and gaining my parents' approval, I told him that I would. The old master then immediately asked me to go to his home at the Highwater Lane (Dashui xiang 大水巷) in Qiaokou District that same morning. There he began to tell me that if I wanted to learn Daoist rites, I must be industrious and serious. He then explained to me the methods and procedures of learning the rituals. The first craft I learned was how to write characters with a brush. This training alone took several years. Next I learned to play the flute and beat the drum and gong, and then came the study of Daoist canonical scriptures, and other fields of knowledge. Of course, I also learned with the master how to conduct myself in society and how to deal with other people and handle business. Later I formally signed the "Compact of Discipleship (*toushiyue* 投師約)" and became a bona fide disciple to my revered master. I am lucky to have a supreme mentor who was very kind and congenial, profoundly learned in Daoist rites and the Great Way, and widely revered for his virtue and reputation. He was none other than Master Luo Guangwan!

Later, Master Luo transmitted to me the Daoist inner secrets and oral instructions (*neimi ji koujue* 內秘及口訣), and told me about the hardships and glories of his lifelong Daoist career. Whenever he did a Daoist rite, he would take me along and allow me to apply what I learned into the actual ritual practice. Through these actual ritual performances, I was able not only to fully understand what I had learned, but also to enrich my own ritual experience. My master took great pains to allow me to learn ritual practice through actual performance of the rites. I have truly benefited from his way of teaching and his ritual practice.[61]

After completing their liturgical training and scriptural studies, the Zhengyi masters may determine that their disciples are ready for ordination whereby they achieve their full status as a Zhengyi ritualist who can set up their own altar to perform independent ritual services to their clients. The ritual process whereby

Xinhua Daoist ritualists are ordained is known as "Petitioning for (priestly) position (*zouzhi* 奏職)" or "Being ordained into a position (*duzhi* 度職)." The ritual ordination lasts for three days and nights. According to Luo, the ritual procedure of the first day includes the following steps[62]:

> Petitioning for water (*qingshui* 請水);
> Commencing the rite (*qishou* 啟首);
> Filing written certificates (*fa wendie* 發文牒);
> Recitation of the Three Lords' Scriptures (*song Sanguanjing* 誦三官經);
> Performing the City God's Litany (*bai Chenghuangchan* 拜城隍懺)
> Audience at noon and submitting Petitions to the Three Lords (*wuchao fa Sanguanbiao* 午朝發三官表);
> Reciting the City God's Litany, and the Southern Peak Litany (*Nanyuechan* 南嶽懺);
> Circumambulating the altar (*raotan* 繞壇);
> Cleansing the altar (*jingtan* 淨壇).

The second day's ritual procedures include the following:

> Summoning the thunder generals for the morning audience (*fa leizaochao* 發雷早朝);
> Filing written certificates (*fa wendie* 發文牒);
> Reciting Lord Lao's Scripture (*song Laojun jing* 誦老君經);
> Performing Lord Guan's Litany (*bai Guandi chan* 拜關帝懺)
> Audience at noon and submitting the written certificates (*wuchao fa wendie* 午朝發文牒);
> Performing litanies (*bai chan* 拜懺);
> Audience at dusk and filing the Petitions of the Masters of the Stars (*wanchao fa Xingzhu biao* 晚朝發星主表);
> Rendering homage to the Lamp of the Seven Stars (*bai Qixing deng* 拜七星燈);
> Performing the Litany for Lengthening Life (*bai Yansheng chan* 拜延生懺);
> Circumambulating the altar;
> Cleansing the altar (*jingtan* 淨壇).

The third day's ritual contents are as follows:

> Summoning the Thunder generals for the morning audience;
> Filing written certificates;
> Reciting scriptures and performing litanies (*songjing baichan* 誦經拜懺);
> Audience at noon (*wuchao* 午朝);
> Interpreting the cast divinatory lots (*jiegua* 解卦)
> Rite of knotting the banners (*jiefan yi* 結旛儀);
> Transmitting oral secrets (*chuanjue* 傳訣);
> Transmitting ritual implements (*chuan faqi* 傳法器)

Returning to the altar (*huitan* 回壇);
Burning incense and paper money (*shaoxiang huazhi* 燒香化紙). [63]

The ritual ceremony usually takes a long time, and requires nearly ten masters to complete, involving the following:

Master of Ordination and Transmission (*chuandu shi* 傳度師);
Master Petitioner (*zoudu shi* 奏度師);
Master who seals the sword (*fengdao shi* 封刀師);
Master who defends the altar (*chatan shi* 插壇師);
Master of Scriptural Recitation (*changdu shi* 唱度師);
Master Usher (*yintan shi* 引壇師);
Master Lecturer of Scriptures (*shuofa shi* 說法師);
Master Recorder (*tenglu shi* 謄錄師);
Master Certifier (*zhengmeng shi* 證盟師);
Altar Assistants (*zhufa shi* 助法師).

The length of the ritual and the hiring of multiple consecration masters cause each ordination altar to be very expensive. To defray the costs, the Baoqing ritualists often pool their resources and money to hold an ordination rite for several initiates rather than just one. On the fourth to seventh of the ninth moon in 1988, Baoqing ritualists Luo Shangjing, Xie Hansheng, and Wang Songsheng from Hankou traveled back to their native hometown of Xinhua and underwent their collective ordination presided by Master Luo Congdao 羅從道 at the Jade Void Altar. At their ordination, they were joined by six native ritualists from Xinhua. Long before the three-day ceremony, Master Luo Congdao and fellow ritual master Chen Zhuquan 陳祝泉 of Xinhua had already begun to closely coordinate with their three disciples from the Baoqing neighborhood in Hankou on the details and logistics of the ordination.

On the day before the ordination, ritual banners for each of the ordinands must be erected on an elevated ground before the ordination ceremony could proceed. During the ordination, the master of ordination not only passes onto the ordinands the ritual crafts and implements, but he also instructs them on how to conduct themselves in the world. At the conclusion of the ordination rite, the ordinands have to ensure that the hanging tassels of the ritual banner must be properly tied or braided by the natural winds into a knot, after the initiated disciples have each performed their ritual mudras and spells. To newly ordained ritualists, this final rite of knotting the flag's tassels in the open air symbolizes the completion of the whole ordination ritual. Based on the patterns or configurations of the wind-formed knot on the banner, it is believed that such knots foretell whether the ordination rite itself is a success or failure, and if the newly ordained ritualist may succeed or fail in his future career. [64]

Luo Shangjin, a middle-aged Zhengyi cleric based in the Baoqing neighborhood remembers his own experience of the 1987 ordination vividly:

As the ordination proceeded to the third day, it was the day when the banner tassels were to be tied. The Master Petitioner divined that the knotting would take place around noon. Our uncle-master informed the three of us that our knotting of banners would manifest the Way at the Wei 未 hours (1–3 pm) in the early afternoon. At the Wu 午 noon hours (11 am–1 pm), we three then hurried up the hill to "hasten the banner knotting (*chuifan* 催旛)" by practicing the spells of the Earthly Administration and Divine Water as instructed to us by our teachers. As soon as it was the Wei hours, our three banners began to flutter and tie up. Wang Songsheng's banner first became knotted up. Then it was my banner, followed by that of Xie Hansheng. But the other six clerics' banners did not knot at all. At the time, there were several hundreds of people who gathered there to watch the banners being knotted. It was an amazing scene. But since the six local clerics' banners did not get knotted, the people there were very unhappy and their feelings tanked to the bottom. They complained that the ordination masters were unlearned and unskilled in the ways of the underworld rituals (*yinjiao* 陰教), and their ordination altar was badly set up. But my uncle master Luo's prediction about our banners being knotted at the Wei hours did come true and quite efficaciously. The banners of his disciple and nephew disciples were all knotted as he predicted albeit with very different knotting configurations. After we brought down the banners from the poles for our uncle master to examine, they each exhibited different patterns. Uncle Master Luo told us that Wang Songsheng's banner was knotted into the Lion's Head Banner (*shizitou fan* 獅子頭旛), while Xie Hanshen's banner and mine were both knotted into the Prince's Banner (*taizi fan* 太子旛), which was the supreme pattern among all knotted banners. How very wonderful that is! At that moment, all the masters of the disciples attending the ordination began to hold uncle master Luo in high regard. That evening, the six local clerics all hurried off to buy new white cloths and then brought them back to uncle master Luo. The Master Petitioner of the ordination then asked uncle master Luo to re-inscribe each of the new banners. His re-scribing the banners took several hours and did not finish until around midnight. It was really arduous and hard work. My uncle master drew unsparingly on his deep erudition in Daoist scriptural classics to accomplish such a great feat in one brush! Yet, quite unexpectedly, the banners of the six local ritual clerics only began to knot around five o'clock early next morning. The results were very unsatisfactory because the knotting process was not witnessed by an audience composed of the local residents. According to local Xinhua customs and traditions, all banner knotting must have been witnessed by local residents in order to have any true potency and efficacy. Otherwise, the knotting is not acknowledged by the local people. Consequently, the ordained cleric's altar will not flourish, as people tend to think that he has not yet mastered the underworld rites, and need to continue to learn and practice. It is a huge loss of face. But our ordination experience shows that our uncle master Luo is truly consummate and unsurpassed in Daoist rites. How superb a Daoist cleric he is![65]

In June of 1994, three other ritualists of the Baoqing Neighborhood, Zeng Mengxiong 曾夢熊, Wu Jihe 伍濟和, and Feng Songwen 封宋文 underwent their ordination at an altar constructed on the sandy beach at the Hankou Pier. The senior clerics of the Baoqing ordination altar were all from the Baoqing neighborhood, except for Master Petitioner Chen Demei who traveled to Hankou for the occasion for the first time. The Master of Ordination was Cai Dongsheng 蔡東生, while the master of swords was Qin Guorong 秦國榮. The Master Usher was Qin Guohua 秦國華. The altar assistants were Zou Zuchun 鄒祖純, Cheng Hengmei 程衡梅, and several other senior ritual masters. At the earlier ordination in Xinhua in 1987, all the ordained ritualists from Hankou and Xinhua did not climb the "sword ladder (*daoti* 刀梯)," which was not instituted because of the budgetary constraints. To make up for it, the Hankou altar masters set up the sword ladder in front of the altar. The sword ladder was made up of two long ladders composed of 36 steps leaned against each other, and a sharp blade was then affixed upward to each of the steps, forming an upward and a downward rungs of sword. With the ordination master ringing the stone bells and reciting the spells, the newly initiated clerics would then climb barefooted up on the rung of the sword ladder and then descend downward on the bladed steps on the side of the ladder. The climbing of the 36 bladed steps of the sword ladder not only signifies the ordained cleric's deliverance out of hell and into the sacred realm, but it also symbolizes his newly acquired ritual prowess and power.[66]

Having descended from the sword ladder, the disciples then had to complete another ritual act: kneeling in front of their masters and eating three mouthfuls of steamed rice which their masters had masticated and then spit out for them to partake of. The act of the ordination masters' sharing the masticated rice carries deep symbolism for the ordained disciples. Similarly, Liu Chih-wan has studied the act of sharing and casting rice in local rituals in Taiwan, and he has argued that such casting of rice signifies not only sowing seeds, and feeding the hungry ghosts, but it also stands for enhanced reproductive fertility and exorcism for the client at the same time.[67] But in the context of the Baoqing Daoist ordination, the master's act of leaving the masticated rice for his disciples to ingest also signals a shared moral economy within the framework of the master-discipleship. First, the act signifies vividly the newly ordained Daoist's livelihood is made possible by the master, that they both partake of the same economy, and that their ritual cooperation can ensure their co-prosperity. Second, the master's feeding of rice to the disciple also insinuates "sowing the seeds (*bozhong* 播種)," signifying the disciple's reception, and continued transmission of the master's lineage.[68]

At the conclusion of the ordination altar, the ordination master confers on the disciple a Daoist title and lineage name, together with the command tablets, the seal, and the ordination certificate. These constitute formal recognition of the disciple's new identity as a fully ordained and certified ritualist who can now independently set up his own altar and operate his ritual business in the neighborhood. The Baoqing ordination was as much an economic enterprise as it was a ritual. For their ordinations at the Baoqing altar, the three ordained ritualists paid 6,000 yuan apiece to their masters. At the time, their payments were by no means a small amount for an average worker in Hankou. The ordination was a spectacular event open to the public, drawing tens of thousands of residents from the Baoqing neighborhood and beyond who poured into the waterfront streets to watch the rare ceremony.[69]

Daoist rituals and daily life in the Baoqing neighborhood

The Baoqing Daoist ritual repertoire is composed of the Yin (*yinshi* 陰事) and the Yang (*yangshi* 陽事) rites. Compared with the pre-1949 era, the Yang rites have been drastically reduced in number. Its present repertoire consists primarily of the Yin rites (for the dead). At present, the Daoist ritualists hold on average two to three ritual services every month, mostly at the requests by the residents from the Baoqing neighborhood and other Hunanese communities in other parts of Hankou, and from the Parrots Shoal neighborhood in Hanyang. They occasionally also travel to the suburbs of Wuhan to perform ritual services for their clients.

The Baoqing ritual masters are sometimes asked by clients to stage large-scale ritual service for which they are often short-handed. When that happens, they often travel back to their hometown of Xinhua and invite the Daoists there to lend a hand. Upon completion of the service, the Xinhua Daoists will then return home. They perform their rites usually in the Xinhua dialect. But recently, as many Wuhan natives have also increasingly requested their ritual service, they sometimes, at their clients' request, perform their rites in Wuhan dialect instead. Their present set of the Yang rites includes the Jade Emperor rite 玉皇醮, the Southern Peak rite 南嶽醮, and the Guanyin rite 觀音醮, though the last is now rarely performed (Figure 6.4).

During the pre-1949 era, the Baoqing Daoist ritualists used to stage their large-scale rites either at the Baoqing Public Yard (Baoqing gongping 寶慶公坪) where most of the communal activities were held or at the dockyard along the Han River. But after the founding of the People's Republic, the Baoqing Public Yard was gradually taken over by the new immigrants who used parts of the yard to construct new residential buildings, while the empty spaces along the river were also used for other purposes, such as bus stations. After the Cultural Revolution, the Daoist ritualists came to hold their ritual services in the streets and alleys of the neighborhood. The post-1980s period witnessed a proliferation of Daoist ritual services throughout the Baoqing neighborhood. But many non-Hunanese residents in the Baoqing neighborhood could not appreciate the religious faith and practices among their fellow residents from Hunan, and viewed the Daoist rites held in their streets and alleys as too noisy, disruptive of traffic and even causing some security problems. They often filed complaints to the relevant municipal agencies. These complaints were taken seriously by the Wuhan Municipal Bureau of Religious Affairs and the Wuhan Municipal Daoist Association. In 1987, they dispatched one of their staff, Mr. Xiao Xinzhu 蕭新鑄, to the Baoqing neighborhood where he conducted extensive interviews with different constituent groups of residents to collect information and opinions from the community. After coordinating with the different groups of residents and obtaining the consent of leading Quanzhen Daoist priests,

Figure 6.4 Baoqing Daoists performing a rite on Mount Wudang, summer 2009 © Xun Liu.

especially Prior Han Gaochao 韓高超 of the Changchun Monastery, the Baoqing Zhengyi ritualists agreed to relocate their ritual venues from the streets and alleys of the Baoqing neighborhood to the Quanzhen Daoist Changchun Monastery in Wuchang. There, on July 13–14 of 1987, the Baoqing Daoist ritual masters held, for the first time, their annual Southern Peak Rite, which was widely regarded as the most important and revered Zhengyi rite among the Hunan residents of the city, to give thanks to the Supreme God of the Southern Peak 南嶽大帝 for making their wishes come true from the previous year. The two-day ritual drew over 2,000 participants. From then on, the Southern Peak Rite together with the Quanzhen Annual Retreat in honor of Patriarch Qiu Changchun 邱長春 became the two major annual retreats at the Quanzhen Daoist temple. It has also since become a highlight of the temple's public brochures complete with an introduction and photographs of the ritual details. Each year since then, it has become a routine that many of the Baoqing residents would come to the Quanzhen temple in Wuchang where they would participate in their annual Southern Peak Rite at the temple after they returned from their pilgrimage to the Southern Peak in central Hunan.

But while relocating the Zhengyi ritual retreat from the Baoqing neighborhood to the Quanzhen temple has solved the problems of lack of ritual space and public security concerns, and made the massive popular ritual event easier to manage, it has also brought up some new issues. For instance, the Quanzhen temple's rather limited legal operating hours from 8 am to 5 pm meant that the Baoqing ritualists could not complete in time their full ritual service which began at 8 am and go on well beyond 11 pm. In addition, the Quanzhen rules prohibits any slaughter of animals and blood sacrifice at the temple, but the Baoqing ritualists heavily steeped in the Xinhua local tradition firmly believed in the efficacy and traditions of blood sacrifice. As a result, both the ritual masters and their lay followers all feel that the Southern Peak Rite performed without blood sacrifice at the Quanzhen temple to be short of something and at variance with their taste. Further, for many followers and devotees living in Hankou and Hanyang, their attendance to the rite held at the Wuchang temple means added time and extra transportation costs. Last but not the least, participating in the rite held at the Wuchang temple also involved extra meal costs and rent for the venue, further stretching the budget and adding to the financial burden of the attendees. For these reasons, the Baoqing ritualists have repeatedly petitioned the Wuhan Daoist Association for a separate and dedicated ritual venue, but to no avail so far.[70]

The Baoqing Daoists and the Nanyue pilgrimage

As shown above, the Southern Peak pilgrimage constitutes yet another major ritual activity popular among the Baoqing residents in Wuhan. From the sixth to the eighth of the eighth moon each year, led by the Zhengyi ritualists, residents of Hunan extraction go on pilgrimage to the Southern Peak in central Hunan, where they burn incense and make offerings in the hope of having their wishes granted by the Supreme God of the Southern Peak. Though we still lack a thorough investigation of the origins of the pilgrimage among the Hunanese residents and sojourners in Wuhan, it is reasonable to surmise that it is most likely a transplanted practice brought by the early migrants and laborers from Hunan who first settled in Hankou in the mid-to-late Qing period.

The Southern Peak pilgrimage is one of the most important religious activities among the populations along the Xiang and Zhi Rivers in western and central Hunan.[71] Baoqing prefecture is no exception. Between the early and mid-eighth moon, many people travel to the Southern Peak to render homage to the Supreme God.[72] The Baoqing residents of Hankou refer to their pilgrimage to the Southern Peak as "paying homage to the Saint Lord Grandpa (*chao Shengdi yeye* 朝聖帝爺爺)." The saint lord is none other than the God of Mount Heng, Zhu Rong 祝融, who is also the God of Fire. Legends have it that Zhu Rong is one of the Five Sovereigns in charge of the south. Such accounts are found in many of the early classics such as *Guoyu, Shanhaijing, Guanzi,* and *Zuozhuan.* They also claim that after his death, Zhu Rong was buried at the Southern Peak, which was also named as the Zhu Rong Peak.

The worship of the mountain God of the Southern Peak began quite early. After the Sui unification, Mount Heng was further affirmed as the Southern Peak of the Five Peaks system, and the worship of the God of Mount Heng entered the imperial state cult. In the fifth year of the Tianbao reign (746) under the Tang dynasty, the Xuanzong Emperor conferred upon the God of the Southern Peak the title of the King Who Administers Heaven (Sitian wang 司天王). From then on, the Tang court routinely dispatched court officials to Mount Heng, where they rendered annual homage to the God. The imperial patronage and the official participation in the rite of homage to the God of Southern Peak further stimulated the local spontaneous cults of the God.[73]

By the Song dynasty, the God of the Southern Peak became further elevated in status after he was granted the title of the Luminously Sacred Emperor Who Governs Heaven (Sitian zhaosheng di 司天昭聖帝) and paired with an celestial empress by the Song court. By then, the temple dedicated to his worship also saw massive expansion to include a main shrine, and 16 other side and subshrines, forming a massive architectural complex composed of more than 800 halls and rooms at the foothill of the Southern Peak. Indeed the architectural pattern of the massive Song expansion has remained unchanged today. Following the Song court, successive Yuan, Ming, and Qing courts heaped additional lavish titles on the Southern Peak God. But the god was known popularly among the locals in Hunan as simply the Sacred Lord, and the God of the Southern Peak.[74]

While serving as an epicenter of Confucian, Buddhist, and Daoist activities through the dynasties, the Southern Peak was also home to the indigenous cult of the Heng Mount God. A host of local traditions, from the audience on the first day of the first moon (*yuandan chaosheng* 朝聖), and its attendant temple fair at the foothill temple, and the Pilgrimage with Incense in the Eighth Moon (*bayue xianghuo* 八月香火), all embody widespread popular piety practices and ritual styles characteristic of Hunan. The autumn pilgrimage to present incense at the Southern Peak Temple is the longest running, most influential, and popular of all the ritual activities centered on the Southern Peak Temple at the foothill. It begins on the 15th of the 7th moon and lasts through the 8th moon, and ends toward the end of the 9th moon, with three climatic moments: the Middle Prime Day, the Sacred Emperor's birthday on the first of the eighth moon, and the Festival of Ascendance on the Ninth Day of the Ninth Moon (*jiujiu denggao* 九九登高).

The pilgrimage by ordinary folk to the Southern Peak is generally believed to have already flourished in central Hunan no later than the Song dynasty.[75] It has remained popular ever since. According to an early Republican era account,

> In lunar eighth moon, the customs in Hengyang is that men and women would go on pilgrimage to the Southern Peak. With incense sticks in hands, they would pause to the left side of the road every three, or five, or seven steps, to perform an obeisance to the Peak. The lyrics of the Song of Advocating Filial Piety (*Quanxiaoge* 勸孝歌) bellowed out by pilgrims could be heard high up in the clouds, lingering in the mountain valleys far and wide.[76]

Another Republican era record offers even more details on the thriving pilgrimage:

> Mount Heng is one of the Five Peaks, and located just above thirty miles from Hengyang prefectural seat. The mountain is dotted with monasteries and temples, most of which honor the Sacred Emperor of the Southern Peak

as the main deity. Each autumn, pilgrims from all places can be seen traveling along the roads to the mountain. Those coming from Hengyang city are the most numerous. Many go on the pilgrimage on behalf of their relatives and friends, but they are not at all different from those devotees who worship the god themselves. Those who seek blessings for their parents routinely go on the pilgrimage for three consecutive years. They usually prepare for the pilgrimage by first having a small wooden incense chair made. The incense chair is about three inches in height and holds three incense sticks. If the pilgrim's parents are still alive, they dress in the red pilgrim garb. If their parents are dead, they then robe in blue clothes. On their first pilgrimage to present the incense to the god, they carry the incense chair in hands and pause every three steps to perform an obeisance. On their second pilgrimage, they pause every five steps to perform an obeisance. On their third pilgrimage to the Southern Peak Temple, they stop every seven steps to pay homage. The obeisance thus performed is known as burning incense while kowtowing (*shaobaixiang* 燒拜香). Even when a pilgrim has a swollen forehead from kowtowing and knees bloody from kneeling, or whether it rains or shines, he or she persists without fail. While such filial piety is commendable, its stupidity is also pitiful *(qixiao gu kejia, qiyu cheng kelian ye* 其孝固可嘉, 其愚誠可憐也).[77]

Republican era accounts estimate that the annual number of pilgrims to the Southern Peak Temple at the time was several tens of thousands.[78] The annual number of pilgrims for present times is about 2 million. The revenue generated from the admission tickets to the foothill Southern Peak Temple is well above 4 million yuan.[79]

Pilgrims to the Southern Peak tend to dress in a certain kind of attires, and sing "Pilgrims' Song (*jinxiang ge* 進香歌)" as they go on pilgrimage. The pilgrims from the Baoqing neighborhood usually wear the same kind of red headdress and dark blue clothes. Those who wear their clothes with red edges typically mean that either one or both of their parents have passed away. They also carry a red incense satchel on the front embroidered with the characters: "Presenting incense to the Southern Peak (*Nanyue jinxiang* 南嶽進香)."

As they walk on the road, each of the pilgrims carries an incense stick and a small chair and sings aloud the Pilgrims' Song. The song is full of local folk tunes. A Daoist cleric who leads the pilgrim group takes up the lead in singing the song, while the pilgrims join the chorus singing all the way until they reach the Main Shrine of the Southern Peak Temple.

During the Republican era, the pilgrims from the Baoqing Pier neighborhood typically took the boat from Hankou all the way to Hengyang. The voyage to and fro took two to three weeks to complete. After 1949, especially after the Land Reforms and the collectivization drive in 1957, the pilgrimage tradition within the Baoqing Pier community was forced to stop. It was not revived until 1983 when Baoqing pilgrims resumed their annual pilgrimage to the Southern Peak. They have either hired a bus or taken the train to the Southern Peak. The itinerary of the pilgrimage is typically arranged by the Zhengyi clerics. The six active Zhengyi ritualists now each have their own pilgrim groups (*xiangke tuanti* 香客團體), ranging from a few dozens to several hundreds. The pilgrims each pay to their Daoist leader a lump sum which cover transportation, admissions, meals, and other pilgrimage related costs. The Daoist leader then makes all the appropriate arrangements for the pilgrimage. The pilgrimage usually sets off on the sixth of the eighth moon and reaches the foothill of the Southern Peak on the same day. After presenting incense to the God of the Southern Peak at the Main Shrine on the following day, they then climb to the top of the mountain to pay homage to the god, before they start off on their home journey on the afternoon of the next day on the eighth.

When going on the pilgrimage, it is also common for pilgrims to bring along their incense sacks (*xiangbao* 香包), which contain paper money and sandalwood chips or powder. The incense sacks have images of gods, Buddha, or immortals painted or decorated on the outside, and they also contain the pilgrims' names, native places, and wishes and signed with the dates. Pilgrims believe that writing down their personal information on the incense sacks makes themselves recognizable to the gods, since these sacks are their offerings to the gods on the Southern Peak.

Pilgrims from the Baoqing neighborhood typically each take 12 incense sacks when they go on the pilgrimage to the Southern Peak. These incense sacks are generally packed and prepared by the Zhengyi ritualists in the neighborhood. Four of the 12 sacks are big ones: the first to be presented at the Zhurong Shrine (Zhurong miao 祝融廟) atop the peak; the second to be offered at the Main Shrine of the foothill Southern Peak Temple reserved for imperial worship; still another is burned at the start of the pilgrimage to ensure safe and propitious journey; and the fourth is preserved at the incense table at home only to be burned and offered to the God of the South Peak when the pilgrims return from their journey. During the pilgrimage, the pilgrims' relatives at home must keep to a vegetarian diet. But the Baoqing Zhengyi ritualists have since made some adaptations to the procedures of the pilgrimage in order to accommodate the conditions of modern life. For instance, the fourth big incense sack is now burned and presented at the Main Shrine of the Southern Peak instead of waiting until the pilgrim returns home. Accordingly, the pilgrims' relatives at home therefore no longer observe a vegetarian diet. The eight small incense sacks are each to be offered and burned at eight small shrines on the Southern Peak. One month prior to their departure, the pilgrims submit to their leading Zhengyi Daoist cleric their wishes and personal information, which are written carefully down on petition forms by the Baoqing clerics, together with their donations, the amount of which is allegedly left entirely up to the petitioners. The Zhengyi Daoists then prepare the incense sacks manually based on their pilgrims-clients' specific requests and personal situations.

Once the incense sacks are made, the Zhengyi ritualists then write down on the sacks relevant information and instructions on how to present incense and perform worship while on the Southern Peak. Once they arrive on the mountain, the Baoqing pilgrims from Hankou then follow these written instructions in making offerings and burning incenses at various shrines and temples on the Southern Peak. While on pilgrimage, the Baoqing devotees abide by established rules and prohibitions. For those who come to repay their wishes that have come true, they would fast, and only drink water or tea during the pilgrimage. They are allowed fruits given to them by others, but they are not supposed to bring any of their own. They are not allowed to smoke or drink. But these prohibitions are no longer followed by everyone. For those who come to present incense, they begin a vegetarian diet at the start of their journey to the Southern Peak. From the foothill to the mountaintop shrine, it is about 15 km in distance. Pilgrims stop every three to four steps to make an obeisance, with each carrying a tiny chair that holds a lit incense stick. In addition to the Southern Peak, Baoqing Daoist clerics have in recent years led their pilgrims groups on pilgrimages to Mount Putuo to pay homage to Guanyin Boddhisattva there.[80]

The Baoqing Daoists' other ritual services

In addition to their collective liturgical services, Baoqing Zhengyi Daoist clerics also routinely employ their liturgical skills and techniques to offer individually tailored service to their clients in the neighborhood. They often perform divination, draw talismans, and chant spells for purposes of calling up divine forces, exorcising ghosts, driving away evil forces, healing illnesses, obtaining geomantic advantages, seeking fortune, and avoiding disasters. Among the Baoqing Daoist ritualists, Zeng Mengxiong and Zou Changzhang have both through their family transmission become adept at drawing talismans, which they both believe to be particularly efficacious. They are much in demand by their clients in the neighborhood to perform tasks of expelling ghosts and evil spirits. Their followers in the neighborhood often wear their hand-drawn talismans on their bodies, or post them on objects or in their homes. Some use the ashes of the burnt talismans to infuse the water they drink for curing illness. Indeed, many of the Baoqing residents are so immersed in the beliefs and practices centered on the culture of talismans that they have developed their cult of the talismans, and the habit of wearing and ingesting talismans. Many residents who have children with frail constitution or chronic illnesses often seek out their Zhengyi ritual masters to draw talismans which they burn into ashes and used them to drink with water. In addition, the Baoqing Zhengyi Daoists also employ spells or oral incantations as ritual instruments in healing and exorcism.

Today, the Baoqing Zhengyi ritualists may not serve on the Baoqing Pier Neighborhood Committee of Residents, the local governance body, but our study shows that they, like their predecessors, continue to exert significant measures of influence in the local community through their ritual skills and service to their clients and the public. Further, they also actively participate in social welfare and public projects. In 1998, when Wuhan suffered a major flood disaster, the six Zhengyi ritualists from the Baoqing community raised a total of 10,000 yuan in support of the flood prevention work. They also mobilized local Baoqing residents to provide cold beverages and water melons to the frontline flood prevention workers working to consolidate the embankments along the Yangzi and Han Rivers.

During the Wuhan city government's anti-SARS drive in 2001, the Baoqing Zhengyi Daoist ritualists made a donation of 2,000 yuan to the city's public health program. In 2002, they contributed more than 1,000 yuan worth of books to the neighborhood library and cultural activity station. In 2003, they not only donated more than 5,000 in cash, but also participated in the construction of an access road to the neighborhood primary school. During the Wenchuan 汶川 earthquake disaster relief drive in 2008, the Baoqing Daoists made a 2,000 yuan cash donation. Through their persistent support for public welfare, disaster relief, and local development projects, their close collaboration with the local government in Wuhan, and their decades of ritual service and commitment to their neighborhood and community, the Baoqing Zhengyi clerics have not only enjoyed public prestige and support, but they have also garnered government recognition.

Yet since the 1990s, with the deepening market economy reforms, public housing commodification drive, urban planning and community development, the city and provincial governments' persistent refusal to allow temple construction by the Baoqing Zhengyi Daoist householders, and the increasingly competitive religious landscape in contemporary China, the six aging Zhengyi clerics based in Baoqing Pier neighborhood as a group are faced now with unprecedented challenges and problems which have rendered the prospect of their survival worrisome and dim.

For their part, the at-home Zhengyi Daoist clerics have long been a thorn in the side of state regulatory and management agencies. Due to a prevalent perception, state regulators and managers have long held rather prejudicial views of the Zhengyi clerics and their largely localized organization, and their management of and policies toward these at-home practitioners have been unavoidably biased.[81] Though the Baoqing Daoists have been allowed to form their own Zhengyi Daoist Self-Governance Council under the Quanzhen dominated Wuhan Daoist Association, and many of them have even held prominent yet largely symbolic positions at various levels and branches of the Hubei provincial and Wuhan municipal political consultative councils, and Daoist associations, they have long been beset with the problem of not owning and operating their own temple for ritual and religious activities. As a result, they have had to rely on the Quanzhen Daoist Changchun Monastery in Wuchang for both their council office and their ritual venue. This lack of their own temple has severely restricted their daily social and ritual activities, and has long held back their overall development as a religious group. Though they have petitioned to the Wuhan municipal Agency of Religious Affairs and to the Wuhan Daoist Association for establishing their own temple in Hankou,[82] the Zhengyi Daoists have not yet been able to build their own temple or even post the nameplate of their Daoist self-governance council.

As a result, the Baoqing Zhengyi ritualists had to work out a compromise with the city religious regulators in order to continue their ritual and social service programs. To do so, they had to surmount an inherent Catch-22 situation.

According to the present state regulations, all ritual activities (with the exception of funerary salvation and memorial rites) must be held at religious venues such as a registered temple. Yet the Baoqing ritualists have never had any formal temple under their names, and had to perform their two major annual retreats, the Jade Emperor's Rite and the Southern Peak Rite at Changchun Monastery owned by the Quanzhen Daoists in Wuchang. For another of their hallmark rites, the incense burning and worship rite prior to the start of the popular annual pilgrimage to the Southern Peak in the fall attended by the Hunan residents in Wuhan, the Baoqing ritual masters would stage the rite at the homes of the pilgrims before they set out on the pilgrimage. The return or repayment incense rite was mostly conducted at the Southern Peak before the Hunan pilgrims return to Wuhan. Other than the funerary and salvation rites, the Zhengyi ritualists could not perform the remainder of their routine ritual repertoire. For many years, they have wanted to restore one of the many Southern Peak shrines that once dotted the tri-cities of Wuhan as their ritual venue, and their Hunanese followers have even offered cash donations to buy the necessary land for the temple restoration. But their initiative has so far failed to gain the approval by the appropriate municipal and provincial agencies. As a result, their lack of dedicated temple has severely restricted their further development as a Daoist ritual group in the Wuhan tri-cities.

State regulatory bias aside, Wuhan's urban planning and development projects have also challenged the Baoqing Daoists' continued development in Hankou. The Hanzheng Street district, which encompasses the Baoqing neighborhood, was one of the oldest districts of Hankou. Lacking any systemic urban planning and design, its neighborhood is notorious for chaotic and shoddily constructed housings and office buildings, overly dense population, and aging and crumbly public infrastructure.[83] These problems were further aggravated by the vigorous growth and overcrowding of small private shops and businesses of small commodity and textile markets. To deal with the overcrowding, fire hazards, business integration, and economic transition, the Wuhan municipal government has launched several phases of urban planning projects since the 1980s to transform the area into a new CBD district that combines commercial and business skyscrapers, office and residential towers, and public markets. As several phases of this urban planning were completed in the 1990s and early 2000s,[84] many Hunan residents and their upwardly mobile children all began to move out of the Baoqing neighborhood into the new middle class and even upscale commercial residential quarters that have since sprung up in select neighborhoods throughout the tri-cities area. This outward remigration or exodus by the second and third generations of the Hunanese residents of the Baoqing neighborhood has not only reduced the sheer physical size of the old Baoqing Pier neighborhood, but it has also significantly eroded the ritual, social, and cultural basis of the Baoqing Zhengyi ritualists. The demographics of the remaining population have also changed, resulting in a new Baoqing neighborhood which has increasingly consisted of mostly elderly, especially elderly women, new rural migrant laborers, and small business owners, and temporary sojourners from non-Hunan as well as Hunan regions that are often not socially and culturally integrated into the Baoqing Pier neighborhood. The outwardly and upwardly mobile children of the Baoqing neighborhood have also become quite diversified in their choices of faith practices, and are increasingly emotionally detached and physically distanced from the religious and cultural traditions of their parents and grandparents who lived in the Baoqing neighborhood all their lives.

On our most recent follow-up visit with the Baoqing Zhengyi clerics in the summer of 2016, we found that they themselves have joined the waves of urban remigration due to the ferocious demolition and redevelopment of their neighborhood. From the spring to the summer of 2013, the Baoqing Pier neighborhood was completely razed to the ground by a real estate development group which had bought the redevelopment rights to the whole neighborhood. Like most of their fellow residents, all six masters of the Baoqing Zhengyi ritual crew could not but move out of the Baoqing Pier neighborhood. They have now relocated and live separately in their new dwellings located in different parts of the Wuhan tri-cities area and beyond. Master Zeng Mengxiong, whose household registration was never completed with the Wuhan authorities, had to return to Jiayu 嘉鱼, a river town along the Yangzi River to the south of Wuhan, where he was retained as a resident Daoist cleric at the local temple, whereas Master Zou went back to his hometown in Xinhua since he never achieved residency in the city either. Master Luo Shangjin informs us during our recent interview that while the new social media such as Wechat has provided much easier and convenient means of communicating and staying in touch with the remaining four Baoqing clerics and their devotees scattered through the Wuhan tri-cities, they feel quite nostalgic about the "good old days" when they could easily run into or call up each other in their old neighborhood where they used to live so close by one another.[85]

These issues aside, the Baoqing Zhengyi ritualists have themselves aged, averaging in the mid- to late-60s. Due to their relatively low income, all six Baoqing Zhengyi clerics have eked out a living by working in construction or operating small businesses such as Xerox copying service and neighborhood retail stores for most of their revenues, and performing ritual services as supplementary incomes. Now with the ever-rising cost of living in the tri-cities of Wuhan, the Baoqing Zhengyi ritualists' traditionally low income makes their profession an even less palatable career choice to their prospective disciples. Confronted by these predicaments, the Baoqing Zhengyi Daoist clerics with their more than 200 years of transmission and practice in Hankou are now facing an uncertain future.

Appendix

Key data on the geography and travel distance on land routes between key towns in Central Hunan and Hubei:

Shaoyang-Xinhua via Zi River: 80 km
Xinhua-Anhua via Zi River: 150 km
Anhua-Yiyang via Zi River: 150 km
Yiyang-Hankou via Changjiang River: 400 km

Notes

We wish to thank the Chiang Ching-kuo Foundation, Agence Nationale de la Recherche (ANR, France), and the American Council of Learned Societies for their financial support which has helped us complete the field observations of and interviews with the Zhengyi Daoist ritualists in the Baoqing Harbor neighborhoods in Hankou of Wuhan between 2007 and 2011. Some findings of the study have been published by Mei Li in her "Yimin, shequ, zongjiao: yi jindai Hankou Baoqing matou wei zhongxin," Hubei daxue xuebao 湖北大學學報 [Journal of Hubei University], 41.3 (May, 2014), pp. 1–8 and 148.

1 See Rowe, *Hankow: Commerce and Society in a Chinese City, 1796–1889* (1984), pp. 213–26; and *Hankow: Conflict and Community in a Chinese City, 1796–1805* (1989).

2 See Wang Ping's entry on social conditions of Daoism during the Republican and socialist periods in *Wuhan shizhi* (1977), pp. 275–78.

3 Liu Xianting, *Guangyang zaji*, p. 193.

4 See *Xiakou xianzhi* (2001), j. 3, p. 31.

5 See Dong Guifu, *Hankou Ziyang shuyuan zhilue*, j. 8.

6 See the Illustrations section of Hou Peijun, *Hankou Shan-Shaan huiguan zhi*, j. 1, pp. 3 and 44; and *Xiakou xianzhi*, j. 3, p. 24.

7 See *Xiakou xianzhi*, j. 3, p. 24. See also Rowe, (1984), pp. 310–17 and 360.

8 In the illustration of the confluence of Changjiang and Han Rivers contained in *Hanyang xianzhi* (1868), Hankou is drawn like a long sand bar or shoal.

9 For the origin and evolution of docks and quays in Hankou, see Wang Jianzhong and Yu Zhong, "Matou shihua"; Wang Dengfu, *Jianghan shihua*, pp. 17–19; Wang Zhifang, "Hanshui matou shihua"; Zhang Dingguo, "Yan Jiang matou yiwang."

10 Ye Diaoyuan, "Shichan 市廛," juan 1 in his *Hankou zhuzhici*, pp. 109 and 105.

11 Peng Yuxin and Jiang Yong, "Shijiu shiji Hankou shangye hanghui de fazhan jiqi yiyi."

12 Rowe, (1984), pp. 213–51.

13 Under the protection and patronage by the newly ascendant militia generals and ranking civil officials from Hunan, the salt, tea, and timber merchants of Hunan became the dominant and wealthiest group in Hankou. But different from their counterparts in salt and tea trades, the Hunan lumber merchants thrived not only on their business know-how, but they also gained competitive advantages by resorting to gang violence and native place alliances among their compatriots. By resorting to violence, the Hunan lumber merchants took over the key docks and storage yards in Hankou and the shoals along the Yangzi and Han rivers. They also maneuvered to use their political influence to protect their hard-gained competitive advantages in the city. See Wang Jiping, *Wan Qing Hunan shi*; Fu Wei, "Wan Qing Hankou difang shehuizhong de shangren he shangren zuzhi"; and anonymous, *Hanyang Yingwuzhou zhumu shichang shilüe*. See also Rowe, (1984), pp. 269–76.

14 Zhang Guoxiong, *Ming-Qing shiqi de liang Hu yimin*, p. 76.

15 Liu Yunsheng, "Hankou kuli zhuangkuang."

16 For a description of how the rough plank boats were built and their sizes, see Su Jinru, "Shaoyang de maobanchuan"; Zhang Qionghua, "Meishan maobanchuan yu Hankou Baoqing matou"; and Li Xiaorong, "Zishui tan-ge yu maobanchuan."

17 The Plank Lane (Banzi xiang) was located in a riverfront neighborhood in Hanyang. See Liu Zhenjie, *Hanyang shihua*, p. 161.

18 Rowe, (1984), pp. 270–73.

19 See *Wuhan magai ziliao huibian*, vol. 1, pp. 38–39.

20 Li Xia, *Fuhe rensheng*, p. 58.

21 Li Shu, "Hankou Baoqing matou he Baoqing huiguan."

22 Guo Ying, "Wan Qing Hankou chengshi kongzhi xitong de yanqian." For studies of the development of Hankou Harbor and its relationship to the internal trade, see Zhang Shanshan, "Jindai Hankougang yuqi fudi jingji guanxi de bianqian, 1862–1936."

23 Li Shu, "Hankou Baoqing matou he Baoqing huiguan."

24 See Yan Xiaorong, "Xinhua wushu yuanliu zongshu"; and You, Liu, and Liang, "Meishan wugong jiqi xinyang chutan."
25 Li Shu, "Hankou Baoqing matou he Baoqing huiguan."
26 Wang Rigen, *Zhongguo huiguan shi*, p. 4.
27 For a recent study of the late Qing and early Republican era migrant labor communities in Shanghai from northern Jiangsu, see Goodman, *Native Place, City, and Nation*; and on new materials for the study of social organizations of the period, see Goossaert, "Matériaux et recherches nouvelles sur les corporations chinoises urbaines traditionelles (des Ming à 1949)," p. 210.
28 Li Shu, "Hankou Baoqing matou he Baoqing huiguan."
29 See *Hankou shijie quantu* (1918), p. 49.
30 See Wuchang Yaxin dixue she, comp., *Xin Hankoushi shice xiangtu (1933); and Hankoushi jiedao xiangtu* (1938), pp. 81 and 85.
31 See *Qiaokou quzhi* (2007), pp. 579–60 and 580.
32 Ning Yi, "Han Wei Nanbeichao Hunan daojiao fazhan yanjiu," p. 15; and Zhang Zehong, "Gudai shaoshu minzu yu daojiao," pp. 33 and 36–39.
33 Hu Nenggai, "Yige juyou wanqiang shengcun yizhi de Yaozu shi weihe yuanli Meishan de?"
34 See Lin Zonghai, "Baoqing maobanshang shihua"; Wu Ruowen, "Maobanchuan: Zijiang shang de Xiangshang chuanqi"; and Yan Ji, "Zijiang shangyeshishang de chuanqi: Maobaochuan yu Baoqing matou."
35 Su Jinru, "Shaoyang de maobanchuan."
36 Based on the sequence of the place names appearing in the ballad, it seems to be sung by boatmen going down the river and goes like this: "寶慶開船下漢口….轄神廟下小連灣…祖師座下蓮花廟…楊泗廟裡把神祝， 卦打三巡三門灘….紙錢落地排八卦…先生送我寺門前…到岸老爺打一敬, 大家兄弟把心寬. 益陽開船往漢口, 抬頭望見鯿魚山. 魏公廟裡把神敬…橘子廟裡算八字…魚骨廟裡香一柱." See Zhou Shaoyao, "Zijiang tan'ge." See also Luo Yuanshi,"Zishui tan'ge," p. 393.
37 The ballad is entitled "Going upstream" and goes like this: "漢口開船走上水, 八卦灘上占一卦….蘇溪有個水府廟， 往來客人燒保香." See Zhou Shaoyao, "Zijiang tan'ge."
38 A folk legend still circulating in the neighborhoods of Hankou seems to have borne out this claim. People in Hubei and Jiangxi still continue to feel that the raftsmen from western Hunan were rather mysterious, and they still enjoy telling stories about how the Hunanese Daoist ritualists vied with the raftsmen for local control and dominance in regions where they each had to make a living. Indeed, some hold the view that sailors and deck hands may have even evolved their own ritual tradition known as "Rafts sect (Paijiao 簰教)," which had its ritual repertoire for healing, demonic suppression, and it circulated widely among the sailors and raftsmen in Hunan and Jiangxi. See the story of the "Songjiashan 宋家山" in *Zhongguo minjian gushi jicheng Hubei Yangxin xian minjian gushiji* (1988), and see also Liu Shouhua, *Daojiao yu Zhongguo minjian wenxue*, p. 210.
39 In the mid-fourteenth century, the Xinhua county Daoist agency was installed at the Palace. See Liang and Liu, *Baoqing fuzhi* (1684), j.9:3b.
40 For an account of Wen Jin's life and career as a county magistrate-turned Daoist immortal, see the entry on the shrine built in his honor "Wen gongci ji 文公祠記" in *Quan Tang wen*, j. 713; and see also the entry on Miaogan zhenrenci 妙感真人祠 in Xu Song, comp., *Song huiyao jigao*, Li, j. 20.
41 See Zeng Yinli et al., *Wen Jin daojiao sanxiu zongpu*. See also Zeng Di, "Xinhua Daojiao yuanliu ji Julan gong leijiao wenshi"; and Ni Caixia, "Zuqun bianqian yu wenhua juhe."
42 For a history of Yuxugong in Xinhua, see Wu Ruowen, "Xinhua Yuxugong yu Dongyuemiao," p. 366; Yang Ziwu, "Shangmei Yuxugong ji qita"; and Zeng Di, "Xinhua Daojiao yuanliu ji Jujilan gong leijiao wenshi."

43 For the evidence of the Longmen lineage's emerging in the late Yuan and the early Ming era, see stele transcriptions: *Wangwushan Tiantan dading Zongxiangong xiuzao Baizhai daoren Zhang gong Taisu xingshi zhibei* and *Changchun zhenren xianpai chuanshoutu* (1524); Qin Yizhen, "Chici Guangfu wanshougong jianli Jiang taishi zhonglie miao daozong yuanliu beiji" (1721). For recent studies on the Quanzhen genealogical studies, see Zhang Guangbao, "Mingdai Quanzhenjiao de zongxi fenhua yu paizipu de xingcheng," and Zhao Weidong, "Henan Jiyuan Quanzhendao zongpai chuancheng kao."

44 This account is based on the interview with Mr. Wang Ping, a local researcher of Hunan Daoism and Baoqing Daoists in Wuhan. The interview was conducted by Xun Liu and Mei Li at Changchun guan in Wuhan on April 15, 2008.

45 For the differences as well as connections between the various local ritualist traditions and practices in Xinhua and central Hunan, see Lü Yongsheng (Wing-Sing Lui) and Li Xinwu, "Shenming, zuxian, yishi zhuanjia."

46 Based on field interview with Mr. Wang Ping at Changchun Monastery in Wuchang, Wuhan on April 15, 2008 by Xun Liu and Mei Li.

47 See Hankou municipal government's Daoist registration records, *Hankoushi zhengfu daoshi dengji*, 9:31:80 (1936); and *Daoshi dengji mingce*, 9:31:1381 (1946), Wuhan Municipal Archives. For a recent study of the Republican census of Daoists in Wuhan, see Mei Li, "Minguo nianjian Hankou difang zhengfu dui huoju daoshi de guanli"; and her "Minguo chengshi Zhengyi huoju daoshi qunti yanjiu: yi Hankou weizhongxin."

48 See Fan Kai, *Hankou congtan jiaoshi*, j. 1, p. 74.

49 Wang Baoxin, *Xu Hankou congtan*, pp. 17 and 209. For more on the flood disasters in Hankou, see *Xiakou xianzhi*, j. 20; Xu Huandou et al., *Hankou xiaozhi*; Fan Kai, *Hankou congtan jiaoshi*, j. 1; and Wang Baoxin, *Zaixu Hankou congtan*, j. 1.

50 For studies on the organization and functions of guilds and native places associations, see Burgess, *The Guilds of Peking*; Rowe, *Hankow: Commerce and Society in a Chinese City, 1796–1889*, and *Hankow: Conflict and Community in a Chinese City, 1796–1805*; and Goodman, *Native Place, City, and Nation*.

51 Wang Rigen, *Zhongguo huiguan shi*, pp. 309–10.

52 See Henansheng gudai jianzhu baohu yanjiusuo and Sheqi xian wenhua ju, comp., *Sheqi Shan-Shaan huiguan.*

53 Wuhan Qiaokouqu dang'an guan, preface to "Wuhanshi Qiaokouqu renmin zhengfu Baoqingjie banshichu," Qiaokou District Archives: File 71.

54 The Baoqing Neighborhood consisted these street blocks: Daxin 大新, Ziyang 紫阳, Guangfu 广福, Yihe 艺和, Xinhe 新河, Shangban 上板, Xiaban 下板, Yanhe 沿河, Sanjie 三街, Zhengjie 正街. See Qiaokou District Archives, Wuhan, Wuhanshi Qiaokouqu Baoqingjie, 1964 nian benjie jumin qungan zonghe dongjibiao, gugan renyuan huamingce, shejiao shoujiaoyu tongjibiao.

55 Wuhanshi Qiaokouqu dang'an guan, "Wuhanshi Qiaokouqu Baoqingjie, 1964 nian benjie jumin qungan zonghe dongjibiao, gugan renyuan huamingce, shejiao shoujiaoyu tongjibiao," File 71, Catalogue 2, Doc 2.

56 Field notes based on interview with Wang Ping taken by Xun Liu, Mei Li and Vincent Goossaert at Changchun Monastery in Wuchang on Nov 19, 2007.

57 Wuhan Qiaokou district gazetteer compilation committee, *Qiaokou quzhi*, p. 530.

58 Interviews with Wang Ping by Xun Liu, Mei Li and Vincent Goossaert at Changchun Monastery in Wuchang on Nov 19, 2007.

59 Field notes based on interview with Wang Ping taken by Xun Liu, Mei Li and Vincent Goossaert at Changchun Monastery in Wuchang on Nov 19, 2007.

60 See Fava, "Han Xin's Revenge: a Daoist Mystery" (a film). See also his *Aux portes du ciel. La statuaire taoïste du Hunan.*

61 Field notes based on interview with Luo Shangjin conducted by Xun Liu and Mei Li in Hankou on June 8, 2008.

62 For recent studies of the Daoist rituals in central and western Hunan, see Mozina, "Daubing Lips with Blood and Drinking Elixirs with the Celestial Lord Yin Jiao"; and Meulenbeld, "Daoist Modes of Perception."

63 Tian Yan, "Gu Meishan Tongquyu Meishanjiao tanjiu," pp. 46–47.

64 Shi Ping, "Hunan Xinhua Guangchan gong nuoyi yinyue yanjiu," p. 16.

65 See field notes by Xun Liu and Mei Li and based on the interview with Baoqing Daoist Luo Shangjin 羅尚金 in Qiaokou district of Hankou on June 8, 2008.

66 "Daoti da jiemi."

67 See Liu Chih-wan, *Taiwan no dōkyō to minkan shinkō*; and see also Rong Shicheng, *Xiqu renleixue chutan: Yishi, juchang yu shequn*, p. 102.

68 Interview by Mei Li and Xun Liu with Luo Shangjin, Sept 26, 2009 at Changchun Monastery in Wuchang; and see also Shi Ping, "Hunan Xinhuaxian Guangchan gong Nuoyi yinyue yanjiu," p. 26.

69 Narratives based on Interviews by Xun Liu and Mei Li with Zeng Mengxiong at his residence in Baoqing neighborhood on June 21, 2008.

70 Our thanks to Zeng Mengxiong for providing the original text of this petition.

71 On the local cults in Hunan, see Zhang Weiran, *Hunan lishi wenshua dili yanjiu*, pp. 97–115.

72 Zhu Yuanxiu and Huang Wenchen, *Guangxu Shaoyang xianzhi*, j.1 (*shilling* 時令 [Festivals]).

73 Xiao Hanping, "Nanyue Hengshan de minsu wenhua."

74 For a recent study of the Southern Peak, see Robson, *Power of Place*.

75 Zhang Weiran, *Hunan lishi wenhua dili yanjiu*.

76 Yu Qian et.al, comp. *Xinxu gaoseng zhuan*.

77 Hu Pu'an, *Hengzhou fengsuji*, p. 581.

78 For Hu Xiazhi 胡遐之's account of the annual temple fair at the Southern Peak, see Xiao Hanping, "Nanyue Hengshan de minsu wenhua."

79 Xiao Hanping, "Nanyue Hengshan de minsu wenhua."

80 This account is based on oral interviews with Zeng Mengxiong at his apartment in the Baoqing neighborhood on June 21, 2008.

81 Deng Hanguang, "Hubei sanju Zhengyipai daoshi de youguan qingkuang ji jinhou gongzuo de sikao."

82 The original of the petition for the Zhengyi temple is kept at Zeng Mengxiong's house.

83 About the housing conditions of the Hangzheng district under the early Republican regime, see Bao Jiaju 鮑家駒's survey, *Hankoushi zhuzhai wenti*, pp. 49991-50546.

84 Zhu Wenyao, *Hanzheng jie shichang zhi*, p. 56.

85 See notes taken of the field interview with Luo Shangjin by Xun Liu, May 21, 2016, at Luo's transitional rental apartment in Hanyang located across the Han River from his old apartment in the Baoqing Pier neighborhood in Hankou. At the time, Luo was still awaiting for his new apartment to be completed in the western Hankou where he was scheduled to move in by end of 2016.

Reference Works

Anonymous 無名氏. "Hanyang Yingwuzhou zhumu shichang shilüe 漢陽鸚鵡洲竹木市場事略 (1964). *Wuhan Municipal Archives* 武漢市檔案館.

Bao Jiaju 鮑家駒. *Hankoushi zhuzhai wenti* 漢口市住宅問題 (1937) in Xiao Zheng 蕭錚 (ed.), *Minguo ershinian Zhongguo dalu tudi wenti ziliao* 民國二十年中國大陸土地問題資料. Taipei: Chengwen chuban gongsi, 1977, vol. 95.

Burgess, John Stewart. *The Guilds of Peking*. New York: AMS Press, 1970.

Changchun zhenren xianpai chuanshoutu 長春真人仙派傳授圖 (1524), stele inscription transcription in Xun Liu's collection.

"Daoti da jiemi 刀梯大揭秘 [Revealing the Secrets of the Sword Ladder]" at: www.ucute .com.tw accessed on April 2, 2011.

Daoshi dengji mingce 道士登記名冊. *Wuhan Municipal Archives*, 9(31), 1946, 1381.

Deng Hanguang 鄧漢光. "Hubei sanju Zhengyipai daoshi de youguan qingkuang ji jinhou gongzuo de sikao 湖北散居正一派道士的有關情況及今後工作的思考," in Hubei Zongjiao Yanjiuhui 湖北省宗教研究會 (ed.), *Hubei zongjiao yanjiu* 湖北宗教研究. Beijing: Zongjiao wenhua chubanshe, 2004.

Dong Gao 董誥, et al., comp. *Quan Tang wen* 全唐文. 1000 juan at Hanchi electronic database 電子漢藉: http://hanchi.ihp.sinica.edu.tw/ihpc/hanji.

Dong Guifu 董桂敷. *Hankou Ziyang shuyuan zhilue* 漢口紫陽書院志略, j. 8 in Zhang Linchuan 張林川 (ed.), *Hubei guji wenxian congshu* 湖北古籍文獻叢書. Wuhan: Hubei jiaoyu chubanshe, 2002.

Fan Kai 范锴. *Hankou congtan jiaoshi* 漢口叢談校釋. 6 juan, (1822). Annot. by Jiang Pu 江浦 and Zhu Zhen 朱枕. Wuhan: Hubei renmin chubanshe, 1990.

Fava, Patrice, dir. "Han Xin's Revenge: A Daoist Mystery" (a film). Paris: CNRS Images and Honolulu, Hawaii, 2005.

———. *Aux portes du ciel. La statuaire taoïste du Hunan*. Paris: Belles Lettres & EFEO, 2014.

Fu Wei 傅威. "Wan Qing Hankou difang shehuizhong de shangren he shangren zuzhi 晚清漢口地方社會中的商人和商人組織," M.A. thesis. Wuhan University, 2009.

Goodman, Bryna. *Native Place, City, and Nation: Regional Networks and Identities in Shanghai, 1853–1937*. Berkeley: University of California Press, 1995.

Goossaert, Vincent. "Matériaux et recherches nouvelles sur les corporations chinoises urbaines traditionelles (des Ming à 1949)," *Revue bibliographique de Sinologie*, 17, 1999, pp. 205–222.

Guo Ying 郭瀅. "Wan Qing Hankou chengshi kongzhi xitong de yanqian 晚清漢口城市控制系統的演遷," *JiangHan luntan* 江漢論壇, 1, 1994, pp. 63–68.

Hankou shijie quantu 漢口市街全圖 (1918), in *Wuhan lishi dituji* 武漢歷史地圖集. Beijing: Zhongguo ditu chubanshe 中國地圖出版社, 1996, p. 49.

Hankoushi zhengfu daoshi dengji 漢口市政府道士登記. Wuhan Municipal Archives: File 9, Catologue 31, 80 (1936).

Henansheng gudai jianzhu baohu yanjiusuo 河南省古代建築保護研究所 and Sheqi xian wenhua ju 社旗縣文化局 comp. *Sheqi Shan-Shaan huiguan* 社旗山陝會館. Beijing: Wenwu chubanshe, 1999.

Hou Peijun 侯培峻. *Hankou Shan-Shaan huiguan zhi* 漢口山陝會館志, 2 juan. N.p.: Hankou Shan-Shaan huiguan, 1896.

Hu Nenggai 胡能改. "Yige juyou wanqiang shencun yizhi de Yaozu shi weihe yuanli Meishan de? 一個具有頑強生存意志的瑤族是為何遠離梅山的?," *Meishan wencui* 梅山文粹 (internal publication), 2, 2001, pp. 198–215.

Hu Pu'an 胡樸安. *Hengzhou fengsuji* 衡州風俗記 in his *Zhonghua quanguo fengsuzhi* 中華全國風俗志, xiabian 下編 [Part 2], vol. 6. (Shanghai: Guangyi shuju, 1923). Reprint edition. Shanghai: Shanghai kexue jishu chubanshe, 2011.

Huang Juan 黃娟, "Hunan jindai hangyunye yanjiu 湖南近代航運業研究," Ph.D. thesis. Wuhan: Central China Normal University, 2009.

Li Shu 李樹. "Hankou Baoqing matou he Baoqing huiguan 漢口寶慶碼頭和寶慶會館," *Wuhan wenshi ziliao* 武漢文史資料, 1, 1984, pp. 179–188.

Li Xia 黎霞. *Fuhe rensheng: Minguo shiqi Wuhan matou gongren yanjiu* 負荷人生:民國時期武漢碼頭工人研究. Wuhan: Hubei renmin chubanshe, 2008.

Li Xiaorong 李曉容. "Zishui tan'ge yu maobanchuan 資水灘歌與毛板船," *Hunan renwen keji xueyuan xuebao* 湖南人文科技學院學報, 5, 2009, pp. 53–55.

Liang Bihai 梁碧海 & Liu Yingqi 劉應祈. *Baoqing fuzhi* 寶慶府志, 38 juan (1684). Reprint edition. Beijing: Shumu wenxian chubanshe, 1988.

Lin Zonghai 林宗海. "Baoqing maobanshang shihua 寶慶毛板商史話," *Shaoyangshi wenshi ziliao* 邵陽市文史資料, 5, 1986, pp. 196–206.

Liu Chih-wan 劉枝萬. *Taiwan no dōkyō to minkan shinkō* 台湾の道教と民間信仰, Tokyo: Fūkyōsha, 1994.

Liu Shouhua 劉守華. *Daojiao yu Zhongguo minjian wenxue* 道教與中國民間文學. Beijing: Zhongguo youyi chuban gongsi, 2008.

Liu Xianting 劉獻廷. *Guangyang zaji* 廣陽雜記, 5 juan. (1879) Reprint edition. Beijing: Zhonghua shuju, 1957.

Liu Yunsheng 劉雲生. "Hankou kuli zhuangkuang 漢口苦力狀況," *Xin qingnian* 新青年, 8(1), 1920, p. 12.

Liu Zhenjie 劉震傑. *Hanyang shihua* 漢陽史話. Wuhan: Wuhan chubanshe, 2004.

Luo Yuanshi 羅元實. "Zishui tan'ge 資水灘歌," *Meishan wencui* 梅山文粹, 1, 1999, p. 393.

Lü Yongsheng 呂永昇 (Wing-Sing Lui) and Li Xinwu 李新吾. "Shenming, zuxian, yishi zhuanjia: Ming yijiang Meishan 'jiazu' yu 'dizhu' xinyang 神明、祖先、儀式專家: 明以降梅山'家主'與'地主'信仰," *Minsu quyi* 民俗曲藝, 187, 2015, pp. 45–104.

Mei Li 梅莉. "Minguo chengshi Zhengyi huoju daoshi qunti yanjiu: yi Hankou weizhongxin 民國城市正一道士群體研究: 以漢口為中心," *Shijie zongjiao yanjiu* 世界宗教研究, 1, 2015, pp. 87–96.

———. "Minguo nianjian Hankou difang zhengfu dui huoju daoshi de guanli: yi dang'an weizhongxin de kaocha 民國年間漢口地方政府對火居道士的管理—以檔案為中心的考察," *Jianghan luntan* 江漢論壇, 3 (2012), pp. 25–33.

———. "Yimin, shequ, zongjiao: yi jindai Hankou Baoqing matou wei zhongxin 移民、社區、宗教: 以近代漢口寶慶碼頭為中心 [Immigration, Community and Religion: the Case of the Baoqing Harbor District in Modern Hankou]," *Hubei daxue xuebao* 湖北大學學報, 41(3), 2014, pp. 1–8 and 148.

Meulenbeld, Mark. "Daoist Modes of Perception: 'Registering' the Living Manifestations of Sire Thunder, and Why Zhuang Zi is Relevant," *Daoism: Religion, History, and Society*, 8, 2016, pp. 35–90.

Mozina, David. "Daubing Lips with Blood and Drinking Elixirs with the Celestial Lord Yin Jiao: The Role of Thunder Deities in Daoist Ordination in Contemporary Hunan," *Cahiers d'Extrême-Asie*, 19, 2010, pp. 269–303.

Ni Caixia 倪彩霞. "Zuqun bianqian yu wenhua juhe: guanyu Meishanjiao de diaocha yu yanjiu 族群變遷與文化聚合:關於梅山教的調查與研究," *Shijie zongjiao yanjiu*, 1, 2011, pp. 97–105.

Ning Yi 寧宜. "Han Wei Nanbeichao Hunan daojiao fazhan yanjiu 漢魏南北朝湖南道教發展研究," M.A. thesis, Hunan Normal University, 2007.

Peng Yuxin 彭雨新 & Jiang Yong 江溶. "Shijiu shiji Hankou shangye hanghui de fazhan jiqi yiyi: *Hankou—yige Zhongguo chengshi de shangye he shehui (1796-1889)* jianjie 十九世紀漢口商業行會的發展及其意義: <漢口:一個中國城市的商業和社會(1796-1889)>簡介," *Zhongguo jingjishi yanjiu* 中國經濟史研究, 4, 1994, pp. 143–53.

Qiaokou quzhi 橋口區志. Wuhan: Wuhan chubanshe, 2007.

Qin Yizhen 秦一溱. "Chici Guangfu wanshougong jianli Jiang taishi Zhonglie miao daozong yuanliu beiji 敕賜廣福萬壽宮兼理姜太師忠烈廟道宗源流碑紀" (1721).

Robson, James. *Power of Place: The Religious Landscape of the Southern Sacred Peak (Nanyue) in Medieval China.* Cambridge (MA): Harvard University Asia Center, 2009.

Rong Shicheng 容世誠. *Xiqu renleixue chutan: Yishi, juchang yu shequn* 戲曲人類學初探: 儀式、劇場與社群. Nanning: Guangxi shifan daxue chubanshe, 2003.

Rowe, William. *Hankow: Commerce and Society in a Chinese City, 1796–1889.* Stanford: Stanford University Press, 1984.

———. *Hankow: Conflict and Community in a Chinese City, 1796–1805.* Stanford: Stanford University Press, 1989.

Shi Ping 石萍. "Hunan Xinhua Guangchan gong nuoyi yinyue yanjiu 湖南新化廣闡宮儺儀音樂研究," M.A. Thesis, Hunan Normal University, 2010.

Su Jinru 蘇緝如. "Shaoyang de maobanchuan 邵陽的毛板船," *Shaoyangshi wenshi ziliao* 紹陽市文史資料, 5, 1986, pp. 207–14.

Tian Yan 田艷. "Gu Meishan Tongquyu Meishanjiao tanjiu—Yi shigong de xinyang wei zhongxin 古梅山峒區域梅山教探究—以師公的信仰為中心," M.A. thesis, Hunan Normal University, 2009.

Wang Baoxin 王葆心. *Xu Hankou congtan* 續漢口叢談, 6 juan. (Wuchang: Yishan shuju, 1933). Reprint edition. Wuhan: Hubei jiaoyu chubanshe, 2002.

———. *Zaixu Hankou congtan* 再續漢口叢談, 4 juan. (Wuchang: Yishan shuju, 1933). Reprint edition. Wuhan: Hubei jiaoyu chubanshe, 2002.

Wang Boxin 王柏心. *Hanyang xianzhi* 漢陽縣志. 28 juan. Privately printed, 1868.

Wang Dengfu 王登福. *Jianghan shihua* 江漢史話. Wuhan: Wuhan chubanshe, 2003.

Wang Jiping 王繼平. *Wan Qing Hunan shi* 晚清湖南史. Changshan: Hunan renmin chubanshe, 2004.

Wang Jianzhong 汪建中 & Yu Zhong 余中, eds. "Matou shihua 碼頭史話," *Wuhan Chunqiu* 武漢春秋, 5, 1983, pp. 17–21.

Wang Ping 王平. "Baoqing shequ de Zhengyi daoshi 寶慶社區的正一道士," *Wuhan shizhi* 武漢市志. Wuhan: Wuhan daxue chubanshe, 1977, pp. 275–78.

Wang Rigen 王日根. *Zhongguo huiguan shi* 中國會館史. Shanghai: Dongfang zhongxin, 2007.

Wangwushan Tiantan dading Zongxiangong xiuzao Baizhai daoren Zhang gong Taisu xingshi zhibei 王屋山天壇大頂總仙宮修造白齋道人張公太素行實之碑 (Early Ming). Stele inscription transcription in Xun Liu's collection.

Wang Zhifang 王志芳. "Hanshui matou shihua 漢水碼頭史話," *Wuhan wenshi ziliao*, 2, 1992, pp. 131–34.

Wuchang Yaxin dixue she 武昌亞新地學社, comp. *Xin Hankoushi shice xiangtu* 新漢口市實測詳圖 *(1933)* in *Wuhan lishi dituji* 武漢歷史地圖集. Beijing: Zhongguo ditu chubanshe, 1998, p. 81.

———. *Hankoushi jiedao xiangtu* 漢口市街道詳圖 (1938) in *Wuhan lishi dituji* (1998), p. 85.

Wuhan magai ziliao huibian 武漢碼改資料彙編, vol. 1. Wuhan: n.p., 1950.

Wuhan lishi dituji 武漢歷史地圖集. Beijing: Zhongguo ditu chubanshe, 1998.

Wuhan Qiaokouqu dang'an guan 武漢礄口區檔案館. "Wuhanshi Qiaokouqu renmin zhengfu Baoqingjie banshichu xu 武漢市礄口區人民政府寶慶街辦事處序," Qiaokou District Archives: File 71 (全宗號 71).

———. "Wuhanshi Qiaokouqu Baoqingjie 1964 nian benjie jumin qungan zonghe dongjibiao, gugan renyuan huamingce, shejiao shoujiaoyu tongjibiao 武漢市礄口

區寶慶街一九六四年本街居民羣幹綜合統計表,骨幹人員華名冊,社教受教育統計表, biaoqi 表七: Jiedao jumin zhengzhi qingkuang diaocha modi tongjibiao 街道居民政治情況調查摸底統計表," Qiaokou District Archives: File 71, Catalogue 2, Doc. 2 (全宗號71 目录號2案卷號2).

Wuhan Qiaokou District Gazetteer Compilation Committee 武漢市橋口區地方志編纂委員會. *Qiaokou quzhi* 橋口區志. Wuhan: Wuhan renmin chubanshe; Wuhan: Wuhan chubanshe, 2007.

Wu Ruowen 伍弱文. "Maobanchuan: Zijiang shang de Xiangshang chuanqi 毛板船:資江上的湘商傳奇," *Chuancheng* 傳承, 9, 2009, pp. 58–60.

———. "Xinhua Yuxugong yu Dongyuemiao 新化玉虛宮與東嶽廟," *Lengshuijiang shi wenshi ziliao* 冷水江市文史資料, 6, 2007, p. 366.

Xiakou xianzhi 夏口縣志, j. 5 in *Hubei fuxian zhi ji* 67 *juan* 湖北府縣志輯 67卷 in *Zhongguo difangzhi jicheng* 中國地方志集成. Nanjing: Jiangsu guji chubanshe, 2001.

Xiao Hanping 蕭漢平. "Nanyue Hengshan de minsu wenhua 南嶽衡山的民俗文化," *Hunan daxue xuebao (shehui kexue ban)* 湖南大學學報(社會科學版), 3, 2000: 14–19.

Xu Huandou 徐煥斗 and Wang Kuiqing 王夔清, comp. *Hankou xiaozhi* 漢口小志 (Hankou: Aiguo tushu gongsi, 1915). Reprint edition, Nanjing: Jiangsu guji chubanshe, 2001.

Xu Song 徐松, comp. *Song huiyao jigao* 宋會要輯稿. Accessed at Hanchi 漢藉 on September 21, 2017: http://hanchi.ihp.sinica.edu.tw/ihpc/hanji.

Yan Ji 鄢吉. "Zijiang shangyeshi shang de chuanqi—Maobaochuan yu Baoqing matou 資江商業史上的傳奇: 毛板船與寶慶碼頭," Accessed at Xinhua xinwenwang 新化新聞網 on Sept 21, 2017: http://www.xhxww.cn/Info.aspx?ModelId=1&Id=30901.

Yan Xiaorong 晏曉榕. "Xinhua wushu yuanliu zongshu 新化武術源流綜述," *Xinhua wenshi* 新化文史, 1, 1985, pp. 193–97.

Yang Ziwu 楊自吾. "Shangmei Yuxugong ji qita 上梅玉虛宮及其他," *Lengshuijiang shi wenshi ziliao*, 4, 2004, pp. 317–18.

Ye Diaoyuan 葉調元. *Hankou zhuzhici* 漢口竹枝詞, 6 juan (1850) in Xu Mingting 徐明庭, Zhang Ying 張穎 & Du Hongying 杜宏英 (eds.), *Hubei zhuzhici* 湖北竹枝祠. Reprint edition. Wuhan: Hubei renmin chubanshe, 2007, pp. 109 and 105.

You Biaoxin 游標新, Liu Zhiyong 劉智勇 & Liang Zhongdong 梁中東. "Meishan wugong jiqi xinyang chutan 梅山巫公及其信仰初探," in Chen Zi'ai 陳子艾 & Hua Lan 華瀾 (Alain Arrault), eds. *Xiangzhong zongjiao yu xiangtu shehui diaocha baogaoji* 湘中宗教與鄉土社會調查報告集, 2 vols. Beijing: Beijing Normal University/Wenhui Digital Publications Center, 2006, v. 2, pp. 889–907.

Yu Qian 喻謙. *Xinxu gaoseng zhuan* 新續高僧傳, in Lan Jifu 藍吉富 (ed.), *Dazangjing bubian* 大藏經補編. Taipei: Huayu chubanshe, 1984–1985, vol. 27.

Zeng Di 曾迪. "Xinhua daojiao yuanliu ji Julan gong leijiao wenshi 新化道教源流暨聚嵐宮雷醮聞事," *Lengshuijiang shi wenshi ziliao* 冷水江市文史資料, 5, 2006, pp. 233–38.

Zeng Yinli 曾胤理. *Wen Jin daojiao sanxiu zongpu* 文斤道教三修宗譜. Privately printed, 1936.

Zhang Dingguo 張定國. "Yan Jiang matou yiwang 沿江碼頭忆往," *Wuhan wenshi ziliao*, 2, 1992, pp. 135–37.

Zhang Guangbao 張廣保. "Mingdai Quanzhenjiao de zongxi fenhua yu paizipu de xingcheng 明代全真教的宗系分化與派字譜的形成," *Quanzhen dao yanjiu* 全真道研究, 1, 2011, pp. 189–217.

Zhang Guoxiong 張國雄. *Ming-Qing shiqi de liang Hu yimin* 明清時期的兩湖移民. Xi'an: Shaanxi renmin jiaoyu chubanshe, 1995.

Zhang Qionghua 張瓊花. "Meishan maobanchuan yu Hankou Baoqing matou 梅山毛板船與漢口慶碼頭," *Dang'an shikong* 檔案時空, 1, 2011, pp. 38–39.

Zhang Shanshan 張姍姍. "Jindai Hankougang yuqi fudi jingji guanxi de bianqian, 1862–1936 近代漢口港與其腹地經濟關係的變遷, 1862–1936," Ph.D dissertation, Fudan University, 2007.

Zhang Weiran 張偉然. *Hunan lishi wenshua dili yanjiu* 湖南歷史文化地理研究. Shanghai: Fudan daxue chubanshe, 1995.

Zhang Zehong 張澤洪. "Gudai shaoshu minzu yu daojiao 古代少數民族與道教," *Zhongguo daojiao* 中國道教, 1, 1990, pp. 33 and 36–39.

Zhao Weidong 趙衛東. "Henan Jiyuan Quanzhendao zongpai chuancheng kao 河南濟源全真道宗派傳承考," *Daoism: Religion, History, and Society*, 5, 2013, pp. 81–110.

Zhongguo minjian gushi jicheng Hubei Yangxin xian minjian gushiji 中國民間故事集成-湖北陽新縣民間故事集 (internal publication, 1988).

Zhou Shaoyao 周少堯. "Zijiang tan'ge 資江灘歌," *Xinhua wenshi*, 2, 1987, pp. 285–96.

Zhu Wenyao 朱文堯. *Hanzheng jie shichang zhi* 漢正街市場志. Wuhan: Wuhan chubanshe, 1997.

Zhu Yuanxiu 諸垣修 & Huang Wenchen 黃文琛, eds. *Guangxu Shaoyang xianzhi* 光緒邵陽縣志, j. 1 (*shiling* 時令 [Festivals]), in *Zhonguo difangzhi jicheng Hunan fuxianzhi ji* 中國地方志輯成·湖南府縣志輯. Nanjing: Jiangsu guji chubanshe, 2002, vol. 50.

Index

Anqing 安慶, 15
Aqamad 阿哈馬, 59, 75n10

Baiyunguan 白雲觀 (White Cloud temple)
　(Shanghai), 18; (Beijing), 35, 141
Bangkok, 120–150
Baopu daoyuan 抱朴道院, 102,
　167–168, 180
Baoqing Guild 寶慶會館, 220–222,
　234–235
Baoqing Pier寶慶碼頭, 6, 16, 213–215,
　217, 220–223, 225, 228, 230–237, 239,
　250, 252–255, 259n85
Beijing, 14, 20, 27, 35, 42n32, 43n53, 53,
　85, 91, 110n83, 111n103, 113n141–142,
　141, 174, 206n13
Buddhism, 12–13, 15–17, 20–21, 26–29,
　34–35, 39, 54, 66, 68, 87, 92–93,
　99–100, 103, 105, 121, 135, 162,
　169–172, 186, 188, 230, 235, 249
Buddhist Associations, 32–33, 41, 102,
　169–172
Bureau of Ethnic and Religious Affairs
　民族宗教事務局(民宗局), 53, 70, 72.
　See also Religious Affairs Bureau
Burials, 36, 109n46, 222

Cankui 慚愧祖師, 120, 135, 137,
　140–141, 151n12, 154n83
Celibacy, 13, 15, 17, 34, 88, 90, 92, 100
Changchun Monastery 長春觀, 45n127,
　149, 232, 238, 247, 253–254,
　258n46;56;58–59, 259n68
Chaozhou, 106, 121, 125, 127
Charities (shantang 善堂), 13, 23–24,
　85–86, 90, 98–99, 112n121, 122–128,
　130, 150
Chengdu, 17, 75n24
Chenghuang: see City God

Chen Yingning 陳櫻寧, 97
City God (Chenghuang 城隍), 12–15,
　21–25, 27–29, 31, 33–34, 36–38, 121,
　126–127, 148, 150, 151n12, 154n102,
　174–175, 208n61, 242
Consecration 受戒, 傳戒, 12, 14, 27,
　90–91, 243
Crouching Dragon Knoll: see Wolonggang
Cultural Affairs Bureau 文化局, 26,
　52–53, 63
Cultural Revolution, 27, 31, 35, 52, 54–57,
　63, 65–67, 71–72, 75n24, 102, 166–167,
　179, 182, 199, 236–238, 240, 246

Dafeng 大峰祖師, 129–130, 150
Daoguan 道官, 12, 60
Daoguan 道館, 16, 22
Daoist associations, 17, 19, 23–41, 54,
　69, 73, 91, 101–103, 121, 124, 148,
　150, 171, 182, 198, 228, 238–239, 246,
　248, 253
Daoist revival, 4–5, 52, 54, 73–74, 238
daotang 道堂, 18, 120
Daoyuan 道院, 16, 43n73
Daoyuan 道院 (redemptive society), 105
Dejiao 德教, 106, 150
Divination, 34, 39, 126, 127, 132,
　134–135, 170, 227, 252
Dongyue: see Eastern Peak
Doumu 斗姆(姥), 18–19, 37, 94

Eastern Peak (Dongyue), 12–13, 19, 27, 30,
　36, 39, 161–206, 230
Exorcisms, 19, 34, 110n74, 190, 230,
　245, 252

Faguan 法官, 13
Fandong huidaomen 反動會道門,
　166, 178

Female alchemy (*nüdan* 女丹), 93
Festivals (*saihui* 賽會), 24–25, 28, 86, 94, 101, 147–148, 165–166, 172–177, 187–194, 199–200
Fuji 扶乩: *see* spirit-writing
Fuxingguan 福星觀, 24, 207n58

Guandi, 60, 84, 121, 123, 125, 127, 135, 140, 145, 148, 151n12, 242
Guangzhou, 3, 16, 19–23, 27, 30, 106, 122, 131, 134
Guanyin 觀音, 102, 125, 130, 145, 246, 252
Guan Yu 關羽: *see* Guandi
Guilds, 1, 4, 12, 14–16, 21–22, 38, 216, 220–222, 233–235

Hangzhou, 14, 17–18, 24–25, 26, 29–30, 32–33, 41, 83, 85, 90, 92–93, 99, 102, 104, 161–206, 238
Hankou: *see* Wuhan
Hanyang: *see* Wuhan
Hanzheng Street 漢正街, 216, 219–220, 254
Healing, 19, 28, 30, 34, 83, 86–87, 92–93, 96, 100, 103–106, 131, 163–164, 205, 230–232, 252
Heavenly Master: *see* Zhang Heavenly Master
Hengshan 衡山, 214, 259n73;78–79. *See also* Nanyue
Hong Kong, 3, 16, 19, 23, 28, 37–40, 45n124, 102, 106, 120, 135, 142, 149–150
Huang gang (Huang bang黃幫), 217–218
Huzhou, 83–106, 196, 201

Inner alchemy (*neidan* 內丹), 85, 92, 96–97, 122, 186

Jade Emperor (Yuhuang 玉皇), 13, 19, 29, 60, 94, 130, 141, 145, 148, 150, 184, 233, 246, 254
Jade Void Palace 玉虛宮, 228–230, 232, 243
Japan, 65, 105
Japanese invasion, 21, 25, 98, 100, 124, 166, 177, 193, 231
Jiao 醮 offerings, 16, 18, 35–36, 89, 94–95, 149, 233
Jigong 濟公, 86, 99–101, 104–106
Jin'gaishan 金蓋山, 83–106
Jingming 淨明, 106

Keshi 客師, 17, 174

Li Lishan 李理山, 24, 44n86
Lineages, 12, 14, 16, 18, 21–22, 26, 30, 62, 83, 87–92, 97, 99–101, 106, 149, 171, 183, 221, 228–230, 237–240, 245
Litanies (*chan* 懺), 34–35, 94–95, 102, 183–187, 198, 233, 242
Liu Chengshan 劉誠山, 52, 69, 74n2
Longhushan 龍虎山, 12, 14, 110n78, 174, 182–183, 225, 229, 232, 238
Longmen 龍門, 52, 62, 83, 87–92, 99–101, 149, 258n43
Lü Dongbin: *see* Patriarch Lü
Lüzu: *see* Patriarch Lü

Macao, 19, 131, 142
Malaysia, 150
Maobanchuan 毛板船: *see* Plank boats
Maoshan 茅山, 25, 40
Martial Marquis Shrine (Wuhouci 武侯祠), 4, 52–54, 56, 58, 62, 64–65, 67–68, 70–73, 77
Medicine, 13, 39, 56, 65, 70, 98, 124, 128–135, 148, 150, 176–177, 182, 231. *See also* healing
mediums: *see* spirit mediums
Meishan 梅山, 225, 230, 256n16, 257n24;33, 259n63
Meizhou 梅州, 120–125, 128–136, 141–150
Min Yide 閔一得, 83, 86–89, 91–93, 95–96, 103, 105
Museums, 14, 27, 52–53, 56, 58, 62–65, 70–72

Nanchang, 225
Nanjing, 104, 218
Nanwu lineage (Nanwu pai 南無派), 62, 75n18–19
Nanxun 南潯, 90, 198
Nanyang 南陽, 3–4, 11, 14, 20, 24, 37, 45n125, 52–54, 56–74, 74n1–5, 75n6;9–10;15;17;22;24–25, 76n27;30–38;40, 76–80, 235
Nanyang Museum 南陽博物館, 52, 56, 58, 62–65, 71–72, 75n24–25
Nanyang Prefectural Administration 南陽行政公署, 62–63, 70
Nanyue 南嶽, 16, 214, 231, 242, 246–252, 254. *See also* Hengshan
Neidan 內丹: *see* Inner alchemy
Northern Expedition (Beifa 北伐), 21–22, 27, 65

Occupation, 14, 62, 66–67, 73–75, 78, 82, 84, 108, 165, 187, 193
Oracles (*lingqian* 靈簽), 94, 121, 125, 130–135, 170
Ordination, 3, 11–12, 35, 149, 174, 182, 238, 240–246. *See also* consecrations

Patriarch Lü, 18–19, 83–155
Pilgrimages, 25, 29, 60, 94, 141, 162, 164–170, 174–178, 180, 187–191, 193–203, 246–252
Plank boats (*maobanchuan* 毛板船), 219–220, 256n15
Possession: *see* spirit possession
Processions, 12, 14, 21–22, 24–25, 33, 103, 165, 188–189, 191–192, 202–205
Putian 莆田, 41n1, 44n105, 205

Qionglongshan 穹窿山, 86
Quanzhen 全真, 12, 14–15, 17–19, 24, 27, 44n99, 52–53, 59, 62, 68–69, 73, 83–84, 87–88, 90–97, 102–103, 105–106, 149, 171, 229–230, 232, 238, 246–248, 253–254

Redemptive societies, 19, 83, 97, 101, 103–106, 178
Religious Affairs Bureau 宗教局, 53–54, 67–68, 77, 170, 238
Religious properties, 76, 87. *See also* Temple properties
Renweimiao 仁威廟, 30
Ritual manuscripts, 180, 187
Rituals: *see* burials, exorcisms, festivals, *jiao* offerings, litanies
Ritual venues, 64, 67, 257–258, 263–264

Saihui: *see* Festivals
Sanyuangong 三元宮, 131, 153n64
Shanghai, 13, 16–22, 24–25, 27–29, 30–31, 33, 39, 85–86, 89–93, 97–99, 103, 176, 189, 196
Shantang 善堂: *see* charities
Singapore, 150
Southern Peak: *see* Nanyue and Hengshan
spirit mediums, 15–16, 18, 28–30, 34, 86, 100, 127, 185
spirit possession, 29, 34, 189
Spirit-writing (*fuji* 扶乩), 5, 14, 16, 18–19, 34, 83–87, 89–106, 120–123, 125–127, 130–146, 150
Squat, 52–54, 63, 67, 72
sublineage (*fang* 房), 14, 22, 88, 229–230

Suzhou, 3, 15, 17, 22, 24–25, 29–31, 36–37, 42n36, 44n84, 84, 86, 90, 93, 108n18, 202

Taicang 太倉, 90, 94, 96
Taiping war, 14, 17, 21, 24, 84, 88, 90–92, 95–96, 109n46, 165, 176, 189, 191, 199, 217–218, 220
Taiqinggong 太清宮, 132
Taiwan, 15–16, 23, 34–35, 37–40, 45n124, 102, 106, 135, 142, 245
Temple expropriation, 14, 52, 62
Temple properties, 57, 63, 68
Tourism, 22, 27–29, 33, 40, 69–70, 169–170

Vietnam, 120, 135–136, 150, 151n3

Wang lingguan 王靈官, 128, 130, 137, 143
Wang Mingzhen 王明真, 17
Wang Yiting 王一亭, 99
Weiyushan 委羽山, 14
Wenchang 文昌, 14, 18, 84–85, 121, 135, 148, 151n12
Wenzhou, 32, 41
White Cloud temple: *see* Baiyunguan
Wolonggang 臥龍崗, 7, 52, 58, 75n9;12;13
Women, 29, 34, 36, 91–93, 99, 100, 103–104, 123, 134, 147, 185, 193, 198, 236, 254
Wuchang: *see* Wuhan
Wudangshan 武當山, 14, 60, 247
Wuhan, 15–16, 22, 40, 149, 213–255
Wuhouci: *see* Martial Marquis Shrine
Wuxi, 42n14, 44n86

Xi'an, 27
xiangtou 香頭, 30, 36, 176, 199, 201–204
xiantan 仙壇, 18
Xiantiandao 先天道, 106, 155n138
Xinhua 新化, 213–214, 217–219, 221, 225, 228–232, 235–240, 242–248, 255, 257n24;39;41;42, 258n45, 259n64;68
Xu Xun 許遜, 84
Xuanmiaoguan 玄妙觀, 12, 14, 20, 22, 24, 25, 29, 37

Yangzi River 長江, 213, 215, 217–218, 220, 225, 232, 237, 255
Yiguandao 一貫道, 178
Yuanhuang: *see* Jade Emperor
Yuhuangshan 玉皇山, 24, 90–91

Zanhuagong 贊化宮, 120–150
Zhang Heavenly Master 張天師, 12,
   44n86, 174, 182, 229, 232
Zheng Guanying 鄭觀應, 96
Zhengyi 正一, 3, 12–14, 17, 19–20,
   27–28, 84, 86, 90, 93–94, 171,
   174, 183, 208n75, 213–214, 225,
   228–232, 235–241, 247–248,
   251–255

Zhenwu 真武, 125, 145, 148
Zhu Zongchang 朱宗長, 52–53, 62, 69,
   71–72, 74n2–3, 75n6;19
Zhuge Liang 諸葛亮, 5, 52, 58–60, 70,
   75n9
Zhuji 諸暨, 91, 93, 95, 99–105, 110n71,
   112n131
Zi River 資水, 213, 215, 217, 219, 225,
   227, 229, 255

For Product Safety Concerns and Information please contact our EU
representative GPSR@taylorandfrancis.com
Taylor & Francis Verlag GmbH, Kaufingerstraße 24, 80331 München, Germany